EFFECTIVE EDUCATIONAL LEADERSHIP

Effective Educational Leadership

The companion volumes in this series are:

Strategic Leadership and Educational Improvement, edited by Margaret Preedy, Ron Glatter and Christine Wise

Leading People and Teams in Education, edited by Lesley Kydd, Lesley Anderson and Wendy Newton

All these readers are part of a course Leading and Managing for Effective Education (E849) *that is itself part of the Open University Masters programme.*

The Open University Masters Programme in Education

The Open University Masters Programme in Education is now firmly established as the most popular postgraduate degree for education professionals in Europe, with over 3,000 students registering each year. The Masters Programme in Education is designed particularly for those with experience of teaching, the advisory service, educational administration or allied fields.

Structure of the Masters Programme in Education

The Masters is a modular degree, and students are, therefore, free to select modules from the programme which best fit in with their interests and professional goals. Specialist lines in leadership and management, applied linguistics, special needs, and lifelong learning are also available. Study within the Open University's Advanced Diploma can also be counted towards a Masters Degree, and successful study within the Masters Programme entitles students to apply for entry into the Open University Doctorate in Education programme.

OU-Supported Open Learning

The Masters Programme in Education provides great flexibility. Students study at their own pace, in their own time. They receive specially prepared study materials, supported by tutorials, thus offering the chance to work with other students.

The Doctorate in Education

The Doctorate in Education is a part-time doctoral degree, combining taught courses, research methods and a dissertation designed to meet the needs of professionals in education and related areas who are seeking to extend and deepen their knowledge and understanding of contemporary educational issues. The Doctorate in Education builds upon successful study within the Open University Masters Programme in Education.

How to apply

If you would like to register for this programme, or simply find out more information about available courses, please write for the *Professional Development in Education* prospectus to the Call Centre, PO Box 724, The Open University, Walton Hall, Milton Keynes, MK7 6ZW, UK (Telephone 01908 653231). Details can also be viewed on our web page http://www.open.ac.uk/courses

EFFECTIVE EDUCATIONAL LEADERSHIP

Edited by
Nigel Bennett, Megan Crawford and Marion Cartwright

The Open University

P·C·P

The Open University   in association with   Paul Chapman Publishing

Paul Chapman Publishing
A SAGE Publications Company
6 Bonhill Street
London EC2A 4PU

SAGE Publications Inc
2455 Teller Road
Thousand Oaks, California 91320

SAGE Publications India Pvt Ltd
32, M-Block Market
Greater Kailash - I
New Delhi 110 048

Library of Congress Control Number: 2002105580

A catalogue record for this book is available from the
British Library

ISBN 0 7619 4055 3
ISBN 0 7619 4056 6 (pbk)

Typeset by Pantek Arts Ltd, Maidstone, Kent
Printed in Great Britain by Cromwell Press,
Trowbridge, Wiltshire

Contents

Acknowledgements   vii

Introduction   ix
Nigel Bennett, Megan Crawford and Marion Cartwright

Part 1 The current context of educational leadership: policy and values   1

1 Leadership in education: losing sight of our interests   3
   Bill Mulford

2 The lifeworld at the center: values and action in educational leadership   14
   T.J. Sergiovanni

Part 2 Understanding educational leadership   25

3 Leadership theory reviewed   27
   Melissa Horner

4 Structure, culture and power in organisations   44
   Nigel Bennett

5 Inventive management and wise leadership   62
   Megan Crawford

6 Networks, cognition and management of tacit knowledge   74
   Mie Augier and Morten Thanning Vendelø

7 The arts of leadership   89
   K. Grint

Part 3 Preparation for leadership   109

8 Mission possible? An international analysis of headteacher/principal training 111
   Brian Caldwell, Gerard Calnin and Wendy Cahill

9 Effective training for subject leaders   131
   Alma Harris, Hugh Busher and Christine Wise

10 Conflict and change: daily challenges for school leaders   143
    Michael F. DiPaola

11 Management development and a mismatch of objectives:
    the culture change process in the NHS   159
    Graeme Currie

CONTENTS

Part 4 Practising leadership   **171**

12 Effective leaders and effective schools   173
    Kathryn Riley and John MacBeath

13 Fostering teacher leadership   186
    Kenneth Leithwood, Doris Jantzi and Rosanne Steinbach

14 Critical studies on men, masculinities and management   201
    David L. Collinson and Jeff Hearn

15 Cross-cultural perspectives on school leadership:
    themes from Native American interviews   216
    Miles T. Bryant

16 Managing ambiguity in further education   229
    Denis Gleeson and Farzana Shain

17 Between hierarchical control and collegiality:
    the academic middle manager in higher education   247
    David Hellawell and Nick Hancock

Part 5 Dilemmas in leadership and management   **265**

18 The emotional side of leadership   267
    Rick Ginsberg and Timothy Gray Davies

19 Leadership challenges and ethical dilemmas in front-line organisations   281
    Patrick Duignan and Victoria Collins

    Index   295

Acknowledgements

The Editors and publishers gratefully wish to acknowledge the following for kind permission to use the following copyright material:

Thomas J. Sergiovanni: The Lifeworld at the Centre. From: T.J. Sergiovanni, *The Lifeworld of Leadership: Creating Culture, Community and Personal Meaning in our Schools*. San Francisco: Jossey Bass. (2000)

Melissa Horner: Leadership Theory, Past, Present and Future. In *Team Performance Management*, vol. 3, no. 4, pp. 270–287. (1997)

Nigel Bennett: An Organisational Perspective on School Effectiveness and School Improvement. From A. Harris and N. Bennett (eds.) *School Effectiveness and School Improvement: alternative perspectives*. London: Continuum (2001)

Mie Augier and Morten Thanning Vendelø: Networks, Cognition and Management of Tacit Knowledge. In *Journal of Knowledge Management*, vol. 3, no. 4, pp. 252–261. (1999)

Keith Grint: The Arts of Leadership. From K. Grint, *The Arts of Leadership*. Oxford: Oxford University Press. (1999)

Alma Harris, Hugh Busher and Christine Wise : Effective Training for Subject Leaders. Adapted from *Journal of Inservice Education*, vol. 27, No. 1, pp. 83–94. (2001)

Graeme Currie: Management Development and a Mismatch of Objectives: The Culture Change Process in the NHS. In *Leadership and Organization Development Journal*, vol. 18, no. 6, pp. 304–311. (1997)

Kathryn Riley and John MacBeath: Effective Leaders and Effective Schools. In J. MacBeath (ed.) *Effective School Leadership: Responding to Change*. Paul Chapman (1998)

Ken Leithwood, Doris Jantzi and Rosanne Steinbach: Fostering Teacher Leadership. In K. Leithwood, D. Jantzi and R. Steinbach *Changing Leadership for Changing Times*. Buckingham: Open University Press. (1999)

David L. Collinson and Jeff Hearn: Critical Studies on Men, Masculinities and Management. From Marilyn J. Davidson and Ronald J. Burke (eds.) *Women in Management: Current Research Issues*. Sage (2000)

Miles T. Bryant: Cross-Cultural Perspectives on School Leadership. From *Educational Management and Administration*, vol. 26, no. 1, pp. 7–20. (1998)

Denis Gleeson and Farzana Shain: Managing Ambiguity: Between Markets and Managerialism – a Case Study of 'Middle' Managers in Further Education. *Sociological Review*, vol. 47, no. 3, pp. 461–490. (1999)

David Hellawell and Nick Hancock: A Case Study of the Changing Role of the academic Middle Manager in HE: between hierarchical control and collegiality. *Research Papers in Education*, vol. 16, no. 2, pp. 183–197. (2001)

Introduction

Nigel Bennett, Megan Crawford and Marion Cartwright

Since the mid-1990s, leadership has become the key concept in work concerned with developing policy and practice in educational systems and organisations. This can be viewed as part of a simultaneous process of centralising key decisions about policy and direction and decentralising the delivery systems for their implementation, which has become widespread across the developed world. In a political context of substantially increased organisational autonomy, it is perhaps not surprising that the discussion of how we might increase the effectiveness of educational and other organisations has increasingly been couched in the language of leadership rather than the more traditional language of management.

This development raises three fundamental questions that we need to consider. First, we have to ask what leadership is for, how it might be conceptualised and what is involved in exercising it. Related to this is whether it should be differentiated from management and, if so, how. Secondly, we need to examine how leaders should be prepared for their work – assuming it is something for which people can be prepared, rather than being something innate to particular individuals. How we answer these two questions will shape our answer to the third question. How and on what basis do we judge leadership to be 'good' or 'bad', and how do we determine whether a course of action in a particular situation or setting is 'right' or 'wrong'? These three basic questions form the foundations of this book.

Leadership is a contested concept. Historically, it has been defined in different ways, and the implications of each definition have created quite different perceptions of what counts as 'good' leadership and what should be involved in leadership preparation. Further, the extent to which leadership can be distinguished from management, and the relative significance of one to the other, varies between understandings or theories of leadership. One key distinction is between those writers on leadership and leadership theory who write about *leaders* and those who write about *leadership*. Those who write about *leaders* assume that it rests upon particular personal skills, knowledge and characteristics of individuals who are placed in particular roles within the organisation. From this assumption, they develop analytical frameworks that see the exercise of leadership by these individuals as resting upon the possession of particular skills or competences, knowledge and understanding, over all of which they demonstrate complete command.

This understanding of leadership makes assumptions about the nature of power in organisations and places a substantial emphasis on vision and direction being provided by a particular individual. Frequently, analysis of leaders is located within a technical-rational model of organisational activity and a hierarchical organisational structure. It also presumes that people follow their leader or leaders. Thus leadership as exercised by leaders locates the activity in individuals rather than in any social setting.

Those who focus on *leadership* discuss it in terms of a function within the organisational setting, which may be performed by a particular individual or, more typically, is provided by individuals appropriate to particular situations or issues. Leadership is therefore seen as a fluid concept: an organisational characteristic or quality, which rests as much upon particular individual expertise as it does on a person's formal position or status within the organisation. Indeed, Ogawa and Bossert (1997) suggest that leadership is exercised not through individual charisma or heroic action, but by creating an organisation that will survive. Leadership, they suggest (1997, p. 19), 'flows through the networks of roles that comprise organisations ... [and] is based on the deployment of resources that are distributed across the network of roles, with different roles having access to different levels and types of resources'. Thus a newly appointed member of staff can provide 'leadership' if his or her particular expertise is unique within the organisation (network of roles) and relevant to the issue or task in hand – always provided his or her colleagues acknowledge this capacity and are willing to accept it as legitimate. Thus, leadership rests on the distribution of resources and is exercised through social relations. It does not assume that individuals have to provide a sense of vision and direction for their colleagues (subordinates) to follow.

Clearly, whichever of these broad understandings of leadership you adopt has profound implications for how you define or identify 'good' or 'effective' leadership, and the kinds of skills or capacities that you identify as necessary. Leadership preparation has become a central question since the early 1990s, with substantial provision being made throughout the world. However, just as there are different perceptions of leadership, so there are different perceptions of what will provide appropriate training or preparation in the most effective way. Arrangements differ from country to country both in structure and content, and these differences do not necessarily reflect the broad division just indicated, but may result from particular interpretations of one view.

This brings us to another factor. How we understand leadership varies not just according to the basic understanding we have of the term, but also according to the cultural background within which it is located. Exporting Western conceptualisations of leadership 'best practice' to other countries was a substantial industry in the later years of the twentieth century. Similarly, we have often observed the uncritical adoption in the West of Japanese propositions and practice. Only recently has the question been raised as to whether the assumptions about organisational structure and interpersonal behaviour made by the 'exporting' nation sit comfortably alongside those of the host nation.

However, this cultural factor need not be located only at the societal level. Different kinds of work may generate different kinds of culture, as may particular organisations. Professionally staffed organisations, such as schools, colleges, universities and hospitals, may reject conceptualisations of leadership that derive from non-professional settings such as manufacturing industry. Indeed, within organisations, different perceptions of good leadership can vary from unit to unit: leadership in a research laboratory may well be viewed differently by the lab's members from the way workers in a manufacturing department may view it. This may relate not just to what is regarded as 'good' leadership, but also to staff attitudes to leadership in general.

We have used the term 'good' several times in this Introduction. By doing so we wish to argue that all of us as individuals have a set of values that allow us to judge what is 'good', and thence what actions are 'right'. Often these values provide us with clear guidance – a course of action is clearly 'right', or clearly 'wrong'. Sometimes, however, this is not the case, and there may be more than one 'right' course of action. For example, should one cause hurt by insisting on a strict application of the rules relating to a particular situation, or break the rules in order to show sympathy and support? Both courses of action are defensible, and both may have unfortunate consequences. People who hold leadership positions in the organisation frequently encounter such dilemmas. Some leadership and management programmes, particularly those that are based on an analysis of individual leader competences, enjoin leaders to develop and articulate a vision and a set of values, which they then draw those whom they lead into sharing (e.g. TTA, 1998).

How, then, does leadership differ from management in its conceptualisation and preparation? In practice, they are closely linked, and indeed the terms are sometimes used almost interchangeably, as is the case in some of the chapters in this book. Some key contemporary concepts relating to the needs and demands of twenty-first century organisations, such as knowledge management, are located in the language of management rather than leadership. It is also the case that some sectors of education still use the language of management to discuss the tensions between traditional professional relationships and the growing emphasis on financial accountability, the emphasis on measurable outcomes, and the pressure to provide and demonstrate value for money that have become the prevailing demands of the new public management. We have therefore included here a number of chapters that use the language of management alongside those that use the language of leadership. The issues they raise, and the discussion they provide, are directly relevant to the development of sound and effective leadership in education.

The set of considerations outlined here has created both the focus and the structure of this book. We begin by introducing the contemporary context within which leadership occurs, before proceeding to explore a variety of ways in which leadership can be analysed. Next we focus on issues in the preparation of leaders, and examine cases of leadership in action in a variety of settings. Lastly, we explore two analyses of dilemmas that leaders typically face.

Part 1 of the book begins with a chapter by Bill Mulford, which examines current policy developments in the field of education. He writes about the 'interests' of education and the importance of defending them against social and political pressures, in particular those relating to accountability. His use of the term 'interests' covers more than the political interests of a professional group whose expertise is being overruled by political administrative decisions; it also refers to the values that underpin the exercise of knowledge-based leadership by practitioners. His use of a 'true story' at the end of the chapter provides a cautionary tale of the possible consequences of the developments he describes.

Chapter 2 provides us with a discussion of the values-base of action. Drawing on Habermas's conceptions of 'lifeworld' and 'systemworld', Tom Sergiovanni examines the implications of basing policy and practice decisions on the systemworld rather than the lifeworld. Sergiovanni suggests that the systemworld relates to the demands of efficiency and administrative relevance, whereas the lifeworld relates to our personal and professional values. Through a combination of argument and case studies, he provides us with examples of the tensions that can exist between lifeworld and systemworld, and what he sees as the potential dangers that will result from allowing systemworld considerations to dominate decisions at the expense of our lifeworld.

The second part of the book explores our understandings of leadership, its organisational context and its relationship with management. In Chapter 3, Melissa Horner gives us a helpful overview of the ways in which leadership has been conceptualised since the early twentieth century. She demonstrates the range of changes, from trait theory through to concepts of transformational leadership, and her analysis suggests that some contemporary emphases, such as the theories of charismatic leadership, hark back to earlier theories. In Chapter 4, Nigel Bennett examines the organisational context in which leadership (and management) is exercised. He suggests that three key concepts – structure, culture and power – help to explore the constraints and opportunities for leaders, and also the boundaries within which leadership as a function can operate. Megan Crawford then broadens the discussion in the way foreshadowed earlier in this Introduction by exploring the relationship between 'leadership' and 'management', drawing on important work by Bolman and Deal and Mintzberg. She suggests that much of what is currently regarded as leadership is really better understood as 'inventive management' and, equally, that there is a need for 'wise leadership' that often has to acknowledge the non-rational world within which organisations function, and the many different bases upon which individuals base their actions.

Two further chapters explore some contemporary understandings of leadership and management. In Chapter 6, Mie Augier and Morten Thanning Vendelø explore the nature of the burgeoning concept of knowledge management, with its implications for the nature of leadership and management and the relationships between members of an organisation. Embedded in their discussion of the relationship between public knowledge and tacit knowledge in knowledge-based organisations, of which educational organisations are prime examples, is the idea of promoting the circumstances in which such knowledge sharing and publicising can take place. Thus there are strong resonances between their discussion and the concept of leadership as an organisational quality that exists in social relationships. Then in the final chapter of this part, Keith Grint provides us with a quite different view of leadership, derived from a constructivist perspective. His emphasis on leadership as an art rather than a science reflects some earlier discussion of teaching by Wise *et al.* (1984), who identified a hierarchy of perceptions of teaching, from the lowest form as labour, through craft to profession to its highest perception, as art. Grint suggests that leadership involves the integration of four kinds of arts – philosophical, martial, fine and performing – in order to persuade followers that they wish to follow.

In Part 3 we explore current issues and provision in leadership preparation. Brian Caldwell, Gerard Calnin and Wendy Cahill draw on their report to the National Center for Education and the Economy in Washington, DC, to outline current provision in four countries – England, Australia, Hong Kong and Sweden – in search of exemplary programmes of headteacher or principal preparation. They identify a wide variety of arrangements, all of which have merits, but all of which rest on a different perception of what principals have to understand and be able to do. They also ask if the problems of headteacher recruitment that have generated this emphasis on principal preparation may lie in the structuring of education as much as in the issue of supply and preparation. Alma Harris, Hugh Busher and Christine Wise then explore the arrangements existing in England prior to the creation of the National College for School Leadership for the training of subject leaders. Through their discussion of the arrangements in existence at the turn of the century, they explore what subject leaders regarded as the significant elements and forms of provision appropriate for their training, and hence their understanding of their middle leadership role. This perception has implications for others involved in leadership or management in schools. Their chapter also enables us to understand what leadership preparation is seen to involve by those who are receiving assistance with a first move into formal leadership or management positions.

Michael DiPaola then looks at the importance of preparing educational leaders for conflict, and looks in particular at how the dilemmas of conflict can be used creatively for the good of the organisation as a whole. Rather than seeing conflict as a dangerous phenomenon to be avoided, he argues that training in how to use cognitive conflict to stimulate schools to better working dynamics should be part of the training of educational leaders. Finally in this part, Graeme Currie examines a management development programme for nursing staff who are being expected to take on more management responsibilities, and asks why it turned out to be very ineffective. Some of the lessons of the mismatch of objectives between the organisation and the participants are particularly relevant to any debate on leadership preparation.

With Part 4, we look in more detail at these ideas and issues in practice. The chapters in this part of the book demonstrate clearly the importance of cultural expectations in the ways in which leadership and management practice is understood and evaluated. Kathryn Riley and John MacBeath report on teachers' perceptions of effective leadership and management in England, Scotland and Denmark. They demonstrate how what is seen as effective leadership depends on what leaders are expected to do, and how that in turn depends on what is seen to be the proper structure and relationship between staff and students in schools. Then Kenneth Leithwood, Doris Jantzi and Rosanne Steinbach present some research findings on the nature of 'teacher leadership', a developing idea at the turn of the century that rests on a progressive diffusion of the leadership function away from the principal and the senior management or administrative staff in schools, and creates a stronger perception of professional leadership. In Chapter 14, David Collinson and Jeff Hearn examine the impact of gendered issues in leadership and management, a continuing concern in the recruitment of senior staff in education and elsewhere, and one that in England has become more of a problem recently. Collinson and Hearn take an interesting perspective on this issue, examining it from the point of view of men and masculinities and the problems they create for leaders and managers, rather than from the point of view that identifies feminine characteristics as simultaneously a potential source of better leadership and a barrier to its achievement. Although cast mainly in the language of management rather than leadership, partly to emphasise the continuing gendered nature of literature and thinking about positions in organisations that involve leading and directing the work of others, their analysis addresses fundamental questions of how both management and leadership should be conceived and enacted. Chapter 15, by Miles Bryant, moves from cultural issues within a culture to cultural issues across cultures. Through an exploration of how leadership is constructed within the communities of Native Americans on the Great Plains, Bryant demonstrates how many of the basic assumptions of most Western leadership thinking can be called into question. Do we need leaders in order to gain direction and achieve? Do organisations need goals? Must leaders and organisations always be concerned about time and the future? By examining cross-cultural understandings of these and related issues, Bryant both raises questions about our own value-systems and priorities and identifies potential concerns about the continued export of Western theories to non-Western cultures.

Collinson and Hearn and Bryant examine leadership issues from a non-educational basis. The last two chapters in this part examine the under-researched world of management and leadership in post-compulsory education. In Chapter 16, Denis Gleeson and Farzana Shain report on work on middle managers in further education colleges in England and Wales. They identify an important issue that is also reflected in Miles Bryant's chapter: that of ambiguity. They demonstrate that the organisational context of the middle managers they interviewed was not one of clear goals, job descriptions and role definitions. In this, their research relates back to the discussion of structure, culture and power in Bennett's discussion of organisations. The consequence of this environment of ambiguity is uncertainty and difficulty for the middle managers interviewed. David Hellawell and Nick Hancock find a similar tension in their detailed study of two faculty deans, whom they classify as middle managers, in a university in England. They observe a contradiction between the public language of professional collegiality that permeates higher education and the reality of increasingly hierarchical structures and decision-making. The tensions this creates for a dean of faculty who is simultaneously trying to sustain collegial practices within the faculty whilst coping with increasing centralisation are clearly delineated.

Parts 3 and 4 demonstrate repeatedly how the cultural context, both nationally and organisationally, is reflected in the judgements that are made about how the tasks of leadership and management should be defined, distributed and executed. Embedded in this cultural context is a set of valuations of good and proper practice. However, it is not always clear what represents good and proper practice, and situations in which there is no 'right' answer – or, more precisely, when there is no 'wrong' answer but all the answers are defensible – create severe tensions and dilemmas for people in authority. Part 5 completes the book with two discussions of these issues. In Chapter 18, Rick Ginsberg and Timothy Gray Davies explore an under-developed area of leadership and management activity, that which is concerned with emotions. Despite the development of an interest in emotional intelligence following on the work of Howard Gardner and Daniel Goleman, little systematic work has been done in this area in relation to management and leadership. Ginsberg and Davies explore a range of emotionally charged situations in which American school principals have been faced with particularly difficult decisions. The study is particularly interesting because it explores the situations through the words of the principals themselves. Then in Chapter 19, Patrick Duignan and Victoria Collins draw on a major Australian study of key service organisations – three different educational organisations and the police – to identify what they call tensions in the work of such organisations, and provide examples from school principals' experiences. They conclude with a set of recommendations for principal preparation programmes.

This book, then, explores a range of issues and perspectives on leadership drawing on work from a range of English-speaking countries, and from both different educational sectors and general management and leadership literature. It provides an overview of the current field of leadership studies, a strong theoretical literature and a range of practical discussions about how to turn theory into practice. It uses theory as both a basis for action and a means of analysing practice as it is observed. In bringing together a range of perspectives and examples, we hope that it will provide both a useful resource for those wishing to study educational leadership and a sound support for those who wish to improve their professional practice.

References

Ogawa, R.T. and Bossert, S.T. (1997) Leadership as an organisational quality. In M. Crawford *et al.* (eds.) *Leadership and Teams in Educational Management.* Buckingham: Open University Press, pp. 7–23.

TTA (1998) *National Standards for Headteachers.* London: Teacher Training Agency.

Wise, A.E., Darling-Hammond, L., McLoughlin, M. and Bernstein, H.T. (1984) *Teacher Evaluation: A Study of Effective Practices.* Santa Monica, CA: Rand.

Part 1

The Current Context of Educational Leadership: Policy and Values

1

Leadership in Education:
Losing Sight of our Interests

Bill Mulford

Introduction

As with 'riding the tiger', we may believe the trick in these days of constant change is not to think about the direction society and its educational institutions are taking but merely to hang on. Unfortunately, in reacting in this way it can become all too easy to lose sight of our interests. Whose interests are being served, for example, when over a 13-month time frame one Australian state minister for education's press releases not once referred to teachers in congratulatory terms (Bishop and Mulford, 1996; 1999)?

Losing sight of one's interests in the leadership of education can take many forms but let me concentrate on three: the use of procedural illusions of effectiveness, especially for accountability; the fostering of dependence, especially on the leader; and the fostering of homogeneity, for example through the use of competency or equivalent frameworks. After discussing each of these I'd like to conclude with a true story. It is the story of the warship *Vasa*. It nicely encapsulates and reinforces the points I am trying to make about the international context within which leadership in educational settings needs to be examined.

The Use of Procedural Illusions of Effectiveness

Meyer and Rowan (1978) point out that procedural illusions can be employed to maintain the myth of education and function to legitimise it to the outside world. In the absence of clear-cut output measures we turn to

---

Source: Commissioned.

processes as outputs. For example, there are precise rules to classify (and credential) types of headteachers, types of teachers, types of students and sets of topics. All these rules and regulations, competency lists, strategic plans, examinations and so on give confidence to the outside (and to many of those inside) that the education system and its schools know what they are doing. The structure of the system or school is the functioning myth of the organisation that operates not necessarily to regulate intraorganisational activity, but to explain it, account for it and to legitimate it to the members outside the organisation and to the wider society. The transactions in educational organisations are concerned with legitimacy.

Structures are offered that are congruent with the social expectations and understandings about what education should be doing, e.g. process goals explicitly stated by an education department to help maintain or develop this legitimacy may influence the use of certain 'approved' consultants, the creation of organisational sub-units such as an audit section or office of review, the setting up of national examination boards and training institutions, including those for leadership, and so on. While such actions may have little proven positive effect on what goes on in the classroom, they do, at the time of their creation, demonstrate congruence with the goals and expectations of the wider society as perceived by the department or authority. Here we are talking about high visibility and the *impression* of decisiveness of action.

Dutch research on conditions that foster the implementation of large-scale centrally determined innovation programmes in schools (Geijsel *et al.*, 2001) is illustrative of the difficulties involved. It found that while teacher implementation was more likely under transformational leadership, participation in decision-making and involvement in professional development activities, there were more changes in attitudes about than practice with the innovation.

Such goal displacement does, of course, raise important moral questions, especially if you believe, as I do, that deception has no place in education and its leadership or administration.

Perhaps the greatest use of procedural illusions of effectiveness in recent times arises from a fascination with accountability. It is as if increased decentralisation in education systems to schools around the world has brought with it increased control by the 'centre' through accountability. Having recently visited the Museum of Law in Nottingham I have learnt that the end of trial by ordeal occurred in 1215 when the church forbade clergy to take part. Trial by ordeal involved throwing a bound male into cold water and if he sank he was innocent but if he floated he was guilty. For women the trial involved walking for nine paces with a red-hot iron in one's hand. If the burn festered then the woman was guilty but if it healed quickly she was innocent. Of course, when trial by ordeal ended we turned to torture to make the accused confess.

Now, what has this got to do with accountability? Talking to many of those on the receiving end of inspections, assessments or quality assurance processes, I have to wonder whether trial by ordeal or torture is still very much with us. Where is the evidence of the various procedures' predictive validity, let alone their cost effectiveness? Have they resulted in improvement in valued student outcomes? Couldn't the resources needed to sustain these monolithic accountability structures be better used in the interests of the country's students?

To take as an example the situation in UK where the cost of national tests for 7, 11 and 14-year-olds topped £24 million last year (*TES*, 2001). Chris Little (2001, p. 17), who teachers at St Vincent sixth-form college in Gosport, Hampshire, and who is a principal examiner in A-level maths for an exam board, has pointed out that 'you can have too much of a good thing: we need to review the unhealthy reliance we place on large-scale external exams and consider the cost-effectiveness of the money we are spending on them'. He continues: 'The plethora of external assessment not only drains schools of valuable resources, but also undermines the status and authority of teachers. We are no longer deemed competent to assess our own pupils ... The emphasis on results and outcomes stifles imaginative teaching' (ibid.). Perhaps the 16-year-old student Rose Heiney (2001, p. 16) said it best when she exclaimed, 'AS-level [examinations] broaden backsides, not minds'.

In his book *Personalising Evaluation*, Kushner (2000, p. 204) clearly presents the choice for educational leaders in the following terms:

> We can ... encourage young people to pass more criterion-referenced assessments
> or strive for intellectual autonomy – they cannot do both at the same time ...
> One demands compliance with a predetermined set of principles (in exchange
> for credentials); the other exposes those principles to critical scrutiny – that is,
> one accepts the authority of government, the other challenges it.

Kushner (ibid., pp. 208–209) concludes that the responsibility of evaluators (educational leaders?) 'is to enhance the quality of intellectual journeys, not confirm, much less rule on, destinations'.

In addition, has anyone wrestled with the possibility of an assess/assist dilemma, that is, that certain forms of assessment (usually, summative, comparative, unqualified) preclude assistance, and precluding assistance tends to preclude learning? Has anyone considered the possibility that such a heavy use, and seeming acceptance, of these forms of accountability may send a message of a lack of trust of those in schools and universities and a disregard for their professionalism? Has anyone considered the possibility that the continued heavy use of these forms of accountability may foster an unacceptable level of dependence?

The Fostering of Dependence

Another way of losing sight of our interests is where the balance between dependence and independence/interdependence in education continually favours dependence. This situation is most easily seen in the overdependence of many of those in educational institutions on 'the leader', often engendered by the overconfidence of 'the leader' in his or her own abilities or importance.

There seem to be a lot of people around these days who want to tell those in schools what to do. This situation is unfortunate. It is unfortunate because many of those doing the telling do not seem to want to accept responsibility for their advice, blaming everything and everybody else (budget cuts is a common excuse) for lack of success. It is also unfortunate because many are not around long enough to take responsibility for their directions – witness the rapid turnover of ministers of education and heads of departments of education each with their unique 'solution' to education's problems (in the Australian state of Victoria there have been eight ministers and nine heads of the department of education in just 18 years, that is, a change on average every two years, compared to every eight years in the previous decades). A week may be a very long time in politics but is a very short time in the education of a child.

We will need to be particularly vigilant regarding a more recent and insidious tactic of some of those who want to tell educators what to do, that is, to prevent fair and open assessment of the changes they promulgate. In 1998 the Melbourne Diocesan Synod of the Anglican church decided to set up an investigative task group to report on Victorian government schools. The subsequent report (Anglican Diocese of Melbourne, 1998) pointed out that they had difficulty in obtaining sufficient reliable information because 'Our State Government seems averse to making available information, which might be used by critics of its policies. Much is only obtained after lengthy Freedom of Information processes. Teachers and others employed by the Department of Education are forbidden to comment on government policies'. The report (ibid.) continues: 'There is strict screening of consultants for the professional development programs of teachers ... Restrictions on undertaking research in schools have been placed on academics who are considered to be critical of recent changes.'

Leadership, like power, has its own corrupting influence. Let me make this point by exploring the reactions of some musicians to those who lead orchestras. Passing judgement on conductors he had known and worked with, the astute and long-suffering violinist Carl Flesch once said that there was no profession that an impostor could enter more easily. Norman Lebrecht (1997) argues that the conductor exists because humankind demands a visible leader or, at the very least, an identifiable figurehead. The conductor's musical *raison d'être* is altogether secondary to that function: 'He plays no instrument, produces no noise, yet conveys an image of music-making that is credible enough to let him take the rewards of applause away from those who actually created the sound' (ibid.). As the flautist, James Galway, was once heard to grumble about conductors: 'Too many of these guys are masters of the brilliant wave.' Of course, the sustenance of such myths requires the connivance of compliant others.

I've come to believe that orchestras don't have a mortgage on 'maestros'. As I reflect on many of the 'leaders' I have known and worked with and their singular lack of success in changing education for the better as well as their unwillingness to take any responsibility for their actions or advice, I conclude that we in education also have many 'masters of the brilliant wave' – whether these be individuals such as education ministers, heads of departments of education, consultants, headteachers or organisations such as ministries of education, leadership institutes, etc. They convey an image or facade that is credible enough to let them take the rewards of applause away from those who actually do the hard work in schools and school systems. They prosper on creating dependence on their services. Unfortunately, the connivance of compliant others in our profession helps sustain the myth of their contribution and greatness.

Dependency on such 'leaders' and connivance of others is a cause of great concern, for the international research is clear on the importance of distributive not dependent leadership for improved outcomes of schooling. Research from Spain (Estebaranz *et al.*, 1999) highlights the importance of teachers' work groups, Australia (Silins and Mulford, 2000; in press) organisational learning, and USA (Goddard *et al.*, 2000) collective teacher efficacy. Case studies of 29 innovative initiatives in school management from nine countries (Belgium, Greece, Hungry, Japan, Mexico, the Netherlands, Sweden, England and USA) conclude that educational leadership that transforms education for the better involves those destined to use changes. As the study (UNESCO, 2001, p. 55) notes: 'it is striking from the case studies, how frequently team-work is cited as a key ingredient to the success of new approaches to school management.' It also warns (ibid.): 'it is risky to rely on the charisma and energy of a single leader to sustain change within a school … When an organisation has progressed sufficiently it is time for other leaders to develop. The ultimate test of any transformation is its durability beyond its original instigator.'

Unfortunately, however, times of uncertainty and relentless pressure prompt an understandable tendency to want to know what to do. This is partly because dependency is a function of insecurity – a matter that, unfortunately, can never be fully resolved while there is uncertainty. Yet, surely, the most effective relationship between an educational maestro and others is where the maestro works him or herself out of a job as quickly as possible by passing on his or her knowledge and skills to those he or she is working for. When the best leader's work is done, the people say, 'we did it ourselves'.

The Fostering of Homogeneity

A third and final observation in respect of losing sight of our interests relates an increasing push for homogeneity. This push is despite the fact that there will be increasingly less need in our societies for large numbers of predictable, interchangeable, don't-ask-why people. Those sought in the future will be the ones who think, question, innovate and take entrepreneurial risk, ones that can work in regularly changing teams and so on.

We need some deviants. Let me illustrate by describing the activities of bees. A worker bee finds a major source of pollen, flies back to the hive, and performs a dance that shows the other bees the direction of the pollen source. The speed of the dance indicates the distance of the find from the hive. Then the queen bee gives the word, and out of the hive fly the workers directly to the newfound pollen. At least, 85 per cent of them do. The other 15 per cent don't follow the swarm. They appear not to have comprehended the message and go wandering off in other directions. And what happens to this 15 per cent? They look for other sources of pollen, and when they find it the story starts all over again. If you look for common denominators in successful educational institutions, you will see that a strong one is to find a way to get some of the people to do a deviant thing. If a system is too tight for this, if every bee is required to go to a particular source of pollen, there will be no search and no development (Pfeiffer *et al.*, 1989).

A well led educational organisation cannot survive without some 'sheet music'. Such overall direction allows the management of complexity, without which it could degenerate into cacophony. Most large-scale human interactions require their specific blueprints, rituals, road maps, scripts, whatever, but for success they need character and that involves improvisation. In other words, development cannot take place in an environment where discretion has been removed.

One lesson here is that reductionist approaches in education, to the complexity that is the world of student, should not go unchallenged. Uniformity for education systems in aims, in standards, in methods of assessment and in training is a complexity-reducing mechanism. It is far tidier to have a single set of aims for all, a single curriculum for all, a single set of standards for all, a single array of tests for all, a single set of training programmes for all than to have locally developed approaches to school and pupil improvement.

How so many education systems and their leaders can rely on such narrow measures of success, usually academic achievement in a few subjects, is difficult to understand, especially when there is growing evidence of the importance of other outcomes of schooling for later life success. For example, Feinstein (2000) has found substantial labour market return in terms of employment/unemployment and earnings as a result of 'non-academic' outcomes such as children's attentiveness, self-esteem and good peer relations.

The use of competency frameworks or lists for headteachers and their training can also constitute a reductionist, one-size-fits-all approach. While there is usually a structure or hierarchy to the levels of competence (for example, the Hay McBer model of excellence for school leaders in England with its characteristics and levels of performance), there appears not to be an equivalent structure or hierarchy to the units of competence. Are some units more important than others, are they sequential in that some are prerequisites for others, and/or are some context bound (primary/secondary; rural/urban; big/small school; age distribution, experience and qualifications of teaching staff; the stage of development of the school when the headteacher takes over; the level of experience of the headteacher)?

I am also worried about the seeming certainty of the competency frameworks. It might be, as some of my early Leadership for Organisational Learning and Student Outcomes (LOLSO) (Silins and Mulford, 1999; 2000; in press) data suggest, that student engagement in school reduces the need for teacher or headteacher leadership and the need perceived by staffs for sharply focused and widely shared school missions. Results also suggest a redistribution of leadership development resources away from those aspiring to or already in the headship to those in teacher and administrator roles. Another early finding suggests the relationship may be curvilinear, i.e. beyond some as yet unclear, optimal level of total leadership, more leadership actually detracts from a school's clarity of purpose, sense of mission, etc. How will competency frameworks take such research findings into account?

Said differently, there is a difficulty in conceptualising leadership as a defined state. The danger with formulaic responses is that they will only function with a given set of variables and these are unlikely to be replicated with any degree of predictability in schools over the next few years. Change in schools also proceeds through some clearly discernible stages. Often things get worse before they get better. If this analysis is accepted then the time at which data are gathered on the headteacher's leadership competencies becomes crucial. If, for example, when the best leaders work is done, the people say, 'We did it ourselves', how will we be able to attribute any success to the leader?

In the varied topography of professional practice, there is a high hard ground overlooking a swamp. On the high ground, manageable problems lend themselves to solutions through structures, plans, curriculum vision, etc. In the swampy lowland, messy, confusing problems involving relationships, values, learning, defy technical solutions. The reality in schools is an organisation characterised by uncertain or contested goals and values, role ambiguity, demands for more for less and so on; the swamp may be the natural habitat for the leader. How do competency frameworks take account of paradoxes in leadership, such as the possibility that effective managers are not in control, the better things are the worse they feel and organisations change most by surviving calamities? Can competencies take account of factors such as caring, passion, sensitivity, tenacity, patience, courage, firmness, enthusiasm, wonder, honesty, trust, spirit and soul?

We need to be supporting diversity, heterogeneity not sameness, homogeneity. Homogeneity of outcome for the future of our society is not necessarily the highest good, and may be impossible to achieve. As Eisner (1991) has argued, the importance of diversity in a population can be compared to the importance of the instruments in this reoccurring orchestra. With only violins, regardless of how broad their range, our musical experience would be impoverished. Each instrument, both individually and in concert with others, makes its distinctive contribution to the whole. Recognising diversity and acknowledging the multiple ways to be and act is a potential source of strength to our culture.

Conclusion: The True Story of the *Vasa* (from Matz, 1991)

Aware that the welfare of his kingdom depended on his navy, on 16 January 1625 King Gustavus II Adolphus of Sweden signs a contract with shipbuilder Henrik Hybertsson for the building of the warship *Vasa*. It is to be the most expensive, largest, most fearsome and richly ornamented naval vessel built in Sweden. The king is anxious to acquire a ship with as many guns as possible on board. He is also keen to have the ship completed as rapidly as possible and certainly in less time than the normal period for building ships of seven to eight years.

During the spring of 1626, work commences on the building of the *Vasa* at Skeppsgarden, the naval dockyard in Stockholm. Some 400 men are employed. Over 1,000 oaks are felled for the project. For three years, carpenters, pit-sawyers, smiths, rope makers, glaziers, sail makers, painters, box makers, woodcarvers and other specialists work on the ship. The hull is constructed from most of the 1,000 oaks, 64 large guns are cast, masts more than 50 metres high are raised and many hundreds of gilded and painted sculptures are carved. The total length of the *Vasa*, including bowsprit, is to be 69 metres. The hull is 12 metres wide. The height at its magnificently carved stern symbolising and idolising the king, his strength, courage and wisdom, his infallibility, his standing above all others, is 19 metres. The *Vasa*'s displacement is 1,210 tons and the sail area 1,275 square metres. It is to carry 145 seamen and 300 soldiers.

In 1628 and almost complete the *Vasa* is moored below the Royal Castle. There, ballast is loaded, as well as the ammunition and guns required for the maiden voyage. The new ship arouses the admiration and pride of

Stockholmers, but as is intended it intimidates the country's enemies. A letter written by Erik Krabble, the Danish Ambassador in Stockholm, reports in awe that the *Vasa* has 48 big guns for 24-pound ammunition, 8 three-pounders, 2 one-pounders and 6 mortars.

By Sunday 10 August, everything is ready. The task of building a mighty warship has been completed. At the king's insistence it has been completed in half the normal time. The weather is fine and the wind light. On board are around 100 mainly conscripted crew members, but also women and children. This is to be a great ceremonial occasion, with pomp and circumstance, so the crew has been given permission to take their families on the first voyage.

As the *Vasa* sails forth, countless Stockholmers stand along the shore to wish her good luck. They have plenty of time to follow the ship's departure. The wind is from the southwest and, for the first few hundred metres, the *Vasa* has to be pulled along using anchors. Then Danish-born Captain Sofring Hansson issues the order: 'Set the foresail, foretop, maintop and mizzen!' The sailors climb the rig and set four of the *Vasa*'s ten sails. The guns fire a salute and slowly, serenely, the *Vasa* sets off. It then capsizes and sinks inside Stockholm harbour. The voyage has lasted only 1,300 metres! Some 50 people follow the *Vasa* into the deep.

News of the disaster does not reach the Swedish king, who was then waiting impatiently in Prussia, until two weeks later. He writes to the Council of the Realm in Stockholm that 'imprudence and negligence' must have been the cause, and that the guilty parties must be punished. 'Were you intoxicated?' 'Had you failed to secure the guns properly?' Questions and accusations echo in the hall at the Royal Castle. Just 12 hours after the loss of the *Vasa* her captain stands before the Council of the Realm. He had been taken prisoner immediately afterwards. As the transcript of interrogation shows, Captain Hansson answers:

> 'You can cut me in a thousand pieces if all the guns were not secured ... And before God Almighty I swear that no one on board was intoxicated ... It was just a small gust of wind, a mere breeze that overturned the ship ... The ship was too unsteady, although all the ballast was on board.'

Thus Captain Sofring Hansson places the blame on the ship's design – and, by the same token, the shipbuilder.

When the crew are questioned, they say the same thing. No mistake was made on board. It was impossible to load more ballast. The guns were properly lashed down. It was Sunday, many people had been to communion and no member of the crew was drunk. 'The ship is top-heavy with her masts and yards, sails and guns,' they declare. Shipmaster Joran Matsson also reveals that the *Vasa*'s stability had been tested before the sailing. Thirty men had run back and forth across the *Vasa*'s deck when she was moored at the quay.

After three runs they had to stop – otherwise, the *Vasa* would have capsized. Present during the test was Admiral Klas Fleming, one of the most influential men in the navy. The admiral's only comment, according to Joran Matsson, was: 'If only his Majesty were at home!'

Those responsible for building the *Vasa* are also questioned. One complication is that the actual builder of the *Vasa*, the very experienced and successful Dutch shipbuilder Henrik Hybertsson, had died the year before. However his replacement, Hein Jakobsson, also swore his innocence. The *Vasa* conformed to the dimensions approved by the king himself and on board were a number of guns as specified in the contract. 'Whose fault is it, then?' asks the interrogator. 'God only knows,' answers the lessee of the shipyard, Arent de Groot.

God and king, both equally infallible, are thus drawn into the case. No guilty party is ever identified, and no one is punished for the disaster. The great, beautiful warship was too large and too strong. It was more massive and had more heavy guns than previous ships. It was an experiment, an innovation that failed spectacularly.

We have in the story of the *Vasa* a reminder of what can happen when one loses sight of one's interests: using procedural illusions of effectiveness in the rushed building of the most expensive, largest, most fearsome and richly ornamented naval vessel, the pomp and circumstance of the launch, and then the looking for a scapegoat, for someone to blame for the disaster; a fostering of dependence on the leader, the infallible king who approved the dimensions and the number of guns, and a fostering of homogeneity with no one, especially the admiral, willing to pass on disquieting information up the line. We also have a spectacular illustration of difficulties of individual and organisational learning, of doing something new, and of failure being part of learning. Those involved with leadership in education and who wish not to lose sight of education's best interests clearly need to stop 'riding the tiger' and start 'remembering the *Vasa*'!

References

Anglican Diocese of Melbourne (1998) *The State of our Schools* (the report of the Synod Schools Task Group on Victoria's Public Education System). Melbourne: Anglican Diocese of Melbourne.

Bishop, P. and Mulford, B. (1996) Empowerment in four Australian primary schools: they don't really care. *International Journal of Educational Reform* 5(2): 193–204.

Bishop, P., and Mulford, B. (1999) When will they ever learn? Another failure of centrally-imposed change. *School Leadership and Management* 19(2): 179–87.

Eisner, E. (1991) My educational passions. In D. Burleson (ed.) *Reflections*. Bloomington, IN: Phi Delta Kappan.

Estebaranz, A., Mingorance, P. and Marcelo, C. (1999) Teachers' work groups as professional development: what do teachers learn? *Teachers and Teaching: Theory and Practice* 5(2): 153–69.

Feinstein, L. (2000) *The Relative Economic Importance of Academic, Psychological and Behavioural Attributes Developed in Childhood*. London: Centre for Economic Performance (London School of Economics and Political Science, Paper 443).

Geijsel, F., Sleegers, P., van den Berg, R. and Kelchtermans, G. (2001) Conditions fostering the implementation of large-scale innovation programs in schools: teachers' perspectives. *Educational Administration Quarterly* 37(1): 130–66.

Goddard, R., Hoy, W. and Hoy, A. (2000) Collective teacher efficacy: its meaning, measure and impact on student achievement. *American Educational Research Journal* 37(2): 479–507.

Heiney, R. (2001) AS-levels broaden backsides not minds. *The Times Educational Supplement* 1 June p. 16.

Kushner, S. (2000) *Personalising Evaluation*. London: Sage.

Lebrecht, N. (1997) *The Maestro Myth: Great Conductors in Pursuit of Power*. London: Simon & Schuster Pocket Books.

Little, C. (2001) Counting the cost of exams. *The Times Educational Supplement* 1 June, p. 17.

Matz, E. (1991) *Vasa*. Stockholm: The Vasa Museum.

Meyer, J. and Rowan, B. (1978) Notes on the structure of educational organisations: revised version. Paper prepared for the Annual Meeting of the American Sociological Association. Reported in J. Hannaway: Administrative structures, why do they grow? *Teachers College Record* 79(3): 416–17.

Mulford, B. (1998) Organisational learning and educational change. In A. Hargreaves *et al.* (eds.) *International Handbook of Educational Change*. Norwell, MA: Kluwer Academic Publishers.

Mulford, B. (2000) The global challenge: a matter of balance. William Walker Oration. ACEA/NZIEA/PNGCEA/CCEAM International Conference, Hobart, September (http://www.cdesign.com.au/acea2000/pages/con03.htm).

Mulford, B. and Silins, H. (2001) Organisational learning effects. A paper in the symposium 'Understanding schools as intelligent systems' chaired by K. Leithwood, ICSEI, Toronto, January.

Mulford, B., Silins, H. and Leithwood, K. (in preparation) *Leadership for Organisational Learning and Student Outcomes: A Problem-Based Learning Package*. Lisse: Swets & Zeitlinger.

Pfeiffer, W. *et al.* (1989) *Shaping Strategic Planning*. San Diego, CA: Scott Foresman.

Silins, H. and Mulford, B. (1999) Leadership for organisational learning and student outcomes: the LOLSO Project. A paper presented at AERA, Montreal, April.

Silins, H. and Mulford, B. (2000) Leadership for organisational learning in Australian secondary schools. In K. Leithwood (ed.) *Understanding Schools as Intelligent Systems*. Greenwich, CT: JAI Press.

Silins, H. and Mulford, B. (in press) Leadership, restructuring and organisational outcomes. In P. Hallinger *et al.* (eds.) *Second International Handbook of Educational Leadership and Administration*. Norwell, MA: Kluwer Academic Publishers.

The Times Educational Supplement (2001) 15 June, p. 13.

2

The Lifeworld at the Center: Values and Action in Educational Leadership

T.J. Sergiovanni

Most successful school leaders will tell you that getting the culture right and paying attention to how parents, teachers, and students define and experience meaning are two widely accepted rules for creating effective schools. We still have to worry about standards, the curriculum, teacher development, tests, resources, and the creation of appropriate management designs that help get things done. But these concerns will not matter much unless the right culture is in place and unless parents, teachers, and students interact with the school in meaningful ways.

School Culture

Culture is generally thought of as the normative glue that holds a particular school together. With shared visions, values, and beliefs at its heart, culture serves as a compass setting, steering people in a common direction. It provides norms that govern the way people interact with each other. It provides a framework for deciding what does or does not make sense. Culture, Louis (1980) points out, is 'a set of common understandings for organizing actions and language and other symbolic vehicles for expressing common understanding' (p. 227).

To be successful at culture building, school leaders need to give attention to the informal, subtle, and symbolic aspects of school life. Teachers, parents, and students need answers to questions such as these: What is this school about? What is important here? What do we believe in? Why do we function

Source: Sergiovanni, T.J. (2000) *The Lifeworld of Leadership: Creating Culture, Community and Personal Meaning in our Schools.* San Francisco, CA: Jossey-Bass. Edited version.

the way we do? How are we unique? How do I and how do others fit into the scheme of things? Answering these questions provides a framework for understanding one's school life, and from this understanding is derived a sense of purpose and enriched meaning. Purpose and meaning are essential in helping a school become an effective learning community – a community of mind and heart. As Thomas B. Greenfield (1973) states, 'What many people seem to want from schools is that schools reflect the values that are central and meaningful in their lives. If this view is correct, schools are cultural artifacts that people struggle to shape in their own image. Only in such forms do they have faith in them; only in such forms can they participate comfortably in them' (p. 570).

If you believe as I do that parents, teachers, and students having faith in a school is critical to its success, then this quotation is worth inscribing on the edifice of every schoolhouse. The best indicator of a good school may well be the extent to which its image reflects the needs and desires of its parents, teachers, and students. To be sure, other interests should appropriately be served. But these interests must be conjoined with those of parents, teachers, and students, whose interests must remain important if not central.

Greenfield (1984) maintains that the task of leadership is to create a moral order that binds a leader and others together.

In 1957 Philip Selznick made several points:

> The art of the creative leader is the art of institution building, the reworking of human and technological materials to fashion an organism that embodies new and enduring values [pp. 152–153] … 'To institutionalize is to *infuse with value* beyond the technical requirements of the task at hand … From the standpoint of the committed person, the organization has changed from an expendable tool into a valued source of personal satisfaction [p. 17].

The institutional leader, then, *is primarily an expert in the promotion and protection of values* (p. 28).

Selznick is pointing to two domains that can exist side by side in a school. One is a technical-instrumental domain and the other is a values domain. One deals with methods and means. The other deals with goals and purposes. When the school places the values domain at the center as the driving force for what goes on and the technical-instrumental domain at the periphery, it becomes transformed from a run-of-the-mill organization to a unique, vibrant, and generally more successful institution. Institutions, Selznick points out, are so important to people and so permeated with values that they become sources of deep meaning and significance and become regarded as ends in themselves.

Organizations, however, are little more than instrumentalities designed to achieve goals – instrumentalities that are constantly at risk. Selznick

(1957) notes that organizations are likely to emphasize methods rather than goals, which results in the substitution of means for ends (p. 12). This happens in schools when rules established to help achieve some purpose, tests designed to provide teachers with information, departmentalized structures intended to bring faculty together as communities of practice, and discipline plans implemented to teach students lessons and enhance civility become ends in themselves.

One of the findings revealed in the successful schools literature (for recent examples, see Bryk and Driscoll, 1988; Meier, 1995; and Darling-Hammond, 1997) is that schools that resemble institutions have central zones of values and beliefs that take on sacred characteristics. As repositories of values, these central zones are sources of identity for parents, teachers, and students from which their school lives become meaningful. Meaningfulness leads to an elevated level of commitment to the school, greater effort, tighter connections for everyone, and more intensive academic engagement for students – all of which are virtues in themselves but which have the added value of resulting in heightened levels of student development and increased academic performance.

The Lifeworld

Culture, meaning, and significance are parts of the 'lifeworld' of the school. This lifeworld can be contrasted with the 'systemsworld'. The systemsworld is a world of instrumentalities usually experienced in schools as management systems. These systems are supposed to help schools effectively and efficiently achieve their goals and objectives. This achievement, in turn, ideally strengthens the culture and enhances meaning and significance. When things are working the way they should in a school, the lifeworld and systemsworld engage each other in a symbiotic relationship.

Symbiotic relationships bring together two dissimilar elements in a way that both benefit. Mutuality is key. Mutuality depends upon a level of intimacy between the elements characterized by trust and respect. Mutuality also depends upon parity. When brought together symbiotically the lifeworld and the systemsworld have equally valuable standing.

An important theme in the discussion that follows is that mutuality can only be achieved in schools, families, friendship networks, faith communities, and other civil associations when the lifeworld drives the systemsworld. But when the systemsworld drives the lifeworld, organizational character erodes. In schools this results in many dysfunctions, including high student disengagement and low student performance.

The terms *lifeworld* and *systemsworld*, as general meanings, are borrowed from the German philosopher and sociologist Jürgen Habermas. Habermas uses the language 'systemsworld' and 'lifeworld' to describe two mutually exclusive yet ideally interdependent domains of all of society's enterprises from the family to the complex formal organization. When contrasted with the lifeworld, the systemsworld, in Habermas's framework, has little to do with 'systems theory' and its postulates of interdependencies, systemic change, and the like.

When we talk about the stuff of culture, the essence of values and beliefs, the expression of needs, purposes, and desires of people, and about the sources of deep satisfaction in the form of meaning and significance, we are talking about the lifeworld of schools and of parents, teachers, and students. The lifeworld provides the foundation for the development of social, intellectual, and other forms of human capital that contribute, in turn, to the development of cultural capital, which then further enriches the lifeworld itself. This is a cycle of 'cultural reproduction'. The systemsworld, by contrast, is a world of instrumentalities, of efficient means designed to achieve ends. The systemsworld provides the foundation for the development of management and of organizational and financial capital that, in turn, contributes to the development of material capital, which further enriches the systemsworld. This is a cycle of 'material reproduction'. The former is a world of purposes, norms, growth, and development, and the latter is a world of efficiency, outcomes, and productivity.

Both worlds have value. Both worlds are important to the school. And both worlds are important to other kinds of enterprises as well. Let's take the family, for example. Families are concerned with purposes, norms, and traditions; they focus on the protection, growth, and development of their members; and they seek to enhance the meaning and significance that members experience, allowing them to lead a more satisfying life. Families also budget, save for college, plan vacations, have schedules, keep calendars, manage tax records, and worry about operating costs. With proper balancing, the systemsworld and the lifeworld of the family enhance each other. For this relationship to be mutually beneficial in enterprises like families and schools, however, the lifeworld must be generative. It must be the force that drives the systemsworld.

■ Center and Periphery

In families, schools, and other social organizations there is a center and a periphery. When social organizations are functioning properly the lifeworld occupies the center position. A good way to visualize this relationship is to recall the old adage 'form should follow function or function will follow form'. When a school makes decisions about means, structures, and policies designed to serve its purposes and values, the lifeworld is at the center. Form follows function. But when school purposes are decided by decisions about school means, purposes, and policies, the lifeworld and systemsworld are no longer properly aligned. Instead the systemsworld dominates the lifeworld. Function follows form.

Let us dig a little deeper into Habermas's theory. Schools grow and maintain their lifeworlds by taking 'expressive' and 'normative' action. Expressive action is when parents, teachers, and students express their individual needs, visions, values, and beliefs within the cultural context of the school. Normative action occurs when they seek to act in ways that embody the school's shared values, visions, and beliefs.

Schools grow and maintain their systemsworld by taking 'teleological action' and 'strategic' action. Teleological action involves the setting of objectives and the creating of systems necessary to achieve them. And strategic action involves making appropriate choices among alternative courses of action with the intent of maximizing value. Schools identify purposes, promote visions and values, plan operations, and engage in teaching and learning by embodying all four forms – expressive, normative, teleological, and strategic – of action. Key to Habermas's theory is that all enterprises can be *simultaneously* understood as both systemsworlds and lifeworlds. Equally key is that teleological and strategic actions of the systemsworld should be determined by and should serve the expressive and normative actions of the lifeworld.

Why is it necessary to engage in this lengthy elaboration of Habermas's ideas? Because noting that schools have both a systemsworld and lifeworld and noting that the two worlds must be successfully balanced to function effectively points to a major problem facing schools across the globe. Habermas (1987) refers to this problem as the 'colonization of the lifeworld' by the systemsworld (pp. 173, 353–356). Colonization occurs when the systemsworld begins to dominate the lifeworld.

Balancing the two worlds does not deny the fact that one of the two will always be generative. Either the lifeworld determines what the systemsworld will be like or the systemsworld will determine what the lifeworld will be like. Either management system is uniquely designed to embody and achieve the purposes, values, and beliefs of parents, teachers, and students in a particular school or the purposes, values, and beliefs of parents, teachers, and students will be determined by the chosen (or more likely state- or district-mandated) management systems. Either unique and locally set school visions and standards determine what testing, curriculum content, and teaching styles will be or testing, curriculum content, and teaching styles imposed from the outside will determine local school visions and standards.

Unfortunately, colonization happens gradually and goes largely unnoticed. As the systemsworld moves to the center, the lifeworld and the systemsworld become separated. This separation is the first step toward colonization. When the systemsworld dominates, school goals, purposes, values, and ideals are imposed on parents, teachers, and students rather than created by them. Further, management systems become ends in themselves, assigning value to schools and students based on adherence to the system's requirements.

Take testing as an example. When the lifeworld dominates, testing reflects local passions, needs, values, and beliefs. Standards can remain rigorous and true but are not presumed to be standardized, universal, or all-encompassing. While tests possess the proper psychometric properties and the integrity of their substance is maintained, the specifics of what is tested reflect local values and preferences. Further, the worth of individuals in schools is not determined by some narrow definition of effectiveness and achievement. Instead, a range of assessments might include not only tests but also students' demonstration of multiple intelligences, performance exhibitions of one sort or another, and other criteria. As the systemsworld dominates, however, what counts is determined more narrowly by bureaucratic mandates, politics, and other outside forces.

▋ Colonization in Rio Vista

The recent closing of the Rio Vista School – a fictional name, as are other names of people and places in this section – in rural Texas provides an example of the tension that often exists between a school's lifeworld and systemsworld and what happens when the lifeworld is colonized by the systemsworld. Rio Vista is nestled next to the Rio Grande River about fifty miles from the town of Sendero, roughly halfway between Big Bend National Park and El Paso (see Stinson, 1995; and Mac Cormack, 1998, for details). Ranch work dominates the economy. Spanish is the first language for most of the children at the school, and many of the roughly forty families who live in Rio Vista maintain close ties with their sister city across the river in Mexico.

The Rio Vista School, part of the Sendero School District, opened about one hundred years ago. It most recently served thirty-eight students on a campus that included a two-room schoolhouse and two trailers. Three certified teachers were employed. The school budget was $173,000 or $4,553 per child. High school students were bussed fifty miles each way to Sendero. In 1995 the Rio Vista School was one of only 254 campuses in the state of Texas that was rated 'exemplary'. The rating is based on test scores, dropout rates, and attendance. Being one of 254 exemplary campuses placed Rio Vista in the top 4 percent of all elementary schools in Texas.

During the summer of 1998, the Sendero School Board voted 7–1 to close the Rio Vista School and bus its students to Sendero. This decision was made without consulting parents, teachers, or students. The district's superintendent gave several reasons for the closing. Sustaining thirty-eight students and three teachers on a budget of $173,000 was not very cost-effective, and money was tight. Further, there was a critical teacher shortage at the Sendero Elementary School campus, and the reassignment of Rio Vista teachers to Sendero would help enormously with this problem. Moreover, in recent years test scores in Rio Vista had dipped to slightly below the scores of Sendero students. And finally, from a management point of view, it was difficult keeping track of things on a campus that was fifty miles away.

Effective and efficient assignment of staff, wise use of resources, assessing the extent to which students are meeting academic and other standards, and providing supervision are in themselves neither good nor bad. At face value they are legitimate systemsworld concerns that can enhance the growth and development of a school's lifeworld. On the other hand, these same systemsworld concerns can erode or even destroy the lifeworld of a school. The latter seems to be the case in this story. In 1995 Stinson asked Linda Whitworth, a twenty-seven-year veteran teacher at Rio Vista, to explain the school's success in being rated as an exemplary school. Her response was, 'We believe in a lot of hard work and we care about our kids. We expect them to be prompt and to do their best work. If they don't, they do it again'. She added, 'I can't say enough about our parents. They are our ace in the hole. They support us completely and really pull together with the school'. Stinson reports that high expectations, hard work, caring discipline, affection, and parental involvement and support were all factors contributing to Rio Vista's success. Clearly small size, sense of community, and the willingness of the faculty to act *in loco parentis* have to be included on this list. Because of its unique history, its way of operating, its clear focus and commitment, and the high level of support it received from the local community, Rio Vista could be described as a school with character.

Mac Cormack asked long-time Rio Vista resident Lupe Hernandez for her reaction to the school closing. 'My father was a student there, and he is ninety now. Some of my brothers and sisters and all eight of my children studied there. It was an excellent school. My children learned a lot, and they were treated very well'. What effect does their children having to make a hundred-mile roundtrip have on the views of Rio Vista residents? Felipe Hermosa told Mac Cormack that 'There are already some children not going to school. They get too sick, throwing up and all that. They get too nervous. My son wakes up at 1 A.M. screaming that the bus is leaving already. What's going to happen by the end of the year? The kids will be all messed up'. Estaban Gonzalez reports that she lets her son Roberto sleep for three hours after coming back from school. Then she wakes him to do his homework and he goes back to sleep. 'He's going to get tired and just hate school'. She told Mac Cormack that her six-year-old son was no longer going to school. 'He vomits before he gets on the bus, and on the bus he vomits twice. So he is staying home with me. For us mothers it is very hard. We have to make our children suffer. How are they going to learn if they come home like this?'

Veteran teacher Linda Whitworth told Mac Cormack that 'I'm heart-broken. It's a very traumatic thing to see the disregard [school board members] seem to have for those little bitty kids and their education. It's the end of a one-hundred-year old tradition'. Mac Cormack says that Whitworth believes the school was closed because of money and politics rather than academics. 'They wanted to close that school forever. I don't think we've had an administration that didn't want to close it at least once.' Whitworth also maintains that criticism of recent dips in the state test scores ignores Rio Vista's long-term success. Historically, she argues, Rio Vista students have outperformed Sendero students.

From the board's perspective they are acting in the best interests of all the children and not just a few. Ironically, one of the board members told Mac Cormack, 'There is no such thing as a bad decision if you have local control'. For him local control means a voice for Sendero but not for Rio Vista.

The Rio Vista story is not about good guys or bad guys. Unfortunately, the systemsworld seems to have a life of its own. Means have a way of strengthening and becoming ends in and of themselves. And that seems to be the case here. Despite what they consider to be good intentions, the policy of the board separates the lifeworld and systemsworld and enables the latter to colonize the former. Colonization erodes the character, culture, and sense-making capacity of the Rio Vista school and the people it serves.

Further Examples

Colonization is not just an American but an international problem. Consider several short examples from abroad. Funding in English schools is on a per capita basis, and parents choose the schools they want their children to attend. Thus whether a school has a decent budget or not depends on its ability to attract students. Funding begins with five-year-olds. Yet it is common for many primary schools in England to admit four-year-olds even though no government support is provided for these students. Head teachers reason that accepting four-year-olds provides an incentive for parents to choose a particular school. The children, however, do not always benefit from this arrangement. The payback to the school occurs if these students stay to become fully funded pupils when they turn age five. Jennifer Nias (1995) quotes one embittered primary head teacher as stating, 'It's alright for you. When you look at a four-year-old, you see a child. When I look at a four-year-old, I have to see bank notes' (p. 2). Nias believes doing something that one has misgivings about contributes to emotional exhaustion, depersonalization, and other symptoms of burnout among English teachers. Teachers react this way because they feel passionately that the moral-person-related basis for their work is being eroded and replaced by formal accountability and the emphasis on cost-effectiveness.

Recently, I visited a secondary school in New Zealand. This school, built in British colonial style, occupies a beautiful campus and enjoys an excellent academic reputation. Even more beautiful than the school are the brochures it has developed to market itself abroad. They are expensive, glossy, and compelling.

Like the English schools, the schools in New Zealand are funded on a per capita basis and compete with each other for students. They are free, however, to fill empty spaces with students from abroad who pay full tuition.

Empty seats are more likely to be filled by wealthy students from other countries than by poor students with social capital deficits who live in the surrounding neighborhoods. But then again, given the financial constraints that schools face and the costs of maintaining this beautiful campus and its enriched educational programs, seeking tuition-paying students seems like a pretty good idea. The struggle to survive, and indeed flourish, in this particular competitive school context overrides any commitment the school might have to serve all New Zealanders. Not only are less affluent students and students from lower social classes worth less in dollars, they are more difficult to teach and might jeopardize the school's academic standing. This in turn would make further recruitment more difficult. The cycle of material reproduction, in other words, would be interrupted.

In Scotland, Catholic and other religious schools are funded either fully or partially by the government. With funding comes the inevitable systemsworld intrusions on the culture and character of the lifeworlds of these schools. Intrusion typically takes the form of regulations and mandates that affect everything from building codes to accountability systems and from curriculum to personnel policies. Consider, for example, the case of a Catholic high school in Scotland that had some unique personnel problems but was not free to deal with them in a way that was consistent with the values the school espoused. Here are the particulars. A twenty-two-year veteran teacher was abandoned by her fifty-one-year-old science teacher husband who moved in with a thirty-year-old language teacher (Savill, 1998). This arrangement was complicated by the fact that the separated couple's seventeen-year-old daughter was a pupil at the school. Her mother complained, 'It does not make it easy having to see the pair on a daily basis at work. It causes division with colleagues who have to choose between me and my husband ... The whole staff cannot condone what my husband is doing to my daughter. All the pupils know about the affair. It is very hurtful to her' (p. 3).

The official policy of the school board is not to interfere in marital problems unless the education of students is affected. But given this school's religious tradition and commitment to teaching certain moral principles and family values by both word and deed, it would seem that some action, perhaps a transfer of one of the teachers involved to another school, might be advisable. A spokesperson for the Scottish Catholic Church, however, stated that the church was powerless to take any action at all. 'Catholic schools in

Scotland are totally run, financed, managed by the state. All the Catholic church has is the right of approval of teachers when they are about to receive an appointment.' In the United States, there is increased interest in providing public financial support for Catholic and other religious schools. Will regulations that prescribe a one best way in terms of required standards, curriculum, testing, and other policies follow? If they do, will the result be the erosion of character in these schools?

Culture, Community, and Person

Habermas distinguishes three dimensions of the lifeworld: culture, community, and person. *Culture* provides us with knowledge, beliefs, and norms systems from which we derive significance. *Community* lets us know that we are connected to others and are part of a social group that is valuable, and thus we ourselves are valuable. This is a kind of solidarity that ensures that our 'individual life histories are in harmony with collective forms of life' (Habermas, 1987, p. 141). Community reminds us of our responsibilities to the common good. *Person* refers to the individual competencies we develop that lead us to reach an understanding of our personal lifeworlds and that help us in our search for individual identity, meaning, and significance.

Erosion of the lifeworld as a result of colonization takes its toll on all three dimensions. As culture wanes in a school, meaning is lost, traditions are ruptured, and parents, teachers, and students are likely to drift in a sea of apathy and indifference. As community wanes in a school, feelings of belonging, of being part of something important, of having a common purpose, are weakened, and parents, teachers, and students experience a lack of connectedness, disorientation, and isolation. Inevitably these developments influence the person. As person wanes in a school, parents, teachers, and students become alienated from themselves, each other, and the school and its work.

'What is the major problem facing schools today?' This was the question asked of students elected to appear in the book *Who's Who Among American High Schools* in 1996. Their worrisome response? Apathy! This is a finding confirmed recently by Laurence Steinberg and his colleagues Bradford Brown and Sanford Dornbusch (1996) in their study of twenty thousand high school students in northern California and Wisconsin. They conclude that curriculum, instructional innovation, changes in school organization, toughening of standards, rethinking teacher preparation, and other reforms will not succeed if students are not engaged – that is, if they do not come to school interested in and committed to learning.

The loss of character in a school that results from an eroding lifeworld forces students to make culture, community, and personal identity for themselves (see Sergiovanni, 1992, 1994). Students turn to their own subculture and its norms in search of meaning and significance. Too often the norms of this sub-culture work against school purposes. Repairing schools and reconnecting youngsters requires that we rebuild culture, community, and person dimensions of the lifeworld of each individual school. Doing so is a way to restore character in a school. If we fail to restore character, then we will fulfill the prophecy of the French philosopher Henri de Saint-Simon: 'The government of man will be replaced by the administration of things' (Kaplan, 1997, p. 15).

References

Bryk, A.S., and Driscoll, M.E. *The School as Community: Theoretical Foundations, Contextual Influences and Consequences for Teachers and Students*. Madison, Wis.: National Center for Effective Secondary Schools, 1988.

Darling-Hammond, L. *The Right to Learn: A Blueprint for Creating Schools That Work*. San Francisco, CA: Jossey-Bass, 1997.

Greenfield, T.B. 'Organizations as Social Inventions: Rethinking Assumptions about Change.' *Journal of Applied Behavioral Science*, 1973, 9(5).

Greenfield, T.B. 'Leaders and Schools: Willfulness and Non-natural Order in Organizations.' In T.J. Sergiovanni and J.E. Corbally (eds.), *Leadership and Organizational Culture*. Urbana-Champaign: University of Illinois Press, 1984.

Habermas, J. *The Theory of Communicative Action*. Vol. 2: *Lifeworld and System: A Critique of Functional Reason*. (T. McCarthy, trans.) Boston: Beacon Press, 1987.

Kaplan, R.D. 'Was Democracy Just a Moment?' *Atlantic Monthly*, Dec. 1997, p. 15.

Louis, M.R. 'Surprise and Sense-making: What Newcomers Experience in Entering Unfamiliar Organizational Settings.' *Administrative Science Quarterly*, 1980, *25*, 226–251.

Mac Cormack, J. 'Schools' Closure Tears Tiny Town,' *San Antonio Express News*, Sept. 7, 1998, p. 4A.

Meier, D. *The Power of Their Ideas: Lessons for America From a Small School in Harlem*. Boston: Beacon Press, 1995.

Nias, J. 'Teachers' Moral Purposes: Sources of Vulnerability and Strength.' The Johann Jacobs Foundation Conference on Teacher Burnout, Marbach Castle, Germany, Nov. 1995.

Savill, R. 'Love-Triangle Teacher "Dreading New Term".' *Daily Telegraph*, Jan. 6, 1998, p. 3.

Selznick, P. *Leadership in Administration*. Berkeley: University of California Press, 1957.

Sergiovanni, T.J. *Moral Leadership: Getting to the Heart of School Improvement*. San Francisco, CA: Jossey-Bass, 1992.

Sergiovanni, T.J. *Building Community in Schools*. San Francisco, CA: Jossey-Bass, 1994.

Steinberg, L., Brown, B., and Dornbusch, S.M. *Beyond the Classroom: Why School Reform has Failed and What Parents Need to Do*. New York: Simon & Schuster, 1996.

Stinson, R. 'Important Discovery Made in Candelaria.' *San Antonio Express News*, Sept. 7, 1995, p. 3A.

Part 2

Understanding Educational Leadership

3

Leadership Theory Reviewed

Melissa Horner

Over the years, leadership has been studied extensively in various contexts and theoretical foundations. In some cases, leadership has been described as a process, but most theories and research on leadership look at a person to gain understanding (Bernard, 1926; Blake, Shepard and Mouton, 1964; Drath and Palus, 1994; Fledler, 1967; and House and Mitchell, 1974). Leadership is typically defined by the traits, qualities, and behaviours of a leader. The study of leadership has spanned across cultures, decades, and theoretical beliefs. A summary of what is known and understood about leadership is important to conducting further research on team leadership.

In a comprehensive review of leadership theories (Stogdill 1974), several different categories were identified that capture the essence of the study of leadership in the twentieth century. The first trend dealt with the attributes of great leaders. Leadership was explained by the internal qualities with which a person is born (Bernard, 1926). The thought was that if the traits that differentiated leaders from followers could be identified, successful leaders could be quickly assessed and put into positions of leadership. Personality, physical, and mental characteristics were examined. This research was based on the idea that leaders were born, not made, and the key to success was simply in identifying those people who were born to be great leaders. Though much research was done to identify the traits, no clear answer was found with regard to what traits consistently were associated with great leadership. One flaw with this line of thought was in ignoring the situational and environmental factors that play a role in a leader's level of effectiveness.

A second major thrust looked at leader behaviours in an attempt to determine what successful leaders do, not how they look to others (Halpin and Winer, 1957; Hemphill and Coons, 1957). These studies began to look at

Source: Team Performance Management, Vol. 3, No. 4, 1997, pp. 270–87. Edited version.

leaders in the context of the organization, identifying the behaviours leaders exhibit that increase the effectiveness of the company. The well-known and documented Michigan and Ohio State leadership studies took this approach. Two primary, independent factors were identified by these studies: consideration and initiation of structure. Research was simultaneously being conducted in other universities and similar results were found. The impact of this work was in part the notion that leadership was not necessarily an inborn trait, but instead effective leadership methods could be taught to employees (Saal and Knight, 1988). These researchers were making progress in identifying what behaviours differentiated leaders from followers so that the behaviours could be taught. Another impact of this line of work dealt with the broadening of management's focus to include both people-oriented activities along with task-oriented activities.

Furthering this work, Blake, Shepard, and Mouton (1964) also developed a two-factor model of leadership behaviour similar to that found at Ohio State and Michigan. They called the factors 'concern for people' and 'concern for output'. They later added a third variable, that of flexibility. According to these studies, managers exhibit behaviours that fall into the two primary categories (task or people). Depending on which category was shown most frequently, a leader could be placed along each of the two continua. The outcome of this research was primarily descriptive and helped categorize leaders based on their behaviour.

A third approach to answering the question about the best way to lead dealt with the interaction between the leader's traits, the leader's behaviours, and the situation in which the leader exists. These contingency theories make the assumption that the effects of one variable on leadership are contingent on other variables. This concept was a major insight at the time, because it opened the door for the possibility that leadership could be different in every situation (Saal and Knight, 1988). With this idea a more realistic view of leadership emerged, allowing for the complexity and situational specificity of overall effectiveness. Several different contingencies were identified and studied, but it is unrealistic to assume that any one theory is more or less valid or useful than another.

One such theory considered two variables in defining leader effectiveness: leadership style and the degree to which the leader's situation is favourable for influence (Fiedler, 1967). Fiedler's concept of situational favourability, or the ease of influencing followers, was defined as the combination of leader-member relations, task structure, and position power. Measuring each as high or low, Fiedler came up with eight classifications of situational favourability. He then developed a questionnaire to measure leader style, called the Least Preferred Co-worker scale. Through his research, he found that certain leadership styles were more effective in certain situations. Although in general this theory is questionably applicable due to its relative simplicity, it initiated discussion and research about matching a leader with a situation that would be most conducive to that leader's style.

Yet another contingency theory deals with an analysis of the people who are led by leaders. The importance of the followers in leadership emerged (House and Mitchell, 1974), and leadership was seen as an interaction between the goals of the followers and the leader. The path-goal theory suggests that leaders are primarily responsible for helping followers develop behaviours that will enable them to reach their goals or desired outcomes. Variables that impact on the most effective leader behaviour include the nature of the task (whether it is intrinsically or extrinsically satisfying), autonomy levels of the followers, and follower motivation. A somewhat limited view of leadership was developed by Vroom and Yetton (1973). The Vroom–Yetton theory described what leader's should do given certain circumstances with regard to the level of involvement of followers in making decisions. Following a decision tree that asks about the need for participation, a conclusion can be drawn about how the leader should go about making the decision to be most effective.

Other leadership theories emerged out of this work, including the vertical dyad linkage theory, also known as the leader-member exchange theory (Graen, 1976). This theory explains the nature of the relationship between leaders and followers and how this relationship impacts the leadership process. Graen categorized employees into two groups: the in-group and the out-group. The relationship between the leader and each group is different, thus affecting the type of work members of each group are given. Research has generally supported this theory, and its value deals with the investigation of each follower's relationship with the leader as opposed to a general or average leadership style.

The broad and varied body of work on leadership, therefore, suggests that there are many appropriate ways to lead or styles of leadership. Contingency theories differ from and build on the trait and behaviour theories, as the philosophy that one best way to lead evolved into a complex analysis of the leader and the situation. For optimal success, both the leader style and situation can be evaluated, along with characteristics of the followers. Then, either the leader can be appointed to an appropriate situation given his/her style of leadership, the leader can exhibit different behaviours, or the situation can be altered to best match the leader.

As leadership research has grown and expanded, an even broader look at leadership has emerged: a focus on the organizational culture (Schein, 1985). For leaders to be effective, according to this view, issues related to the culture must be clearly identified. For example, one aspect of a culture is change. Leaders must be able to adapt to change, depending on the culture, as the environment shifts and develops. In one study it was found that organizations that have tried to resist change in the external environment have experienced more difficulties than organizations that have responded posi-tively to change (Baron, 1995).

As a different example of the importance of culture, culture management is another important aspect of leadership. Culture management deals with the ability of leaders to know and understand what the organizational cul-ture is, modifying that culture to meet the needs of the organization as it progresses. Baron (1995) found in his research that organizations that have tried to proactively exploit new opportunities in the environment experi-enced successful culture change. Additionally, Baron found that the rise of the professional manager over the past several decades suggests that increas-ing and different management and leadership skills are high on the agenda for effective culture management. In other words, additional skills are needed in today's leaders so that they will be able to manage the organiza-tional culture. Part of the culture change found in this research consisted of a drive for greater flexibility and the development of employee empowerment and autonomy. Leaders are also involved in managing the culture by estab-lishing an explicit strategic direction, communicating that direction, and defining the organizational vision and values. This line of research, however, has not identified a model for different styles of leadership given different cultural factors. The application of these ideas is difficult, in part due to the organizational specificity of culture and the difficulty in defining culture. One conclusion that can be drawn is that leaders need to work within the culture to be most successful.

With regard to leadership and motivation, the leadership research and the-ories reviewed above depend heavily on the study of motivation, suggesting that leadership is less a specific set of behaviours than it is creating an envi-ronment in which people are motivated to produce and move in the direction of the leader. In other words, leaders may need to concern them-selves less with the actual behaviours they exhibit and attend more to the situation within which work is done. By creating the right environment, one in which people want to be involved and feel committed to their work, lead-ers are able to influence and direct the activities of others. This perspective requires an emphasis on the people being led as opposed to the leader. A review of some of the major theories of motivation can help provide a better understanding of how a leader might create such an environment.

A well-known motivation theory is that of Herzberg (1964). Through his research, Herzberg differentiated between elements in the work place that led to employee satisfaction and elements that led to employee dissatisfaction, such that satisfaction and dissatisfaction are thought of as two different con-tinua instead of two ends of the same continuum. Those elements that cause satisfaction can be thought of as motivators, because employees are moti-vated to achieve them. The other set of elements Herzberg labelled hygiene factors, because they are necessary to keep employees from being dissatisfied.

This theory ties to leadership, because leaders may be interested in reducing dissatisfaction and increasing satisfaction to develop an environment more conducive to employee satisfaction and perhaps performance.

Other motivation theories also apply to leadership in terms of offering arguments for what leaders need to do to influence others' behaviour. For example, need theories suggest that people have needs for certain results or outcomes, and they are driven to behave in ways that will satisfy these needs (Alderfer, 1969; Maslow, 1943; Murray, 1938). Maslow proposed a need hierarchy in which certain needs are more basic than others and people are motivated to satisfy them (for example, physiological and safety needs), before they will feel a drive to satisfy higher-order needs (belongingness, esteem, and self-actualization). Alderfer (1969) built on this work, suggesting that there may be only three needs (existence needs, relatedness needs, and growth needs) in a hierarchy of concreteness. He theorized that people could move up and down the hierarchy, and people may be motivated by multiple needs at any one time. Another related theory is Murray's (1938) manifest needs theory. This theory suggests that people experience a wide variety of needs (for example, need for achievement, need for power, and need for affiliation), and everyone may not experience the same needs. The appropriate environmental conditions activate certain needs. Relating this to leadership, work typically satisfies some needs, and the question is whether leaders can develop an environment that helps meet people's more advanced or immediate needs.

Additional motivation theories include expectancy theory, equity theory, goal setting, and reinforcement. Each of these has implications for the approach leaders take to dealing with their followers. Expectancy theory proposes that people engage in particular behaviours based on the probability that the behaviour will be followed by a certain outcome and the value of that outcome (Vroom, 1964). As leaders understand what people value, they can impact people's actions by defining what behaviours will produce desired outcomes. Equity theories suggest that people are motivated to balance their input/output ratio with others' input/output ratio (Adams, 1965). This indicates a delicate balance based on individual perceptions that may or may not accurately represent reality. Goal setting theory takes a somewhat different approach, suggesting that people are motivated to achieve goals, and their intentions drive their behaviour (Locke, 1968). Performance goals, therefore, set by either leaders or individuals themselves contribute to determining what behaviours will be exhibited. Finally, reinforcement theory stems from a behaviourist viewpoint and states that behaviour is controlled by its consequences (Skinner, 1959). Leaders are certainly in a position to provide either positive or negative consequences to followers, and reinforcement theory has had a significant impact on developing effective leadership style.

Motivation is not seen as the only element involved in eliciting certain behaviours from followers or employees; knowledge and abilities certainly play a role as well. However, the motivation theories add to the body of leadership work because of the emphasis on the followers themselves and what causes them to act, instead of focusing on the leaders and their traits, behaviours, or situations. Leadership, then, is not only the process and activity of the person who is in a leadership position, but also encompasses the environment this leader creates and how this leader responds to the surroundings, as well as the particular skills and activities of the people being led.

Using motivational theories as support, additional leadership theories then emerged, represented by the comparison of transactional versus transformational leadership, for example. Transactional leadership stems from more traditional views of workers and organizations, and it involves the position power of the leader to use followers for task completion (Burns, 1978). Transformational leadership, however, searches for ways to help motivate followers by satisfying higher-order needs and more fully engaging them in the process of the work (Bass, 1985). Transformational leaders can initiate and cope with change, and they can create something new out of the old. In this way, these leaders personally evolve while also helping their followers and organizations evolve. They build strong relationships with others while supporting and encouraging each individual's development.

A definition of leadership from Gardner (1990, p. 38) holds that 'leadership is the accomplishment of group purpose, which is furthered not only by effective leaders but also by innovators, entrepreneurs, and thinkers; by the availability of resources; by questions of value and social cohesion'. By this definition, then, leadership can be thought of as an even broader phenomenon. Gardner begins to challenge the idea that leadership exists within a single designated person and a situation. Instead, he positions leadership as moving toward and achieving a group goal, not necessarily because of the work of one skilled individual (i.e. the leader) but because of the work of multiple members of the group. Not only does leadership require someone who helps set the direction and move the group forward while serving as a resource, but it involves the contributions of other great thinkers and doers, access to the right resources, and the social composition of the group.

Manz and Sims also offer a revised, integrative perspective on leadership. Using the term 'SuperLeadership', they challenge the traditional paradigm of leadership as one person doing something to other people (Manz and Sims, 1991). Instead, they suggest that another model exists for leadership today: 'the most appropriate leader is one who can lead others to lead themselves' (p.18). With this view, leadership exists within each individual, and it is not confined to the limits of formally appointed leaders. They suggest that, for leaders to be most successful, they need to facilitate each individual in the process of leading himself or herself. Leaders become great by unleashing the potential and abilities of followers, consequently having the knowledge of many people instead of relying solely on their own skills and abilities.

Is there a clear, single profile that exists for a great leader? Most likely there is not. Based on the reviewed theories, there is not a consistent definition of a successful leader or one best understanding of what causes people to act as they do at work. This helps explain why leadership is one of the most widely studied phenomena, yet there seem to be no clear answers. So why do people keep studying leadership? Because there seem to be some differentiating factors that can be assessed, trained, and developed that contribute to making great leaders great. There are differences among individuals in leadership effectiveness, and researchers strive to identify, quantify, and predict such differences. Although it is hard to define and capture, the belief clearly prevails that interventions will help develop and improve leadership in today's organizations. Some work has been done to understand what makes good leaders successful with the intent of developing better leadership in organizations. Such qualities are discussed next. In relation to the characteristics of a successful leader, several hypotheses have been made about what makes a leader successful. For example, measures of personality have been shown to correlate with ratings of leadership effectiveness (Hogan, Curphy, and Hogan, 1994). Specifically, these authors suggest that the big-five model of personality structure that is commonly accepted provides a common language that encompasses the personality factors found to relate to leadership. The big-five model holds that personality, as observed by others, can be described by five broad dimensions (extraversion, agreeableness, conscientiousness, emotional stability, and intellect). Using this common terminology, research on leadership can be integrated more easily. Stogdill (1974) and Bentz (1990) found significant correlations between multiple measures of leadership effectiveness (ratings by others, advancement, and pay) and extraversion, emotional stability, conscientiousness, and agreeableness. These findings may be due to a wide variety of reasons, however, because the relationship has not been found to be causational. This line of research can be linked to trait theories of leadership, suggesting that personal qualities, such as dimensions of personality, are somehow related to effectiveness as a leader. Although significant results have been found, the application of this research to leadership development is limited due to the relatively stable nature of personality within individuals over time.

Other empirical work determining what makes a leader successful is disappointingly slim, in part because measures of effectiveness are very difficult to identify and isolate (Hogan, Curphy, and Hogan, 1994). Some general attributes have been identified and agreed upon to some extent; for example, Bennis (1989) described leaders as people who know what they want and why they want it, and have the skills to communicate that to others in a way that gains their support. Lappas (1996, p. 14) states that 'the leadership focus of knowing what you want and when you want it distinguishes exceptional from average leaders'. Yet other approaches look to the productivity of the followers to measure leadership effectiveness (Fiedler, 1967; House, Spangler, and

Woycke, 1991). Productivity, however, has consistently been difficult to use as a variable in field research due to the multitude of variables that impact it.

Although not much research exists on why leaders fail, it appears that leadership success depends on a combination of both exhibiting positive behaviours and also not exhibiting negative or derailing behaviours (Hogan, Curphy, and Hogan, 1994). Some of these negative behaviours include arrogance, untrustworthiness, moodiness, insensitivity, compulsiveness, and abrasiveness (Bentz, 1990). These characteristics are more difficult to quickly identify in an assessment process, because they may or may not exist in the presence of the big-five personality traits. It appears, however, that if they emerge, regardless of the extent to which the leader demonstrates positive leadership behaviours, the leader will be less effective and potentially will fail if the behaviours are not changed.

Given the repeated and recent emphasis on identifying attributes and behaviours associated with successful leadership (Lappas, 1996; Hogan, Curphy, and Hogan, 1994; Wilson, George, and Wellins, 1994), it appears, so far, the objective of defining successful leadership has not been satisfactorily accomplished. Perhaps a different angle can be taken that will add insight to the search for understanding about leadership.

These leadership models have been designed for the 'typical American worker': a white male with a high school education working in manufacturing (Hogan, Curphy, and Hogan, 1994). The economy continues to shift more toward service and away from manufacturing, the workforce becomes older and more ethnically diverse, and competition for highly educated, talented people increases. Organizations rely on innovation and creativity more heavily than they have before (Wilson, *et al.*, 1994).

Because of the changes in the workforce, the nature of work, and the structure of organizations, it is important to re-evaluate the concept of leadership in this context. Characteristics that made leaders successful in the twentieth century may or may not be the same characteristics needed in the future. For example an explosion has occurred in the amount of knowledge that exists: 'the transformation of an industrial-based economy into an information-based economy' (Wilson *et al.*, 1994, p. 18). Therefore, capitalizing on the talents and intellectual potential of employees is increasingly important for organizational success (Wriston, 1990). Another major shift deals with the need to increase speed and efficiency. Not only in taking ideas to market, but also in responding quickly to changes internally and externally, organizations are being forced to move faster (Stalk and Hout, 1990).

Most definitely, there are some additional, different skills and behaviours needed, because of the changes mentioned above, along with the increasing movement toward creating a team-based environment. As put by Lappas (1996, p. 15), 'identification and definition of attributes and behaviours associated with leadership in the public and private sectors are essential to success'. Prior research and theory on leadership, while it provides a strong foundation and basis to work from, is not enough to fully understand what makes leaders successful in changing environments. Leadership has proven to be an area that changes over time as organizations and individuals change, and therefore needs to be continually studied so that assessment and training processes are appropriate for current leadership contexts.

Another area of theory on leadership looks at leadership as a process in which leaders are not seen as individuals in charge of followers, but as members of a community of practice (Drath and Palus, 1994). A community of practice is defined as, 'people united in a common enterprise who share a history and thus certain values, beliefs, ways of talking, and ways of doing things' (p. 4). This definition may be thought of as a variation of organizational culture. These authors believe that the vast majority of leadership theories and research has been based on the idea that leadership involves a leader and a group of followers, and dominance, motivation, and influence are the primary vehicles of leadership. Building on and modifying this view, Drath and Palus (1994) propose a theory of leadership as a process. Instead of focusing on a leader and followers, they suggest studying the social process that happens with groups of people who are engaged in an activity together. With this view, leadership is not so much defined as the characteristics of a leader, but instead leadership is the process of coordinating efforts and moving together as a group. This group may include a leader, per se, but the dynamics are dramatically different than traditional leadership theories have suggested; everyone involved in the activity is assumed to play an active role in leadership.

The work of Manz and Sims supports this notion of leadership as a process, as they focus on self-leadership within each individual more than the behaviours and actions of a few select people designated as formal leaders in an organization (Manz and Sims, 1989). As theories turned toward looking at the environment of leaders (for example, Fiedler, 1967), the relationship between leaders and followers (House and Mitchell, 1974), and even the organizational culture (Schein, 1985), researchers have been acknowledging the highly complex, interdependent nature of leadership. These theories have laid the groundwork for examining leadership as a process, taking the emphasis away from an individual.

Drath and Palus (1994), Bruner (1986) and Kegan (1982) suggest that all members of an organization continually construct knowledge of themselves and the world around them. In constructing views of the world, people working together in an organization need to develop socially understood interpretations, so they can be effective as a group. This is the foundation from which people interpret, anticipate, and plan. By the nature of this definition, leadership requires participation from everyone so that all members are engaged in creating meaning and acting on that meaning (Drath and Palus, 1994).

Perhaps this is the most appropriate way to view leadership in organizations that largely consist of work teams who have taken on significant decision-making responsibility (Bednarek, 1990; Dumaine, 1990). As organizations become flatter and teams of employees are empowered with more decision-making responsibility, the need for traditional supervisors is rapidly decreasing (Fisher, 1993). Because many of the responsibilities typically held by supervisors and managers are gradually being turned over to team members (for example, scheduling work, making assignments, and evaluating performance against goals or standards), people holding these positions have questioned their role and purpose in the organization. However, this does not mean that people who were leaders in traditional hierarchical organizations are no longer needed.

The key in organizational transformation to teams lies in the evolution of the role of leadership. More tightly integrated with the teams themselves, successful leaders take on new and different responsibilities, such as facilitation, coaching, and managing relations outside the group (Fisher, 1993). No matter how advanced the team is, there is still a need for leadership to enable the team to be optimally successful (Wilson, et al., 1994). In fact, 'teams probably need more coaching, guidance, and attention in their early stages than the same individual contributors would need in a traditional structure' (Wilson, et al., 1994, p. 6). Leaders are in the best position to provide this support and direction. The method used in doing so, however, is drastically different. Through collaboration, openness, and the creation of shared meaning, leaders can elicit the commitment of others and guide the work process, allowing members to expand their skills and contributions to the organization more broadly (Hackman, 1987). Perhaps, then, viewing leadership as a process gives a framework within which this evolution of leadership responsibility can be examined further.

'Teams' and 'leadership' may arguably be two of the most frequently used terms in management literature and discussion. They may also be two of the most misunderstood words, as there are almost as many definitions of each word as there are authors that write about them (Bass, 1981; Lappas, 1996). Combining the two words to create the concept of team leadership or leadership of teams remains a challenging, yet necessary, next step in the development of organizations and their structures. According to Millikin (1994, p. 3), 'as more organizations are looking at self-managed work teams as a way of doing business, questions arise about what leadership style is effective and where the locus of power is within modern organizations'. This locus of power shift suggests that leadership may be taking on a significantly different appearance in modern organizations than it has in the days of scientific management, mass production, and command and control styles.

With the emergence of self-directed teams, the question of leadership arises in a different context. Self-directed teams can be defined as 'a group of employees who have day-to-day responsibility for managing themselves and the work they do with a minimum of direct supervision' (Fisher, 1993, p. 15). This term is typically used to describe teams in a highly empowered environment. The idea of leadership as a person may no longer be appropriate due to the highly collaborative, involved nature of the workforce. Looking at leadership as a process may offer a better fit for organizations following the philosophy of Drath and Palus (1994). This is due in part to the shift organizations may take in which team members hold significant responsibility over their work. When looking at self-directed teams, team members are by definition involved in the leadership of their work. Consequently, viewing leadership as contained within an individual outside the team significantly limits our understanding of what actually happens in the work process.

In addition to the nature of leadership, the description of formal leaders has become much more heterogeneous over time, adding to the complexity of the leadership environment. A formal leader does not take the same shape or form in different organizations, different departments, or even in the same team over time. Although organizational hierarchies often show formal lines of authority and accountability from one individual to another, and a formal leader or manager is designated for any team, the role of that person within the team's functioning varies widely (Ayres, 1992). More and more we are seeing that this formal leader is only minutely involved in the daily activities of the team. More often, the true leadership of the team, in terms of day-to-day activities, comes from other sources. In some situations, the leadership may be rotated among some or all of the team members over time. In other situations, each person may hold leadership responsibility for a certain aspect of the work. In yet other situations, informal leaders may simply emerge from within the boundaries of the team (Wilson, *et al.*, 1994).

Consequently, in team environments, researchers may have a difficult time identifying a leader in the team. The behaviours that represent leadership, for example setting direction or managing conflict, can be, and often are, exhibited by anyone and everyone in the group. Therefore, the focus of 'leadership research cannot be a specific person, even if that person is designated as the team leader, if a comprehensive understanding of the leadership process is expected. To understand leadership in teams, the entire team must be studied. The leadership behaviours may come from one person or multiple people within the team or external to it. According to Hackman (1987), as team members practise self-management, they take personal responsibility for outcomes, feel personally accountable, monitor and manage their own performance, and help others improve their performance. As self-managing activities contribute to setting and pursuing the direction of the team, all members of a team have the potential to add to the leadership of the team. It is important to understand what leadership as a process consists of and the ramifications this has for the team's overall performance.

The line between leaders and followers in this environment has become less clear and more flexible.

As organizations move from more traditional, hierarchical structures to a more team-based structure, the role and function of leadership is thought to change as well (Nygren and Levine, 1995). The 'command and control' models of leadership do not fit these re-engineered and empower organizations (especially for those people responsible for the front-line employees). As Fisher (1993) explains, individuals responsible for managing employees that are organized into self-managed teams need different leadership skills from those used by traditional managers.

In understanding what is important for successful team leadership, a consideration of employee motivation may be helpful. The concept of motivation plays a key role in team-based organizations as well as team leadership, although it may be defined somewhat differently. According to Senge, Ross, Smith, Roberts, and Kleiner (1994), self-awareness and motivation toward a common goal are two factors essential for a learning organization to exist, which they define as the most productive type of organization, continually working toward a state of development and growth. Each employee, not just the formal leaders, needs to be aware of their values, motives, and goals. They also need to commit to a common goal and feel ownership of that goal to be motivated to produce and move the organization forward. Such commitment and motivation will allow a broader spectrum of individuals to participate in leading the organization into the future.

Because every employee must be motivated and committed to reaching organizational goals, not just the leaders, leadership takes on a different form. No longer do formal leaders exist to monitor employee behaviour correct problems. Everyone is charged with showing some leadership qualities. This empowerment is the beginning phase of developing a leadership process in which everyone can engage.

An interesting aspect of team leadership, as opposed to individual employee leadership, is that success does not seem dependent solely on applying the right behaviour given the right situation, as the contingency theories suggest. The nature of work is changing, requiring much more innovation, creativity, and individual thought and initiative. The same is true for the work of leaders. Prescriptions, policies, and procedures no longer exist to help leaders decide what to do in what situation, if they ever did exist in reality. It is less likely than in the past that leaders will face the same situations frequently enough that prescriptions would be of value. Given the increased complexity of work on so many levels (such as technological, interpersonal, and environmental), employees are required to apply their judgment to evaluate situations and make decisions instead of relying on established structure or routine.

It is suggested that future leaders may need to hold visions, values, assumptions and paradigms that are in agreement with having a team-oriented, empowered workforce in order to be most successful. For the decisions to be aligned with the organization, each member's paradigms and assumptions must also be aligned with those of the organization. Only when this exists will a leader act consistently in ways that support the team environment.

Team leadership can potentially take on a multitude of shapes and forms, adding a dimension of complexity that may not have existed in the past. By combining the research of the past, current trends and methods, and practical experience with teams there is hope for making the process of team leadership consistent, modifiable, and valuable in organizations.

Manz and Sims (1989), researched the changes in leadership as a result of team structures. They defined a new management style that is essential for team-based organizations: SuperLeadership. Instead of one formal leader holding the power, this theory suggests that the locus of control is shifted over time from the leader to the team. Taking this idea a step further, they believe that employee self-leadership is a critical aspect of successful teams. Self-leadership is described as a set of strategies for leading oneself to higher work performance and effectiveness, taking on increasing amounts of responsibility internally.

The relationship between self-leadership and productivity has been studied to test these ideas. In 1994, Millikin hypothesized that teams with members who experienced high levels of self-leadership would be more productive than teams exhibiting less self-leadership. He found a positive relationship, indicating that higher levels of team self-leadership (measured as a combined total of individual measures of self-leadership) were related to increased levels of productivity in a manufacturing environment. This finding lends support to the theory of self-leadership as an effective way to operate in a team-based organization.

The idea of leadership as a process, therefore, appears to provide a theory that connects teams and leadership by integrating the efforts of team members with the efforts of management and allowing responsiveness to change. Consistent with the ideas of SuperLeadership, individual team members are taking on more responsibility, more power, and more leadership qualities. According to Drath and Palus (1994), leadership involves the entire group of people working together, which may be called the team. Such shared meaning then guides the group's behaviour and helps them work toward a common goal. The applications of this idea for practice are clear (Drath and Palus, 1994, p. 6):

> Instead of focusing leadership development almost exclusively on training individuals to be leaders, we may, using this view, learn to develop leadership by improving everyone's ability to participate in the process of leadership.

One approach may be to question teams about leadership behaviours and who in the team exhibits those behaviours. In this way, leadership is not assumed to reside in one individual member of the team, or someone outside the team. At the same time, it is not assumed to reside in every member of the team. Instead, leadership may be thought of as a component of organizational culture. Given the theory that leadership is a process, it is important to ask what that process looks like, so it can be refined and replicated.

The general concept of team leadership is not new, and several authors have written about potential behaviours that are important for effective leadership in team-based organizations. Kozlowski, Gully, Salas, and Cannon-Bowers (1995) suggest a wide range of behaviours that are needed for leading teams. Their list includes developing shared knowledge among team members, acting as a mentor, instructing others, facilitating group processes, providing information, monitoring performance, promoting open communication, providing goals, and allocating resources efficiently. Dew (1995) identified several skills needed for democratic leadership: the ability to lead participative meetings, listening skills, the ability to handle conflict, measurement skills, group-centred decision-making skills, teaching skills, and team building skills. Temme (1995) reinforced the aspect of coaching by stating that team leaders need to create a high-expectations climate through coaching and developing others.

Other authors emphasize the boundary management and structural aspects of leadership. Frohman (1995) described the importance of the bridge between top management and teams, suggesting that leaders need to coordinate work, obtain support resources, and negotiate for time and availability of members. With regard to managing upward in the organization, Brown (1995) discusses the importance of the need for leaders to challenge others' ideas and decisions, creating an environment in which people are not afraid to take risks. Kolb (1995) adds that leaders must avoid compromising the team's objectives with political issues, they must stand behind the team and support it, and they need to be influential in getting outside constituencies to support the team's efforts.

Wilson and Wellins (1995) discuss both tactical and strategic skills that are required in today's team-based organizations. From a tactical perspective, they specify communication skills, performance management, analysis and judgment, coaching, and championing continuous improvement and empowerment. Strategic skills essential for leading in high-involvement environments include leading through vision and values, building trust, facilitating learning, and building partnerships with other parts of the organization. In a study of the importance of various leadership qualities, Donnelly and Kezsbom (1994) found that managerial competence (not specifically defined) was found to be most important, followed by collaborative and analytical competence, and communication and interpersonal competence were found to be next most important.

As can be seen by this review, various perspectives have been taken in trying to define and characterize leadership. Going back to two-factor theories, justification seems to exist for giving continued attention to both task-related and people-related behaviours, because neither one has been shown to be the primary determinant of leader success. At the same time, these authors indicate a stronger emphasis on influence and support, as opposed to directing and commanding behaviours of leaders. From coaching and training to developing a learning environment to managing boundaries, these theories add support for a shift in what comprises effective leadership in empowered, team-based organizations.

References

Adams, J.S. (1965). Inequity in social exchange. In L. Berkowitz (ed.), *Advances in experimental social psychology* (vol. 2). New York: Academic Press.

Alderfer, C.R. (1969). A new theory of human needs. *Organizational Behavior and Human Performance*, 4, 142–175.

Ayres, C.L. (1992). *The relationship between productivity and work team autonomy and team process effectiveness.* Unpublished doctoral dissertation, University of Texas, Austin.

Baron, A. (1995). Going public with studies on culture management. *Personnel Management*, 1(19), 60.

Bass, B.M. (1981). *Stogdill's handbook of leadership.* New York: Free Press.

Bass, B.M. (1985). *Leadership and performance beyond expectations.* New York: Free Press.

Bednarek, D.I. (1990). Go, team, go. *Human Resource Executive*, 21, 45.

Bennis, W. (1989). *On becoming a leader.* New York: Addison-Wesley.

Bentz, V.J. (1990). Contextual issues in predicting high-level leadership performance: contextual richness as a criterion consideration in personality research with executives. In K. E. Clark and M.B. Clark (eds.), *Measures of leadership* (pp. 131–143). West Orange, NJ: Leadership Library of America.

Bernard, L.L. (1926). *An introduction to social psychology.* New York: Holt.

Blake, R.R., Shepard, H.A., and Mouton, J.S. (1964). *Managing intergroup conflict in industry.* Houston, TX: Gulf Publishing Co.

Brown, T. (1995). Great leaders need great followers. *Industry Week*, pp. 24–30.

Bruner, J. (1986). *Actual minds, possible worlds.* Cambridge, MA: Harvard University Press.

Burns, J. (1978) *Leadership.* New York: Harper and Row.

Dew, J. (1995). Creating team leaders. *Journal for Quality and Participation*, 18(6), 50–54.

Donnelly, R.G., and Kezsbom, D.S. (1994). Overcoming the responsibility-authority gap: an investigation of effective project team leadership for a new decade. *Cost Engineering*, 36(5), 33–41.

Drath, W.H., and Palus, C.J. (1994). *Making common sense: leadership as meaning-making in a community of practice.* Greensboro, NC: Center for Creative Leadership.

Dumaine, B. (1990, May 7). Who needs a boss? *Fortune*, 34, 52–60.

Fiedler, F.E. (1967). *A theory of leadership effectiveness.* New York: McGraw-Hill.

Fisher, K. (1993). *Leading self-directed work teams: a guide to developing new team leadership skills.* New York: McGraw-Hill, Inc.

Frohman, M. (1995). Nothing kills teams like ill-prepared leaders. *Industry Week*, pp. 72–76.

Gardner, J.W. (1990). *On leadership*. New York: Free Press.

Graen, G. (1976). Role-making processes within complex organizations. In M.D. Dunnette (ed.), *Handbook of industrial and organizational psychology*. Chicago: Rand McNally.

Hackman, J.R. (1987). The psychology of self-management in organizations. In M.S. Pollock and R.O. Perloff (eds.), *Psychology and work: productivity change and employment* (pp. 85–136). Washington, DC: American Psychological Association.

Halpin, A.W., and Winer, B. J. (1957). A factorial study of the leader behavior description. In R.M. Stogdill and A.E. Coons (eds.), *Leader behavior: its description and measurement*. Columbus, OH: Bureau of Business Research, Ohio State University.

Hemphill, J.K., and Coons, A.E. (1957). Development of the Leader Behavior Description Questionnaire. In R.M. Stogdill and A.E. Coons (eds.), *Leader behavior: its description and measurement*. Columbus, OH: Bureau of Business Research, Ohio State University.

Herzberg, F. (1964). The motivation-hygiene concept and problems of manpower. *Personnel Administrator*, 27, 3–7.

Hogan, R., Curphy, G.J., and Hogan, J. (1994). What we know about leadership. *American Psychologist*, 49, 493–504.

House, R.J., and Mitchell, R.R. (1974, fall). Path-goal theory of leadership. *Journal of Contemporary Business*, 3(4), pp. 81–98.

House, R.J., Spangler, W.D., and Woycke, J. (1991). Personality and charisma in the U.S. presidency: a psychological theory of leadership effectiveness. *Administrative Science Quarterly*, 36, 364–396.

Kegan, R. (1982). *The evolving self: problem and process in human development*. Cambridge, MA: Harvard University Press.

Kolb, J.A. (1995). Leader behaviours affecting team performance: similarities and differences between leader/member assessments. *Journal of Business Communication*, 32 233–248.

Kozlowski, S.W.J., Gully, S.M., Salas, E., and Cannon-Bowers, J.A. (1995, September). *Team leadership and development: theory, principles, and guidelines for training leaders and teams*. Paper presented at the Third University of North Texas Symposium on Work Teams, Dallas, TX.

Lappas, G.E. (1996). *A comparison of the transformational attributes of community college presidents with selected American corporate chief executive officers*. Unpublished doctoral dissertation, University of Texas, Austin.

Locke, E.A. (1968). Toward a theory of task motivation and incentives. *Organizational Behavior and Human Performance*, 3, 157–189.

Manz, C.C., and Sims, H.P., Jr. (1989). *SuperLeadership*. NY: Prentice Hall Press.

Manz, C.C., and Sims, H.P, Jr. (1991). *SuperLeadership: beyond the myth of heroic leadership*. *Organizational Dynamics*, 19, 18–35.

Maslow, A.H. (1943). A theory of human motivation. *Psychological Review*, 50, 370–396.

Millikin, J.P. (1994). *The role of self-leadership in empowered work teams*. Unpublished doctoral dissertation, Arizona State University, Tempe.

Murray, H.A. (1938). *Explorations in personality*. New York: Oxford University Press.

Saal, F.E., and Knight, PA. (1988). *Industrial/organizational psychology: science and practice*. Pacific Grove, CA: Brooks/Cole Publishing Co.

Schein, E.H. (1985). *Organizational culture and leadership*. San Francisco, CA: Jossey-Bass.

Senge, P., Ross, R., Smith, B., Roberts, C., and Kleiner, A. (1994). *The fifth discipline fieldbook: strategies and tools for building a learning organization*. New York: Doubleday.

Skinner, B.F. (1959). *Cumulative record*. New York: Appleton-Century-Crofts.

Stalk, G., Jr., and Hout, T.M. (1990). *Competing against time*. New York: Free Press.

Stogdill, R.M. (1974). *Handbook of leadership: a survey of theory and research*. New York: Free Press.

Temme, J. (1995). Building teams: becoming an effective team means listening, counselling. *Plant Engineering*, 49, 154–156.

Vroom, V.H. (1964). *Work an motivation*. New York: Wiley.

Vroom, V.H., and Yetton, P.W. (1973). *Leadership and decision-making*. Pittsburgh, PA: University of Pittsburgh Press.

Wilson, J.M., George, J., and Wellins, R. S. (1994). *Leadership trapeze: strategies for leadership in team-based organizations*. San Francisco, CA: Jossey-Bass, Inc.

Wilson, J.M., and Wellins, R.S. (1995). Leading teams. *Executive Excellence*, 12(6), 78.

Wriston, W.B. (1990). The state of American management. *Harvard Business Review*, 68(1), 78–83.

4

Structure, Culture and Power in Organisations[1]

Nigel Bennett

Introduction

Although both school effectiveness and school improvement research are concerned with schools as organizations, both pay relatively little attention to the insights that organizational theory can bring. School effectiveness research, despite strenuous attempts to move away from broad-brush statistical correlation's, remains locked into a view of schools that emphasizes their structural aspects, while school improvement writing focuses on the need to change the culture of the school if improvements are to occur, so establishing an emphasis on process. The two orientations ought to complement each other but, in practice, despite a series of attempts to bring the two fields of study together, little has yet been achieved. Creemers (e.g. 1994) has made strenuous attempts to generate a theory of effectiveness but the movements have paid insufficient attention to theorizing about what schools are – that is, organizations.

Organization theory, however, can provide a means for achieving this synergy if the view taken of the school as an organization is broadened to take account of a third, frequently ignored aspect – power. This can provide ways forward by raising alternatives to bring into consideration, challenging orthodoxies and offering new frameworks.

In this chapter, I will outline the twin concepts of structure and culture. showing how in each case the missing concept of power can provide a dynamic element that is frequently missing. I will then bring the three elements together in a three-dimensional model of schools as organizations, and conclude by indicating briefly how this model might provide a basis for the linkage that has been sought so unsuccessfully to date.

Source: Harris, A. and Bennett, N. (eds.) (2001) *School Effectiveness and School Improvement: Alternative Perspectives*. London: Continuum. Edited version.

Organizations

Organizations as 'systems'

The field of organization theory is enormous and one reason for this is that there is no clearly agreed view of what an organization is, nor how it should be analysed. Scott (1987) adopts a broadly systems perspective, distinguishing between 'rational' 'natural' and 'open' systems. Rational systems, he states (p. 22–3), are 'oriented to the pursuit of relatively specific goals' and exhibit 'a relatively highly formalised' social structure. In natural systems, participants are little affected by formal structures and official goals but 'share a common interest in the survival of the system and ... engage in collective activities, informally structured, to secure this end'. Open systems are strongly influenced by their environment, which reduces the organization's structural fluidity.

Other writers, such as Hanna (1988), argue for a much tighter and more structured definition of an open system than Scott, suggesting that the key dimension of a system is the interdependence of its different parts and the complexity of the transactions that take place within it as 'inputs' become converted through a 'process' into 'outputs'. The school effectiveness movement rests on a rational open systems model. This makes it easy to see the process of educational activity as one of 'adding value' to the 'raw material' of the input. When Gray *et al*. (1999), for example, examine the basis on which we can judge the effectiveness of a school and the extent to which it can be seen as an 'improving' school, they are concerned with what it does with its 'raw material' of the children it receives each year. In their emphasis on a limited set of measurable outputs, as expressed in examination results, school effectiveness researchers adopt this organizational view of the school very comfortably and leave to one side a lot of process-related issues.

School improvement writers can also find much to encourage them in an open systems view of schools and colleges. Whether this is in the looser terms offered by Scott and developed more fully in the concept of the 'loosely coupled system' by Weick (1976; see also Orton and Weick, 1990) or in the tauter view expressed by Hanna (1988), there are some significant emphases that are important to school improvement efforts. First, it stresses a process as much as a product: organizational members do things to the resources that are obtained for them and without resources ('inputs') the organization cannot survive. Second, it stresses the interdependence of the different parts of an organization – sometimes referred to as its structure – but also emphasizes that this is not a fixed and unchanging arrangement. As the inputs or the processes change, so the possibility develops of changes to the structure. Third, it stresses that not only are the constituent parts of an organization interdependent, but organizations are also, to an extent, interdependent. It isn't possible for a school to strike out on its own – for example, by deciding to apply for permission to change from being an 11–16 school to an 11–18 school and start a sixth form – without affecting those around it. Related to this, the open systems model sees organizations as needing to be kept in a reasonably stable condition. Consequently, when the environment becomes very turbulent, as some might describe the educational policy scene in England and Wales since 1980, an important management responsibility is to reduce the impact of that turbulence in order to create internal circumstances that do not interfere with the basic task of the organization's members. And lastly, it is important that each part of the organization is kept informed of what is going on elsewhere that might affect its work. All of this emphasizes that organizations should not be seen as static forms but as dynamic processes.

Unless they retain what Levačić et al. (1999) define as a strongly rational–technicist view, writers using the open systems model tend away from a mechanistic view of the organization towards one which is more organic (Burns and Stalker, 1961). However, much recent official writing about managing and leading schools as organizations has placed a strong emphasis on more mechanistic approaches, as is visible in some of the official utterances about professional development for headteachers and 'subject leaders' (e.g. Teacher Training Agency [TTA] 1998a, b). Following Taylor (1911) and Fayol (1949), mechanistic views of organizations emphasize detailed task specification, routinized work, uniform procedures and consistency, and see management as oversight, ensuring that routines are correctly adhered to and procedures (not processes) followed. By comparison, organic views of the organization see them as possessed of members rather than tasks and therefore capable of developing a life of their own. Organizational members who view their organization as organic see it as having the capacity to adapt and grow in relation to its environment, rather than having to be changed by management decision. Further, management becomes an activity within the organization, rather than standing more or less outside it, as the mechanistic view might sometimes suggest.

Underlying these ideas on how to think about organizations are certain basic propositions. They:

■ have members;
■ have a purpose, which gives rise to both the core task of the organization and the technology or technologies through which it is carried out;
■ have to acquire and retain resources;
■ require some sort of structure through which to ensure that the tasks are carried out and the purpose met.

Further, organizations are both identifiably similar and different. Something makes one distinguishable from another.

Members

If an organization must have members, then it ceases to exist without them (Greenfield, 1989). In a fundamental way, therefore, the members *are* the organization. Members might be volunteers, choosing to participate in its activities and often paying for the privilege, or they might be employees, providing services to the organization in return for a reward. Goffman (1961) identified 'total organizations' as those organizations in which key members had no choice over membership or the right to leave. Prisons and mental hospitals were the most obvious example but pupils might argue that schools also qualify.

Membership of any organization places certain obligations on the member, which may be written down in the shape of rules and regulations or communicated in other less formal and tangible ways. These informal norms and expectations may be officially sanctioned and universal across the whole organization or may be limited to specific tasks or areas of work. We will return to this later when we examine the concept of organizational culture.

Purpose

The clarity with which the purpose of an organization can be defined varies, as does the ease with which the core task and its associated technologies can be derived from it. At one level, organizations can be said to exist simply to survive; at another, they may exist to provide rewards to the founder or founders. Such rewards may not be financial but derive, for example, from the organization fulfilling a social need perceived or defined by the founder(s). This raises the question of how the purpose and its associated task and technologies are defined.

In addition, organizational purposes, tasks and technologies may be influenced, if not indeed defined, by agencies external to the organization itself. For example, schools that progress their children from class to class according to their levels of attainment rather than their age run into difficulties in societies that expect children of similar ages to be taught together. This pressure to conform to wider societal institutional norms (Meyer and Rowan, 1977; Rowan, 1995; Ogawa and Bossert, 1997) is sometimes referred to as establishing wider legitimacy and creates pressure for organizations expressing similar purposes to conform to similar definitions of purpose, task and technology.

Resources

Resources are often understood as either financial resources or as 'raw material' to be processed. But the term can be taken more widely to include the range of expertise that can be purchased with the financial resources that are obtained. Members are also part of an organization's resources. However, obtaining such resources carries a cost. Further, once obtained, they can be used more or less efficiently and this will affect the extent to which the purposes of the organization are achieved within the resources available.

Structure and tasks

The tasks involved in fulfilling the purposes of the organization have themselves to be organized. Structures imply that tasks and responsibilities are allocated and that resources reach the right place at the right time. They imply a means by which the activities of organizational members are influenced or directed. They also imply accountability.

Mechanistic views of organizations see structures as fixed, static entities that only change as the result of specific decisions by those who control them. Organic views see structures as capable of developing in an almost living way.

Structures, then, should be seen as dynamic entities, even when there is no change apparently taking place. This is what open systems theorists call 'dynamic equilibrium'. When we describe something as dynamic, we are also stating that there is something that is making it so. Hence the word 'dynamic' can be both an adjective, describing the characteristic, and a noun, identifying something or some things as giving it that dynamism. In the discussion that follows, I will try to identify both the range of structural elements that might impact on a person's work in an organization and also the dynamic that is at work, which I suggest is power.

■ Structures as dynamic entities

Physical structures

Organizations use and respond to structures in a number of ways. First, there is the physical structuring of work. New office blocks are usually built as open spaces, to be organized as each renting business sees fit, and some companies no longer assign individual employees to specific desks, so that they 'hot desk' wherever there is space when they need to be in the office. Those employees may do a lot of their work 'on the road', or from home, and only come into 'the office' from time to time. Such structures are deliberately constructed to organize what work is done and how it is done.

Work structures

Within that physical structure other structuring decisions are taken that affect how work is done. Secondary schools may decide to structure their pastoral work horizontally on year-group or key-stage lines or vertically through house systems. They may organize the academic teaching through departments or faculties or in some other way. Children may be organized in mixed-ability groups or banded or setted in some way according to some criteria that are determined by particular individuals or groups within the school. These are structural decisions. They influence the way that organizational members do their work and the colleagues with whom they have to interact on a formal, work-related, non-social basis.

Task structures

A third, significant set of structural decisions relates to the responsibilities that individuals discharge and the tasks they carry out. Learning how to write good job descriptions is an important part of much management training. As well as defining responsibilities and tasks, good job description are supposed to demonstrate the managerial accountability of the jobholder, defining the lines of accountability and control that govern the work.

Job descriptions should also state the salary of the post being described. In this way, structures also state the valuation placed upon the work being undertaken, not just in terms of its formal seniority but in terms of the resources being allocated to it. In the public sector, salary structures are frequently imposed nationally and may, therefore, restrict the freedom with which such valuations can be made.

Structural responses to external factors

Other external structural factors also act as constraints on individual action. Legal requirements such as health and safety legislation and laws relating to child protection both place direct structural obligations on organizational decision makers and act as definitions of 'proper' behaviour by organizational members.

In all these ways, then, organizational structures define both the constraints and the formal relationships within which individual members of the organization can take action. They also demonstrate how the organization's decision makers have responded to the external constraints upon the organization.

What becomes clear from this is that organizational structures only start to have any meaning when they relate to individual actions. Despite their apparent rigidity and formality, the significance of organizational structures for organizational members lies in the ways in which they define their *relations* with colleagues and the *arenas* within which they are able to make decisions.

These interpersonal relations are not between equals. A crucial dimension of the relations which are formally defined by the structure is the power which each individual in the relationship brings to it.

We shall explore the concept of power in more detail below. For the moment, we shall take it to depend on two things. First, there is how central the individual is to the issue under consideration and the decision that has to be taken. Second, there is the extent to which the structure allows them free-dom to decide how to act in response to decisions that are taken – what is usually referred to as 'discretion'. The more discretion that is created struc-turally – for example, by putting individuals into independent classrooms with closed doors, rather than operating in open-plan settings – the more power is held by the junior member of the relationship. How this power is used depends on how each individual then interprets the situation. Young (1981) proposed that we bring to every situation a number of elements:

- cognitive knowledge of the situation and of ways in which it might be possible to act;
- an affective valuation of the situation, leading to a judgement of the potential worth of any given action in the situation;
- the 'cathectic' sense of how we ourselves relate to the situation, interpret it and understand it: the combination, if you like, of the cognitive and affective elements;
- the directive sense of being required to decide on a course of action and take it – which might, of course, be to leave things as they are.

Young suggested that we actively deploy these four elements in a process of construction through which we come to an understanding of the situation, our freedom to act in it and our sense of what is the 'right' action in that set-ting. He calls this our 'assumptive world'. Since it is an active and continuous process of construction and reconstruction, it is clear that the individual assumptive world of our organizational members is another dynamic ele-ment in our organizational picture.

Structures, then, both create and are created by power relationships. They are dynamic: simultaneously static and fluid, fixed and changing. But exactly how an organization distributes responsibilities and responds to and priori-tizes between the multitude of external pressures it faces will vary, depending upon the beliefs and assumptions of the individuals who are involved in deciding how to arrange its internal workings. It is to this dimension of organizations that we turn now.

Cultures as dynamic entities, reflecting power distribution

What is organizational culture?

Organizational culture is taken in the literature to mean almost anything from 'the way we do things around here' (Bower, 1966) through Bolman and Deal's (1991) shared values which give rise to shared behavioural norms, to

Heck and Marcoulides' (1996) proposition that it is the way that an organization solves problems to achieve its goals and maintain itself. More all-embracing concepts of organizational culture incorporate not just the norms which are supposed to govern members' actions but also the concept of what the organization is about which gives rise to them. Schein (1992) includes within an organization's culture what members believe their work involves and requires and the consequent organizational decisions that result, both structural and physical.

Culture as distinctive rather than integrative

Most analyses of organizational culture from a management perspective focus on the norms which bind together individual behaviour into a pattern, stressing what Meyerson and Martin (1987) describe as the integrative dimension of culture (e.g. Schein, 1992; Bolman and Deal, 1991; Nias *et al.*, 1989: Wallace, 1989; Campbell. 1989). However, cultures need not be integrative: rather, they might more usefully be understood as what define organizations as distinctive from one another. Each organizational culture is unique but, as Meyerson and Martin (1987) argue, it may be a culture which differentiates sub-units and elements, producing subcultures at odds with one another, or one which accepts and copes with ambiguity, rather than attempting to relate events and actions to clearly defined goals and purposes. Each is likely to generate a different structural pattern or artefact (Schein, 1992, p. 17). Integrative cultures are more likely to be associated with tighter coupling, stronger lines of accountability and control and more emphasis on uniform practice.

Externally generated norms

The norms and rules that culturally govern the actions of organizational members derive in part from the concept of the work in which the organization is engaged. This understanding originates outside the organization, in the environment in which the organization is located. Cultural norms rest, in many cases, upon wider societal or 'institutional' definitions (Meyer and Rowan, 1977; Rowan, 1995; Ogawa, 1996).

The culture of an organization, then, is a construct made up of a range of expectations about what are proper and appropriate actions. Such expectations are both external to the organization and internal to its members, who 'transact' them (Archer, 1980) into the culture. Just as structures generate the degree of freedom or constraint of individuals, so cultures shape how they act within those freedoms or constraints. That is to say, they shape what is seen as legitimate action in a given setting.

Two views of power as sources of norms: hegemony and discipline

This outline of the institutional and environmental origins of many organizational norms reflects two major views of power in society, which it is appropriate to outline here. One is the concept of hegemony (Gramsci, 1971; Lukes, 1974) and the other is Foucault's (1977) concept of disciplinary power with its associated concept of bio-power. Hegemony is a concept that rests on the idea that domination and control rest simultaneously on both coercion and consent. This requires what Clegg (1989) describes as 'the active consent of dominated groups'. This active consent needs to be both generated and sustained, which Clegg suggests requires four key activities:

1. Taking systematic account of popular interests and demands;
2. Making compromises on secondary issues to maintain support and alliances in an inherently unstable political system (whilst maintaining essential interests);
3. Organizing support for national goals which serve the fundamental long-term interests of the dominant group;
4. Providing moral, intellectual and political leadership in order to reproduce and form a collective will or national popular outlook. (Clegg, 1989, p. 160)

Certain organizations are particularly significant in generating this active consent, notably the Church, schools, trade unions and the mass media.

An important way in which Foucault's (1977) view of power in particular differs from many others is that it does not see power as negative. Power is typically analysed in a negative way and the discussion of structure and culture so far in this chapter has used the language of constraint and control, thus appearing to link it with that view. But a view of power based on Foucault will argue that it is not concerned with delimiting and proscribing activities so much as converting the body into something both useful and docile. To achieve this, according to Burrell (1998), power resides in a network of interconnected relationships. It is through the day-to-day working out of these 'minute and diffuse power relations' that our organizational members' assumptive worlds are formed and influenced.

Power and the creation of organizational culture

This view of power relates comfortably to my earlier argument that saw structures as operating through relationships. It also connects easily to more traditional views of culture within organizations. These argue that the values of individual members and their concepts of the work of the organization, embedded in wider institutional contexts, may give rise to the cultural norms and so to the behavioural rules which limit individuals' freedom of action, but this does not explain how such norms are established and maintained. Schein (1992) is quite clear that they derive initially from the founder, who gathers together like-minded people who then continue to recruit similarly like-minded colleagues as the organization expands. Writers on corporate culture also see the role of the chief executive as crucial for the development of cultural norms (Deal and Kennedy, 1982; Bolman and Deal, 1991).

These views of culture creation and maintenance as a deliberate activity invest particular individuals with a great deal of power to direct the actions and behaviour of others. Deal (1985, p. 607) refers to the 'informal network of priests and priestesses [note, again, the presence of religion], gossips, story-tellers, and other cultural players' who sustain the culture of 'how we do things around here'. Such direction, as Foucault suggests, is frequently concerned with creating a strong and disciplined collectivity and need not be seen, as Ball (1987) for example would suggest, as individuals seeking power over others for their own ends. In organizational settings the power which drives and shapes the cultural and structural constraints on individual action is exercised by individuals – 'cultural players' – who possess particular forms of power resources, which they have acquired by first accepting particular norms and then developing, articulating and sustaining a particular interpretation of them.

Culture as observed is the pattern of rules and norms that derive from the basic understanding of the work that is done, and which shape the actions of those in the organization. As structures are enacted and create formal and publicly accepted rules, so cultures are also enacted and create informal and often unstated rules. Both represent forms of constraint upon the individual, and as such represent statements of power relationships between members of the organization. However, just as structures are susceptible to both direct and organic change, so cultures are not fixed either. The possibility of advocates of a new corporate culture creating a new set of norms to replace those of the old organizational culture is one potential form of change.

Power as the dynamic linking structure and culture

I have suggested that 'cultural players' deploy power resources in order to maintain and create the organizational culture. It is necessary to explain a little more the means by which they do this. It is suggested that we should view the acting out of relationships within organizations as an endless sequence of exchanges between parties. Each party brings a range of 'resources' to each exchange. Their distribution within the organization and the value attributed to them by the parties to each exchange are simultaneously a key determinant and consequence of culture as it is both a determinant and a consequence of structure. Even if we adopt a view of power built on Foucault's analysis, we still have to explain the particular pattern of power relationships within any given organizational setting and the results of the exchanges between parties to each relationship. I suggest that the way to do this is to examine what individuals can draw upon in their exchanges with their colleagues that cause some to be seen as more powerful than others. In other words, power in organizations becomes a resource that is brought to bear on the exchanges that make up the relationships between their members. The greater the disparity of resources between the two parties to an exchange, the more likely it is that one will be able to cause the other to act in the manner desired.

Kinds of power resources

Hales (1993) has distinguished between four kinds of power resource – physical, economic, knowledge and normative – which may be available to an individual in any exchange, and the section that follows draws heavily upon Hales' development of this idea.

Physical resource power represents the ability of one person to use physical force to coerce another to comply. *Economic* resource power rests upon the ability to provide or withhold things that someone else needs, such as a salary or the means of doing a job. In organizational terms, it is usually associated with a formal role rather than an individual. Because it rests upon the ability to call upon the formal resources of the organization, this is the form of power most closely associated with the functioning of formal structures.

Knowledge power can take two forms: administrative or technical knowledge. *Administrative* knowledge relates to the operation of the organization, whereas *technical* knowledge relates to the core of the work which the individual does. It is a resource because it can be used to provide assistance and support to a colleague who lacks it or as a counterweight to the planned exercise of economic resource power. The last form of power resource Hales identifies is *normative* power. This should be distinguished from norms in the cultural sense: rather, it is access to scarce values or desired ideas. Normative power can also rest upon personal friendships and broader reputation: the colleague who is able to persuade colleagues to do something as a personal favour calls upon normative power resources when this happens. Clearly, then, such normative power resources, like knowledge power resources, rest in individuals rather than the positions they may hold.

Compliance

The variable distribution of economic, knowledge and normative power resources accounts for the disparity in power which exists between individuals and, through the activities of individuals within them, of units within an organization. When the disparity is great, it is likely that the result will be a substantial element of what theorists of power call 'compliance' on the part of the person or persons with fewer power resources at their disposal. When there is a more equal distribution of these resources, compliance may have to be obtained through a more negotiative process. In such circumstances of relative equality, the structure is likely to provide for substantial levels of discretion for the individuals in discharging their technical activities, which makes it more difficult for managers to influence directly what they do. Economic power resources may have to fight the influence of knowledge power resources when this occurs.

Compliance may come in several forms, depending on the power resources being exercised and the legitimacy accorded to them. Normative power resources are, by definition, deemed legitimate and Hales (1993, p. 30) suggests that they result in a values-based commitment to act: compliance linked to a cognitive or emotional attachment to the task. Physical power resources, however, are non-legitimate and result in 'alienative compliance' and a search for countervailing power resources to deploy against them. Economic and knowledge resources result in a more calculative response, which might be 'cognitive compliance', wherein the person is persuaded that what is being required is correct, or 'instrumental compliance', which rests purely on a calculation of benefits and disadvantages.

Making the exercise of power legitimate

It is also important to take account of the ways in which power might be deployed. Power can be deployed overtly or covertly: covert power can be direct, in the sense of an immediate action, or provisional, in the sense of a threat or promise. All methods of deployment can be positive or negative. Table 4.1 provides examples of these methods, using examples of economic power resources.

Thus in this formulation, power resources come in four different forms, each capable of deployment in three ways, and of being positive or negative in their use. For managers and consultants it is important to invest their power resources with as much legitimacy as possible, since only power resources deemed legitimate are likely to produce positive forms of compliance. Structures and cultures are crucial ways of attempting to provide legitimacy for power resources. Structures provide in particular the legitimation of economic resources, and the deployment of economic resources in ways not permitted by the structure is likely to be seen as corrupt and therefore non-legitimate. However, cultural norms may permit such corruption. Power resources whose deployment is legitimated through the structure of the organization tend to be used overtly.

Cultures provide the legitimation of normative and much knowledge power, since these forms of power reside in the individual rather than their

Table 4.1 *Examples of means of power deployment*

Use of economic power resources	Example	Methods of deployment
Manager provides additional resources	'I would like you to take on this additional work and will provide you with supply cover so you can do it.'	Overt, direct, positive
Manager withholds resources	'I asked you to do this additional work and you have not done so. I am therefore penalizing your department by reallocating 50 per cent of your budget.'	Overt, direct, negative
Manager promises resources	'I would like you to take on this additional work and intend to provide you with supply cover so you can do it.'	Overt, provisional, positive
Manager threatens to withhold resources	'If you do not do the additional work I have asked you to do, then I will penalize your department by reallocating 50 per cent of your budget.'	Overt, provisional, negative
Manager implies that resources will be promised	'If you do this additional work then it is possible that I might be able to find you a responsibility point when one becomes available.'	Covert, positive
Manager implies that resources will be withheld	'I hope that you will feel able to do this. I would not like to think that you had caused a reduction of 50 per cent in your departmental budget next year.'	Covert, negative

office. They also provide crucial means of aligning legitimate normative and knowledge power with the wider institutional norms within which organizational members live, and which organizations have to acknowledge (Ogawa, 1996; Rowan, 1995). It is important to remember that institutional norms can be a major source of organizational cultural norms. Indeed, I argued earlier that members transact institutional norms into the culture of the organizations to which they belong. Such transactions can cause shifts in the norms embedded in organizational cultures and subcultures and, with them, changes in the power resources that are deemed legitimate. Cultures have to be continuously re-enacted and restated and the act of restatement gives room for the statement to be changed. Hence cultures live in the assumptive worlds of individual organizational members.

This process provides a tool for examining the process of cultural change and for explaining how organizational culture can be at once an agent of change and stasis. I suggest that there is also a relationship between the kinds of power resource and their associated compliance and the issue of power disparity. The greater the power disparity, the less countervailing power can be brought to the exchange by the weaker party. Weaker parties to a relationship are more likely to possess elements of knowledge and normative power than they are economic or physical power, and so are less likely to recognize economic and physical power resources as legitimate. Consequently, when economic or physical resource power is brought to bear in an exchange, the response is likely to be one of compliance rather than commitment. Indeed, a characteristic of cultural knowledge power is that it is widely shared – hence its high level of legitimacy.

It is important to emphasize, then, that this view of power resources sees them as being exercised repeatedly through an endless series of exchanges between individuals and therefore variable in their extent and distribution between each exchange. Thus the power resources possessed by an individual can grow or diminish through a series of exchanges or vary in an almost random way depending on the context and the parties to the exchange. Power in organizations, therefore, just like structures and cultures, is fluid and dynamic.

Power, conflict and exchange

It is easy to present this view of power as necessarily operating through conflict, as one person persuades another person to act against their will or perceived self-interest in a particular way that favours the self-interest of the more powerful partner to the exchange. Unfortunately, the term 'compliance' strengthens this interpretation. However, although it is clearly an effective analysis for conflict situations, it has relevance in other circumstances too. What is important to this understanding of power is not the idea of *conflict* but the principle of *exchange*, which usually but not necessarily occurs in a situation of unequal possession of resources. For example, within a rational action model, one might expect an individual's response to the exercise of power resources upon their actions to move from instrumental compliance, to cognitive compliance, to commitment, as it became clear that their interests were best served by acting in the way that the other party desired. All that is necessary for this process to begin is an uncertainty in the mind of the person complying as to what the most appropriate or desirable course of action is. Faced with uncertainty and a colleague who has greater certainty, the individual is likely to follow 'advice' or instructions.

This discussion of power, which is summarized in Table 4.2, has attempted to demonstrate how I believe it is a crucial variable which needs to be incorporated into our analysis of structures and cultures, and why I argue that an analysis of organizations along all three dimensions is important. However, I would also stress the interconnected nature of the three dimensions.

Table 4.2 *Characteristics of power resources in organizations*

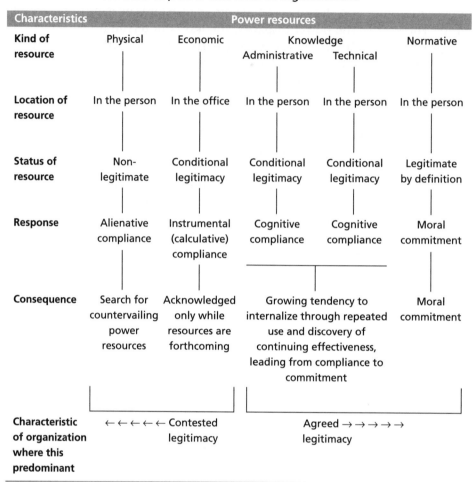

Characteristics	Power resources				
Kind of resource	Physical	Economic	Knowledge		Normative
			Administrative	Technical	
Location of resource	In the person	In the office	In the person	In the person	In the person
Status of resource	Non-legitimate	Conditional legitimacy	Conditional legitimacy	Conditional legitimacy	Legitimate by definition
Response	Alienative compliance	Instrumental (calculative) compliance	Cognitive compliance	Cognitive compliance	Moral commitment
Consequence	Search for countervailing power resources	Acknowledged only while resources are forthcoming	Growing tendency to internalize through repeated use and discovery of continuing effectiveness, leading from compliance to commitment		Moral commitment
Characteristic of organization where this predominant	← ← ← ← ← Contested legitimacy		Agreed → → → → → legitimacy		

Structures can be understood as artefacts generated by the particular combination of values and assumptions that comprise the basic elements of the culture. Structures can be both formally created and informally established as networks of social relations. Cultures develop as they do because of the particular disposition of power resources among their members and the ways in which those resources are used over time. Formal and informal structures provide the vehicle through which power resources can be deployed. Legitimacy is accorded to particular forms and content of power resources depending upon the previous exercise of power resources and the extent to which they are perceived as reflecting external expectations and pressures. This interrelationship is summarized in Figure 4.1.

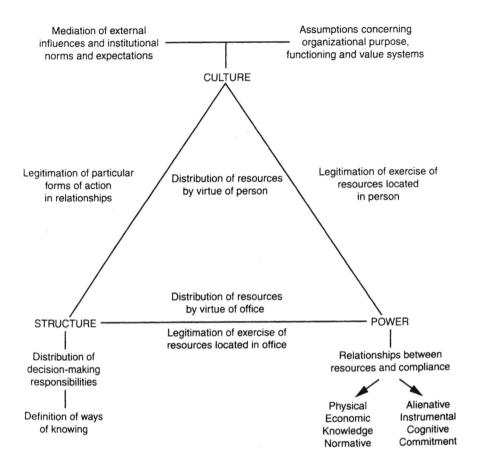

Figure 4.3 *The three dimensions of organizational operation*

The conceptualization of power laid out in this chapter is not rooted in a conflict model of organizational behaviour, and allows a wide sense of the resources which individual parties to an exchange recognize as legitimate and relevant. It provides a means of understanding how structures and cultures exist and function, and how they might be altered.

▍Note

1. Parts of this chapter draw on material previously published in *The Open University* 1996 and Bennett and Harris (1999).

References

Archer, M.S. (1980) 'Educational politics: a model for their analysis', in P. Broadfoot, C. Brock and W. Tulasiewicz (eds.) *Politics and Educational Change: An International Survey*, pp. 29–55. London: Croom Helm.

Ball. S.J. (1987) *The Micropolitics of the School*. London: Methuen.

Bennett, N. (1991) 'Change and continuity in school practice: a study of the influences affecting secondary school teachers' work, and the role of local and national policies within them.' Unpublished PhD. thesis, Department of Government, Brunel University.

Bennett, N. (1995) *Managing Professional Teachers*. London: Paul Chapman Publishing.

Bennett, N. and Harris, A. (1999) 'Hearing truth from power? Organisation theory, school effectiveness and school improvement', *School Effectiveness and School Improvement* 10(4): 533–30.

Bolman, L.G. and Deal, T.E. (1991) *Reframing Organizations: Artistry, Choice, Leadership*. San Francisco, CA: Jossey-Bass.

Bower, M. (1966) *The Will to Manage: Corporate Success through Programmed Management*. New York: McGraw-Hill.

Burns, T. and Stalker, G.M. (1961) *The Management of Innovation*. London: Tavistock.

Burrell, G. (1998) 'Modernism, postmodernism and organizational analysis: the contribution of Michel Foucault', in A. McKinlay and K. Starkey (eds.) *Foucault, Management and Organization Theory*. London: Sage.

Campbell, J. (1989) 'Towards the collegial primary school', in T. Bush (ed.) *Management in Education: Theory and Practice*. pp. 57–65. Milton Keynes: Open University Press.

Creemers, B.P.M. (1994) *The Effective Classroom*. London: Cassell.

Deal. T.E. (1985) 'The symbolism of effective schools', *Elementary School Journal* 85(5): 605–20.

Deal. T.E. and Kennedy, A.A. (1982) *Corporate Cultures. The Rites and Rituals of Corporate Life*. Reading, Mass.: Addison-Wesley.

Fayol. H. (1949) *General and Industrial Management*. London: Pitman (originally published 1915).

Foucault. M. (1977) *Discipline and Punish: The Birth of the Prison*. Harmondsworth: Penguin.

Foucault, M. (1984) *The History of Sexuality: An Introduction*. Harmondsworth: Peregrine.

Goffman, E. (1961) *Asylums*. Harmondsworth: Penguin.

Gramsci. A. (1971) *Selections from the Prison Notebooks*. London: Lawrence and Wishart.

Gray. J., Hopkins. D., Reynolds, D., Wilcox, B., Farrell, S. and Jesson, D. (1999) *Improving Schools: Performance and Potential*. Buckingham: Open University Press.

Hales. C. (1993) *Managing through Organisation*. London: Routledge.

Hanna. D. (1988) *Designing Organisations for High Performance*. Reading, Mass.: Addison-Wesley.

Heck. R.H. and Marcoulides. G.A. (1996) 'School culture and performance: testing the invariance of an organisational model', *School Effectiveness and School improvement* 7(1): 76–95.

Lukes. S. (1974) *Power: A Radical View*. London: Macmillan.

Meyer, J.W. and Rowan, B. (1977) 'Institutionalized organizations: formal structure as myth and ceremony', *American Journal of Sociology* 83(2): 340–63

Meyerson, D. and Martin, J. (1987) 'Cultural change: an integration of three different views". *Journal of Management Studies* 24(6): 623–47.

Nias. J., Southworth, G. and Yeomans, R. (1989) *Staff Relationships in the Primary School*. London: Cassell.

Ogawa, R.T. (1996) 'The case for organisation in highly-institutionalised settings'. Paper presented to the American Educational Research Association Annual Meeting, April, New York.

Ogawa, R.T. and Bossert, S. (1997) 'Leadership as an organizational quality', in M. Crawford, L, Kydd and C. Riches (eds.) *Leadership and Teams in Educational Management*, pp. 9–23. Buckingham: Open University Press.

Orton, J.D. and Weick, K.E. (1990) 'Loosely coupled systems: A reconceptualisation', *Academy of Management Review* **15**(2): 203–23.

Rowan, B. (1995) 'Institutional analysis of educational organizations: lines of theory and directions for research', in *Advances in Research and Theories of School Management*, vol. 3, pp. 1–20. Greenwich, CT: JAI Press.

Schein, E.A. (1992) *Organizational Culture and Leadership*. San Francisco, CA: Jossey-Bass.

Scott, W.R. (1987) *Organizations: Rational, Natural and Open Systems* (2nd edn). Englewood Cliffs, NJ: Prentice-Hall.

Taylor, F.W. (1911) *Principles of Scientific Management*. New York: Harper.

Teacher Training Agency (TTA) (1998a) *National Standards for Subject Leaders*. London: Teacher Training Agency.

Teacher Training Agency (TTA) (1998b) *National Standards for Headteachers*. London: Teacher Training Agency.

The Open University (1996) *E838 Leadership and Management in Education: Study Guide*. Milton Keynes: The Open University.

Wallace, M. (1989) 'Towards a collegiate approach to curriculum management in primary and middle schools', in M. Preedy (ed.) *Approaches to Curriculum Management*, pp. 182–94. Milton Keynes: Open University Press.

Young, K. (1981) 'Discretion as an implementation problem; a framework for interpretation', in M. Adler and S. Asquith (eds.) *Discretion and Welfare*, pp. 33-48. London: Heinemann.

5

Inventive Management and Wise Leadership

Megan Crawford

Introduction

The interplay between management and leadership has always been an important one for me. In writing this chapter, I want to look afresh at management and leadership in educational contexts, and offer some thoughts for you to consider. This chapter explores the proposition that educationalists need to reflect again on both management and leadership if educational organizations are to be effective in the current climate.

Bolman and Deal (1997) are the starting point of this chapter. They write:

> Both managers and leaders require high levels of personal artistry to respond to challenge, ambiguity and paradox. They need a sense of choice and personal freedom that lets them find new patterns and possibilities in everyday thoughts and deeds ... they need the capacity to act inconsistently when consistency fails, diplomatically when emotions are raw, non-rationally when reason makes no sense, politically when confronted by parochial self interest, and playfully when fixation on task and purpose seems counter-productive.

Their hope was that their book would inspire both inventive management and wise leadership, with a concentration on artistry. It is this essence of creativity that I want to bring back to the debate by looking at management and leadership not as rational and formulaic, but as resourceful, imaginative and sometimes inspirational. Discussing what it means to inspire inventive management and wise leadership, and in particular looking again at management, is one way of focusing on these issues more closely. The chap-

Source: Commissioned.

ter will indicate strongly the interdependence of leadership and management and will suggest that leaders need to attend more closely to those things that are to do with management if they are to have the capacity to be more creative and effective leaders within a variety of contexts and a changing educational environment.

Leadership as a concept has deep societal significance, with discussion of it stretching back as far as the Bible and Ancient Rome and Greece. Even the word 'leadership' has the feel of a movement to it, with its own myths such as the 'great leader'. Grint (1999) suggests that we might visualize leadership as a talisman we use because we can never be sure whether it works or not. So, just to make sure, if one leader fails, followers instinctively look for another. Leadership is a 'buzz' word in education, whilst management in education is deeply unfashionable. Even the title of this book doesn't allude to it. Whereas in the 1980s leadership might have been seen as an aspect of management, it now appears that without leadership there is no management in education. Newman and Chaharbaghi (2000, p. 65), indeed argue that leadership has now become a quasi-consumable product that we are invited to want, and aspire to, as if it was a better house or smarter car. This is despite the fact, they state, that most of us know that we will never be able to have that thing to which we aspire. Gronn (forthcoming) offers an interesting metaphor of sibling rivalry:

> Leadership is one of a family of terms in both academic and common usage, which is invoked to designate modes of human conduct and engagement. Other close family members include power, authority, influence, manipulation, coercion and force, with persuasion, a term usually associated with rhetoric, as a first cousin. Within this discursive family leadership has always been the favourite offspring. None of its siblings command anything like the reverence and respect with which leadership is adorned.

He does not deal specifically with management, which may in itself be significant as the concept could currently be portrayed as the youngest stepdaughter, who really is not worth noticing. The danger inherent in the aggrandisement of leadership is that potentially good leaders in education may be daunted by the view of leadership that they see being offered as exemplars for them. It also raises the question of whether all educational leaders can be very effective at their jobs all, or even most, of the time.

It has been suggested (Law and Glover, 2000) that managers need to be good at everything that leaders are not, perhaps because management is viewed as something that fills in the gaps. Others go further and argue that being able to see the differences between the two is a key differentiating tool of organizational analysis (Levicki, 2001). Quoting Kotter (1999), Levicki (2001, p. 145) says that management brings order and consistency to key dimensions of an organization. Leadership, in contrast, is about coping with change. The policy context in which schools and colleges work at the time of writing is full of tensions and inconsistencies that have resulted in a growing emphasis on, if not a belief in, leadership, and a shying away from educational management. This chapter will suggest that educational management and effective leadership are symbiotic, but should be differentiated, and that chasing the chimera of leadership should only be part of the picture.

Returning to some of the business literature on leadership and management will enable us to rethink what we mean by effective management in education, an issue of crucial importance for effective educational organizations. To do this, two organizing constructs will be utilized:

1. Mitzberg's (1990) emphasis on leadership and cerebral and insightful management as one of the functions of management.
2. The concept of frames (Bolman and Deal, 1997), as an organizational basis for considering cerebral and insightful management as defined by Mintzberg.

▌ Management Theory – a brief background

Writing and thinking about general management was at first dominated by the ideas of 'scientific' management, which were developed in the first half of the last century by theorists such as Taylor (1911) and Fayol (1949). Taylor, working in industrial settings, emphasized the idea of the worker as machine. If the worker's tasks were defined and controlled, and their rewards tied to the quality of output, then the most efficient ways of working could be structured by the manager. Fayol identified the five key elements of managerial behaviour as to:

- plan
- organize
- command
- co-ordinate
- control.

The emphasis was on rationality and control rather than creativity and innovation. 'From a technical rational perspective, organisations exist to attain specific, predetermined goals: ... they develop technologies to attain goals ... and generate structures to enhance efficiency' (Ogawa and Bossert, 1997). It was soon argued that this view was limited and mechanistic and, as the century progressed, there was much more of an emphasis on the humanist, people side of management, and the creation of the right conditions for people to work best (Mayo, 1933). The assumption was that people are more strongly motivated to work by affective factors rather than by fear of sanctions and direct monetary reward (Hertzberg, 1966). Apart from a much stronger emphasis on motivation and the role it plays, much of this viewpoint still relied on a rational view of systems and control. Adair (1983) pointed out that, crucially, the manager had to be aware of the tensions between the needs of the task, the team and the individual. This highlights the importance of socially constructed meanings in influencing how people work and the importance of creating an organizational culture within which people are motivated and enabled to work effectively.

These views of management have in common a focus on *control* – that the task of managers is to direct in some way or other. An alternative view (Morris, 1975; Cuthbert and Latcham, 1979) is to see organizations as systems which can self-regulate once they are established. A manager, therefore, was someone who problem-solved in a system, sorting out the problems that cannot be dealt with in the normal arrangements of day-to-day activities. For Cuthbert and Latcham (1979), this is the most important focus of management – coping with the non-routine, keeping an eye on demand and planning new work in order to resource the organization successfully.

The influential competency movement (MCI, 1991; HayMcBer/TTA, 1998) is the strongest recent example of rational management models. It focuses on what managers do rather than what is known. Different models exist within the competency movement but they share a basic premise that it is possible to identify and separate the key components of effective performance, and that this can be done by a process of analysis, identifying tasks and items and the skills that are required for them. It also claims that the competency framework is applicable to all forms of analysis of all aspects of work, management or anything else. This approach runs the risk of losing sight of the broader integrative skills that managers also need, although it can be used creatively. The competency movement has had a significant effective on leadership and management training in England. There are National Standards for certain groups in education, and standards in this sense are a type of competency statement, though less behaviourist than some competency models. In schools, the National Professional Qualification for Headship (NPQH) takes a minimum competency approach laying out the basic requirements for satisfactory performance. This is differentiated from the Leadership Programme for Serving Heads (LPSH) which is based on the Hay/McBer competency approach. This approach seeks to identify the components that are needed for superior performance and concentrates on the skilled behaviours required to be highly effective. Its competency approach emphasizes integrating rather than itemizing the elements.

A serious challenge to rational models of management is made by Henry Mintzberg (1979; 1990). He has suggested that the tenets of rational manage-

ment are more like vague objectives that managers have when they are working, rather than the characteristics of a manager. Initially, he argued that role
rather than skills were the key to different aspects of a manager's work. By
identifying ten key management roles (Figurehead, Leader, Liaison, Monitor,
Disseminator, Spokesperson, Entrepreneur, Disturbance Handler, Resource
Allocator and Negotiator), Mintzberg hoped that they would be seen as working together to form an integrated whole, with leadership as a role that a
manager had in a particular situation. Revising his conceptualization, he
sought to make the model more interactive (1997). Some of the work of leaders involves the application of rationality – which Mintzberg calls the *cerebral*
aspects – and some rests on the development of vision and encouragement of
others – which he refers to as the *insightful* aspect. The insightful aspect
stresses commitment and sees the world as an integrated whole, using a language that emphasizes the personal values of the individual. The cerebral
approach stresses calculation and tends to see the world as if it were the components of a portfolio, using the language (words and numbers) of
rationality. Mintzberg's view of balance concurs with that of this chapter. He
produced a new framework based on a review and integration of the various
roles described in the management literature. At its heart is the person with
his or her own values, experiences and knowledge. This person then makes a
'frame' for the work that needs to be done. This consists of what the person
views as:

■ The purpose of the job;
■ The perspective on what needs to be done;
■ A specific set of strategic positions for doing (Mintzberg, 1997, p. 132).

He perceived this idea in a particular way, which can be examined with educational examples in mind. Framing a management task in this context can be
specific (a new curriculum initiative) or more nebulous (the building needs
updating). These tasks can be either self-generated (e.g. a whole organization
vision day) or applied by external agencies (e.g. national targets). He suggested
that all this could be thought of as the essential centre of managing.

In order to place this concept of a core in context, Mintzberg conceived
two further ideas. There are the three levels through which management
activity can take place – information, people and action. He represents these
as concentric circles since the manager works from the inside out, beginning
with the processing of information, hoping that this will make people take
action. In a more concrete sense in the next circle, the manager works with
people in order to help them take action. Finally, in the outer circle the manager can manage action directly. Managerial effort can be directed either
internally or externally in terms of the organization. Thus there is a core of
person, his or her frame and the agenda, and the three levels.

He then suggested that there are five roles rather than his original ten – *communicating, controlling, leading, linking,* and *doing* – that overlap on to these three concentric circles or levels.

1. **Information level** – *communicating* is concerned with the flow of information and the sharing of it, while *controlling* is using information to control people's work, either through structures directives or formal systems.
2. **People level** – *leading* is encouraging people inside the workplace to take effective action, whether by focusing on the individual, the team or the whole organization. *Linking*, on the other hand, relates to the external environment and gaining useful contacts to help drive external impact, or to linking externally to gain information that is important to the workplace.
3. **Action level** – *doing* relates to the taking of action more or less directly. Taking control in a crisis would be an extreme example of this.

So, rather than there being an irreconcilable tension between these rational and non-rational views of management, the work of leading an organization draws upon essentials of both rationality and culture. For Mintzberg, leading has that essential people component, a view that reoccurs in much of the literature (Horner, 1997).

█ Framing

Bolman and Deal (1997) take up these concepts in relation to organizational culture. They use a concept they call reframing and, in particular, describe four frames, or ways of looking differently at the same situation. They have suggested that because organizations are thoroughly difficult to understand and manage, this four-frames model offers a way of building the ability to understand what is going on in the organization, or building personal capacity. They suggest that viewing an organization from differing perspectives or 'frames' is a very useful tool for leaders and managers faced with complexity: 'No single story is comprehensive enough to make an organization truly understandable or manageable. Effective managers need multiple tools, the skill to use each of them, and the wisdom to match frames to situations' (ibid. p. 13). In fact it is the overlap between leadership and management that makes both so powerful because they allow for movement and synergy.

A brief overview of each frame is given here in a simple form in order to help further the debate. Readers should refer to Bolman and Deal's original for further elucidation.

Each frame illuminates a different aspect of organizational activity:

1. **Structural frame** – this has its focus on structure, strategy, environment, implementation, experimentation and adaptation. Bolman and Deal suggest that an organization's structure at any point in time represents its resolution of an enduring set of organizational dilemmas – such as are we overworked/underworked, are standards too high/too low? Such resolutions are then subject to change, as newer and perhaps competing claims for the organization arrive both from within and outside the organization.
2. **Human resource frame** – this has its focus on the relationship between people and organizations – using this frame can be optimum when considering such activities as increasing participation, support and information sharing. A good fit between individual and organizational needs means that people are satisfied at work, and the organization gets what it needs from its workforce to succeed.
3. **Political frame** – this focuses on the idea that organizational goals, structures and policies emerge from an ongoing process of bargaining and negotiation among major interest groups. There is an emphasis on building linkages to other stakeholders. From this perspective, Bolman and Deal argue, every significant organizational process is inherently political.
4. **Symbolic frame** – this frame is most closely concerned with organizational culture and values and utilizes symbols to capture attention. The frame is about providing plausible interpretations – by communicating a vision, by redefining what we see in the organization. The task of leadership is to understand, create and communicate in symbolic terms that help people to understand the world and the meaning of their involvement with the organization.

Bolman and Deal maintain that these frames are a useful insight culled from organizational theory on to the culture of an organization: 'They are both windows on the world and lenses that bring the world into focus. Frames filter out some things whilst allowing others to pass through easily' (p.12). They also argue that reframing should be viewed as a tool, each frame having its own strengths and weaknesses.

There are, of course, many differences of view about how far organizational culture exists and what it comprises (Bennett, 1995; Morgan, 1998). This chapter takes the premise that cultures are socially constructed realities (Berger and Luckmann, 1991). Members of an organization may share basic assumptions and beliefs. These then operate unconsciously, and therefore define an organization's view of itself and environment. Meyerson and Martin (1997) argue that the definition of what culture is and how cultures change depends on how one perceives and enacts culture. They stress the importance of looking at culture from more than one paradigmatic perspective and, in particular, they focus on aspects of cultural change they see as not amenable to managerial control.

Elsewhere (Levačić *et al.*, 1999) the author and colleagues have argued that only in the case of an integrated organizational culture will be found shared and stable norms, values and meanings that relate to the organization's purposes, how human relationships are conducted and how work is done. So, the creation and maintenance of an integrated culture as an organizational control device requires the insightful aspect of leadership (Mintzberg), while the development and operation of formal systems for planning, implementation and review require 'cerebral' capacities. Bolman and Deal's frames offer unique images of the leadership process, and they then extend this discussion into 'rules of thumb' successful leadership practice (1997, p. 303). The idea of building personal capacity is crucial, because it gives room for the manager to change and develop his or her skills and capabilities in an insightful way in order to understand the situations that arise. The personal internal cohesion of the educational manager is thus enhanced. This utilizes both of Mintzberg's cerebral and insightful aspects. This is rather a shorthand way for describing how to move towards wise leadership and inventive management, which I now want to go on to look at further.

Levicki (2002) states that being able to see the differences between leadership and management is a key differentiating tool of organizational analysis. Managers, in his definition, are the chief motivators of an organization, by being able to understand themselves at a high level and the concerns of those they work with. He dubbed the manager as 'strategic messenger … translators of the (leader's) vision' (p. 148). The quality that an effective manager has, he suggests, is 'the capacity to transform the complex and difficult into the simple and doable' (p. 149). A leader, in contrast, must be continuously strategic and have a vision of how the organization can be at its very best. Thus he suggested the transition from manager to leader involves moving from just relaying the message to that of communicator; from motivator of groups to inspirer of the organization; from small-scale tactician to overall strategist. So if we return to Mintzberg, we could view what happens not as a transition, but as a means of identifying when the effective manager has moved into a leadership-level task. If we think more closely about educational management, even using Levicki's framework, we can suggest that most of the time those we currently name leaders are in reality being managers, with many of them working quite effectively within their organizational contexts. Leadership, at any level of an organization, might then be seen as the part of actions that inventive managers perform. The most effective leaders may be those who can be inventive and creative at times, as Bolman and Deal suggest, but have developed wisdom through their experience of management of information, people and action. This concept of wise leadership is one that can be much more readily achieved by those who work in educational organization, because it asks the leader to examine his or her own practice rather than looking for ways to be exceptional. In other words, wise leadership must be viewed in connection with inventive management as a whole and not as a separate entity. Management is inextricably bound up with leadership, but the debate has become too one-sided of late, and this may be less helpful to those who actually have to exercise management and leadership within educational organizations. Personal framing may be done on an unconscious level, but an inventive manager can use reframing deductively in order to learn more both about management contexts and his or her own capabilities. This is what Bolman and Deal (1997, p. 3) call a 'sense of choice and personal freedom that lets [leaders and managers] find new patterns and possibilities in everyday thoughts and deeds'. Inventive managers use this reframing as a tool for looking at their work consistently, and with increasing veracity. The idea of personal artistry leaves room for exceptionality and great leaders, whilst recognizing that this is the exception rather than the norm. It also means that inventive managers who are not in positions of great personal power within an organization are still able to use the skill of finding new patterns and possibilities in the context within which they work.

Bolman and Deal wanted to inspire 'inventive management and wise leadership'. Much debate could go on into the precise meanings of these terms. But if we were to imagine inventive management and wise leadership as twin concepts, it might help provide a plausible interpretation for people to understand the meaning of their involvement with the organization. Other concepts could also be used, of course, but the purpose of the idea as described here is to help build their own morale as managers. This is because it can serve both to differentiate between management and leadership, as well as stressing their inter-relatedness. As Levicki (2001) demonstrates, managers have a need for the cerebral and insightful, just as leaders do. Utilizing inventive management and wise leadership signifies that management can be extended beyond the boundaries of faithful implementation of procedures, and leadership can be viewed as a possibility for the inventive manager. Unlike the discussions of leadership referred to by Newman and Chaharbaghi (2000), inventive management can be learnt with experience. This occurs as the person learns the purpose of the job, the different perspectives on what needs to be done in various situations; and it can develop a toolkit of specific strategic positions for doing it. Mintzberg suggests that managers' performance is significantly influenced by their insight into their own work that can take place within his three spheres – information, people and action. Inventive management starts from the premise that an inventive manager develops through acquiring information, developing people skills and learning through reflection on action. In this sense it could be seen as effective management but involving a high degree of personal capacity. Inventive management uses wise leadership, or personal artistry, as necessary to make things happen within situations, usually but not always where an integrated organizational culture already exists. Wise leadership as defined here can be connected to Mintzberg's concept of action through people or directly, for example, in terms of managing external relationships. Wise leadership is therefore very important to the inventive educational manager, but it is also highly achievable because the skills involved can be developed through reflecting on action (Schon, 1983). Because an inventive manager can expand his or her own personal capacity through personal reflection, he or she is then able to be more effective as a leader when the situation demands it. An effective inventive manager, who has built up the skills in both insightful and cerebral management from direct experience, may well be able to address the difficulties that some organizations find themselves in. Helping a school move out of special measures may be an example of this process. But as Mintzberg (1990, p. 170) states, examples of outstanding management success achieve their success precisely because it is exercised in specific organizations that may bear no relation to where we ourselves actually work.

Conclusion

Understanding the importance of the complementarity of the leadership and management functions helps us to understand why people with very different personalities can be equally effective. This chapter sees much of what is commonly called 'leadership' as highly effective inventive management. Those who single in on 'leadership', therefore, are, in reality, looking for exceptionality. This view could lead to the problem of education being unable to supply enough very effective leaders to fulfil perceived demand. If leadership and management were promoted as more usable and versatile, in fact inventive and wise, perhaps many more educationalists would see it as within their capacity to achieve.

I have my own personal 'frame' (Mintzberg) based on what I believe to be the purpose of the job and the perspective on what needs to be done. 'Wise leadership and inventive management' is in itself a form of reframing I have chosen to use because, for me, it illuminates certain key aspects. It is, in itself, using Bolman and Deal's symbolic frame, and yet at the same time draws on their other frames. By changing the lens and reframing, other ideas emerge, although my own personal frame will be more fixed because it has to do with core values and beliefs about education.

This discussion has focused on making some creative connections between views of reality and the complex world of educational organizations.

Pursuing wise leadership and inventive management is about using the insightful to illuminate the cerebral. Elsewhere in this book, Grint suggests that leadership is part of a ritual that followers appear to require and, as long as followers believe they need leaders, leaders will be necessary. Perhaps inventive managers are those who are skilled at performing the ritual of leadership for the organization.

The idea of personal artistry leaves room for exceptionality and great leaders. It also means that inventive managers who are not in positions of great personal power within an organization are still able to use the skills of finding new patterns and possibilities in the context within they work. Distributed leadership might then be seen as the part of the core of inventive management, and one that can be much more readily achievable by those who work in educational organizations. Thus, pursuing inventive management for effectiveness is about using the insightful to illuminate the cerebral.

References

Adair, J. (1983) *Effective Leadership*. Aldershot: Gower.

Bennett, N. (1995) *Managing Professional Teachers*. London: Paul Chapman.

Bennis, W. and Powell, S. (2000) Great group and leaders. *Team Performance Management* 6(1/2): 34–37.

Berger, P. and Luckmann, T. (1991) *The Social Construction of Reality*. London: Penguin.

Bolman, L.G. and Deal T.E. (1997) *Reframing Organisations: Artistry, Choice and Leadership*. San Francisco, CA: Jossey-Bass.

Cuthbert, R.E. and Latcham, J. (1979) Analysis managerial activities. Combe Lodge Information Bank (1410).

Fayol, H. (1949) *General and Industrial Management*. Pitman.

Grint, K. (1999) *The Arts of Leadership*. Oxford: Oxford University Press.

Gronn, P. (forthcoming) Distributing and intensifying leadership in schools. In *Rethinking Educational Leadership: Challenging the Conventions*. London: Paul Chapman.

HayMcBer/TTA (1998) *Leadership Programme for Serving Headteachers*. London: TTA.

Hertzberg, F. (1966) *Work and the Nature of Man*. Cleveland, OH: World Publishing.

Horner, M. (1997) Leadership theory, past, present and future. *Team Performance Management* 3(4).

Law, S. and Glover, D. (2000) *Educational Leadership and Learning*. Buckingham: Open University Press.

Levačič, R. Glover, D., Bennett, N. and Crawford, M. (1999) *Modern headship for the rationally managed school: combining cerebral and insightful approaches*. In T. Bush *et al.* (eds.) *Educational Management. Redefining Theory, Policy and Practice*. London: Paul Chapman.

Levicki, C. 92001) *Developing Leadership Genius*. London: McGraw-Hill Educational.

Mayo, E. (1933) *The Human Problems of an Industrial Civilization*. Boston, MA: Harvard Business School.

MCI 91991) *Management Standards Implementation*. London: MCE.

Meyerson, D. and Martin, J. (1997) Cultural change: integration of three different views. In A. Harris *et al.* (eds.) *Organisational Effectiveness and Improvement in Education*. Buckingham: Open University Press.

Mintzberg, H. (1979) *The Structuring of Organizations*. Englewood Cliffs, NJ: Prentice-Hall.

Mintzberg, H. (1990) The manager's job, folklore and fact. *Harvard Business Review*, March–April: 163–76.

Mintzberg, H. (1997) Managing on the edges. *International Journal of Public Sector Management* 10(2): 131–53.

Morgan, G. (1998) *Images of Organizations*. New York: Sage.

Morris, J. (1975) Developing resourceful managers. In B. Taylor and G.L. Lippit (eds.) *Management Development and Training Handbook*. New York: McGraw-Hill.

Newman, V. and Chaharbaghi, K. (2000) The study and practice of leadership. *Journal of Knowledge Management* 4(1): 64–73.

Ogawa, R.T. and Bossert, S.T. (1997) Leadership as an organisational quality. In M. Crawford *et al.* (eds.) *Leadership and Teams in Educational Management*. Buckingham: Open University Press.

Schon, D. (1983) *The Reflective Practitioner*. London: HarperCollins.

Taylor, F.W. 91911) *The Principles of Scientific Management*. New York: Harpers.

6

Networks, Cognition and Management of Tacit Knowledge

Mie Augier and Morten Thanning Vendelø

Introduction

It is an unsurprising premise that we live in a world of change and surprises, as the pace of change in industry and society constantly increases. This was already reflected in the very beginning of Greek philosophy, particularly in Heraclitus' famous dictum, that we cannot step in the same river twice as the river is always in flux, in a stage of becoming. Many years later Knight (1921, p. 311) phrased it in the following way:

> We live in a world full of contradiction and paradox, a fact of which perhaps the most fundamental illustration is this: that the existence of a problem of knowledge depends on the future being different from the past, while the possibility of the solution of the problem depends on the future being like the past.

Today, this is especially true in high-tech industries, such as biotechnology and information technology, where individuals and organizations continue to discover new technological potentials and develop new ideas for application of the technology, which enters and destroys existing landscapes by processes of 'creative destruction' (Schumpeter, 1975). Ergo, in an environment with a rapidly changing technology knowledge is often subject to distortion and uncertainty and is of paramount importance as the future is difficult to predict. Firms in these industries find themselves facing 'hypercompetition' (D'Aveni, 1994), and in order to survive they try out new combinations of resources (Ilinitch *et al.*, 1996). In doing so they must carefully avoid competence traps (Levitt and March, 1988) by finding a balance between what is often termed 'exploration' and 'exploitation' (March,

---

Source: Journal of Knowledge Management, Vol. 3, no. 4, 1999, pp. 252–61. Edited version.

1991a). Also, this is reflected in recent studies in organization (cf. e.g. Nonaka, 1994; Nonaka *et al.*, 1996; Tsoukas, 1996; 1998; Chia, 1998; Kreiner, 1998) where knowledge, uncertainty and change are prominent themes, and a large part of the research in the management of knowledge and organizations has focused on organizational designs embodying these qualities.

Most students of organization would assign organizations a particular role within this framework, viewing organizations as the source of relative stability and predictability. We extend this idea to cover knowledge networks, because as noted by Powell (1998, p. 229):

> When uncertainty is high, organizations interact more, not less, with external parties in order to access both knowledge and resources.

Hence, it is relevant to view knowledge networks as providing stability in a rapidly changing and highly uncertain world. Therefore, we consider the implications of change and uncertainty for designing and managing knowledge networks.

Knowledge in Organizations

Being the driver of much of the modern world, knowledge itself is anything but easy to grasp. When knowledge becomes specialized, markets increase in diversity, and make knowledge even further dispersed. Underlying cognitive frames[1] are being destroyed and undergoing constant change; those cognitive frames, or categories, are critical to effective use of knowledge (Langlois, 1998), since knowledge, to be of value, has to be interpreted within some frame. Thus, there can be little doubt that knowledge is the fundamental issue when we talk about 'technology' and 'organization' (Kreiner, 1998). Technology is a kind of 'knowing how' – a set of beliefs, routinized knowledge and artifacts (Garud and Rappa, 1994, 1995). Technologies manifest themselves as representers of knowledge (Garud and Rappa, 1994, 1995; Rosenberg, 1982). Change, particularly technological change, is equally important. But change only makes sense when compared to something existing, something already present, and hence, relatively stable. Knowledge represents something existing; something already given (although it may be complex, tacit and even unexplored). It is perhaps a symptom of these facts that it is often said that technological evolution has brought us to the age of a (rather unspecified) 'knowledge society', 'knowledge economy' or 'post-industrial society'. Here, knowledge is supposed to be the key to understanding this society as well as the technological developments taking place (Kreiner, 1998). Bell (1973) explains the 'post-industrial society' in opposition to the 'industrial society', which 'is the coordination of machines and men for the production of goods', whereas:

Post-industrial society is organized around knowledge, for the purpose of social control and the directing of innovation and change; and this in turn gives rise to new social relationships and new structures which have to be managed politically (Bell, 1973, p. 20).

To Bell (1973), the central category of knowledge is theoretical knowledge:

the change in the character of knowledge itself. What has become decisive for the organization of decisions and the direction of change is the centrality of theoretical knowledge – the primacy of theory over empiricism and the codification of knowledge into abstract systems of symbols that, as in any axiomatic system, can be used to illuminate many different and varied areas of experience.

A profound characteristic of knowledge is that it is a non-consumable resource, i.e. it is possible to use knowledge without using it up (Adler, 1989; Sadler, 1988). Ergo, the more knowledge is used the more there is of it. Kreiner (1992, p. 62) adds complexity:

Knowledge is a transient type of resource, as its relevance and credibility are time and context dependent. We cannot regard knowledge as something that we once for all have collected and constructed. Knowledge must constantly be reproduced through execution.

Hence, the knowledge possessed by an organization is a dynamic entity, which alters over time as new knowledge is added and knowledge not in use fades (March, 1991b; Nystrom and Starbuck, 1984; Winter, 1987; Prahalad and Hamel, 1990). Thus, to survive, organizations must sustain their capability to produce through ongoing maintenance and development of their knowledge, and to do so they utilize their knowledge, which otherwise degenerates.

In organizations, knowledge is typically an immeasurable resource, such as technological knowledge, market knowledge, knowledge about how to organize production, coordinate diverse skills and integrate multiple streams of technologies. We often find knowledge to be embedded in routines, structure, culture, etc. (Walsh and Ungson, 1991). Therefore, the knowledge possessed by an organization does not constitute a homogeneous mass. Instead, within an organization one can find islands of specialized knowledge possessed by sub-units. Such knowledge needs to be combined or cross-fertilized with knowledge from other sub-units to stay viable and valuable to the organization and perhaps even more important prevent sub-units from getting caught in competence traps. In turn, this implies that the character of the knowledge networks within an organization determines its ability to both exploit knowledge and explore new business opportunities, and thereby, its ability to cope with uncertainty and change.

Tacit Knowledge and its Management

The issue of tacit knowledge has been dealt with within many disciplines and by many authors. Polanyi (1958), for example, sees tacit knowledge as a personal form of knowledge, which individuals can only obtain from direct experience in a given domain. Tacit knowledge is held in a non-verbal form, and therefore, the holder cannot provide a useful verbal explanation to another individual. Instead, tacit knowledge typically becomes embedded in, for example, routines and cultures. Opposite to explicit knowledge, which can be expressed in symbols and communicated to other individuals by use of these symbols (cf. Schulz, 1998). We might assess the tacitness of knowledge by measuring its level of codification (Zander and Kogut, 1995), describing the level of codification as the degree to which the knowledge is expressed in writing at the time of its transfer. We usually refer to knowledge characterized by a low degree of codification as tacit knowledge. Such knowledge is typically believed to be hard to articulate and can solely be acquired through experience. Thus, it is more difficult to transfer tacit knowledge than explicit knowledge. Consequently, individuals or organizations might choose to keep their knowledge tacit in order to prevent its transfer and diffusion, and thereby, maintain a competitive advantage.

The emphasis on tacit knowledge is not novel to studies of organization (Kreiner, 1998). Indeed, it has been present since Adam Smith's (1776) famous argument that division of labor made specialization of knowledge possible. von Hayek (1948a, b) later reminded us that the important knowledge was 'the knowledge of the particular circumstances of time and place' (von Hayek, 1948b, p. 60) – the tacit, subjective, idiosyncratic knowledge that individual actors hold. It is precisely this kind of knowledge, which is important for understanding organizational routines (Nelson and Winter, 1982).

The organization of knowledge (e.g. in routines and artifacts) is matters of 'beliefs' (such as heuristics for search, cf. Nelson and Winter, 1982). Just as von Hayek emphasized that different individuals hold different bits of knowledge – so do we hold different perceptions of this knowledge, and therefore, of technology and organization. The cognitive processes by which knowledge is created, distributed and shared thus become important to studies attempting to deal with the organization of technological knowledge (cf. Garud and Rappa, 1994, 1995). And by stressing the importance of shared knowledge, we emphasized the importance of knowledge networks since we will argue that such knowledge networks can be seen as representing the cognitive frames and categories by which we structure new knowledge and thus, manage it.

Knowledge Networks

In the knowledge society access to new knowledge is a critical factor to all organizations. However, there is not enough time to develop all knowledge internally, and thus, to acquire new knowledge organizations and individuals depend on knowledge networks. About this Powell (1998, p. 230) notes:

> Firms in technologically intensive fields rely on collaborative relationships to access, survey and exploit emerging technological opportunities.

Knowledge networks may take the form of more or less loose cooperation with other organizations and individuals. In fact, it has been shown that loose and informal networks among organizations may represent significant sources of new knowledge (Kreiner and Schultz, 1993). Another string of research shows that the network open to an organization is determined by its social position (Podolny, 1993), implying that its reputation determines the opportunities open to it. Taking this further it has been suggested that to develop a favorable social position organizations must demonstrate both social skills and technological knowledge in cooperation with other organizations (Christiansen and Vendelø, 1998).

We regard knowledge networks as transmitters of knowledge among both individuals and organizations. In contrast to formal organizations networks represent loose couplings among the entities included. Such networks (technological ones) are defined by Wright (1999, p. 296):

> … a technological learning network composed of people who are not necessarily acquainted with each other personally, but who share a common technical language and problem-solving environment.

Descriptions like those above explain that oftentimes networks are activated by occasions like the need for favors or services, incidental meetings, etc. This has at least two implications for how we can manage knowledge networks. First, as networks are of a loose kind they are difficult to manage in the strict sense of this word. Rather than being an issue of controlling and directing flows of knowledge, then the task of managing knowledge networks is one of creating accessibility. For example, it is commonly assumed that technological learning in firms is enhanced when technically skilled employees are encouraged to collaborate with like-minded individuals elsewhere. This leads us to assume that exchange of tacit knowledge improves the result of learning processes. In fact, Schulz (1998) noted that knowledge flows in organizations are important because they feed into sub-unit learning processes. Thus, to organizations there are many reasons to encourage the exchange of tacit knowledge in networks. Second, as it cannot be known in advance which knowledge will be needed in the future, and when indications exist about what kind of knowledge is needed, then that knowledge might exist at a different place than expected in advance. Thus, more traditional ideas about management will not do well, and instead, we must look elsewhere.

Basically, these two implications concern search for and transfer of knowledge among individuals and organizations. Recently, Hansen (1999) found that finding and acquiring knowledge places different demands on networks. Using the concepts of weak versus strong ties and the notion of tacit versus explicit knowledge Hansen (1999) investigated the role of weak ties in sharing knowledge across organizational sub-units. His findings show that weak interunit ties help a sub-unit search for useful knowledge in other sub-units, but impede the transfer of tacit knowledge, which requires strong ties between the two parties to a transfer. Also, according to Granovetter (1973) distant and infrequent relationships, i.e. weak ties, are efficient for knowledge sharing because they give access to novel information by bridging otherwise disconnected groups and individuals in organizations. Opposite strong ties are likely to provide redundant information as they often exist among a small group of actors in which everyone knows what the others know (Hansen, 1999, p. 83).

Turning to the concepts of tacit and explicit knowledge, then it is commonly assumed that the difficulties with and the length of the transfer go up as the tacitness of the knowledge to be transferred increases. Therefore, tacit or non-codified knowledge is best transferred through strong ties, whereas when weak ties exist among the two parties involved then transfer of tacit or non-codified knowledge is difficult. This is so because strong ties allow for face-to-face interaction between the two parties involved in the transfer, and thus the richness of the media used for the knowledge transfer is high and better suited for transfer of tacit knowledge (Daft and Lengel, 1984). Also, the existence of strong ties between the parties involved in a knowledge transfer makes it more likely that they understand each other, because they share cognitive frames and hold common heuristics. One important effect of this might be that the receiver holds the absorptive capacity (Cohen and Levinthal, 1990) needed to use and benefit from the knowledge transferred. In contrast, codified knowledge is equally well transferred through weak and strong ties, and in both cases knowledge is most easily searched for through weak ties. In total, this means that strong ties are best for transfer of non-codified knowledge, but inhibit efficient search, whereas weak ties impede transfer of non-codified knowledge, but provide a more advantageous search position in the network than strong ties as these ties are less likely to provide redundant knowledge (Hansen, 1999, p. 84) (see Figure 6.1).

This represents a paradox to organizations operating in rapidly changing environments. In such organizations product development teams are likely

	Tie Strength	
	Strong	Weak
Tacit (non-codified)	Low search benefits moderate transfer problems	Search benefits severe transfer problems
Knowledge	Low search benefits few transfer problems	Search benefits few transfer problems
Explicit (codified)		

Figure 6.1 *Search and transfer effects associated with combinations of knowledge tacitness and tie strength*

Source: Adapted from Hansen, 1989; 1999

to depend on novel, and thus, non-codified knowledge to succeed with their effort. If a product development team can obtain useful knowledge from other sub-units then it might be able to shorten completion time for its product development effort. Especially, as knowledge from other units can help these teams avoid duplication of efforts (e.g. by using an existing software module) or provide them with complementary expertise, as when an expert helps solve a technical problem (Teece, 1986; cf. Hansen, 1999). However, that novel knowledge might not be found if the product development team has networks consisting of strong ties, useful for transfer of tacit knowledge.

Another drawback of focusing on networks consisting of strong ties is that they are significantly more costly to maintain than weak ones. They require frequent visits to and meetings with employees in other sub-units on a regular basis. Also strong ties are likely to commit a sub-unit to help other sub-units and spend time on their problem solving. These routine activities are often not directly related to a specific project and hence distract a project team from its task, and thereby, affect its completion time.

On the other hand, weak ties are likely to be valuable product development teams undertaking innovative projects, because weak ties can point to useful knowledge which the teams did not know about in advance (Hansen, 1999, p. 101). Thus, sub-units with networks consisting of weak ties are likely to be able to find novel knowledge; however, if this knowledge is non-codified they will not be able to acquire it.

The efficiency of strong and weak ties for knowledge sharing depends on the tacitness of the knowledge to be shared. Strong ties are best if the knowledge to be shared is tacit and non-codified whereas the opposite is true for weak ties. Thereby, the two types of ties affect project completion time in different ways.

Concluding on this section, we assess that to meet the demands for creation of information and knowledge, organizations rely on knowledge networks to access knowledge, skills and resources that cannot be produced by firms internally in a timely fashion (Powell, 1998, p. 228). Yet, although knowledge networks exist they might not be of the right kind to facilitate search and transfer of knowledge. Thus, when organizations consider their strategy for building knowledge networks they should take into account that strong ties may constrain flows of new knowledge and inhibit the search for new knowledge outside established channels. Such inflow and search might be very important in changing environments where competence traps arising from restrictive interpretive schemes are the likely result of strong tie networks.

Knowledge networks and cognition

Crucial to knowledge networks is, well, knowledge. What characterizes the knowledge we have in mind is that it is tacit and subjective, and dependent upon the cognitive schemes of the individual (von Hayek, 1948a). Thus, it can only be transferred through routines or direct interactions among individuals and organizations. Knowledge networks of strong ties are constituted by shared tacit knowledge, and thus involve shared cognitive categories and schemes. These cognitive categories are the beliefs that the individuals hold about the world – or, in North's terminology, their 'mental models' (Denzau and North, 1994). Since they constantly change, knowledge and knowledge networks are also changing.

The idea that agents have different cognitive categories and hold different knowledge about the world is an idea that goes back at least to von Hayek (1948a, b). As he noted, this is the kind of knowledge which 'by its nature cannot enter into statistics, and therefore, cannot be conveyed to any central authority' (von Hayek, 1948b, p. 80). It is knowledge which cannot be explicitly stated, and thus must be interpreted and therefore dependent on the context in which this interpretation takes place (Schutz, 1932). Cognitive categories serve the task of making this context more stable and less disposable; they create a network of shared beliefs about the world which is largely reliable as a basis for interpretation of knowledge. The key point – and here we come to the essence – in understanding knowledge is thus to understand the process by which it is shared among individuals and organizations through cognitive networks. von Hayek, of course, was well aware that some highly abstract and anonymous categories might be more likely to be shared. This sharing element is what holds the world together:

> If the social structure can remain the same although different individuals succeed each other at particular points ... this is because they succeed each other in particular relations, in particular attitudes they take toward other individuals and as the objects of particular views held by other individuals about them. The individuals are merely the focuses in the network of relationships and it is the various attitudes of the individuals toward each other ... which form the recurrent, recognizable and familiar elements of the structure (von Hayek, 1952, p. 59).

Thus, cognitive schemes represent shared tacit knowledge (and thus, networks). In organizations, this may manifest itself when individual agents through shared beliefs and cognitive categories can reach a better mutual understanding, and thus, reduce some of the inherent ambiguity. Furthermore, it is only a small amount of the total stock of knowledge, which will be articulated in such a process of sharing. As a result, organizations may differ significantly on the degree to which they are able to produce such networks of knowledge (Winter, 1987).

Managing knowledge networks in times of uncertainty and change

From above it should be evident that how organizations choose to organize knowledge and design networks has implications for the knowledge that they can organize and subsequently manage (Loasby, 1992; Kreiner, 1998). Organizations are often seen as providing relative stability and consisting of structures which are aimed at matching the complex environment (Ciborra, 1996). As we have indicated, this is so because organizations and networks consisting of strong ties are constituted by shared cognitive categories. This view on the organization seems similar to what von Hayek (1978) described as 'organized complexity':

> Organized complexity here means that the character of the structures showing it depends not only on the properties of the individual elements of which they are composed, and the relative frequency with which they occur, but also on the manner in which the individual elements are connected with each other (von Hayek, 1978, p. 26).

The structures of the organization are thus not technical regularities, but are products of complex relations and interactions between individual beliefs and perceptions and organizational routines (Garud and Rappa, 1994, 1995). The organization is an adaptive entity, which through learning and experimentation adapts to its environment. This continuous adaptation to change is necessary for the organization and requires flexibility on all levels. From this perspective it follows that sub-units come and go, and thus networks among individuals in the organization become a central source to internal stability, which is much needed as individuals tend to learn better in stable settings. But the organization is not a static entity. It is a dynamic system of rules in which change is at the center, including 'the change in the character of knowledge itself' that Bell (1973) pointed out.

In studies of organizations concepts like play (March, 1971) and improvisation (Ciborra, 1999; Moorman and Miner, 1998, Weick, 1993, 1998) emphasize the inherent unpredictability and change in human nature; the 'becoming' element. But what is the role of knowledge networks in a world where improvisation, play, uncertainty and change matter? It is widely recognized that play and improvisation are important sources of both novel ideas for new products and for carrying these ideas into reality. This may be especially true for organizations operating in changing and uncertain environments. Play, according to March (1971), is when an organization for a moment steps outside its routines, skips rational behavior and fools around, hoping that this will produce new ideas for products, etc. Hence, play is likely to be a precondition for becoming the organization that sets the pace for the change in its industry. Improvisation, according to Moorman and Miner (1998, 698), is 'the degree to which the composition and execution of an action converge in time', and according to Ciborra (1999) it is 'a situated performance where thinking and action emerge simultaneously and on the spur of the moment. It is purposeful human behavior which seems to be ruled at the same time by intuition, competence, design and chance'. Therefore, improvisation can be considered as a rapid problem-solving technique used by organizations to cope with sudden technological changes. From this it can be said that improvisation is stimulated by the context coming through the time-pressure. Ergo, it is lack of time to solve an unexpected problem that leads humans to improvise.

The question then becomes how knowledge networks might support play and improvisation in organizations. Going back to Granovetter's (1973) distinction between weak and strong ties, we suggest that weak ties support play in organizations, whereas strong ties support improvisation. This is because for playing organizations, weak ties are advantageous, as they allow the playing individuals to search widely for input to their play. In addition, the ability to capture the received knowledge 'correct' does not matter, as there is no criteria for efficiency in play. Instead play can be said to be effective to the extent that it generates new interesting ideas, and then later organizations can start thinking about their relevance. By contrast, improvisation typically comes about as an organization faces a problem that needs to be solved here and now, and with whatever is at hand. As the organization may be genuinely 'surprised' in the Shacklian (Shackle, 1972) sense, there is typically little time for search, although effective improvisers never worry about (lack of) time, they just act at the appropriate time (Ciborra, 1999). Yet, because time is scarce improvisers must draw on their existing repertoires of skills and knowledge to come up with a solution to the problem facing them. Hence, it is important that they share cognitive frames and can absorb the received knowledge. In sum, improvisations will benefit from knowledge networks consisting of strong ties.

From the above it follows that an appreciation of unpredictability is required to deal with continual change and complex organization factors (Loasby, 1992; Kreiner, 1998). As a result we devoted attention to the context within which elements of shared understandings are developed. Networks consisting of strong ties reflect such shared understandings (March and Simon, 1958, 1993), common beliefs and procedures. Shared understandings may lead to new knowledge through new combinations of knowledge, which might come about through both play and improvisation in organizations, and thus, involve both stability (combinations of existing knowledge) and change (the generation of new knowledge).

Now turning to the role of management in organization, especially with regard to knowledge networks, we may view it as being that of sense making and design in coping with unexpected events (Kreiner, 1998). Also important is the role of play and improvisation in experimenting with existing knowledge and new ideas. Individuals in organizations may pick up pieces and leftovers of past plans, marketing choices and goals, and paste them together in order to make new sense of technologies and markets. By improvising organizations act on the basis of attention, rather than intention (Weick, 1993); since 'the only things we can sense are enacted events that have already taken place, attention rather than intention becomes central' (Weick, 1993, p. 351). Those enacted events represent, and embody, knowledge. Consequently, the role of management in relation to knowledge networks is that of suiting the organization to cope with unpredictability and chaotic environments where sudden events can tilt established patterns of routines and capabilities (Ciborra, 1996, p. 113).

Conclusions

In this chapter we focused on some characteristics of knowledge – in particularly on the tacitness of knowledge which is so crucial to modern organizations, and yet so difficult to manage. The focus in our treatment of knowledge networks was this because '... technological know-how is often tacit and is best transmitted through personal relationships' (Powell, 1996, p. 55), making management of knowledge networks both important and difficult. Therefore, our chapter represents an attempt to do more justice to the nature and characteristics of tacit knowledge and networks, and to show that there is still much to learn about knowledge, in particularly about managing knowledge.

Focusing on tacit knowledge we emphasized the importance of shared cognitive categories – networks of knowledge which make knowledge, if not manageable, then at least easier to structure and understand. We argued that tacit knowledge is hard to articulate and difficult to transfer, and thus its transfer demands that the parties involved in the transfer share cognitive frames. Furthermore, we proposed that shared cognitive frames are equivalent to knowledge networks consisting of strong ties. Knowledge networks of this kind make it possible for organizational sub-units to evaluate ideas, knowledge and skills made available through the network, and thus, absorb them (Powell, 1996; Cohen and Levinthal, 1990). Hence, it is such knowledge networks that make tacit knowledge possessed by other sub-units valuable to the focal sub-unit.

Then directing our attention towards environmental uncertainty and change we described how weak and strong tie knowledge networks support firms in both coping through improvisation, with uncertainty and change imposed on them by the environment and in creating uncertainty and change in their environment through play. Nevertheless, in both cases change in knowledge and knowledge structure is the result. Whether imposed from the outside or created internally, such change pre-supposes the existence of knowledge structures and cognitive frames, but the intimate relationship between these remains untouched (March, 1995, 1996). It seems clear, therefore, that if we intend to build a theory of the constitution and the management of knowledge, we need to invoke considerations that go beyond 'knowledge' and also consider the process of sharing knowledge (networks) and the importance of cognitive frames and categories.

Regarding recommendations for organizations hoping to design effective knowledge networks, Hansen (1999) concludes that if a sub-unit does not know in advance what kind of knowledge it will need in the future then focusing on knowledge networks of a certain strength (weak or strong) is likely to cause problems. Hence, designing knowledge networks for future and uncertain needs is not a simple and straightforward task. One solution to the design problem might be to identify if the sub-unit relies foremost on tacit (non-codified) or explicit (codified) knowledge and then use this as the basis for development of the needed kind of ties. However, as the need for knowledge in the future is subject to both change and uncertainty, this solution should be applied with care. Consequently, as an alternative managers may choose to remember that human judgment and intuition (Knight, 1921), which are both central to play and improvisation, by nature are rather unpredictable in their effects, and may thus be sources of unexpected change confronting the organization. Hence, as change is not only environmental (and external), but also comes from internal sources (cf. March, 1995) then the whole act of organizing knowledge networks may be an act of creating and discovering new organizational goals and targets (March, 1971, 1988, 1994), e.g. through improvisation and play.

Note

1. Cognitive frames represent those stable patterns of ideas that characterize organizations and other networks of individuals.

References

Adler, P.S. (1989), 'When knowledge is the critical resource, knowledge management is the critical task', *IEEE Transactions on Engineering Management*, Vol. 36 No. 2, pp. 87–94.

Bell, D. (1973), *Coming of Post-Industrial Society: A Venture in Social Forecasting*, New York, NY.

Chia, R. (1988), 'From complexity science to complex thinking: organization as simple location', *Organization*, Vol. 5 No. 3, pp. 314–69

Christiansen, J.K. and Vendelø, M.T. (1998), 'The role of reputation building in international R&D project cooperation', paper presented at the 2nd International Conference on Corporate Reputation, Identity and Competitiveness, Amsterdam, January 16–17, pp. 1–19.

Ciborra, C.U. (1996), 'The platform organization: recombining strategies, structures, and surprises', *Organization Science*, Vol. 7 No. 2, pp. 103–18.

Ciborra, C.U. (1999), 'Notes on improvisation and time in organizations', *Accounting, Management and Information Technology*, Vol. 9 No. 2, pp. 77–94.

Cohen, W.M. and Levinthal, D.A. (1990), 'Absorptive capacity: a new perspective on learning and innovation', *Administrative Science Quarterly*, Vol. 35 No. 1, pp. 128–52.

D'Aveni, R. (1994), *Hypercompetition*, Free Press, New York, NY.

Daft, R.L. and Lengel, R.H. (1984), Information richness: a new approach to managerial behavior and organizational design', in Staw, B.M. and Cummings, L.L. (eds.), *Research in Organizational Behavior*, Vol. 6, JAI Press, Greenwich, CT, pp. 191–223.

Denzau, A.T. and North, D. (1994), 'Shared mental models: ideologies and institutions', *Kyklos*, pp. 3–3.1

Garud, R. and Rappa, M. (1994), 'A socio-cognitive model of technology evolution: the case of cochlear implants', *Organization Science*, Vol. 5 No. 3, pp. 344–362.

Garud, R. and Rappa, M. (1995), 'On the persistence of researchers in technological development', *Industrial and Corporate Change*, Vol. 4 No. 3, pp. 531–54.

Granovetter, M.S. (1973), 'The strength of weak ties', *American Journal of Sociology*, Vol. 78 No. 6, pp. 1360–80.

Hansen, M.T. (1999), 'The search-transfer problem: the role of weak ties in sharing knowledge across organizational subunits', *Administrative Science Quarterly*, Vol. 44 No. 1, pp. 82–111.

Ilinitch, A.Y., D'Aveni, R.A. and Lewin, A.Y. (1996), 'New organizational forms and strategies for managing in hypercompetitive environments', *Organization Science*, Vol. 7 No. 3, pp. 211–20.

Knight, F. (1921), *Risk, Uncertainty and Profit*, Houghton-Mifflin, Boston, MA.

Kreiner, K. (1992), 'Organisering af Vidensproduktion', in Kreiner, K. and Mouritsen, J. (eds.), *Teknologi og Virksomhedsudvikling*, Samfundlitteratur, Frederiksberg, pp. 59–99.

Kreiner, K. (1998), 'Knowledge and mind: the management of intellectual resources', in Porac, J.F. and Garud, R. (eds.), *Advances in Managerial Cognition and Organizational Information Processing*, Vol. 6, JAI Press, Greenwich, CT, pp. 1–29.

Kreiner, K. and Schultz, M. (1993), 'Informal collaboration in R&D: the formation of networks across organizations', *Organization Studies*, Vol. 14 No. 2, pp. 189–209.

Langlois, R.N. (1998), 'Rule following, expertise and rationality: a new behavioral economics?', unpublished manuscript.

Levitt, B. and March, J.G. (1988), 'Organizational learning', *Annual Review of Sociology*, Vol. 14, pp. 319–40.

Loasby, B. (1992), 'How do we know?', working paper, University of Stirling, Stirling.

March, J.G. (1971), 'The technology of foolishness', *Civiløkonomen*, Vol. 18 No. 4, pp. 7–12.

March, J.G. (1988), 'Variable risk preferences and adaptive aspirations', *Journal of Economic Behavior and Organization*, Vol. 9 No. 1, pp. 5–24.

March, J.G. (1991a), 'Exploration and exploitation in organizational learning', *Organization Science*, Vol. 2 No. 1, pp. 71–87.

March, J.G. (1991b), 'Organizational consultants and organizational research', *Journal of Applied Communication Research*, Vol. 19 No. 1/2, pp. 20–31.

March, J.G. (1994), *A Primer on Decision Making*, Free Press, New York, NY.

March, J.G. (1995), 'The future, disposable organizations and the rigidities of imagination', *Organization*, Vol. 2 No. 3/4, pp. 427–40.

March, J.G. (1996), 'Continuity and change in theories of organization action', *Administrative Science Quarterly*, Vol. 41 No. 2, pp. 278–87.

March, J.G. and Simon, H.A. (1958), *Organizations*, Basil Blackwell, Oxford.

March, J.G. and Simon, H.A. (1993), 'Organizations revisited', *Industrial and Corporate Change*, Vol. 2 No. 2, pp. 229–316.

Moorman, C. and Miner, A.S. (1998), 'Organizational improvisation and organizational memory', *Academy of Management Review*, Vol. 23 No. 4, pp. 698–723.

Nelson, R.R. and Winter, S.G. (1982), *An Evolutionary Theory of Economic Change*, Harvard University Press, Cambridge, MA.

Nonaka, I. (1994), 'A dynamic theory of organizational knowledge creation', *Organization Science*, Vol. 5 No. 1, pp. 14–37.

Nonaka, I., Takeuchi, H. and Umemoto, K. (1996), 'A theory of organizational knowledge creation', *International Journal of Technology Management*, Vol. 11 No. 7/8, pp. 833–45.

Nystrom, P.C. and Starbuck, W.H. (1984), 'To avoid organizational crises, unlearn', *Organizational Dynamics*, Vol. 12 No. 4, pp. 53–65.

Podolny, J.M. (1993), 'A status-based model market competition', *American Journal of Sociology*, Vol. 98 No. 4, pp. 829–72.

Polanyi, M. (1958), *Personal Knowledge – Towards a Post-Critical Philosophy*, Chicago University Press, Chicago, IL.

Powell, W.W. (1996), 'Trust-based forms of governance', in Kramer, R.M. and Tyler, T.R. (eds.), *Trust in Organizations – Frontiers of Theory and Research*, Sage, Newbury Park, CA, pp. 51–67.

Prahalad, C.K. and Hamel, G. (1990), 'The core competence of the corporation', *Harvard Business Review*, Vol. 68 No. 3, pp. 79–91.

Rosenberg, N. (1982), *Inside the Black Box: Technology and Economics*, Cambridge University Press, Cambridge.

Sadler, P. (1988), *Managerial Leadership in the Post-Industrial Society*, Gower, Aldershot.

Schulz, M. (1998), 'The uncertain relevance of new knowledge: organizational knowledge flows in multinational corporations', paper presented at the *SCANCOR Conference, Samples of the Future*, September 20–22, Stanford University, pp. 1–36.

Schumpeter, J.A. (1975), *Capitalism, Socialism and Democracy*, Addison-Wesley, Reading, MA.

Schutz, A. (1932), *The Phenomenology of the Social World*, Heinemann, London.

Shackle, G.L.S. (1972), *Epistemics and Economics*, Cambridge University Press, Cambridge.

Smith, A. (1776), *Inquiry into the Nature and Causes of the Wealth of Nations*, Penguin Classics, London.

Szulanski, G. (1996), 'Exploring internal stickiness: impediments to the transfer of best practices within the firm', *Strategic Management Journal*, Vol. 17 No.1, pp. 27–43.

Teece, D. (1986), 'Profiting from technological innovation: implications for integration, collaboration, licensing and public policy', *Research Policy*, Vol. 15 No. 6, pp. 285–305.

Tsoukas, H. (1996), 'The firm as a distributed knowledge system: a constructionist approach', *Strategic Management Journal*, Vol. 17 No. 1, pp. 11–25.

Tsoukas, H. (1998), 'Introduction: chaos, complexity and organization theory', *Organization*, Vol. 5 No. 3, pp. 291–313.

von Hayek, F.A. (1948a), 'Economics and knowledge', in von Hayek, F.A. (ed.), *Individualism and Economic Order*. Routledge & Kegan Paul, London.

von Hayek, F.A. (1948b), 'The use of knowledge in society', in von Hayek, F.A. (ed.), *Individualism and Economic Order*, Routledge & Kegan Paul, London.

von Hayek, F.A. (1952), *The Sensory Order: An Inquiry into Foundations of Theoetical Psychology*, Routledge & Kegan Paul, London.

von Hayek, F.A. (1978), 'The presence of knowledge', in von Hayek, F.A. (ed.), *New Studies in Philosophy, Politics, Economics and the History of Ideas*, Routledge & Kegan Paul, London, pp. 23–24.

Walsh, J.P. and Ungson, G.R. (1991), 'Organizational memory', *Academy of Management Review*, Vol. 16 No. 1, pp. 57–91.

Weick, K.E. (1993), 'Organizational redesign as improvisation', in Huber, G.P. and Glick, W.H. (eds.), *Organization Change and Redesign*, Oxford University Press, New York, NY, pp. 346–79.

Weick, K.E. (1998), 'Improvisation as a mindset for organizational analysis', *Organization Science*, Vol. 9 No. 5, pp. 543–55.

Winter, S. (1987), 'Knowledge and competence as strategic assets', in Teece, D.J. (ed.), *The Competitive Challenge: Strategies for Industrial Innovation and Renewal*, Ballinger, Cambridge, MA, pp. 159–84.

Wright, G. (1999), 'Can nations learn? American technology as a network phenomenon', in Lamoreaux, N.R., Raff, D.M.G. and Temin, P. (eds.), *Learning by Doing in Firms, Markets and Countries*, National Bureau of Economic Research, Chicago, IL, pp. 295–331.

Zander, U. and Kogut, B. (1995), 'Knowledge and speed of the transfer and limitation of organizational capabilities: an empirical test', *Organization Science*, Vol. 6 No. 1, pp. 76–92.

7

The Arts of Leadership

K. Grint

Socratic Thinking about Leadership

In 1986, before I first began to study leadership in a serious manner, my knowledge of it was complete. I knew basically all there was to know and I had already spent over a decade practising it. I should have stopped then, because ever since, in effect, the more I read, the less I understood. This was partly to do with a Socratic problem: the more I read, the more I realized how ignorant I was. But there was something else at work: the more I read, the more *contradictory* appeared the conclusions I came to. Despite all my best efforts to analyse the data as objectively as possible, the results refused to regurgitate any significant pattern except one banal truism: successful leaders are successful. Then, when I stopped trying to read everything about leadership and began to try and think through the implications of my problem and started my quest for understanding, a light of some form began to emerge.

That light was not an answer but a series of questions that undermined whatever faith I had previously had in traditional 'objective' forms of analysis. In general these comprise three approaches that remain popular in the conventional literature: *trait* approaches, *contingency* approaches, and *situational* approaches. The fourth approach, *constitutive*, forms the basis of this chapter. These are summarized in Fig 7.1. In the *trait* approach, the 'essence' of the individual leader is critical but the context is not. Thus, providing we select the right leader with the appropriate leadership traits, everything should be plain sailing on our metaphorical journey. In short, a leader is a leader under any circumstances and it is more than likely that such traits are part of the individual's genetic makeup – otherwise the circumstances of the

---

Source : Grint. K. (1999) *The Arts of Leadership*. Oxford: Oxford University Press. Edited version.

situation that faced the individual at some time in his or her life would have had an influence upon his or her leadership 'traits'. This kind of model implies that organizations should concern themselves with the *selection* of leaders rather than their development, though *traits* can, presumably, be honed, as one's singing can be improved through training or one's athletic ability can be improved.

In the *contingency* approach, both the essence of the individual and the context are knowable and critical. Here one would expect individuals to generate an awareness of their own leadership skills and of the context so that they can compute the degree of alignment between themselves and the context. Where the permutation of the two suggests a high level of alignment – for instance, where a strong leader and a crisis situation coincide – then the leader should step into the breach, only to step out when the situation changes and the context and the context is no longer conducive to his or her vigorous style. Self-awareness and situational analysis are the two developmental areas for such approaches to concentrate upon.

The third variant, the *situational* approach, reproduces the essentialist position with regard to the context – certain contexts demand certain kinds of leadership – so we do need to be very clear about where we are. However, in this model the leader may be flexible enough to generate a repertoire of styles to suit the particular situation. Consequently, development work is required both in terms of situational analysis and in terms of expanding the variety or versatility of the leader.

The final, and most recent, model here, the *constitutive* approach, questions the significance of the allegedly objective conditions that surround

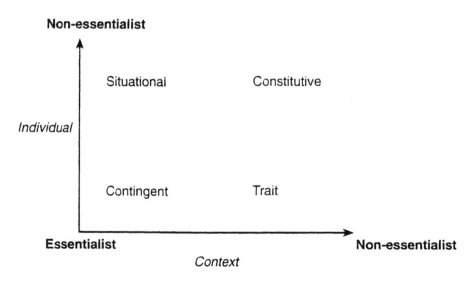

Figure 7.1 *Essentialist and non-essentialist leadership*

leaders and implies that the 'conditions' are as contested as any other element. For example, contingency models suggest that, under certain
conditions, a particular form of leadership which is the most appropriate –
that is, a crisis requires 'firm' leadership. But the problem with this is
twofold. First, it is no different from the scientific-management approach
pursued by F.W. Taylor at the beginning of the century in which 'the one best
way' of organizing production became synonymous with good management
– and leadership. But Taylor was never able to prove what this best way was,
nor can contingency theory. Secondly, and the probable reason for the problem, what counts as a 'situation' and what counts as the 'appropriate' way of
leading in that situation are interpretive and contestable issues, not issues
that can be decided by objective criteria. This might sound counter-intuitive
– for example, surely in war we know when a crisis exists? Yet one argument
for leadership would be that those people who can operate calmly because
they do not consider the situation to be critical – while the rest 'lose their
heads' because they perceive a catastrophe about to happen – will provide
the most successful forms of leadership.

Contrarily, those leaders seeking to exercise greater control over their population might construe (imagine/invent) a situation as critical in order to
legitimate their action. Under these circumstances it becomes impossible to
know what is contingently the best form of leadership because the information to assess the situation is monopolized by the leaders. Despite this,
leadership must still be perceived as 'appropriate', but what that means is an
interpretive issue. By implication, leaders must respond to the culture within
which they operate, but they are also capable of changing that culture.

The *constitutive* approach, therefore, is very much a pro-active affair for
leaders. It is they who actively shape our interpretation of the environment,
the challenges, the goals, the competition, the strategy, and the tactics; they
also try and persuade us that their interpretation is both correct – and therefore the truth – and, ironically, not an interpretation but the truth. But
because this is essentially an interpretive affair, it casts doubt upon those
claiming scientific legitimations for their claims and buttresses an approach
to leadership that is firmly within the arts, not the sciences. I am suggesting
here that one of the main reasons that we have so much difficulty in explaining leadership and in trying to enhance the leadership qualities and skills of
those who are leaders is that we have adopted a philosophical perspective
that obscures rather than illuminates the phenomenon. The more 'scientific'
our methods of analysis become, the less likely we are to understand leadership because it is not accessible to scientific approaches. This would be the
equivalent of trying to measure the merit of a picture by reference to a scientific system that evaluates the objective use of colour, form, and definition.

There have been experimental forms of leadership research, but either they
have been very limited in their numbers and replicability, or, while replicable,

the results have been less than compelling (Sherif 1967). As a result, most leadership research has tended to be either a review of successful leaders or grounded in survey approaches. Either way, the results are often informative but not definitive. The major problem seems to be the very complexity of the subject. There are so many potentially significant variables in establishing what counts as successful leadership that it is practically impossible to construct an effective experiment that might generate conclusive evidence on the topic.

It is also important to note here the limits of leadership, in particular the capacity of leaders to make mistakes. In effect, for organizations to succeed, the followers must play their part and cannot rely upon the leader or leaders to secure success alone, both because that success is a social not an individual achievement and because followers carry the responsibility of compensating for leaders' errors. It is this mirroring of followers' responsibilities that Heifetz (1994) concentrates upon as the proper role of leadership and the motivation and mobilization of this responsibility distinguish the successful from the unsuccessful leaders.

That, surely, is one of the greatest ironies of leadership, for, while we traditionally look to leaders to solve our problems, it would seem that leaders are most likely to be successful when they reflect the problems straight back to where they have to be solved – at the feet of the followers.

If, then, leadership is an art – or rather an array of arts – more than a science, then that might account for the four paradoxes that have bedevilled its understanding:

- it appears to have more to do with invention than analysis, despite claims to the contrary;
- it appears to operate on the basis of indeterminacy whilst claiming to be deterministic;
- it appears to be rooted in irony, rather than truth;
- it usually rests on a constructed identity but claims a reflective identity.

Let me explore these four paradoxes a little and suggest how we might adopt the metaphors of art as a way of understanding them better, first by beginning with that most elusive of questions: *who* are we?

The Who Question: Constructing Identity and the Construction of Truth

Leadership is not simply about leaders. Leadership is an essentially social phenomenon: without followers there are no leaders. What leaders must do, therefore, is construct an imaginary community that followers can feel part of. In this case the imagination of the followers is critical, because few will ever know their fellow community members well enough really to know whether they have anything in common either with them or their putative leader (Anderson 1991: 6). We can probably take this further to suggest – ironically – that imaginary communities may well be considerably stronger than 'real' communities. By this I mean, for example, that we may feel we have more in common with a community that we do not know intimately than with one that we do. Take, for instance, the problem of moving house: if I think about moving locally – within my 'real' community – I know that I should avoid living in 'that' part of town or down 'this' particular street or next door to 'them' because I *know* what kind of people live there. But if I intend to move a hundred or a thousand miles away, I am quite happy to live near anyone because I *don't know* what they are like. Thus, in my imagination, I construct my unknown destination rather more generously than I do my known destination. Paradoxically, then, when I am called to defend my national community against 'foreigners' (who have allegedly invaded a country that I had not heard of until the invasion), I again have to imagine that I have more in common with my fellow nationals than with 'the enemy' – even if my lifestyle, chances, and culture are actually much closer to those in the 'enemy' camp than in my own. Solidarity is constructed in the imagination and does not mechanically reflect the material similarity of conditions.

Leaders, then, must spend at least some of their time constructing not just followers, but a *community* of followers. Whether that community is held together by love of the leader or of the community, by hate of the 'other', by greed, or by honour is less relevant than that identity is an issue that successful leaders address. Yet few people will ever really know their leader, least of all those at a national level. As Machiavelli (1981: 56) pointed out: 'everyone is in a position to watch, few are in a position to come in close touch with you.'

However it is but a short distance from the imaginative construction of a community of followers to the distorting invention of a community. For example, S. James (1999) has argued that much of the ancient history of the Celts as a discreet ethnic people is a myth, constructed for political purposes in the early eighteenth century by a Welsh patriot, since historically, linguistically and ethnically they have nothing in common.

In effect, because a national population hardly know each other, they have to imagine the similarities that apparently bind them together. But, to follow Jenkins (1996: 28), to say that something is imagined does not mean that it is imaginary. In effect, identity is constructed not discovered; it is imposed upon a population rather than emerging from one; it does not reflect what is a deep essence within a people but is essentially steeped upon a people. It is not an event but a process, for 'social identities exist and are acquired, claimed and allocated within power relations. Identity is something over which struggles take place and with which strategies are advanced' (Jenkins 1996: 25).

War is a particularly powerful crucible for identity construction because it often denudes the possibilities of difference; it makes us choose between them and us. In war, there can be a 'forging of identities.' A consequence of this 'forging' is a tendency for the complete stripping of all critical faculties, such that an identity based in a balanced construction of the admirable and distasteful elements of a group becomes rendered down to an infatuation, where the group or nation can do no wrong.

Secondly, identities are 'forged' in the sense of being 'not a true likeness', in that national identities are superimposed upon a myriad of competing local, regional, class, religious, ethnic, status, and any other identities that pre-exist the national construction. They are also 'forged' in the sense that identities do not exist as 'facts' or as 'things' – that is, independently of people; rather they have to be reproduced by people if they are to survive, though identities, like groups, may survive irrespective of who the particular individuals are that make them persist (Barth 1969). The only essential element of identities are that they are essentially contested, and that contestation is the context within which leaders vie to impose their own version of identity upon populations.

This particular approach to identity owes much to constructivism. Constructivism in its most radical formats rejects the notion of essences entirely (see Grint and Woolgar 1997). That is to say, it rejects the idea that we can ever have an objective account of an individual or a situation or a technology – or in this case an identity – because all such accounts are derived from linguistic reconstructions. Instead the approach suggests that what the identity (or situation or leader or whatever) actually is, is a consequence of various accounts and interpretations, all of which vie for domination. In effect, we know what an identity or leader or situation actually is only because some particular version of it or him or her has secured prominence. The relativism at the heart of the approach does not mean that all interpretations are equal – and that what the leader/context is, is wholly a matter of the whim of the observer – because some interpretations do appear, to misquote Orwell, to be more equal than others. For example, my version of an identity – individual or collective – must fight for dominance along with the others. Similarly, my account of a popular individual may be that he or she is an incompetent charlatan, but, if the popularity of this person rests upon the support of more powerful 'voices' (including material resources), then my negative voice will carry little or no weight. The critical issue for this approach, then, is not what the identity or leader or the context 'really' is, but what are the processes by which these phenomena are constructed into successes or failures, crises or periods of calm. For example, when the Chief Executive declares an impending crisis based on information that must remain confidential to prevent the crisis deepening, how are we subordinates to evaluate the claim? The point of this approach, therefore, is to suggest that we may never know what the true essence of an identity, a leader, or a situation actually is, and must often base our actions and beliefs on the accounts of others from whom we can (re) constitute our version of events.

Furthermore, even the most powerful leaders are restricted by the social discourses within which they operate. In other words, leaders cannot invent a completely new world or identity but are constrained by the language, the customs, the social mores, the dress codes, and so on with which we operate. For example, in gardening, to try to define 'weeds' in a scientific way is impossible, because weeds are merely plants in the wrong place. To encourage consumers, seed-sellers label them 'wild flowers'. The difficulty is that the form of discourse encourages us to consider plants as 'weeds' or 'not weeds', as if they were objectively different; when weeding it is far from clear what criteria are being employed to differentiate between wanted and unwanted green things. Thus the identity of a green thing cannot be secured against an objective weed-measurer; it is culturally constructed. However, the gardening discourse encourages us to identify plants in this bipolar way – weed/not weed – in precisely the same way that we appear to perceive people as one identity or another.

This would not be the case if we could get to the world, in this case the plant or the person, without first going through language, but we can get to them only through the words that describe them or explain them or categorize them and so on. The implication of this mediated approach to the world is that our assessment of the validity of the account lies not in the world itself but by reference to other words. It looks as though we are then forced to conclude that there is no objective way of assessing which account of the world is true or closer to the truth because every account has to be adjudged by other accounts. And from this 'relativist' conclusion we may conclude that every definition of a weed, every version of identity is as good as any other. The relativist's dilemma is usually taken to mean that an anarchic free for all exists with no mechanism for establishing truth from falsehood, morality from immorality, weeds from plants, or true identities from false. In some ways this is an accurate conclusion: there is no objective way to be absolutely and permanently sure of the truth. On the other hand, this does not necessarily mean that any morality is as good as any other or that we must abandon attempts to analyse the world. On the moral problem it simply means that we need to agree a form of morality that we can all live with – this includes agreeing what to do about those people who refuse to accept this agreement. On the analytic problem the issue is surely not that every account of the world is as good as any other because some accounts are taken to be more reliable and robust than others and thus the issue is: what makes successful accounts successful? For our purposes this means that we might want to investigate why British versions appear to be more *persuasive*.

It is also important to remember *how* identities are forged not just why they are forged. For instance, we should be alert to the way symbols are deployed in organizations, uniforms, songs, in clothing, and in corporate images. Indeed, A.P. Cohen (1985) has suggested that the symbolic construction of a community is especially relevant where the apparent equality of community has to transcend the inequalities that exist in collective hierarchies. In short, the greater the difference between individuals in a community, the more the symbolic element is likely to be deployed to persuade people that the differences are less relevant than the similarities.

The emergence of the 'true' identity of a character in a play is often constructed through a particular revelation: one's origins are revealed to lie in a 'handbag' or one's natural father is revealed as the individual whom you previously murdered and whose wife you married, and so on. In practice, however, there is no single final truth, only different interpretations that construct, rather than reflect, the phenomenon. The struggle is to persuade others that your own version of their identity is true, and it is also a struggle to convince them that they have not been convinced – in effect, that it is not through argument that their identity exists, but through revelation of the 'truth'. Identity is not essentially embodied by actions and words; it is constructed by people and those around after them. Significantly for us, it may well be that whichever leader can most successfully 'construct' – as opposed to 'tap' – the identity of his or her followers in a way that generates maximum effort may also be the most successful leader.

To some extent leaders seem to forge not just a community or a common ideology but a parallel practice. For example, many military leaders take personal risks in an attempt to galvanize their troops to do the same. But leaders do not need to resemble their followers to remain as successful leaders. For example, many leaders purposefully adopt clothes or styles of speech that differentiate them from their followers. Even some of the most long-lived leadership systems have not necessarily been rooted in a physical or social alignment between followers and leaders.

To sum up, the constructivist approach does not necessarily deny the importance of leadership. However, it does assert that an epistemological question mark hangs over all issues, human and non-human, and, particularly for us, the issue of – and literally the invention of – identity. And for this reason we may regard the construction of identity both as a critical element and task of leadership and as one that is appropriately captured by the image of the philosopher's study, for it is in philosophical endeavours that one's identity is considered and constructed and it is through philosophy that we begin to answer that slippery question: *who* are we? But there is more to leadership than answering this question, for, having constructed an answer, we are then forced to consider the *what* question: *what* do we want to be and do?

The What Question: Strategic Vision and the Invention of Leadership

Leadership is an invention. I do not mean that this implies leadership is a trick or is unnecessary or false in some sense – although it might be any or all of these at times; rather, I mean that leadership is primarily rooted in, and a product of, the imagination. Imagination is the 'faculty or action of producing mental images of what is not present or has not been experienced' (*Collins English Dictionary* 1979). To imagine 'what is not present' is to concern oneself both with what may be and what was but is no longer. It is to look at *what* – the content of the vision – but also to consider *where* this will be achieved, *when* it will be achieved, and *why* it should be achieved. In other words, this aspect of the imagination can look backwards as well as forwards; leaders may rekindle the activities of their followers by recalling some golden age of the past, quite possibly mythical – or imagined – but which nevertheless mobilizes people to move from one situation to a different one. To imagine 'what has not been experienced' is to relay to one's followers the hope of a better future, or again, quite possibly to remind them that a preferable state of affairs did once exist but that such a state has not been experienced by the current generation. In this sense the imagination of the leader is very much locked into notions of utopia – imaginary other worlds that are literally 'no place' at the present but may be in the future. Utopian thought has attempted to transcend the present rigidities and construct a better future. And, although many have criticized utopian thought on the grounds that it is impossibly naïve, there are good reasons to suggest it has a kernel of critical importance to leadership; for, if leaders cannot imagine a preferable alternative to the status quo, why should followers follow them? Thus, if we ensure that utopias must be capable of realization then we can utilize the creative potential of the imagination and not suffer from it or suffer from its absence (see Bloch 1986 and Grint 1995: 90–123).

Most leaders do not actually do a great deal – in the sense, for example, that they regularly lead a political party by speaking on the doorstep to voters. Instead, the role of the leader tends to be one where the imagination, not the body, is required to act; for example to dream up new strategies for expansion.

The imagination is also crucial in the construction of what may be the most important element of leadership: the community narrative or myth. I mean myth in the sense of a narrative that roots a community in the past, explains its present, and conjures up a preferred future. A leader without a persuasive account of the past, present, and future is unlikely to remain a leader for long. They must persuade their followers that life under them is preferable to life under an imaginary alternative.

The level of leadership is less relevant than the process. A trade-union shop steward or a locally elected politician face the same form of problems: who are we, how did we get here, where do we want to go to, why should we go there, and what do we need to do to get there? These are all problems of the imagination in the first place.

The imagination of followers is also relevant because they have to interpret events, gestures, speeches, texts, and so on to mean something similar to that which the leader implies. There cannot be a way of *ensuring* that followers interpret a leader's actions or words in precisely the same way that the leader intends, but there are methods for trying to limit the discrepancy between the two and it is this discrepancy, this gap of the imagination, upon which leaders need to concentrate.

Naturally, there will be followers who cannot or will not close this gap of imagination to join the community and facilitate its goals. Here the leader may well fail in his or her attempt to mobilize the entire community, but is this critical? Not necessarily, and for several different reasons.

First, there are many examples where only a limited proportion of the community are ideologically mobilized in line with the leader. Indeed, a majority of followers may be disinterested in the issue, but, providing a sufficient core of people is mobilized, they can persuade or coerce the rest into undertaking the action necessary to achieve the goal. For example, office workers may simply disbelieve the vision and mission statements of their employers and take no interest in what the organization is trying to achieve, but, providing the line managers are true believers, the goal may still be achieved (see Abercrombie *et al.* 1980). In this case the imagination of the front-line staff must be mobilized by the top leadership, but it may not be necessary to fire the imagination of all and sundry. In short, a critical mass of subordinate leaders may need 'to believe' but the mass need only obey.

Secondly, self-interest may generate the necessary response on the part of followers without mirroring the interests of the leaders. For instance, office-cleaners may have no real interest in providing the cleanliness that their boss says the cleaning company guarantees – but, if the cleaner's jobs are suddenly on the line then they may make the effort, not because they are concerned for the customer or their boss but for self-interest. But even here the leader must get inside the head of the follower to ascertain what will persuade the follower to undertake the necessary action.

However, even though we may have established that gaps between the imagination of the leader, manifest in the strategic vision, and the action of the followers in pursuit of that vision can be transcended, it is still the case that the most successful leaders appear to be those whose inventiveness is rooted in, rather than separate from, the imagination and lived experience of their followers. By that I mean that leaders are most likely to be followed when their strategic vision is not simply clear but also resonates with the desires of the follower. Furthermore, where the strategic visions of a community or organization become aligned with the personal agenda of the leader, we have the potential for a very seductive message: followers should sacrifice themselves to the required merits of the leader, not because this will fulfil the leader's private ambitions but because it will further the social needs of the collective.

To summarize, the role of invention is so significant that we should perhaps attempt to formalize its role in metaphorical terms. In this sense, not only is leadership an art in general; it is a particular form of the arts, in effect, fine art. This art is the one responsible for constructing the strategic vision of an organization; it is, in effect, the world of the artist's studio. Moreover, in drawing for the future by drawing on the past, involving the imaginative use of the paintbrush, distinguishes the powerful from the indifferent vision. Furthermore, where the fine artist/leader manages to construct a vision that superimposes his or her own agenda onto the collective agenda, the imaginative vision can be crucial in explaining the success or failure of a leader. But there is more to leadership than constructing an identity and imagining the future – that is, answering the *who* and the *what* questions. To achieve the *what*, leaders need to consider the *how* as well.

The How Question: Organizational Tactics and the Indeterminacy of Leadership

The indeterminacy of leadership, this inability to predict the outcome of events on the basis of objectively analysing the resources available to each side, is a second critical weakness in conventional approaches to leadership.

Indeterminacy concerns the political gap between theory and practice – that is, between the issuing of requests and achieving appropriate action. The requests may appear perfectly logical to the leader but not necessarily to the followers, and even if they do appear logical that is not a sufficient reason to expect them to be carried out. I may understand that completing my task is essential for the success of the organization, but if that also means losing my job once the task is completed then I have a logical reason for not completing the task that is contrary to the logical reasoning of the organization's. In short, the logic of the leader is seldom sufficient to persuade followers to follow.

The suggestion that a gap exists between theory and practice, between dream and reality, and between what you want and what you get is hardly new. The assumption that political conflicts are an inevitable component of all organizations – and therefore that leaders should take cognizance of their inevitabilty – is something that many writers seem to have understood – but not many leaders. The assumption that technology is shot through with the same problem is something that few writers have even discussed.

For Clausewitz (1976), for instance, army commanders naturally and normally commanded unswerving obedience from their troops despite the breakdown of supplies or even of the troops themselves, but these were abnormal issues that could be resolved through the appropriate application of corrective techniques.

For Marx, the corrosion or friction between what workers were paid to do and what they did, between labour power (theory) and labour (practice), ensured that workers' discretion remained an essential element in the so-called labour process (see Marx 1954 and Grint 1998a). Boreham (1983) applies a related notion of indeterminacy to the professions.

Adopting the original Greek word, *agon*, meaning contest, Foucault suggests that conventional power relations can be classified as 'agonism', a permanent struggle between two sides in which neither side dominates. Further, Foucault (1980: 39) insists that power is not a property but a relationship. That is, power is not something that you can hold or have, but, rather, is a relationship between people. This 'capillary power', then, works through us rather than upon us: we are both held in place by – and responsible for holding in place – power. Another French writer, Latour (1986), has suggested that between the 'principle' of power, or its 'ostensive existence', and the 'practice' of power, or its 'performative existence', lies this same gap. This gap also generates the distinction between power as a *cause* of subordinate action and power as *consequence* of subordinate action: followers can almost always refuse to carry out the leader's requirements – and suffer the consequence – so whether a leader has power over his or her followers depends upon the action of the followers more than the order of the leader (see Grint 1995). This is critical because it implies that networks of power are the foundations of success. That is to say, only a sufficiently extensive network is strong enough to deter subordinates from resisting superordinates and widening the gap between theory and practice, orders and actions, demands and results. The gap is also one that Strauss (1978) talks of as facilitating 'the negotiated order' of organizational existence.

When we move from the problem of accounting for people's inability to do what they are supposed to do, to the problem of accounting for the equivalent issue in non-human phenomena, such as machines – usually an essential element of any kind of leadership – the same kind of debate recurs. Hence, what a machine is, what it will do, and what its effects will be tend to be more or less a direct result of the essence of an unmediated or self-explanatory technology. A technology's capacity and capability are never transparently obvious and necessarily require some form of interpretation; technology does not speak for itself but has to be spoken for. Thus our apprehension of technical capacity is the upshot of our interpreting or being persuaded that the technology will do what, for example, its producers say it will do. The crucial role of interpretation and persuasion suggests we need to attend closely to the process of interpretation rather than assuming that we are persuaded by the effectiveness of the technology. Again, this does not mean that any interpretation is as good as any other. Rather, the point is to analyse why some accounts seem more persuasive than others. Very often the most powerful accounts are those rooted in the strongest and most heterogeneous networks.

In sum, all of these writers recount a similar problem: between the order and the execution, between the leader's wishes and the followers' actions, there is a form of political corrosion that undermines leadership as a systematically recurrent problem. This means that subordinates may comply with leaders' requests for their own reasons and in pursuit of their own interests. It is this that undermines the direct link between the request and the act; the leader and the led.

Even if we can ensure that followers do what leaders want them to do it may still not secure the wishes of the leader, because the resources available may be inadequate. Conventionally, of course, success tends to be associated with accumulating sufficient power and resources to bludgeon the opposition or competitor into submission. In business, this kind of success through dominating the market is achieved by monopolistic firms such that consumers have little choice but to buy the products of the monopoly producer.

The sporting arena is a useful way of thinking about the different forms of organizational tactics, especially if we adopt the idea of the Martial Arts and its requisite site: the dojo. And at an individual level this approach is captured in karate's traditional reliance upon the development of sufficiently overpowering strength and technique to deliver a single strike to a pressure point of an opponent that will effectively terminate an attack. But not many of us are blessed with the physical strength or technical skill to dominate all others. Very often we may find that the competition is just as well equipped and resourced and skilful as we are. The victor may well be the side with the marginally superior resources or tenacity or stamina or just better luck, but the tactical aim remains the same – to eliminate or undermine the opponent.

And what happens if we are significantly weaker than the opposition? Well at least two possibilities remain open beyond submission or retreat. (Although for leadership, submission or defeat ought to be regarded as a proactive decision, not something forced upon the weaker side if damage limitation is something leaders are concerned with.)

Neutralization of the opposition's resources is one such possibility beyond defeat or failure. Here the other's resources are not resisted but rather avoided. Aikido tends to rest upon this tactic of neutralization – the intention is to neutralize the attacker and prevent further attack. There is no first strike and the aim is to return the attacker to a position of stability where no further aggression will occur. It is inherently a reactive system designed solely for personal protection and promotes a version of moral action intended to minimize damage to an attacker. But if we consider aikido as a metaphor for organizational tactics rather than simply a personal self-defence system we can see how applicable it can be. For example, in business Swatch managed to survive the onslaught of cheaper Asian products by neutralizing the primary resources of the producers – their cheap labour. By redesigning the Swatch product, the company reduced the proportion of costs taken up by labour down to 10 per cent – a point at which quality and fashion aspects became the main selling point, not the costs of the watch.

It is also possible to consider indeterminacy in which it is not just that the weaker side wins but that the weaker side's victory is premised upon using the strength of the stronger against itself. We can see the significance of this resource inversion with Dell computers, for example. When Michael Dell first began considering the idea, he faced the giants of IBM, Apple, Compaq, and DEC, all of which had a large slice of the market and delivered through conventional shops. There was little hope of Dell meeting this competition head-on because he had no network of shops to sell through and little hope of developing a traditional distribution channel. However, by choosing to market his computers through direct mail he not only avoided a direct clash with the giants but he ensured that the giants remained stuck with distribution channels that proved increasingly inefficient. In short, the more they used their traditional strengths against him, the more Dell benefited.

It is, then, this resource inversion that appears to explain some of the more remarkable examples of leadership when the resource imbalance is considerable, when the determinate is reversed. Here, the closest martial art is probably something like T'ai Chi, a 'soft' martial art where the aim is to use an opponent's strength to defeat him or her rather than attempting to stop him or her head-on, or neutralize his or her efforts to continue the attack. Now that we have established *who* we are, *what* the vision is, and *how* we can overcome opponents, we have still to consider that group without whom there are no leaders: the followers – for *why* should they follow a leader?

The Why Question: Persuasive Communication and the Irony of Leadership

One of the most interesting scenarios in everyday life is purchase; sales representatives do not sell on the basis of the benefits to themselves. Yet the irony is that so often leaders at all levels assume that they can persuade their subordinates to change on the basis of the leader's problems, or rationale, or advantages. So, for example, leaders regularly demand belt-tightening efficiencies or sacrifices on the basis of their own budgetary problems – and such leaders are just as regularly surprised when their subordinates appear unimpressed by such impeccable business logic or corporate needs. What is so often missing from business leadership is any attempt to *persuade* followers to follow, to *sell* them the future.

This brings us to a further element of irony, in which not only must a leader fire the imagination of the followers in their own identity, induce them to seek their future destination, and develop the organizational tactics to get them there, but he or she must also ensure that, within that imaginary alternative, the followers are sufficiently motivated to get there. That motivation is partly constructed through the envisioning of an identity, a strategic vision, and set of organizational tactics that enhance the chances of success and reduce the risks of failure, but it is primarily achieved through the fourth form of leadership art: the performing arts. In this we can include the theatrical performances that leaders must engage in if they are to achieve the necessary mobilization of followers and it is also derived from the skills of rhetoric and the skills of negotiation. Thus having a persuasive message, delivering it effectively, and deploying negotiating skills to achieve movement are also critical elements of leadership. But again, although science and rational argument can be used to support these practices, they are fundamentally rooted in emotional and symbolic grammars, not the language of science. Thus the irony of leadership includes an acknowledgement that persuasive communication is the bedrock of achieving change. For example, it may well be that managers and workers will agree with the rational logic that suggests the company must remain efficient and effective – but when that same logic also requires the dismissal of those same people somehow the logic falls to work. So leaders can be successful only if their followers come to believe in the collective identity, the strategic vision, and the organizational tactics of the leader. For that to happen the skills of the performing arts are crucial. Leadership, therefore, is more a performance than a routine: it is the world of the theatre and it has to be continually 'brought off' rather than occasionally acted out.

Theatre is overwhelmingly a rhetorical communication but is not solely rhetorical. That is to say, the focus is usually upon the words and the way that the words persuade the audience to accept the stage and its narrative as 'real', but that 'reality' has to be brought off in the imagination of the audience.

A performative approach to communication seems a long way from the earliest academic business research where 'how to win friends and influence people' was the order of the day, but actually the two are not that far apart. The critical issue was how to persuade someone of something. Much of the writing in the field of communication is still locked into the persuasive issue but often premised on quite different axioms from those considered here. In the main, most business research still seems rooted in what has been called the 'transmission' or 'conduit' model, in which the crucial point of communication is to ensure that the message from the origin to the destination, usually from (active) superordinate to (passive) subordinate, is transmitted or carried in as undistorted a fashion as possible. This essentially means that all kinds of organizational problems can be explained away through 'communication failures' –

that is, because of distorted or misperceived messages. Hence the solution is to clarify communications as much as possible, to simplify and repeat messages because the subordinates have not understood. That the subordinates have not understood the message perfectly well (for example, 'you are our greatest asset'), but may construe it as a blatant lie, is seldom part of this approach.

A second way of considering communication is as a lens or filter, in which the information flying around an organization is of such a great quantity that some form of quality filtering is necessary to make sense of it all (Putnam *et al.* 1996). In this case the filtering may be by the individual receiving the message or it may occur at a higher level in the hierarchy. At its most obvious, this occurs through censorship; at its least obvious we may never know whether the communication has been censored.

A third way of considering leadership is as a performance. A performance is not just uttering words from a script, though these are obviously important. A performance involves the script, the props, the players, the audience, the interpretations, the context, the shared cultures, and so on. Reading this or any other book on leadership will not provide you with everything you need to know about leadership. It is something to be experienced rather than simply read. The text and the performance are not identical.

However, the error of reducing the performance to the text should not be taken to mean that a clear and significant difference exists between rhetoric and reality. On the contrary, it is only through language, only through rhetoric, that we can experience, nay imagine, what reality really is. These interpretations differ, so we must choose between them or accept that the confusion is an inevitable reflection of the complexity of the case. Either way, our knowledge of the 'reality' is one constituted by the language of others, which we, in turn, interpret.

Sometimes a particular speech by a leader is held to be responsible for a radical change of direction in a community, but usually when it was a performance not merely a speech act.

The significance of persuasive rhetoric echoes Foucault's (1980) argument about the relationship between power and knowledge in discourse. Since, for Foucault, power is implicitly encased by knowledge, and vice versa, we cannot secure a true representation of the world that is untainted by power relations. Discourse, then, is not so much a reflection of material reality but a construction of it, a particular way of representing the world through language and practice.

Leadership *performance* is inevitably reproduced, expanded, distorted, and reconstructed through rhetoric of one form or another. Performances are not necessarily objectively good or bad or brave or stupid but simply performances that are adjudged by others – once communicated – to be one thing or another.

It may be that actions speak louder than words; Ralph Waldo Emerson's *The Poet* thought that 'words are also actions, and actions are a kind of words'. This is why persuasive communications are so important to leadership, for without a persuasive *why* there is little to mobilize followers further than you can push them.

Philosophical, Fine, Martial, and Performing: Leadership Arts

To summarize, therefore, I am suggesting that leadership might better be considered as an art rather than a science, or, more specifically, as an ensemble of arts. Under this approach we might consider how four particular arts mirror four of the central features of leadership: the invention of an identity, the formulation of a strategic vision, the construction of organizational tactics, and the deployment of persuasive mechanisms to ensure followers actually follow. In sum, leadership is critically concerned with establishing and coordinating the relationships between four things: the *who*, the *what*, the *how* and the *why*:

- *Who* are you? – An identity.
- *What* does the organization want to achieve? – A strategic vision.
- *How* will they achieve this? – Organizational tactics.
- *Why* should followers want to embody the identity, pursue the strategic vision, and adopt the organizational tactics? – Persuasive communication.

Science may help the leader and the organization achieve these but fundamentally, they are all subjective issues and are better considered as various arts.

- *Identity* is constructed out of the amorphous baggage of myth and the contested resources of history; it is not a reflection of the world but a construction of it. It is rooted in the philosopher's stone not the scientist's microscope.
- *Strategic visions* are designed through the imagination not the experiment, they are the equivalent of the fine arts not physics, for they involve imagination rather than experimentation, they are paintings not photographs.
- *Organizational tactics* are rather better envisaged as martial arts than mathematics, for here the leader must evaluate the organizational forms and manoeuvres suitable for the competition and must take account of the likely indeterminacy of outcome.
- *Persuasive communication* can certainly be supplemented by scientific knowledge, but fundamentally this is the world of the performing arts, the theatre of rhetorical skill, of negotiating skills, and of inducing the audience to believe in the world you paint with words and props.

Fig. 7.2 summarizes the four areas of concern.

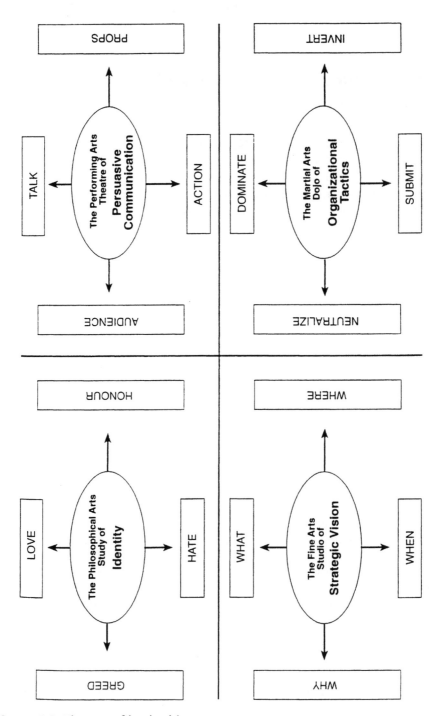

Figure 7.2 *The arts of leadership*

To return to a previous question: how do we know that leaders make any difference? Could it be that leaders are like talismans? That is to say, that everyone has one, that no one really knows whether they are necessary but, just to be on the safe side, we keep them close to our hearts. Whether they actually work or not is irrelevant. The same might be said of leaders – we may not actually need them, but, just in case they do act beneficially, we feel obliged to keep them.

Conventional science would resolve the problem by experimental methods in which the variable (talisman) was removed in a controlled environment to establish its significance. We do not have that luxury – or dangerous power – but it might be possible to establish to some extent what significance leadership makes if we could find a series of cases where parallel scenarios are played out with what appears to be marginal differences – except in terms of leadership. This could help us to decide whether leadership is itself critical, and, if it is, whether there are resemblances between its formation in different walks of life – in effect, whether leadership is similar in political, social, military, and business environments.

References

Abercrombie, N., Hill, S., and Turner, B.S. (1980), *The Dominant Ideology Thesis* (London: Tavistock).

Anderson, B. (1991), *Imagined Communities: Reflections on the Origin and Spread of Nationalism* (London: Verso).

Barth, F. (1969) (ed.), *Ethnic Groups and Boundaries* (Oslo: Universitetsforlaget).

Bloch, E. (1986), *The Principle of Hope* (Oxford: Oxford University Press).

Boreham, P. (1983), 'Indetermination: Professional Knowledge, Organization and Control', *Sociological Review*, 31/4: 693–718.

Clausewitz, C. Von. (1976), *On War* (Princeton: Princeton University Press).

Cohen, A.P. (1985), *The Symbolic Construction of Community* (London: Tavistock).

D'Este, C. (1996), *A Genius for War: A Life of General George S. Patton* (London: HarperCollins).

Foucault, M. (1980), *Power/Knowledge* (Brighton: Harvester).

Grint, K. (1995), *Management: A Sociological Introduction* (Cambridge: Polity Press).

Grint, K. (1998a), *The Sociology of Work*, 2nd edn. (Cambridge: Polity Press).

Grint, K. and Woolgar, S. (1997), *The Machine at Work* (Cambridge: Polity Press).

Heifetz, R.A. (1994), *Leadership Without Easy Answers* (Cambridge, Mass.: Belknap Press).

James, S. (1999), *The Ancient Celts: Ancient People or Modern Invention?* (London: British Museum Press).

Jenkins, R. (1996), *Social Identities* (London: Routledge).

Latour, B. (1986), 'The Powers of Association', in J. Law (ed.), *Power, Action and Belief* (London: Routledge).

Machiavelli, N. (1981), *The Prince* (Harmondsworth: Penguin).

Marx, K. (1954), *Capital*, i (London: Lawrence & Wishart).

Sherif, M. (1967), *Group Conflict and Co-operation* (London: Routledge & Kegan Paul).

Strauss, A. (1978), *Negotiations: Varieties, Processes, Contexts and Social Order* (London: Jossey-Bass).

Part 3

Preparation for Leadership

8

Mission Possible? An International Analysis of Headteacher/Principal Training

Brian Caldwell, Gerard Calnin and Wendy Cahill

Factors Shaping Interest in the Role of the Headteacher/Principal

There has been, and continues to be, considerable change in the role of the headteacher. While change was endemic in the profession for the last quarter of the twentieth century, the acceleration of change and its pervasiveness for schools meant that there is now concern about how we prepare candidates for headteacher status and the shortage of suitable applicants for the available positions. The literature suggests that the ubiquity of change, complexity of the role, level of remuneration, status of the profession, legal constraints and impact on family life are all reasons why there is a dearth of candidates seeking leadership roles in schools.

Daresh and Male (2000) explored the changes that affected headteachers in both the UK and America as they moved into their first year. The candidates reported that they were not prepared for the life-changing event of assuming the role of head and felt that there had been a lack of preparation for major decisions which require reflection and assistance, with a strong emphasis on personal values and ethical stances. Importantly, the personal lives of new leaders were altered significantly, with most reporting feelings of alienation, isolation and frustration in their work. The UK and USA have quite distinct models of preparing prospective leaders, but Daresh and Male (ibid., p. 99) conclude that neither method has prepared aspiring leaders adequately:

> British headteachers do not feel as if they were prepared totally for their posts simply because they had years of experience in roles similar to but not the same

---

Source: Commissioned.

as headteachers. And American headteachers report that academic preservice training does not prepare them completely for their jobs. The issue, therefore, is not one of suggesting that one is prepared either by previous practice or by courses. It is an issue of finding appropriate balance.

Davis (1996) identified a number of impediments to the role of the modern headteacher, but gives weight to the problem of values in a postmodern and pluralist society where absolutes are replaced by relativism, and legislation has sought to mandate much in the public and private lives of its citizens. Davis (ibid., pp. 10–11) sees potential problems for headteachers when they are faced with a values vacuum and overzealous litigation: 'No condition could give more opportunity for debate and disagreement ... There is no doubt that the first part of the next century will see litigious proceedings become commonly accepted responses to schools' management of such areas as student misbehavior, curriculum choice and attendance at class.'

James and Whiting (cited in Gunter, 1999) report research into the decision to become a headteacher at a time of a shortage in recruits. They argue: 'the notion that there is a large pool of potential heads out there who have the capacity to assume leadership and who will, of course, choose to do so in sufficient numbers is unsustainable' (Gunter, 1999, p. 261). They go on to show that the decision not to become a headteacher is related to contextual reasons, from job satisfaction through to family commitments, combined with a view of headship that was not professionally or personally attractive. The formal utilitarian aspect of the training and the projected life of a headteacher remain unattractive and are not helped by the ridiculing of both educational values and those who 'resist' business management.

Consider some of the changing dimensions within the professional practice of a headteacher in Britain over the last ten years:

■ competitive tendering for cleaning and canteen facilities;
■ the hiring, firing, promotion and dismissal of staff;
■ the selection, recruitment, retention, discipline and exiting of pupils;
■ bidding for resources from external funding agencies;
■ the installation and operation of information systems to measure and report on performance;
■ inspection of the school by a privatized team according to the OFSTED (Office for Standards in Education) framework; and
■ buying in training and consultancy to support staff training and development.

These tasks are typical of those carried out by senior executives in other fields. It is therefore understandable that 'school headteachers are increasingly regarded as the equivalents of senior managers in medium-sized business enterprise ... The message which the government wishes to emphasize is that of schools as businesses in a market-led economy for education' (Thody, 1998).

Centralization and decentralization are apparently competing trends in education introduced from the late 1980s onwards. Reflecting centralization of the system in Britain, there is now a national curriculum for all public schools, national standards to be attained are set by the central government and all schools are subject to frequent inspections that operate according to nationally set requirements. To decentralize, schools have become individually self-managed. If centralized control is the intention of the government, as it appears to be, then the nationalization of the training of school headteachers could be seen as yet another part of the control mechanism.

Olson (2000) reported that some of the reasons for a shortage of appropriate qualified candidates for school leadership in the USA were related to the quality of training programmes. Sibyll Carnochan, director of policy and research for the Broad Foundation, argues that 'new training programs, should blend coursework and on-the-job experience; provide ongoing support for novices; and combine a deep knowledge about instruction with management training' (ibid.).

A Review of Headteacher/Principal Training Programmes

This section of the chapter provides a review of developments in a number of nations, with particular reference to England, Australia, Hong Kong and Sweden.

England

National professional qualification for headteachers/principals

The trend in aspirant headteacher training programmes has been towards a centralized, compulsory, competency-based training scheme based on the National Standards for Headteachers. In 1997, launched by the Teacher Training Agency (TTA), the National Professional Qualification for Headteachers (NPQH) was introduced to address the professional development needs of aspiring and practising headteachers. This programme has moved away from conventional models of training, which have traditionally served the profession through diverse and pluralistic provision with multiple providers and an emphasis on voluntary participation. The move towards a centrally determined and accredited training programme is seen as a break with the past and a sense of the failure of traditional programmes to meet the needs of the modern headteacher.

The National Standards for Headteachers (TTA, 1998) contained five sections that prescribe criteria a candidate needs to meet and training that will facilitate such attainment. The five sections are:

1. Core purpose of headship.
2. Key outcomes of headship.
3. Professional knowledge and understanding.
4. Skills and attributes.
5. Key areas of headship, which are:
   A. strategic direction and development of the school;
   B. teaching and learning;
   C. leading and managing staff;
   D. efficient and effective deployment of staff and resources; and
   E. accountability.

Training centres and providers were established in ten NPQH Training and Development Centres in England and Wales and Regional Assessment Centres. Alternative training was provided through the partnership between the Open University and the National Association of Headteachers. Training focused on activities which were both practical and relevant to school improvement and provided by accredited trainers. It is useful to note at this point that the scale of the project is very large indeed since there are about 25,000 public schools and about 3,000 private schools in England and Wales.

The NPQH had six stages and was based on the separation of assessment from training:

Stage 1: Application and selection. The eligibility of the person to become an NPQH candidate was determined by the local education authority (or an assessment centre if the person was in a grant-maintained school – a classification abolished in 1998 – or independent school).

Stage 2: Needs assessment. The candidates attended an assessment centre where they underwent needs assessment and produced an action plan for their training.

Stage 3: Training and assessment. All candidates undertook the compulsory module for training related to key areas A and E and produced four assessment tasks.

Stage 4: Assessment for any remaining standards for candidates not following the training. All candidates had to complete the assessment tasks for key areas B–D, a total of six tasks. Training modules were available for candidates who had these areas identified in their action plan.

Stage 5: Final assessment. Candidates returned to the assessment centre having demonstrated that they had met the national standards through the ten assessment tasks. The decision to award was based on a day at the assessment centre in which through 'group and individual exercises', the candidates demonstrated that they were ready for headship. The emphasis was on the core purpose of headship in which they 'demonstrate their overall readiness for headship by showing that they are capable of exercising the professional judgment and leadership qualities of a headteacher' (TTA, 1997, p. 4).

Stage 6: Award of the qualification. The award of the NPQH signalled readiness for headship so that: 'Governing bodies can be confident that anyone who has successfully completed this programme of training can perform effectively in post. The NPQH will also give aspiring headteachers the confidence to know they are ready for the top job' (TTA, 1997) (adapted from Gunter, 1999, p. 256).

Anthea Millett, former Chief Executive of the TTA responsible for headship training programmes, claimed that 'the programme is unique in bringing together development of personal leadership effectiveness with school improvement strategies' and that the programme is right to 'aim at raising the game of all headteachers, and that trials so far suggest this has been a very successful outcome' (Millett, 1998).

But not all commentators subscribe to her sanguine views. Gunter (1999) reviewed some of the literature that has evaluated the NPQH programme. An initial concern is that the type of training offered by the NPQH programme fails to provide candidates with sufficient differentiation in terms of their needs and those of their schools, ranging from gender issues to those of spiritual leadership which might be essential in religious or denominational schools. A further concern (Bush, 1998) related to the 'deficit model' of sorting out potential/weak candidates or effective/failing headteachers which has little appeal for educational professionals. So, too, the emphasis in the training programme is more on achieving competence rather than drawing on what has been learned about the importance of mentoring in such a role.

Another criticism was that there was an assumed causal connection between what the head does and the outcomes achieved. The emphasis on organization, management and the production of measurable facts (Gunter, 1999, p. 259) suggests a managerial process devoid of issues related to values, power and relationships. Gunter (1999, p. 259) argues that 'we have been moved radically, perhaps tragically, from what traditionally has been known as the preparation of headteachers to the training of headteachers and in doing so all the debates that have gone on nationally and internationally about pedagogy and purpose are being marginalized'. The adoption of business competencies and strategies has, in part, served to alienate those candidates who hold firm to the centrality of their educational role in their professional identity.

A further perceived problem with the NPQH training programme was that it assumed a rational/linear view of change and change management. The teaching of or training in competencies presupposes that these skills in areas of technical expertise will effectively equip the headteacher to initiate and implement change in a turbulent school environment. Other writers (for example, Stacey, 1992; Fullan, 1993) argued that the pace of change, the degree to which it is externally imposed or arises internally, and the complexity of large organizations such as schools, mean that the management of change is far more complex, that there is no clear relationship between input and outcomes, and that change management in the future will be far less linear or rational. In this environment, change management will involve a complex interplay of skills, motivation, the capacity to provide meaning and animate others; change then is more about a journey, making and refining plans to achieve a particular set of objectives, rather than setting a predetermined pathway. Leaders, then, will be required to be flexible, responsive, and adaptive to the increasing turbulence of the school milieu. Ouston (1998, p. 128) argued that 'incremental approaches to organizational change are more likely to be successful in a complex environment: decisions made rationally are those that are most likely to *contribute* to achieving long-term objectives'. It would be difficult to see how the skills of flexibility, adaptability, motivating and providing meaning for others could easily be achieved in a rational, universal, competency-based model of headteacher training.

Leadership programme for serving headteachers/principals: the Hay/McBer programme

Another initiative in England is the Leadership Programme for Serving Heads (LPSH) that commenced in November 1998. The LPSH was developed for the Teacher Training Agency by private consulting organization Hay/McBer, in partnership with the National Association of Headteachers (the professional body that serves elementary school headteachers) and the Open University. As described by the Department for Education and Employment (2000, p. 2), the programme:

■ Draws on the national standards for headteachers and research evidence on the characteristics of highly effective headteachers;
■ Begins with a thorough and confidential analysis of personal and school performance, providing a sharp focus for subsequent training and development;
■ Features a four day residential workshop followed by further professional development and support;

- Directly links personal target-setting by the headteacher and school target-setting for raising pupils' achievements; and
- Combines challenge and support in a neutral and confidential setting, where heads can share expertise with colleagues from other types of school and different parts of the country.

The programme is conducted in four stages, with pre-workshop preparation requiring participants and members of staff in their schools to complete a questionnaire on leadership style (providing 360° feedback), a four-day residential workshop, post-workshop support including electronic networking and the use of a development guide, and a follow-up day that calls for preparation by the participant and members of their school community. The programme is delivered through seven national training providers, most of which are consortia that include at least one university among their members. The University of London Institute of Education through its Leadership Centre is the only university acting in its own right. It is an expensive programme, costing £2,000 per participant, with an optional £250 in order to be matched with a business partner through the Partners in Leadership scheme. Participants may seek support from their local education authority or they may self-fund their involvement.

The programme is selected for recommendation as an exemplar for two reasons. First, for its evident success on a national scale and, secondly, because it is the outcome of a successful adaptation from another country. The Hay/McBer organization successfully tendered for its role in the scheme on the basis of its success with an almost identical programme in Victoria, Australia, brief details of which are given in another section of this chapter. There are, however, three points of difference. In England, the target population is all serving heads, numbering about 25,000 in public schools, to participate at the rate of 3,000–4,000 per year, whereas for Victoria the programme is intended for experienced heads only. In England, the programme is implemented through seven national providers, with staff trained by Hay/McBer, whereas Hay/McBer conducts the Victorian programme with its own staff. The Partnership in Leadership scheme has no counterpart in Victoria.

The framework and other aspects of the programme are derived from the work of David McClelland, formerly a professor at Harvard and founder of the McBer practice in the Hay Group. It is based on the view that four variables – individual characteristics, job requirements, leadership styles and school climate – come together and impact on performance. Early evidence cited by Hay/McBer in both Victoria and England suggests that there is an association of this kind.

National College for School Leadership

The programme in England described above may be viewed as exemplary, despite the reservations and critiques, for it is national in scope and it has been implemented. However, it is the next stage that is attracting considerable international attention. In mid-1999 the government released a prospectus for a National College for School Leadership (NCSL) (Department for Education and Employment, 1999).

The main purpose of the following short account is to establish the significance of the initiative on the world stage, for the UK has a population of more than 50 million, with about 25,000 public schools and about 3,000 private schools whose leaders will be involved in the programme of NCSL in one way or another.

The NCSL has been given responsibility for the NPQH but, more broadly, for the design and delivery of a range of programmes at its site in Nottingham and around the country. Building a capacity for online learning is clearly a priority, as is ongoing research about school leadership. A feature is the international linkage and this alone is exemplary, with scores of people from many nations invited to contribute their ideas so far. Particular features of the programme are likely to include problem-based learning, mentoring, international travel and exchange, and use of the 'master class' approach. The government committed £10 million to building the headquarters of NCSL in Nottingham and £100 million per year for three years for mounting its programmes.

At the time of writing, the NCSL was gathering momentum in each of the areas in its mandate, with plans for delivery now including scores of local and regional learning networks. Leadership in middle management has been added, increasing the number of potential clients at any one time to more than a quarter of a million people.

Australia

We would wish to include reports of exemplary practice in our own nation but there is no coherent and comprehensive strategy in place at this time. There are elements of such a strategy and these are briefly described below. The situation in Australia is that, constitutionally, education is a state responsibility. The national government has an influence on policy and practice through the provision of grants to states and other bodies that have particular conditions attached to them in terms of utilization and accountability. This report of training programmes in Australia is divided into three sections. The first describes a range of noteworthy practices in Victoria. The second summarizes efforts to develop a competency-based approach. The third provides an overall assessment, highlighting the fragmentation of effort around the country.

Noteworthy practices in Victoria

An example of best practice in the 1980s was the programme of the Institute of Educational Administration (IEA) in Victoria, the centrepiece of which was a four-week intensive residential experience modelled on practice in management colleges in the business sector. Its building in Geelong was purpose designed around 45 people assigned to syndicates of 15 people. Some of the leading international experts in the field of educational administration served as major consultants for two of the four weeks. Other consultants assisted in particular fields of administration, including developments of local (state) interest. A problem-based or case-study approach was preferred in syndicate work and the programme was noted for its coherence. The IEA also conducted short programmes and developed resources for use or purchase by others. About 2,000 people participated in its extended residential programmes over nearly 15 years, prior to its closure in early 1993. While its impact was likely a very powerful one for participants and the institutions they served, the number of participants was but a small fraction of the population of school leaders during the time of its operation. This was a function of programme design. Aside from the issue of impact, the IEA was dependent to a large extent on state grants, and was placed under pressure as the financial circumstances in Victoria deteriorated in the late 1980s and early 1990s. A change in government in 1992 saw closure and sale of the property.

The government that closed the IEA had a commitment to headteacher development that was manifested in several noteworthy ways. The focus was the package of reforms from 1993 known as Schools of the Future that brought together a state curriculum and standards framework, local selection of teaching staff who remained under contact with the state education department, the decentralization of more than 90 per cent of the state's education budget to schools for local decision-making, the introduction of state-wide assessment tests in key learning areas at two points in elementary schooling and one point in secondary schooling (there is also the programme for the Victorian Certificate of Education at the end of secondary schooling), and a system of annual and triennial reviews with external validation. An integrating mechanism is the school charter, being a document outlining school priorities over a three-year period, reflecting agreement between the school and its community on the one hand and the school and the education department on the other.

Several large-scale training efforts were mounted. Brian Caldwell and the late Max Sawatzki were contracted to provide five-day residential training programmes for more than 1,000 headteachers from 1994 to 1997 on the theme 'Creating a School of the Future'. The programme was conducted in three parts, the first a three-day residential, the second a work-based project and the third a two-day residential. Major themes fell into the broad areas of strategic leadership and management; self-management in the personal sense, with opportunities for gaining 360° feedback and personal career planning; performance management and quality assurance; and team-building. Mean ratings were invariably in the high 4s on a 5-point scale.

Other large-scale efforts centred on various curriculum initiatives, commencing with literacy. The Early Literacy Research Project (ELRP), led by Peter Hill and Carmel Crévola, yielded valuable findings that underpinned programmes for headteachers and teachers in most schools. Impact on learning outcomes has been demonstrated. Related projects have been implemented in several cities in the USA. A similar effort is underway for school improvement in the middle years, based on findings in the Middle Years Research and Development Project (MYRAD) led by Peter Hill. Hill and Crévola have proposed a general design for improving learning outcomes that includes standards and targets; monitoring and assessment; classroom teaching programmes; professional learning teams; school and class organization; intervention and special assistance; and home, school and community partnerships – all underpinned and centred on beliefs and understandings (Hill and Crévola, 1999, p. 123). Training programmes based on the notion of school design have been conducted and these show promise as an integrating mechanism for a major component of headteacher development.

Two other initiatives in Victoria are noteworthy, namely, the creation of the Australian Principals Centre (APC) and the Hay/McBer programme that was the forerunner of the Leadership Programme for Serving Heads (LPSH) in England, described earlier. The APC was created as a limited company in 1995 with directors drawn from the Education Department of Victoria, the Victorian Association of State Secondary Principals, the Victorian Primary Principals Association and the University of Melbourne through its Faculty of Education (which provides the site of the enterprise at its Hawthorn campus). The organization has a small core staff and offers a range of programmes, including several under contract to the education department. It has pioneered a programme of peer recognition with various grades of fellowship. Like the former Institute of Educational Administration it is dependent on the state government for much of its funding. An attempt to develop the APC into a national organization has not succeeded, with other states preferring to establish their own centres or institutes. It links well with other organizations in Victoria with an interest in teacher and headteacher development. Its future may be resolved in the next year or so in the context of plans by the new state government to establish an institute of teaching. It is interesting to note that the longest-serving Chief Executive Officer of the APC, Bruce Davis, served as the Senior Consultant to the Education Department in Hong Kong in the design of a comprehensive programme for headteacher development (see account later).

The final development in Victoria reported here is the Hay/McBer programme described earlier in connection with the LPSH in England. It is likely that success in Victoria led to its adoption in England. The Hay/McBer Leadership Development Programme (LDP) in Victoria was, in turn, based on programmes conducted for major corporate clients including ICI, IBM, PepsiCo and Mobil. It was introduced in Victoria as part of a package of programmes to support the Schools of the Future initiative. The programme was piloted and refined in 1994 with more than 400 experienced headteachers and 80 senior managers in the education department taking part thus far. The Hay Group provided the author with the findings of an independent review that suggested it was an efficient and effective professional development programme with a positive impact on the performance of headteachers and the climate of the school. More recently in Victoria, Hay/McBer was invited to develop a programme for aspiring headteachers. It is interesting that a trigger for this work was the decline in number and quality of teachers seeking to be headteachers. Hay/McBer was also chosen to conduct research and prepare a school leadership competency model for headteachers and others who hold positions of responsibility in schools.

A competency-based approach

A competency framework for standards of headteachers' work has been adopted in two states, Queensland and, in a modified form, Western Australia. The competency framework identifies seven key areas of responsibility, including areas such as 'curriculum management' and 'people management'. Within each of these key areas there is a subdivision of a further six or eight competencies, for example, 'develop an effective performance management process for all staff'. The standard of performance in each competency is to be judged by indicators such as a 'performance management process is in place which is clearly understood by all staff and is consistent with the regulatory framework' or 'staff are encouraged to reflect on their performance and identify strengths and areas for development'. The competency-based model developed in these states is therefore one that describes observable behaviours based on a close scrutiny and analysis of the role of headteacher (Louden and Wildy, 1999).

Louden and Wildy (ibid.) have three concerns about the competency approach. First, the 'standards frameworks attempt to divide complex professional performances into hierarchical lists of dispositions, knowledge, or duties' (ibid., p. 102) with seven key responsibility areas, under each are three to eight competencies, and then a further subdivision into indicators, with a total of 134 items on the lowest level of the hierarchy. The problem remains, despite caveats which suggest that these items are not to be viewed in isolation, that 'the consequence of long hierarchical lists is to fragment professional performance. Careful warnings not to see the lists as fragmen-

tary do not overcome the problem of fragmentation. Within a single incident, headteachers may demonstrate a whole range of competencies that
appear as separate items on separate lists' (ibid.).

Louden and Wildy's second objection is that such standards and competencies 'separate the performance from the context within which it occurs'.
The context in which a specific competency is required will impact on the
skills and knowledge brought to bear on the situation:

> For example, quite different knowledge and skills would be required to
> demonstrate the competency 'provides and receives regular and constructive
> feedback' in the context of well established collegial relationship than the
> knowledge and skills required in giving feedback in the context of an alleged
> moral impropriety by a teacher ... A performance that appears to be an obvious
> and separate competency when stated in a general form may require a range of
> different knowledge and skills in different contexts. (ibid., p. 103).

The third concern about the competency model, with its lists of duties or dispositions, is the degree of precision required in evidencing the operation of
such competencies. It is difficult to determine absolute degrees of competence: one has the skill or not, within a professional role which requires a
more detailed and nuanced understanding of particular skills or dispositions
and the complex environment in which they are performed. The impact of
the list of competencies, therefore, is to dichotomize the skill rather than
estimating where a person's skill level sits on the continuum of development
or progression.

In Victoria, a range of leadership programmes described in the previous
section supported the introduction of Schools of the Future. A performance
management system based on the specification of competencies was also
introduced. It has two components: accreditation – which certifies the
demonstration of key skills and competencies and evidence of their application to the job; and assessment – the achievement of agreed outcomes.
Former Director of Schools and Secretary for Education, Geoff Spring (1996,
p. 28), reported on the role of mentors or coaches and the intended outcome:

> The widely accepted model of mentoring and coaching is being implemented
> with a pool of experienced headteachers receiving training to act as coaches and
> mentors for their colleagues. The performance management system is the
> centrepiece for ensuring quality management practices and links improving
> student learning to performance management.

Though not a programme designed for aspiring headteachers, the
Performance Standards for School Headteachers is an attempt in Western
Australia to explore an alternative to the competency-based models described

above by using a probabilistic standards framework to support the judgements made by headteachers. The project is a collaborative research and development project undertaken by Edith Cowen University and the Department of Education of Western Australia.

Rather than describing in detail the work of a headteacher, the purpose of the project was to specify and illustrate the range of performance within the headteachers' work. After initial research into selecting trial dimensions of headteachers' work (for example, 'managing staff') and establishing a continuum of performance, the second phase provided an account of the content of headteachers' work, the duties to be undertaken and the skills and dispositions required to perform the duties at a high level of performance. The third phase was designed to develop progress maps that describe the progression in performance on each of the dimensions in the standards framework (Louden and Wildy, 1999).

The project attempted to deal with several weaknesses identified in competency-based standards, namely, the hierarchical lists, the decontextualizing of performance and the promise of false dichotomies of those who reach a prescribed standard and those who fail. Dimensions representing duties, interpersonal skills and moral dispositions have been developed inductively, based on headteachers' reactions to reading and rating a series of case studies of headteachers' work. Louden and Wildy (ibid., p. 118) are optimistic that the project has the potential to offer an alternative and more rewarding response to the professional development of headteachers, and suggest that rather than listing duties and responsibilities as competencies:

> they abstract from commonly shared experiences and familiar dilemmas those interpersonal skills and moral dispositions that appear to differentiate the quality of headteachers' performance. For these reasons, the rich reality of the case studies appears to engage headteachers at a deeper level than lists of duties and dispositions.

Research such as that associated with the Performance Standards for School Headteachers may well provide insight into alternative training programmes for aspiring headteachers.

A fragmented effort

Neither across the nation as a whole nor within a single system is there a coherent and comprehensive approach to the preparation and professional development of headteachers. In Victoria, where reform has been relatively coherent, even if controversial in some respects, there are many commendable initiatives but they do not come together in the way envisaged, for example, with the National College for School Leadership in Engalnd. This may have been the intention with the Australian Principals Centre, which is essentially a Victoria-based organization, but it has not been achieved. Leadership development for learning and teaching in literacy, numeracy and the middle years is designed and delivered in other agencies, as is the Hay/McBer programme. Units of the education department, variously named in recent years, have served as the co-ordinating mechanism to the extent that state funding and the needs of leaders in government or public schools are involved. There is, however, a high level of co-operation with professional associations and organizations serving non-public schools.

Hong Kong

Hong Kong, while having a dynamic East–West culture, is now a Special Administrative Region of the People's Republic of China. It has about 1,200 schools in its public education system, which is large by US district standards, and has a mix of mostly urban and some small rural schools. While most of these schools are almost fully publicly funded, only about 8 per cent of students attend schools that are publicly owned, administered by the Education Department. Almost all the remaining 92 per cent attend schools in the so-called aided sector, set up and managed by a trust or foundation or church.

The relevance of Hong Kong arises from a similarity between a substantial package of reforms that has been evolving in recent years and those found in the nations to which detailed attention has been given in this chapter. An Education Commission of representatives of major stakeholders has been in place for many years and has issued seven major reports, the most recent of which (Education Commission, 2000) brings together a number of proposals to reform the curriculum, improve assessment mechanisms, remove obstacles to learning especially in the middle years, and reform the university admission system, with a resource strategy that takes account of the costs of reform. A high level of school-based management is intended for all schools. The driving force for change is similar to that in other nations, namely, recognition of the importance of lifelong learning and the need for an education system that responds to the needs of all students in every setting.

There was recognition in 1999 that changes such as those foreshadowed 'will require headteachers to take on new leadership roles in quality development and quality assurance. They also highlight the need for a more focused and systematic leadership training and development program to enhance the quality of school leadership' (Education Department, 1999). A consultation paper of the Task Group on Training and Development of School Leaders proposed that all newly appointed headteachers participate in such a programme from 2000–2001. Five core modules were proposed (learning and teaching, human resource development, financial management, strategic management, school administration). The seven elective modules included school visits outside Hong Kong; international perspectives on educational development; professional responsibility and the law; future economic development and its impact on education; education in the age of information and technology; equality issues in education; and education development in the mainland. It was proposed that participants be attached to a school with good practice and that there be an eight-month experiential school project, facilitated by a headteacher, academic or senior manager from the public or private sector. The complex role of headteacher was organized in three domains: the headteacher as leader of the school, the headteacher as leader of teaching and learning, and the headteacher as leader of the wider educational community. The proposal is noteworthy for its connection to systemic reform at the same time that it provides for exposure to developments elsewhere in society, nationally and internationally; and the connection to a mentor/facilitator.

The merit of the approach lies in its coherence, links to a comprehensive school reform movement, recognition of a context beyond the immediate school system extending internationally and to other sectors of public and private endeavour, and the connection between training/development and career.

Some qualifications on this assessment of progress in Hong Kong are offered at this point. One is the potential for reductionism and fragmentation in an approach based on a detailed specification of role. This is a criticism offered of some programmes elsewhere (see Louden and Wildy, 1999, on developments in Australia). Another is the capacity of 'the system' to drive through the implementation. Hong Kong is exemplary in the manner it puts almost all proposals out for community consultation, but stakeholders are many and powerful. The Education Department is relatively small, as noted at the outset, and this contrasts with the situation in England, where there is a relatively powerful central government that is clearly bent on implementation of existing programmes and intentions for the National College for School Leadership.

It is intended that universities be the main providers in Hong Kong, with three institutions likely to be the main sources (Chinese University of Hong Kong, Hong Kong Institute of Education, University of Hong Kong). While there will be substantial public funding to support the endeavour, it is likely that participants will contribute substantially to the costs of their involvement, for the programme is viewed as individual career advancement. It is noteworthy that many Hong Kong headteachers are already engaged in professional development in Mainland China through a highly regarded programme offered at East China Normal University in Shanghai. The Director of Education in Hong Kong assisted in the launch of the programme.

Sweden

Programmes for preparation and professional development of headteachers in Sweden were viewed as exemplary a decade or so ago. The authors gained new insights through their meetings with study groups of headteachers from Sweden who visited Melbourne on a regular basis. These visits are of interest in their own right, being organized for secondary school headteachers by their professional association. The Victorian Association of State Secondary Principals worked with particular schools, school systems and the University of Melbourne in making local arrangements. These tours are part of a systematic approach that has emerged in England in the programme of the National College for School Leadership.

Headteachers in Sweden are appointed by local government and undertake a two-year induction programme. It is significant that Sweden does not pre-train headteachers *per se*. The local board of education appoints its leaders after a suitable recruitment programme. They want to be able to make a choice based more on the 'integrity' of the person, rather than have to select from those applicants who may have had specific training and hold a certificate to say that this makes them suitable.

Recruitment programmes are in operation at the local level, and local government boards of education are encouraged to identify the qualities that they require in the leadership of their schools. One approach for the 'would-be leader' is the opportunity to undertake a ten-meeting study circuit to enhance their educational background. This adds to their professional profile, but it is an opportunity open to all educators and is not set up specifically for potential headteachers, nor is it focused entirely on leadership.

When headteachers are appointed in Sweden, as the first step in their formal induction programme, they are brought together with four others, under the guidance of a tutor, who is a very experienced school leader. The tutor is freed from normal responsibilities for a month in order to assist the new headteachers on the job. Ten per cent of a new headteacher's working time is to be used on exercises set by the induction programme organizers. The entire induction is closely mentored yet is sufficiently flexible to provide for individual differences. It aims at developing individual strengths.

After the two-year induction programme, the still-new headteacher undertakes a three-year 'deepening' programme. As well as studying school-focused leadership, the school leader must concentrate on studying leadership in two other organizations. One is to be a business or a factory, the other should be another public service organizations such as a welfare agency. This three-year programme is co-ordinated through the School Leader Education Project (SLEP) that has overall responsibility for school leader training in Sweden.

There are two noteworthy features of this approach in Sweden. The first is the matching with an experienced school leader and the second is the extended period of time in the 'deepening' programme. The latter conveys a sense of 'formation', a concept that is explored in another section of this chapter.

International initiatives

International linkages and partnerships of one kind or another are starting to emerge on a large scale and ought to feature in the design of new programmes. These reflect the globalization of education but also indicate the extent to which reform proposals have much in common across the world and that leaders can learn from leaders in other settings.

Several universities and professional associations have organized such partnerships in recent years, including the three-nation International Principals Institute at the University of Southern California (Australia, Britain, USA) conducted for five years in the mid to late-1990s; travel programmes organized for secondary headteachers in Sweden; and similar ventures organized in England by the University of Hull and by the National College for School Leadership.

Universities are starting to form strategic alliances for the delivery of their programmes and one such alliance is emerging for the training and professional development of school leaders. This will involve the University of Hull, the University of Nottingham, the University of London through its Institute of Education, the University of Toronto through the Ontario Institute for Studies in Education, Claremont Graduate University and the University of Melbourne. London, Melbourne and Nottingham are members of the Universitas 21 global alliance that currently has 19 partners on four continents. It is intended that this global leadership alliance will be connected to the programme of the National College for School Leadership based at Nottingham.

■ The Formation of Leaders

The concept of 'formation' is helpful in describing how capacities for the headteacher are acquired and sustained, with a role for university-based diploma and degree programmes as well as specialist professional development opportunities, but the emphasis is on systematic 'formation', with opportunity for mentoring along the way. It is given most eloquent expression in the work of Gronn (1999), based on studies of headteachers in the non-public sector, and Ribbins (2000).

Gronn's 'career model' of leadership identifies four stages of a leader's career – formation, accession, incumbency and divestiture – that are set in three macro-contexts – historical, cultural and societal. These macro-contexts account for the differences in practices across nations, how approaches that may have been effective in one era may not be effective in another and how biographies of leaders who succeed in different eras and in different settings may differ in respect to the conclusions that may be drawn about the development of leaders.

Formation can be understood at two levels, according to Gronn. For society and key sectors within society, formation is 'the totality of the institutionalized arrangements which either by intention or effect, serve to replenish or reproduce cohorts of leaders' (Gronn, 1999, p. 32). For individuals, formation 'means those preparatory socialization processes and experiences which served to later position them in their previous incarnation as leadership aspirants in a state of social and psychological readiness to assume responsibility and authority' (ibid.). Accession is 'the stage of grooming or anticipation in which candidates for leadership roles rehearse or test their potential capacity to lead by comparison with existing leaders and the field of potential rivals for advancement' (ibid., pp. 35–36). Incumbency or leadership proper, as Gronn describes it, is the stage where 'leaders have developed and honed their public personas, they have learned to project their authoritativeness, and they now seek to give further expression to their quest for mastery and self-realization by gaining experience through circulating amongst various elite postings and leadership roles' (ibid., p. 39). Divestiture is simply the process of 'letting go', which may 'come about voluntarily or involuntarily' (ibid.).

It is readily apparent, in this view of leader development, that formal programmes of training may be entirely inadequate, especially those that do not take account of context and do not provide for or recognize in an aspirant the rich range of experiences and particular constellation of personal qualities that come from an extended process of formation.

Ribbins (2000, p. 87) advocates the 'career model' proposed by Gronn and argues for an approach to development which:

- is centrally concerned with improving the quality of schooling and the achievement of pupils
- is systematic and comprehensive and of high quality
- makes available continuing professional development opportunities for every career phase
- has a concern for practical skills but also for a more philosophical approach
- involves a range of providers, with the universities engaged fully at a variety of levels
- provides core training, but supports development opportunities that mean more than this
- is based on the best available evidence and fosters the research that generates this.

Conclusion

Despite the promise of practices such as those summarized here, there remains an underlying concern that the role of the headteacher, as it is emerging in several nations, is essentially unfeasible, and that this, more than limitations in training and development, is the fundamental reason for the shortage in number and quality of applicants. This seems to be the case in non-public schools as well as public schools, even those in highly favourable circumstances. Some may argue that the whole approach to schooling, still based on models developed in the last century or even the century before that, is no longer relevant, and that problems such as those addressed here will remain until a fundamental re-engineering of schooling occurs. This re-engineering may have over-arching priority, but training and development along the lines explored here may make a significant contribution to the quality of schooling and the satisfaction of those who lead the effort.

Note

This chapter is based on a report to the National Centre for Education and Economy (NCEE) in Washington, DC, prepared in 2000 as a resource for the NCEE in the design of leadership programmes in the USA.

References

Daresh, J. and Male, T. (2000) Crossing the border into leadership: experiences of newly appointed British headteachers and American headteachers, *Educational Management and Administration* 28(1): 89–101.

Davis, B. (1996) Leadership in the next millennium. *The Practising Administrator* 18 (1): 6–11.

Department for Education and Employment (UK) (1999) *National College for School Leadership: A Prospectus*. London: Department for Education and Employment.

Department for Education and Employment (UK) (2000) *Leadership Programme for Serving Headteachers*. London: Department for Education and Employment.

Education Commission (HK) (2000) *Review of Education System: Reform Proposals. Consultation Document of the Education Commission, Hong Kong Special Administrative Region, People's Republic of China*. May.

Education Department (HK) (1999) *Leadership Training Program for Headteachers. Consultation Paper, Task Force on Training and Development of School Headteachers*. June.

Fullan, M. (1993) *Change Forces: Probing the Depths of Educational Change*. London: Falmer Press.

Gronn, P. (1999) *The Making of Educational Leaders*. London: Cassell.

Gunter, H. (1999) Contracting headteachers as leaders: an analysis of the NPQH. *Cambridge Journal of Education* 29 (2).

Hill, P. and Crévola, C. (1999) The role of standards in educational reform for the 21st century. In D. Marsh (ed.) *Preparing our Schools for the 21st Century. ASCD Yearbook 1999*. VA: Alexandria ASCD.

Louden, W. and Wildy, H. (1999) Short shrift to long lists: an alternative approach to the development of performance standards for school headteachers. *Journal of Educational Administration* 37 (2): 99–120.

Millett, A. (1998) New leadership programme takes shape. http://195.44.11.137/coi/coipress.nsf (visited on 25 March 2000).

Olson, L. (2000) New thinking on what makes a leader. *Education Week* 19 January. http://www.edweek.org/ew/ewstory.cfm?slug=19lead.h19 (visited on 30 March 2000).

Ouston, J. (1998) Management in turbulent times. In A. Gold and J. Evans (eds.) *Reflecting on School Management*. London: Falmer Press.

Ribbins, P. (2000) Understanding leadership: developing headteachers. In T. Bush *et al.* (eds.) *Educational Management: Redefining Theory, Policy and Practice*. London: Paul Chapman.

Spring, G. (1996) System support for self-managing schools: Victoria's Schools of the Future. *The Practising Administrator* 18 (1): 14–17, 28–30.

Stacey, R. (1992) *Managing the Unknowable*. San Francisco, CA: Jossey-Bass.

Teacher Training Agency (UK) (1998) *National Standards for Headteachers*. London: TTA.

Thody, A. (1998) Training school headteachers, educating school governors. *International Journal of Educational Management* 12 (5), http://www.emerald-library.co./brev/06012ed1.htm (visited on 25 March 2000).

9

Effective Training for Subject Leaders

Alma Harris, Hugh Busher and Christine Wise

Introduction

The pressure upon schools to improve and to raise achievement is unlikely to recede over the next few years. Educational policy remains firmly focused upon securing increased pupil and school performance. However, it has become increasingly apparent that for schools to develop and improve in rapidly changing times, issues of leadership and management can no longer simply be seen as the exclusive preserve of senior staff. Staff at all levels in an organisation need to be involved in decision-making and policy formation (Earley, 1998; MacBeath, 1999; Day *et al.*, 2000). Successive research studies have shown that within the most effective schools, leadership extends beyond the senior management team to encompass other levels within the school organisation (Harris, 1999; Busher and Harris, 2000).

One important source of leadership resides at the middle management level. In both primary and secondary schools, subject leaders are uniquely placed to influence the quality of teaching and learning within their subject areas (Busher and Harris, 1999). As team leaders they have a powerful influence over classroom practices, and are important gatekeepers to change and development within the subject. The importance of the subject leader's management role was formally acknowledged by the Teacher Training Agency (TTA) with the publication of the 'National Standards for Subject Leaders' (TTA, 1998). These Standards were part of a much wider initiative to establish a professional development framework for teachers.

The Standards define both the nature and the scope of a subject leader's role in Primary and Secondary schools. These are categorised into four sections:

Source: Journal of In-Service Education, Vol. 27, no. 1, 2001, pp. 83–94. Edited version.

- strategic direction and development of the subject;
- teaching and learning;
- leading and managing staff;
- efficient and effective deployment of staff and resources (TTA, 1998).

The Subject Leader Standards represent not only a change of terminology, but also a major re-definition of the role, expectations and performance of middle managers. The Standards highlight the importance of the subject leader in securing *high quality teaching and improved standards of achievement* (TTA, 1998). They also acknowledge the centrality of the subject leader in contributing to whole school policy and development:

> While the headteacher and governors carry overall responsibility for school improvement, a subject leader has responsibility for the subject curriculum and for establishing high standards of teaching and learning in their subject as well as playing a major role in the development of school policy. (TTA, 1998, p.3)

In September 2001, the DfES published the *Teaching Standards Framework* in which they state:

> Subject leaders provide professional leadership and management for a subject to secure high quality teaching, effective use of resources and improved standards of learning and achievement for all pupils.

The main thrust of both sets of Standards is to secure higher pupil achievement by meeting clearly defined organisational, curriculum and pedagogical goals. As a result, the expectations of middle managers have changed dramatically, and the leadership and management challenges they face are extensive. At the same time, the effect of educational changes on the Senior Management Team (SMT) within schools has resulted in the delegation of some tasks from senior to middle management (Brown and Rutherford, 1996).

The introduction of performance management has recently extended the responsibilities subject leaders face. It is clear that team leaders will have a major role in assessing and monitoring the performance of others (Hammond and Harris, 2000). Such developments have serious and far-reaching implications for the professional development and training of middle managers in schools across England and Wales. In order to meet the requirements of the Standards and to cope with the additional demands placed upon them by performance management, subject leaders will require an extensive and substantive programme of professional development. However, the training and development provision for middle managers in schools has, to date, been relatively limited.

More than 10 years ago Earley and Fletcher Campbell (1989) identified the paucity of research into middle management and they highlighted the inadequate preparation for the role. They found that *many new heads of department seem to be ill prepared for the role* and that few training programmes were available for aspiring or new heads of department (Earley and Fletcher Campbell, 1989, p. 7). Recent research has shown that despite some improvement, there continues to be a lack of adequate and effective training for middle managers. Research by Adey (2000) found that of 112 middle managers surveyed, 57.4% indicated that they had received no training to prepare or equip them for their role.

This level of provision seems wholly inadequate given the important contribution middle managers make to school performance and improvement (Harris, 1999; Busher and Harris, 2000). In order to meet the new demands of the role in a much more coherent way a comprehensive training programme for subject leaders would seem to be long overdue. Two important questions need to be addressed. First, what is the current extent and scope of professional development and training opportunities for subject leaders? Secondly, what are the most effective forms of professional development and training available to subject leaders?

This chapter outlines the findings from research funded by the TTA that considered both of these questions within the context of the United Kingdom. The research explored the nature, scope and impact of professional development and training opportunities available to subject leaders in England and Wales (Harris *et al.*, 2000). Its central purpose was to identify the types of professional development and training opportunities that were most effective in changing subject leaders' professional practice. While the research was undertaken in England and Wales, the broad implications for professional development and training emerging from this study are applicable to other countries and other educational contexts.

▌ Research Design

The research was conducted in two phases. The first phase involved a national survey of training opportunities for subject leaders. The purpose of the survey was to establish the extent of the provision of subject leader training by Local Education Authorities (LEAs) and Higher Education Institutions (HEIs) in England and Wales (Harris *et al.*, 1999). Within the survey, data was collected on the dual dimensions of course type (i.e. short courses and long courses; accredited and non-accredited courses) and course delivery (i.e. sole provider, partnership, outside trainer, other provider). It was recognised that partnerships between LEAs and HEI providing courses might result in some duplication of information and this was factored into the data analysis. The central aim of the survey was to obtain a comprehensive picture of provision that indicated the range of courses on offer to subject leaders.

From the survey four main types of training courses for subject leaders emerged:

■ LEA delivered short courses – non-accredited;
■ HEI delivered long courses accredited at higher degree level (diploma, masters, etc.);
■ partnership courses offered jointly by LEA and HEI – long, non-accredited;
■ school-based courses led by HEI – long, accredited (diploma, masters, etc.)

These courses formed the basis of phase two of the research. This phase explored the relative impact of each type of course upon the professional practice of subject leaders. Within this phase, the prevalent models of training identified in the audit were subjected to further exploration and scrutiny. This was to establish whether and to what extent, the different modes of training had a positive impact upon subject leaders' practice. The LEA 'short course' approach to training proved difficult to investigate as participants generally felt that the impact of a 1-day course would be difficult to detect. Consequently, courses were selected from the audit data in the three main categories. These categories were HEI higher degree level courses, partnership courses (offered jointly by LEA and HEI) and school-based courses.

Semi-structured interviews were conducted with 15 subject leaders (nine male and six female), 12 senior staff and 19 team members across the three course types. The participants in the interviews were spread across 12 secondary schools. The views of subject leaders were triangulated with the views of their team members and senior staff. In particular, the impact of the training upon the subject leader's practice was investigated. This was the main criterion in judging the effectiveness of the course.

The impact of the training was considered at three different levels, the whole school, the department and the classroom level (Harris *et al.*, 2000). Subject leaders, team members and senior managers were asked to provide evidence of impact at each of these levels, where it was available. This evidence was used to judge, first, whether the course had resulted in any positive changes in the practice of the subject leader and secondly, whether these changes had led to tangible improvements, particularly at the classroom level.

Findings

The survey data revealed that the majority of LEAs and HEIs had yet to develop a comprehensive range of specialist training courses for subject leaders. While there was a proliferation of LEA short course programmes available to schools, only a small percentage of these courses matched the Subject Leader Standards (TTA, 1998) and addressed the specific training needs of subject leaders. The majority of LEA short courses identified in the survey reflected a range of subject and curriculum focused topics. Relatively few short courses were designed to address the particular professional development needs of subject leaders. The long course provision offered by LEAs similarly focused upon topics of a broad and general nature. The audit found that the majority of long courses tended to focus upon general issues of management, rather than to be tailored to the professional needs of a particular group.

In terms of Higher Education Institutions (HEIs) 83% of courses were higher degree courses that reflected the interests and expertise within the respective institution of higher education. There was a predictable pattern of MA, diploma and MEd courses within the various HEIs and a number of taught doctorate programmes with management or leadership themes. Generally, the higher degree courses were not designed to address the needs of a specific group but were aimed at a wider population. A small proportion of HEIs offered school-based higher degree courses that were delivered on site. However, the majority of HEIs tended to offer traditional higher degree courses of a general nature.

The survey data showed that there were a significant number of partnership courses on offer across England and Wales that involved both LEAs and HEIs. Fifty-one per cent of all LEA provision was in partnership with HEIs. This figure reflects a growing trend towards training that comprises the expertise of both HEI and LEA personnel.

The responses to the open-ended questions in the survey provided some interesting findings about the general features or attributes of effective continuing professional development (CPD) courses. Effective training courses for subject leaders were considered to be those that offered evidence of a focused and relevant curriculum that helped participants develop better understanding of their professional role. A consensus emerged around the features of effective training courses for subject leaders. Effective training courses were considered to:

■ involve an action research component where participants focused upon a particular problem or issue;
■ encourage participants to analyse data and to scrutinise evidence;
■ ask participants to identify areas of action/development on returning to school;
■ be integrated into school improvement programmes;
■ stimulate debate about pedagogy and the quality of teaching and learning within the subject area;

- assist subject leaders to change their practice and the practice of others within the subject area;
- provide advisory support throughout the course and school visits;
- develop good rapport and trust between teachers;
- establish supportive networks for teachers and coordinators;
- provide support to participants to help them follow up work in schools.

Three dominant aspects of effective training for subject leaders emerged from the audit phase of the study. The first aspect concerned the importance of immersing subject leaders in a process of 'urgency, agency, action'. The most effective form of training was considered to involve subject leaders in some change requiring external agency and subsequent action. The second aspect focused upon the centrality of encouraging subject leaders to reflect on their practice in a systematic and rigorous way. Effective training programmes were considered to involve subject leaders in self-reflection and analysis. Finally, the third aspect related to professional networks for subject leaders. Effective training programmes were considered to be those that provided a means of support for sustained professional collaboration and networking.

Effective Training Approaches

One of the central purposes of the research was to ascertain the relative effectiveness of different models of training upon the professional practice of subject leaders. In order to achieve this, evidence was sought from subject leaders, team members and senior managers about the impact of the training upon the whole school, department and classroom level. Using this empirical evidence it was possible to gauge the relative effectiveness of different forms of training using a staff development framework created by Joyce and Showers (1988). They suggest that different staff development activities have an impact on different levels of teachers' thinking and practice:

- awareness;
- knowledge:
- understanding;
- behaviour.

Using this model of evaluating professional training and development, the four training courses identified in this study were analysed. A summary of this analysis appears in Table 9.1.

From the data analysis, there was evidence to suggest that both courses facilitated changes in subject leaders' awareness, knowledge, understanding and behaviour. Within the LEA/HEI partnership model, there was evidence of

Table 9.1 *Impact of training courses on professional practice.*

	LEA-based (short)	HEI-based (long)	LEA/HEI partnership (long)	School /HEI partnership (long)
Awareness	*	*	*	*
Knowledge		*	*	*
Understanding		*	*	*
Behaviour			*	*

* denotes available evidence.

changes at each of these four levels. For example, one senior manager commented that the subject leader in question:

> has greater awareness of what is going on elsewhere. He looks to the school as a whole. He has taken on more responsibility in the whole school realm. (Senior Manager)

At a personal level, the LEA/HEI courses were found to have a positive impact upon subject leaders' knowledge and understanding of their role and responsibilities:

> I am now more confident and less unsure about my role. Because I have a plan in place and real targets to work to . . . the confidence is there. (Subject Leader)

> His confidence has grown. He thinks the course has transformed him. He probably could have done the work without the course but it has helped him to know that he is doing the right things. (Team member)

In addition, it was acknowledged that the course had assisted subject leaders to understand the process of change and to instigate new developments:

> The training has allowed me to work closer with the senior management team and to get my department noticed. (Subject Leader)

> The direct result of the training has been the formalisation of plans for initiating the new assessment schedules in the department with specific allocated responsibilities with time scales attached. (Subject leader)

There was evidence that subject leaders had changed their views on pedagogical processes as a result of the course:

> [It] has sharpened his focus on the classroom and aspects of good practice that need to be developed. (Team member)

In one case this led to the implementation of more consistent assessment and tracking procedures for students within a department. In another it led to a re-written departmental plan and the implementation of a lesson observation plan for the department.

In the school-based model of partnership, the training was perceived to have affected the work of subject leaders in a variety of ways. At whole school level it had raised awareness and assisted subject leaders to take a broader picture of their work:

> *my awareness has certainly improved. I can see the wider picture. (Subject Leader)*

> *had alerted [the subject leader] to an awareness of major educational issues at a higher level. (Senior manager)*

Within their subject areas, there was evidence that subject leaders had become more inclusive in their processes of decision-making and had placed greater emphasis on building teams. Some subject leaders were considered to be more aware of the needs of their team colleagues:

> *She is more reflective and thoughtful . . . Good at involving department members and spending time with them. Knows how to use team members to best effect. Excellent development of team-members for what is expected of them. [She] is very clear and consistent in setting expectations. (Senior manager)*

> *Very supportive towards his team… acts as a 'critical friend' which I appreciate. (Team member)*

> *We now all support and encourage each other. For example, over GCSE coursework moderation or display work… we often share ideas and see each others' work. (Team member)*

There was also evidence to suggest that subject leaders attending school-based programmes developed better understanding of the learning needs of pupils. In some cases this led to subject leaders revising schemes of work or developing new assessment processes. In others it led to a better understanding of the different learning orientations pupils have when taking a subject:

> *She now gives strategies [to teachers] to help with classroom management and is concerned with how children are learning in lessons. (Team member)*

> *He now monitors pupil performance more carefully. He makes sure that pupils receive schemes of work as intended. There is a careful checking of pupils' work to judge whether their work is being assessed properly. (Team member)*

*The course has changed the way I teach because it has required me to analyse the way
I teach a project over [across] several groups [of students]. (Subject leader)*

*It has enabled me to find out a little more about the variety of teaching and learning
styles. (Subject leader)*

With both partnership models of professional development, a number of
common elements emerge. The elements were as follows:

- an emphasis upon collaboration;
- involvement and support of senior management;
- flexible and intermittent training points;
- external agency;
- context related planning and development;
- necessity of enquiry and reflection;
- use of research to inform practice;
- evaluation and data analysis.

For both types of training course, there was an emphasis upon change at the
subject and classroom level. In particular, the clear focus upon teaching and
learning within these courses resulted in tangible improvements within different subject areas.

Discussion

From the analysis of effective training programmes a number of conclusions
can be drawn. Firstly, that an important component of both the partnership
training models is an emphasis upon reflection. Day (1999) highlights the
importance of the relationship between reflection and professional growth
and learning. The importance of reflection in enabling teachers able to take
control of their own practice within different organisational frameworks is
well established. Professional learning is understood to be as much a process
of critical reflection on ideas and practices offered for scrutiny, as it is a
matter of encountering the ideas themselves. Schön (1983, 1987) argues that
people not only need to think critically about practice, but also to think practically about it.

In order to learn successfully, subject leaders need to construct and reflect
on their own learning pro-actively. They need to take some time to inter-
nalise new knowledge if it is to influence practice directly. As Steadman *et al.*
(1995, p. 49) note:

*Change in the classroom practice involves more than extending the repertoire by
acquiring new skill. It will mean changing attitudes, beliefs and personal theories.*

The partnership models of training provided subject teachers with the
expertise and support to instigate changes in attitudes, beliefs and personal
theories. To realise these changes the training programmes assisted subject
leaders in developing a clear understanding of the importance of particular
styles of interpersonal relationships that assisted staff and students to work
successfully together.

A second important feature of these training programmes concerned the
provision of some 'external agency'. Changes in behaviour and practice are
not achievable in isolation (Joyce and Showers, 1988). Such developments
need to be facilitated and nurtured by some external agency. Joyce and
Showers (1988) argue that it is difficult to transfer teaching or management
skills from INSET sessions to classroom settings without adequate support
through mentoring or the guidance of critical friends (Golby and Appleby,
1995). Smyth (1991) argues that such approaches encourage teachers to be
more creative and flexible in solving problems because it encourages them to
take ownership of the problems and their preferred solutions. This 'external
agency' assists subject leaders to reflect upon the changes in practice and to
evaluate the outcomes of implementing change within their subject area. In
some cases, this may be the link advisor from the LEA, or a HEI tutor or a colleague from another school. Whatever the source of this external agency, the
existence of external pressure and support is an important contributory
factor in changing teachers' practice and behaviour.

A third feature of these effective training courses concerned the linkage
between the 'workshop and the workplace'. While it may be relatively easy to
give subject leaders a range of perspectives on what it means to lead a subject
area in a school, one of the key problems is how to help them to transfer and
translate that knowledge into practice. Indeed, the impact of much in-service
training remains variable because of the lack of connection between what
Joyce and Showers (1988) term 'the workshop and the workplace'. Often the
workshop or training ground for developing new skills and knowledge is
divorced from the workplace, the classroom, department or school where
new skills and knowledge are utilised.

In both partnership models of training, an emphasis was placed upon the
direct application of ideas presented in the 'workshop' sessions. There existed
clear expectations that the course was intended to prompt action and to
facilitate change. As a consequence, subject leaders made explicit linkages
between the 'workshop and the workplace' and were able to secure beneficial
development and change within their subject area.

Coda

As schools face continuous change in the years ahead, the need and demand for supportive leadership and management at all levels within the school organisation will become even stronger. The reality is that those responsible for leading and managing others will have further and higher expectations placed upon them to improve schools. For subject leaders, this presents the opportunity to secure high standards within the subject area by improving the quality of teaching and learning. This will only be achieved if adequate and effective models of training are in place to equip subject leaders to meet these challenges. This research has illustrated some of the important components of effective training provision and has demonstrated how this impacts upon professional development and growth. Clearly, there is further work to be undertaken but the need for high quality professional development for subject leaders remains incontestable.

References

Adey, K. (2000) Professional development priorities: the views of middle managers in secondary schools educational management and administration, *Educational Management and Administration*, 28, pp. 419 ff.

Ball, S.J. (1999) Labour, learning and the economy: a policy sociology, *Cambridge Journal of Education*, 29, pp. 195–206.

Brown, M. and Rutherford, D. (1996) Leadership for school improvement: key issues for the head of department, paper presented at the British Educational Research Association Annual Conference, September, University of Lancaster.

Busher, H. and Harris, A. (1999) Leadership of school subject areas: tensions and dimensions of managing in the middle, *School Leadership and Management,* 19, pp. 305–317.

Busher, H. and Harris, A. (2000) *Leading Subject Areas Improving Schools*. London: Paul Chapman.

Carr, W. and Kemmis, S. (1986) *Becoming Critical: education, knowledge and action research*. Lewes: Falmer Press.

Day, C. (1998) *Developing Teachers: the challenge of lifelong learning*. London: Falmer Press.

Day, C., Harris, A., Hadfield, M., Tolley, H. and Beresford, J. (2000) *Leading Schools in Times of Change*. Buckingham: Open University Press.

Earley, P. (1998) Middle management – the key to organisational success? in D. Middlewood and J. Lumby (eds.) *Strategic Management in Schools and Colleges*. London: Paul Chapman.

Earley, P. and Fletcher-Campbell (1989) *Time to Manage*. Slough: NFER.

Golby, M. and Appleby, R. (1995) Reflective practice through critical friendship: some possibilities, *Cambridge Journal of Education*, 25, pp. 149–160.

Hammond, P. and Harris, A. (2000) Caught in the middle, *The Times Educational Supplement*, 1 September.

Harris, A. (1999) *Effective Subject Leadership: a handbook of staff development activities*. London: David Fulton Press.

Harris, A., Busher, H. and Wise, C. (1999) *Interim Report to the TTA on the Effective Training of Subject Leaders*. Nottingham: University of Nottingham, School of Education.

Harris, A., Busher, H. and Wise, C. (2000) *Effective Subject Leadership: final report to the Teacher Training Agency*. London: Teacher Training Agency.

Joyce, B. and Showers, B. (1988) *Student Achievement through Staff Development*. New York: Longman.

Macbeath, J. (ed.) (1999) *Effective School Leadership Responding to Change*. London: Paul Chapman.

Schön, D. (1983) *The Reflective Practitioner: how professionals think and learn*. New York: Basic Books.

Schön, D. (1987) *Educating the Reflective Practitioner: towards a new design for teaching and learning in the professions*. San Francisco, CA: Jossey Bass.

Smyth, J. (1991) *Teachers as Collaborative Learners*. Buckingham: Open University Press.

Steadman, S., Eraut, M., Fielding, M. and Horton, A. (1995) *Making School Based INSET Effective: research report no. 2*. Brighton: University of Sussex, Institute of Education.

Teacher Training Agency (TTA) (1998) *National Standards for Subject Leaders*. London: HMSO.

10

Conflict and Change: Daily Challenges for School Leaders

Michael F. DiPaola

Introduction

This age of reform, standards and accountability creates higher expectations and increased demands on school administrators. Meeting the demands for increased effectiveness of schools cannot occur without systemic change. Innovative solutions are necessary for school organizations to cope with these changes in expectations (Tjosvold, 1997). As school leader, the principal plays the major role in planning and implementing changes (Hall and Hord, 1987; Fullan and Stiegelbauer, 1991). However, change arouses emotions. Because the natural response to change initiatives, even those that have promise to serve students more effectively, is resistance, tension and conflict, a principal's leadership is key (Fullan, 2001).

Conflict begins when an individual or group feels negatively affected by another person or group. It may occur in interpersonal encounters between two colleagues, in decision-making teams, between work groups or in board meetings. The larger and more diverse the group, the greater the potential for conflict because diversity among members of groups results in differences in goals, perceptions, preferences and beliefs. Thus it should not be surprising that conflict is common in schools, and that conflict is particularly likely to occur at the boundaries or interfaces between different groups or units within organizations.

As children we are often taught not to argue or disagree and that people shouldn't quarrel. As adults, this often translates into behavior that attempts to avoid conflict by sweeping it under the rug or smoothing it over. Discomfort and uncertainty are natural responses to conflict for two princi-

---

Source: Commissioned.

pal reasons: first, most people are unaccustomed to confronting conflict; and, secondly, there is a cultural tendency to avoid uncomfortable situations (Folger *et al.*, 1993).

Burns (1978: 37) captures the essence of the problem: 'The potential for conflict permeates the relations of humankind, and that potential is a force for health and growth as well as for destruction and barbarism.' Conflict will not disappear nor should it be ignored; indeed, it is on the daily menu of school administrators. In any conflict people think and feel differently from one another. The real issue isn't whose perceptions are true and whose are false, but how to deal with the way people think and feel about the conflict. Understanding differences in conflict issues and the relationships between conflict and change can help practicing administrators improve the climate in schools.

Many school administrators seek to eliminate conflict because it '... has been given a bad reputation by its association with psycho-pathology, social disorder, and war. However, it is the root of personal and social change; it is the medium through which problems can be aired and solutions arrived at' (Deutsch, 1991, p. 27). Some argue that 'conflict holds the potential for change, for better or worse' (Folger *et al.*, 1993, p. 163). The issue, then, is not the inevitability of conflict but rather how to avoid destructive conflict while promoting constructive conflict. The purpose of this chapter is to examine how different kinds of conflict interact with different types of formalization to promote or hinder change. To that end, a typology of the likely consequences for change is developed and then discussed in terms of its implications for the preparation and training of school administrators.

Conflict

Conflict is usually thought of as negative and often destructive, but that need not be the case. Conflict can be destructive or constructive.

Conflict: a destructive force

Rational systems theorists emphasize organizational goals, roles, technologies, social control and norms of rationality. In this view, conflict is a problem that interferes with achieving organizational goals because it threatens hierarchical authority; a pathology to be diagnosed and treated (DeDreu, 1997). Gardner (1990, p. 16) contends that most leaders attempt to eliminate conflict because social functioning requires 'some measure of cohesion and mutual tolerance'. From this view 'educational organizations exist only to foster cooperative human endeavor in order to achieve goals that cannot be achieved individually ... their organizational ideals normatively emphasize cooperation, harmony and collaboration' (Owens, 1998, p. 230). The elimination of conflict seemed to be the ideal goal for administrators who presumed that it was dysfunctional to school organizations (Getzels and Guba, 1957). Managers and scholars continue to highlight the detriments of disputes despite the fact that conflict theorists argue that disagreements are essential to the formation and maintenance of organizational life (Putnam, 1997).

Conflict: a constructive force

A peaceful and harmonious organization, however, very well may be an apathetic, uncreative, stagnant and unresponsive organization (Heffron, 1989). The tendency to emphasize the potential negative consequences of conflict distracts attention from its potential benefits. When appropriately dealt with conflict can generate many positive results for the organization (Barge, 1994); in fact, Dewey called conflict the 'gadfly of thought ... a *sine qua non* of reflection and ingenuity' (cited in Johnson *et al.*, 1996, p. 45). A Deweyian perspective sees conflict as an inevitable, healthy force of change. According to this view, conflict should result in attempts to resolve disruption and be used as a creative force for positive change; indeed, in some organizations, dissent is desirable and conflict resolution is used as a creative force for positive change (Labich, 1988; Johnson and Johnson, 1994).

Political theorists see power, conflict and distribution of scarce resources as central. Organizations are competitive environments in which managers achieve cooperation using power, coalitions, bargaining and conflict. Bolman and Deal (1991) argue that because of scarce resources and enduring differences, conflict is critical to organizational dynamics, and power is the crucial resource. The political perspective doesn't view conflict as either a problem or sign that something is amiss. In this perspective, resources are in short supply; individuals compete for jobs, titles and prestige; and conflict is natural, inevitable and not necessarily bad. The focus in this view is not on the resolution of conflict but on the strategy and tactics of conflict.

Strategy and tactics

Conflict is an everyday reality with both benefits and costs. It is a way of confronting reality and creating new solutions to tough problems; in fact, Tjosvold (1997, p. 23) asserts that 'Conflict is necessary for true involvement, empowerment and democracy. Positive conflict develops our individuality so we feel more fulfilled and capable'.

Conflict is as critical as consensus (Burns, 1978). The general norm is to behave peacefully, but conflict brings issues into the open and can sharpen insights into interests and goals. Conflict plays the role of a catalyst in the development of groups. Moreover, suppressing conflict may lead to 'groupthink', a tendency to produce uncritical like-mindedness (Janis, 1985). Administrators who seek to create a homogeneous faculty and suppress minority dissent are reducing creativity and innovation (DeDreu, 1997).

There is strong evidence that suppressing conflict leads to its escalation in the longer run. Conflict, however, can be used to balance power, improve communication and enhance organizational development, as well as to facilitate the understanding of complex problems, broaden perspective of organizational life and develop a foundation to manage differences (Putnam, 1997).

Administrators spend much time each day dealing with conflicts. Proactive administrators sense when a problem exists, identify it and move to action. But what action holds most promise to yield a positive impact from the conflict? Conflicts handled in a cooperative, problem-solving manner are more likely to have positive outcomes because they generate solutions, promote insight and help individuals grow and strengthen emotionally. Conflicts handled in a competitive way, however, usually result in the disputants moving farther apart and investing more energy in perpetuating the conflict. Burns (1978, p. 39) summarizes this position as follows: 'Leaders, whatever their professions of harmony, do not shun conflict; they confront it, exploit it, ultimately embody it. But leaders shape as well as express and mediate conflict … by influencing the intensity and scope of conflict.'

Ideally, school administrators can sort out the perceptions on all sides, understand them and get in touch with them. This is critical in order to use conflict constructively, to maintain organizational harmony and to lead school organizations successfully in the twenty-first century. A successful conflict strategy includes:

■ agreeing on the basics;
■ searching for common interests;
■ experimenting;
■ doubting your own fallibility; and
■ treating differences as group responsibility (Bolman and Deal, 1991).

Types of conflict: cognitive and affective

Groups operate at two levels: the overt, conscious level where task is the focus, and the subtle, process level where group maintenance and interpersonal dynamics are foci. One may categorize conflict issues in terms of being task-related (cognitive) or being social-emotional (affective). Evidence suggests people are able to detect whether conflict is characterized by strong emphasis on ongoing relationships rather than elements of the task, and whether conflict contains attention to affective states such as hatred and jealousy (Thomas, 1992; Jehn, 1997).

The distinction between cognitive and affective conflict issues is key to understanding productive conflict. DeDreu (1997) reported the findings of several studies on the influence of cognitive versus affective conflict. He and his colleagues found that affective conflict lowers decision quality, reduces performance and satisfaction, while cognitive conflict enhances decision quality and overall group performance (Turner and Pratkanis, 1994; Amason, 1996; Jehn, 1995; 1997). Table 10.1 compares and contrasts cognitive and affective conflict. Cognitive issues tend to be task-related, focus on roles, policies, resources and enhance group performance. Affective issues, in contrast, are social-emotional, focus on norms and values and reduce performance and satisfaction. The problem with maintaining and promoting cognitive conflict is that cognitive debates easily evoke affective issues.

The first step in managing conflict effectively is to develop a constructive context, one that determines whether the conflict is managed constructively or destructively (Johnson *et al.*, 1996). Conflict management impacts the amount and nature of conflict. The more constructive conflict strategy is problem-solving, and its aim is to integrate interests of disputants to achieve mutually satisfying outcomes.

The strategy of contending produces dominant assertive behavior in which one party is coerced into accepting the opposing position. This strategy results in the consideration of fewer alternatives, rigidity and an increased tendency to perceive threat and use power. Research has shown that cognitive issues produce more problem-solving and less contending behaviors than affective issues do. It also reveals contending behaviors produce more affective issues, while problem-solving behaviors produce fewer of them (DeDreu, 1997).

Types of Formalization: Enabling and Coercive

School administrators often feel pulled in opposite directions by the compliance and control requirements of standardization and formalization, which call for the elimination of conflict, and management models that advocate collaboration, teamwork and employee involvement in decision-making,

Table 10.1 *Conflict Issues*

Cognitive	Affective
Task related	Social emotional
Roles, policies, resources, goals	Norms, values, group identity
Enhance performance and satisfaction	Reduce performance and satisfaction

which generate conflict. Adler and Borys (1996) argued that formal procedures do not have to be coercive and controlling. In fact, they propose a typology that includes two contrasting types of formalization: enabling and coercive.

In *enabling formalization*, procedures provide organizational memory that captures lessons learned from experience. It provides employees with best practice templates and the benefits of accumulated organizational learning. Deviations and conflicts are risks but are also learning opportunities (Adler and Borys, 1996). In contrast, *coercive formalization* is 'designed to force reluctant compliance and to extract recalcitrant effort' (ibid., p. 69). This type of formalization 'stifles creativity, fosters dissatisfaction, and demotivates employees' (ibid., p. 61). Deviations and conflict are not tolerated.

Formalization, conflict, and consequences

Table 10.2 illustrates types of formalization, kinds of organizational conflicts and their likely consequences for organizational change. *Enabling formalization* welcomes *cognitive conflict* and uses it as a springboard for change and improvement. Administrators in such structures explore the task-related conflicts concerning roles, policies, resources and/or goals with staff members in attempts to create greater understanding and efficiency. Here cognitive conflict has the greatest potential to effect positive change because this situation is most likely to be a *catalyst* for change. An enabling structure encourages innovation, expression of new ideas and empowerment; in fact, administrators work through cognitive conflict in this context and typically see the process as an opportunity to engage in joint problem-solving with teachers.

When *cognitive conflicts* are suppressed, however, as they are in *coercive formalization*, the potential for positive, constructive change is *frustrated*. Individuals who have the potential to make significant contributions toward enhancing group performance become stifled by the coercive and controlling manner of the administration. The organization misses opportunities to improve and stagnates as teachers become embroiled in and frustrated by destructive conflict.

Table 10.2 *Formalization and organizational conflict: a typology of likely consequences for change*

Types of formalization	Types of conflict	
	Cognitive	Affective
Enabling	Catalyst for change	Facilitator of change
Coercive	Frustrator of change	Inhibitor of change

Enabling formalization recognizes that *affective conflict* has the potential to diminish performance and satisfaction; thus, administrators are encouraged to work through conflict issues with teachers. Trying to deal with the affective conflict increases the potential for greater efficiency by limiting disruptions and assuaging conflict. Thus affective conflict is diminished; values, norms and group cohesiveness are enhanced; and change is *facilitated* in the process.

Coercive formalization attempts either to control or ignore *affective conflict*. Because there is no place for conflict in this type of organization, it is neither recognized nor dealt with. As a result, the dysfunctional effects of affective conflict are exacerbated as the conflict festers and grows and the potential for constructive change is *inhibited*.

Administrative impact

Administrators in schools with coercive formalization have little hope of reaping the fruits of cognitive conflict. The restrictive rules, policies and/or procedures require control and afford little latitude to 'sanction' conflict by recognizing it and attempting to work through it. Such organizations are destined to be plagued by the dysfunctional affects of untended affective conflict. The tension between administrators and subordinates is likely to be especially strong when superiors attempt to control the behavior of teachers who are professionals because teacher professionals will see administrative attempts to control as infringements on the autonomy they need to fulfill their professional role.

In schools that have an enabling formalization, administrators utilizing a problem-solving strategy, attempt to manage effectively the affective conflict issues that emerge and encourage cognitive conflict. Conflicts handled in a cooperative, problem-solving manner are most likely to have positive outcomes (Nicotera, 1995). People generate new solutions, gain insight and perspective, and grow and strengthen emotionally. In schools with little conflict, there is no sense or urgency, no necessity to look for alternatives and no incentives for conciliatory overtures (DeDreu, 1997).

Administrators who attempt to work through conflict by creating win–win scenarios are *catalysts* for the positive growth and change that can be generated by cognitive conflict. They create forums for the task conflicts to be aired, explained, discussed and worked through to resolutions that usually have a positive impact on the growth and efficiency of the school.

In recognizing and confronting affective conflict issues, these administrators create opportunities to work through the social/emotional conflicts that have the potential to sap energy and efficiency from the school. Although this is often messy work, it keeps the focus on the overall goals and uncovers the potential for positive change. By working through issues that normally prevent individuals from being productive, administrators *enable* those employees to focus on the task-related conflicts that naturally emerge.

School administrators, who believe conflict has no place, attempt to suppress and drive out all conflict. When the conflict is task related, such behavior *inhibits* the potential positive, productive change that cognitive conflict can generate. Ignoring or avoiding affective conflict not only encourages conflict escalation, but also communicates disinterest in shared values, beliefs and norms. Teachers will ultimately focus more energy on the festering, *escalating* and personal conflict issues than on the goals of the schools.

▌ Conflicts in Schools

Conflict in schools is a reality, but the time teachers spend in conflict with each other and the administration appears to me much less than many believe it to be (Corwin, 1966; DiPaola, 1990). Both Corwin and DiPaola found that schools had little disruptive conflict. The conflict that was revealed was primarily cognitive, that is, contributing to school improvement by questioning the status quo. This interpretation is consistent with the findings that teacher militancy was related to conflict (DiPaola and Hoy, 1994). Militant teachers were found to be slightly more conflict oriented. These are likely teachers who are catalysts of change.

Proactive administrators spend energy in efforts to build enabling formalization, for example, by making sure that the rules and regulations enable rather than frustrate innovative action. This will make it possible to mediate affective conflict as it arises and manage cognitive conflict, which has greater potential to produce positive change. Those administrators who are overly concerned with harmony within the school are likely to be missing, and perhaps preventing, the leadership initiatives necessary to produce healthy organizational change.

School administrators can strive to get optimal level of conflict through conflict management techniques. Employing problem-solving techniques to integrate interests of all parties can result in achieving mutually satisfying outcomes: a win–win situation. However, such a strategy will likely not succeed unless the structure of the school is enabling. Some structures doom conflict resolution regardless of the best of intentions of administrators and in spite of a constructive, positive strategy. Administrators must recognize that conflict in and of itself is neither bad nor good. Moreover, its impact on the school and the behavior of teachers largely depends on three factors – the kind of conflict (cognitive or affective), the kind of formalization (enabling or coercive) and the way conflict is handled.

Administrators who want to cultivate a climate of professionalism and change in their schools should avoid reliance on their authority to control teachers and instead nurture a professional teacher perspective of autonomy. Such an orientation may increase cognitive conflict, but the conflict generated by professional teacher action will likely lead to constructive change and help avoid rigidity and stagnation in schools (Pondy, 1989).

Understanding the task as conflict management rather than conflict resolution is major shift in perspective (Fisher *et al.*, 1994). Building principals see the school in its entirety, a dynamic interaction of competing elements, as it functions day to day. Although external forces press for continued bureaucracy, the professionalization of teachers is a reality. Principals must coordinate and integrate individual efforts, while encouraging a community of learners committed to common goals. By working with teacher professionals in aligning their individual goals with those of the school organization, win–win situations are created.

One of the basic challenges in organizations like schools (institutions staffed with highly trained professionals) is to construct an enabling work environment where professionals can perform their tasks relatively unencumbered by administrative scrutiny and control. The conflict between administrative control and teacher independence is a fundamental dilemma that cannot be completely resolved; rather a balance between the two is necessary.

District-level administrators must recognize that there will be conflict in any well led organization because leaders marshal, organize and use conflict. When leadership is present, teachers can experience conflict as a normal part of organizational life (Owens, 1998). Conflict is not only functional for the organization; it is essential to its very existence (Pondy, 1989, p. 96). Changing administrators and organizations to be positive about conflict is a tough, long-term pursuit requiring informed persistent action and ongoing research (Tjosvold, 1997, p. 34). In summary, principals and those charged with their training and preparation should consider the following:

■ Cognitive and affective conflict have different consequences for change.
■ Cognitive conflict has the potential for constructive change.
■ Affective conflict inhibits constructive change and is destructive.
■ Formalization can either enable or hinder change.
■ Constructive change is most likely when conflict is cognitive and formalization is enabling; in fact, this combination produces a catalyst for constructive change.
■ Constructive change is least likely to occur when conflict is affective and formalization is coercive; in fact, this combination inhibits constructive change.

Effective Administrators: Change Agents

The increasing emphasis in the past quarter century on the school as the unit of change has created a more complex role for principals. No longer are they able to rely on traditional ways of thinking and working on one task at a time. Effective school administrators are catalysts of change (Hall and Hord, 1987; Fullan and Stiegelbauer, 1991) and recognize that conflict is essential to any successful change effort (Fullan, 1993). When 'People spark new ideas off each other when they argue or disagree – when they are conflicting, confused, and searching for new meaning – yet, remain willing to discuss and listen to each other' (Stacey, 1992), a positive, meaningful outcome will likely result. Consensus may seem more desirable, but is ordinarily achieved only through superficial agreement (Fullan, 1999).

By challenging the status quo and championing continuous improvement, principals create a milieu in which the potential for conflict is great. Therefore, creating a school environment where people in conflict remain willing to discuss and listen to each other is a real administrative challenge. Because change arouses emotions, a principal's leadership is key (Fullan, 2001). Principals must act not only with the intention of making a positive difference in the lives of students, but also with an understanding of the change process. Fullan (ibid., p. 6) argues that 'moral purpose without an understanding of change will lead to moral martyrdom', not the desired change. Principals must be aware that, as people confront change, they experience two kinds of problems – 'the social-psychological fear of change, and the lack of technical know-how or skills to make the change work' (ibid., p. 41). During these times, principals should be coaches and recognize that overall goals will not be achieved if these problems aren't worked through.

When emotions run high during a conflict the likelihood of positive, constructive outcomes decreases. Strong emotions such as anger can often be dampened or reduced by reminding the parties that it is perfectly acceptable to 'agree to disagree' about the issue; that the disagreement should not be interpreted that they don't personally like one another or that they can't work effectively together. Maintaining focus on why all the individuals are in school, to help students, often moves the conflict into the cognitive realm.

Building positive relations is a key to effective school leadership. Fullan believes '... the single factor common to every successful change initiative is that *relationships* improve'. When relationships improve, thing get better. If they remain the same or get worse, no progress is made. Thus leaders must be consummate relationship builders with diverse people and groups. Building and maintaining strong relationships require a real commitment and involve hard, labor-intensive work and a lot of time. Successful administrators model and encourage sincerity in day-to-day interactions. They also routinely provide explanations for seemingly confrontational actions or behaviors (Baron, 1997). In conflict situations, there is a tendency for the parties to engage in stereotype-driven thinking. Administrators should encourage everyone to think about others as individuals, with unique characteristics, rather than as members in or affiliates of various groups (Neuberg, 1989).

Implications for Training and Practice

Schools are all about teaching and learning. These goals should be supported and enhanced by all other activity. In preparing individuals for the role of principal, it is imperative to stress these goals and focus on instruction and effective pedagogy. Instructional improvement is a long, multi-stage process involving awareness, planning, implementation and reflection. Implicit in improvement is instructional change. Principal trainees must not only have a strong instructional focus and background, but must also create a culture of change – and recognize such change has the potential to be a breeding ground of cognitive conflict. Fullan (2001) calls establishing this culture of change reculturing. He argues (ibid., p. 44) that effective leaders recognize that the hard work of reculturing is the sine qua non of progress.

Reculturing also brings the potential for great conflict, which, if not worked through, can undermine positive reform efforts. People's reactions to change include fear, anxiety, loss, danger, panic – but they also include exhilaration, risk-taking and excitement: '… Change arouses emotions, and when emotions intensify, leadership is key' (ibid., p. 1).

Creating this culture of change by constantly challenging the status quo is a contact sport involving hard, labor-intensive work and a lot of time. Fortunately, in enabling organizations, most novice principals can tap the collective expertise of the faculty to drive instructional innovation. Effective leaders know that systemic improvement occurs when good ideas, coming from talented people working together, are implemented. In such a scenario collegiality, caring and respect are paramount (Elmore and Burney, 1999).

In order to achieve school goals school leaders need to plan effectively. Planning for the future for both students and teachers is a critical process. The job of the principal is primarily about enhancing the skills and knowledge of people in the school. It includes creating a common cluster of expectations around the implementation of those skills and knowledge, holding the various components of the school together in a productive relationship with one another, and holding individuals accountable for their contributions to the collective outcomes (Elmore, 2000, p. 15).

Preparation programs should provide experiences that will help potential administrators hone skills to help them use conflict effectively. Skills related to establishing an effective working relationship with all members of the school community are critical, and communication, trust, and creating an enabling formalization seem essential elements in using conflict constructively. Skills related to establishing a cooperative problem-solving attitude among the conflicting parties as well as skills involved in developing a creative group process and group decision-making are essential tools for successful administrators (Deutsch, 1991).

In the process of leadership development principal candidates should have authentic experiences with effective leaders through internships and/or mentoring. It is important to work with and observe leaders who effectively work with people and communicate unambiguous goals and expectations. Opportunities to interact with principals who have successfully mobilized people to tackle tough problems that had not yet successfully been addressed can provide invaluable learning experiences. By integrating traditional preparation with hands-on experiences, prospective principals learn from exposure to real-world problems and challenges (Gates, *et al.*, 2000). Principals must be equipped with the ability to challenge teachers to face problems for which there are no simple, painless solutions – problems that require them to learn new ways (Heifetz, 1994). Relevant case studies and simulations have great potential to enhance preparation in these areas.

Preparing principals who know 'what to do', however, is insufficient. The 'how to do it' is just as critical. Transforming a coercive organization to an enabling structure requires long-term strategic thinking and planning. The anticipation and understanding of conflict and its potential positive and negative consequence in different types of school organizations are essential. Principals work directly with everyone within their school, as well as act as liaison between the school and the school district, parents, community members, social service organizations, vendors and suppliers. As the number of times they interact with others within and outside the organization grows, the opportunities to model behaviours that are indicative of enabling structures increase. Principals must not only be verbal advocates of change, but must 'walk the talk' daily by building relationships and modeling the communication so essential for progress.

Conflicts also arise as a result of the stresses created by inadequate resources, lean staffing and higher accountability. This creates an environment primed for differences in values, beliefs and viewpoints, and miscommunications that lead to arguments and conflicts. Conflicts can arise over small matters that are easily resolved and soon forgotten, but they can also arise and then escalate to the point where the hostile emotions affect the job performance of the parties involved or that of spectators who either are distracted or take sides in the issue. The current focus within schools on collaboration and teamwork to achieve higher expectations creates additional opportunities for conflicts to emerge and be useful in enabling school structures or destructive in coercive school organizations.

Preparation programs must equip principals with effective decision-making, problem-solving and communication strategies. Effective school leaders view conflicts as problems and employ problem-solving approaches to work through them. They strive for a solution that will satisfy both parties' needs. They believe that relationships can be retained if both parties are satisfied. They work for a mutually satisfactory solution to the conflict, which they view and treat as a problem rather than confrontation. Not only does such a solution represent the best interests of all in the conflict, it also serves the best interests of the organization. The parties to the conflict develop into partners; they no longer are adversaries.

Hoy and Miskel (2001, p. 357) caution that 'Not all school problems involve unsuccessful communication'. Yet, communication skills are essential tools of effective administrators and must be addressed in preparation programs. Successful principals have a repertoire of communication strategies and are creative and selective in moving from one approach to another as individuals, situations and content change (Burbules and Bruce, 2000). In order to prepare principals effectively to communicate a vision, to challenge the status quo, to reculture the school and to use conflict constructively, preparation programs should provide opportunities to hone communication skills including sending (making oneself understood), listening (ability to understand others) and feedback.

Imbedded in all administrative actions are decisions. 'Deciding is a sine qua non' of educational leadership because the school is a decision-making structure (Hoy and Miskel, 2001, p. 317). Effective principals know when to act unilaterally and when to include others; whom to include in decision-making and whom to leave out; when no decision is the best decision; and how to evaluate alternatives to maximize the achievement of goals and objectives. Preparation programs must included decision-making models and a general framework for decision-making in the toolkit of principals in training. There is no one best way to decide. By successfully completing a preparation program, administrators should have a repertoire of strategies to select from, as circumstance dictates, so that quality decisions result.

Conflicts are an inevitable part of school and daily life. Effective leaders employ strategies to minimize the frequency of affective conflicts, but can't entirely prevent them. Any time two people get together, eventually there will be disagreement. Well prepared school leaders minimize affective conflict, encourage cognitive conflict, and work to maintain a school organization that enables all participants to develop and grow in a process of continuous improvement.

In summary

One aim of this analysis was to make school leaders aware of the relationship between change and conflict and the potential benefits of both. To that end, distinctions were made between constructive and destructive conflict. Next, a typology of change was constructed by first conceptualizing conflict in terms of cognitive and affective types. To illustrate the potential impact of the school's organizational structure on conflict and change, formalization was viewed as enabling or coercive. These two dimensions (types of conflict and formalization) form a typology that predicts their impact for potential change ranging from being a catalyst to an inhibitor of change.

Another goal of this analysis was to highlight the role of school leader as an agent of change and discuss the implications of the resulting conflicts that are generated in the change process. Effective school leaders understand the change process and work daily to reculture their school organizations. They appreciate the significance of building strong relationships between and among all members of their school community. They also know that the potential impact of both cognitive and affective conflicts has much to do with the organizational context in which they occur.

In order to maximize constructive change, administrators must create formatlization (rules, regulations and policies) tht enables rather than hinders change. Effective leaders build enabling school organizations and use change, and the conflicts that result, to improve the quality of instruction as well as the overall milieu of the school: 'The litmus test of all leadership is whether it mobilizes people's commitment to putting energy into actions designed to improve things' (Fullan, 2001, p. 9).

The final purpose of this endeavor was to use the conceptual framework to determine the implications for the training and preparation of school leaders. Certainly the role of principal has evolved into a collection of multidimensional, day-to-day tasks that seem impossible for one person to perform. In order to be prepared adequately for the role, individuals must understand and appreciate the overarching dimensions of the role that make it possible for a school leader to orchestrate the completion of daily tasks while achieving multiple goals. By creating an environment in which individuals work together constructively and tap each other's creative energy, true progress is possible. Orchestrating such an endeavor, however, requires leadership with strong skills in communication, decision-making, problem-solving and relationship-building. Although traditional preparation programs have focused on content knowledge, the ability to create the context for continuous improvement in schools is a dimension of the role that cannot be ignored. To prepare effective school leaders, training programs must assist individuals in building a clear, individual leadership identity while honing the skills necessary to create learning communities responsive to the diverse populations of students and educators, as well as to the increased expectations of the public.

References

Adler, P.S. and Borys, B. (1996). Two types of bureaucracy: enabling and coercive. *Administrative Science Quarterly* 41: 61–89.

Amason, A.C. (1996). Distinguishing the effects of functional and dysfunctional conflict on strategic decision making: resolving a paradox for top management teams. *Academy of Management Journal* 39: 1.

Barge, J.K. (1994) Managing organizational relationships. In S.P. Weir *et al.* (eds.), *Leadership: Communications Skills for Organizations and Groups*. New York: St Martin's Press.

Baron, R.A. (1997) Positive effects of conflict: insights from social cognition. In C. DeDreu and E. Van De Vliert (eds.) *Using Conflict in Organizations*. London: Sage.

Bolman, L. and Deal, T. (1991) *Reframing Organizations: Artistry, Choice, and Leadership*. San Francisco, CA: Jossey-Bass.

Burbules, N.C. and Bruce, B.C. (2000) Theory and research on teaching as dialogue. In V. Richardson (ed.) *Handbook of Research on Teaching* (4th edn). Washington, DC: American Educational Research Association.

Burns, J. (1978) *Leadership*. New York: Harper & Row.

Corwin, R.G. (1966) *Staff Conflicts in the Public Schools. Cooperative Research Project* 2637. Columbus, OH: The Ohio State University.

DeDreu, C. (1997) Productive conflict: the importance of conflict management and conflict issue. In C. DeDreu and E. Van De Vliert (eds.) *Using Conflict in Organizations*. London: Sage.

Deutsch, M. (1991) Subjective features of conflict resolution: psychological, social, and cultural influences. In R. Vayrynen (ed.) *New Directions in Conflict Theory*. London: Sage.

DiPaola, M.F. (1990) Bureaucratic and professional orientations of teachers: militancy and conflict in public schools. Doctoral dissertation, Rutgers, The State University, 1990. *Dissertation Abstracts International* AAG9124964.

DiPaola, M.F. and Hoy, W.K. (1994) Teacher militancy: a professional check on bureaucracy. *Journal of Research and Development in Education* 27(2): 83–89.

Elmore, R.F. (2000) *Building a New Structure for School Leadership*. Washington, DC: Albert Shanker Institute.

Elmore, R.F. and Burney, D. (1999) Investing in teacher learning: staff development and instructional improvement. In L. Darling-Hammond and G. Sykes (eds.) *Teaching as the Learning Profession: Handbook of Policy and Practice*. San Francisco, CA: Jossey-Bass.

Fisher, R., Kopelman, E., and Schneider, A. (1994) *Beyond Machiavelli*. Cambridge, MA: Harvard University Press.

Folger, J., Poole, M. and Stutman, R. (1993) *Working through Conflict*. New York: HarperCollins.

Fullan, M. (1993) *Change Forces: Probing the Depths of Educational Reform*. London: Falmer Press.

Fullan, M. (1999) *Change Forces: The Sequel*. London: Falmer Press.

Fullan, M. (2001) *Leading in a Culture of Change*. San Francisco, CA: Jossey-Bass.

Fullan, M. and Stiegelbauer, S. (1991) *The New Meaning of Educational Change*. New York: Teachers College Press.

Gardner, J.W. (1990) *On Leadership*. New York: The Free Press.

Gates, S., Ross, K. and Brewer, D. (2000) *School Leadership in the 21st Century: Why and How it is Important*. Oak Brook, IL: North Central Regional Educational Laboratory.

Getzels, J. and Guba, E. (1957) Social behavior and the administrative process. *School Review* 65: 423–41.

Hall, G.E. and Hord, S.M. (1987) *Change in Schools: Facilitating the Process*. New York: State University of New York Press.

Heffron, F. (1989) *Organization Theory and Public Organizations: The Political Connection*. Englewood Cliffs, NJ: Prentice-Hall.

Heifetz, R. (1994) *Leadership without Easy Answers*. Cambridge, MA: Harvard University Press.

Hoy, W.K. and Miskel, C.G. (2001) *Educational Administration: Theory, Research, and Practice* (6th edn) Boston, MA: McGraw-Hill.

Janis, I.L. (1985) Sources of error in strategic decision making. In J.M. Pennings (ed.) *Organizational Strategy and Change*. San Francisco, CA: Jossey-Bass.

Jehn, K.A. (1994) Enhancing effectiveness: an investigation of advantages and disadvantages of value-based inter-group conflict. *International Journal of Conflict Management* 5: 223–38.

Jehn, K.A. (1995) A multimethod examination of the benefits and detriments of inter-group conflict. *Administrative Science Quarterly* 40: 56–82.

Jehn, K.A. (1997) Affective and cognitive conflict in work groups: increasing performance through value-based intergroup conflict. In C.K.W. DeDreu and E. Van De Vliert (eds.) *Using Conflict in Organizations*. Thousand Oaks, CA: Sage.

Johnson, D.W. and Johnson, R.T. (1994) *Creative Controversy: Intellectual Challenge in the Classroom* (3rd edn). Edina, MI: Interaction Book Company.

Johnson, D.W., Johnson, R.T. and Smith, K.A. (1996) *Academic Controversy: Enriching College Instruction through Intellectual Conflict*. ASHE-ERIC Higher Education Report 25(3). Washington, DC: The George Washington University.

Labich, K. (1988) 'The seven keys to business leadership.' *Fortune* October: 62.

Neuberg, S.L. (1989) The goal of forming accurate impressions during social interactions: attenuating the impact of negative expectancies. *Journal of Personality and Social Psychology* 56: 374–86.

Nicotera, A.M. (1995) Thinking about communication and conflict. In A.M. Nicotera (ed.) *Conflict and Organizations: Communicative Processes*. Albany, NY: State University of New York Press.

Owens, R. (1998) *Organizational Behavior in Education*. Needham Heights, MA: Allyn & Bacon.

Pondy, L.R. (1989) Reflections on organizational conflict. *Journal of Organizational Change Management* 2: 94–98.

Putnam, L. (1997) Productive conflict: negotiation as implicit coordination. In C. DeDreu and E. Van De Vliert (eds.) *Using Conflict in Organizations*. London: Sage.

Stacey, R. (1992) *Managing the Unknowable*. San Francisco, CA: Jossey-Bass.

Thomas, K.W. (1992) Conflict and the negotiation processes in organizations. In M.D. Dunnette and L.M. Hough (eds.) *Handbook of Industrial and Organizational Psychology* (2nd edn). Palo Alto, CA: Consulting Psychologists Press.

Tjosvold, D. (1997) Conflict within interdependence: its value for productivity and individuality. In C. DeDreu and E. Van De Vliert (eds.) *Using Conflict in Organizations*. London: Sage.

Turner, M.E. and Pratkanis, A.R. (1994) Social identity maintenance prescriptions for preventing groupthink: reducing identity protection and enhancing intellectual conflict. *International Journal of Conflict Management* 5: 207–304.

Management Development and a Mismatch of Objectives: The Culture Change Process in the NHS

Graeme Currie

Introduction

The chapter is concerned with the contribution of management develop-ment to the culture change in the health service which the Griffiths Report (DHSS, 1983) and subsequent reforms (DHSS, 1986; DHSS, 1989a; DHSS, 1989b; DoH, 1991a; DoH, 1991b) have promoted. It examines a management development programme aimed at a middle management group, 'Patient Services Managers', in a single case study, 'Florence Hospital'. It suggests that the cultural change promoted in government policy reforms is not translated to the organizational context. The reason suggested is a mismatch between the expectations and desires of those managers who are the participants in the management development programme and other stakeholders in the process: the Executive Directors, the Organization Development Department and the facilitators of the programme.

Government Reforms and Management Development

Policy reforms in the UK health service since the Griffiths Report have repre-sented a major policy shift since they seek to challenge the hegemony of professional groups within the National Health Service (NHS) (Ferlie *et al.*, 1996; Reed and Anthony 1991). The statements which stand out in the Griffiths Report are the ones which present a scenario whereby Florence

Source: Leadership & Organization Development Journal, Vol. 8, no. 6, 1997, pp. 304–11.
Edited version.

Nightingale returns to the health service in the early 1980s and cannot identify who is in charge. In response to this 'problem' the Griffiths Report and associated documentation (for example, NHSTD (1991)) have argued that cultural change is necessary in the NHS to address the problem. Under the Griffiths Report a new cadre of general (line) managers are given the strategic role of 'change agents' in initiating a cultural metamorphosis within the NHS.

In the management of organizational culture, management development has a key role (Albert and Silverman, 1984a, 1984b; Trice and Beyer; 1993; Williams *et al.*, 1993). If management development programmes broadcast a consistent set of cues (as dictated by the vision of senior executives) then they represent an important means of strengthening, reorienting, and in the long term possibly changing culture (Brown, 1994, p. 135). The application of business management approaches into spheres such as health care seeks to transform such an organization into a managerial organization (Holmes, 1995).

However, the transformation of health care organizations into managerial organizations is problematic (Newman and Clarke, 1994; Pollitt, 1990). It has been suggested that normative control strategies in the public sector, of which management development is an example, exist largely as symbolic and rhetorical artefacts towards which the majority of staff are highly cynical (Hoggett, 1996). Many aspects of the reforms which do not fit local managers' conceptions of 'good' management may be rejected and labelled an ideology or reshaped in ways which fit existing values and assumptions (Ranade, 1995). This chapter examines the extent to which existing values and assumptions impact on the cultural change desired by the reforms.

Context

The case study organization ('Florence Hospital') is a large acute hospital (37,000 inpatients and 61,000 out-patients in 1995/96) which occupies a city centre site. It has existed as a hospital since 1895 and had gained Trust status in 1992. The hospital trust board saw a need for management development as part of a culture change programme to support the ongoing change which had initially emanated from the Griffiths reforms. They decided to implement management development for their 'general management group'; that is, General Managers, Service Managers, Ward Sisters. It was decided by the Organization Development Manager, in conjunction with the Director of Human Resources and Director of Nursing, that separate programmes would be provided for each of the management groups. The focus of this chapter lies with one of the three levels of management programme delivered to the Service Managers named the 'Patient Service Managers Development Programme'.

The Organization Development Manager held initial discussions with a number of potential providers. Following this a competence based approach to management development was decided on. Two of the providing organizations were invited to tender for the design and delivery of the programme.

The providing organization which was successful was a new university with substantial experience in the competence based area. A programme defined by the Management Charter Initiative (MCI) as National Vocational Qualification Level Four (NVQ4) would be delivered and there would be dual certification for a Certificate in Management and a NVQ4 in Management.

Thirty-five participants were nominated and accepted for the programme. The Certificate in Management would be awarded following attendance at the development workshops and successful completion of assignments associated with the workshops. As a start to the programme all participants took part in a one-day development centre from which they identified their strengths and weaknesses as they related to generic competences. There then followed 16 development workshops over nine months under headings of: managing people, managing operations, and personal effectiveness; delivered over a ten-month period. These were interspersed with one-to-one counselling workshops every two months which facilitated development of the portfolio of evidence for NVQ purposes.

Research design

This chapter is the result of a 12-month longitudinal study which evaluates the impact of management development on culture change in the health service. The study is broadly ethnographic. As such it is an interpretation of organizational processes from the standpoint of the actors involved, collected and retold by the researcher, also representing a certain standpoint. The research focuses on middle managers; and particularly on clinical services managers with a nursing background.

Access to the single case study, the 'Florence Hospital', was negotiated via the Organization Development Manager and agreed with the Chief Executive. The researcher observed planning meetings, development centres and delivery of the management development programme. Analysis after observation was followed up by 25 informal interviews with participants and other stakeholders in the process. At the end of the observation period Trust Board Directors, General Managers, Service Managers, as well as the Organization Development Manager and some Ward Sisters who had been exposed to management development in the Florence Hospital were formally interviewed.

Programme outcomes

The most appropriate point to start the analysis of the management development programme is to describe the outcomes of the intervention. This provides evidence of a programme failure and a starting point for analysis of what went wrong.

Before the half-day introduction at the beginning of the programme the number of participants was 35. Following the half-day introduction to outline the programme to interested parties a number of participants had obtained their manager's support for non-participation. Following the development centre, before the programme began, others requested significant amounts of accreditation of prior learning and thus non-attendance at the formal sessions. During the delivery of the programme there were frequent discussions between the organizational stakeholders and the providers of the programme. In some of these sessions representatives of the group of participants were invited along to state their views. In the face of criticism from the participants, the providing organization modified the programme content and delivery. However, by the time this occurred a number of participants at Service Manager level had dropped out.

The Organization Development Manager and the Human Resource Director seriously debated cancelling the programme at one stage. The Organization Development Manager experienced 'a great deal of flak' over the programme. Participants were complaining directly to their General Managers, Clinical Directors and to the Director of Nursing.

Following such criticism, the programme continued with a rump of participants attending the formal workshops. Of over 30 participants who started the programme attendance dropped to around 12. These consisted of Administrative Managers and Ward Sisters rather than the Patient Service Managers at whom it had been aimed. The formal delivery of the programme has been completed for the Certificate in Management for around half the original number of nominated participants. The one-to-one counselling sessions set up for portfolio development have been very poorly attended throughout. The remaining participants are currently developing their portfolios for the NVQ4 in Management to varying degrees. Over 12 months since the programme started, a significant number of those remaining have made little progress in the development of their portfolios. The Organization Development Manager has left to take up a similar post for another health trust.

On the evidence above, the question is posed as to why the programme was a failure. The seeds of failure were evident at the beginning of the programme in its planning stage. There were differences in the perceived objectives of management development interventions particularly between the participants and other stakeholders.

Objectives of the management development programme

It is important to recognize the different stakeholders. The 'formal' organizational objectives are taken as those espoused by the Chief Executive and other Executive Directors. The objectives of the Human Resource Department as put forward by the Director of Human Resources and the Organization Development Manager, also reflect formal organizational objectives. Besides these, we have the objectives of the facilitators of the providing organization who invoke the Management Charter Initiative (MCI) agenda. In addition there are the participants themselves who have a different interpretation of what the organization is hoping to achieve in putting on the programme.

Executive directors

The four influential figures in relation to organization development and management development in the Trust were the Chief Executive, the Director of Nursing, the Director of Business Development, and the Director of Human Resources. The researcher expected the Executive Directors to formulate strategy in response to government policy. However, the relationship of management development to the government policy reforms was not made explicit by the Executive Directors. Instead they invoked a need for cultural change which was inherent in the policy reforms.

The Executive Directors emphasized the importance of shifts in thinking as to how things should be done in the health service. The Chief Executive saw leadership as a key lever in change. Middle management were seen as a blockage to changes he wished to implement. He felt that although nurses were the best people for the role of Patient Services Managers (if they were up to it) they suffered from professional blinkeredness. The management development programme would address this problem. The Chief Executive talked of 'core competences' which were service specific and patient-focused, covering both professional and managerial areas.

The Director of Business Development also saw middle management as needing to see the big picture. She regarded Nurse Managers, particularly those at ward level, as not having reference to any influences which lay outside their ward. She wanted the beliefs of some of the middle managers challenged. They needed to move away from their 'Ivory Towers' perspective and think about the future of their service.

The Director of Nursing saw the big picture as being one of optimizing resource use. She recognized the difficulties in doing this. She saw many nurses as wishing to remain in clinical roles. She argued that good nurse managers were going to be needed if nursing was to have a voice in the changes. She saw a need for nurse managers to develop skills and competences. She suggested those skills were those which enabled them to stand back and look at what they do, when they do it and why they do it.

The Chief Executive also saw Service Managers' organizational commitment as fragile. The reason is that they feel they can get a job elsewhere on the basis of their professional clinical skills. He wanted them to identify with the Florence Hospital rather than the NHS in general, or a particular ward. Many of the participants still felt uncomfortable with leaving their previous professional values behind and taking on what they perceived as a new set of managerial values.

Human resource department

The Director of Human Resources gave the Organization Development Manager responsibility for any management development within the Trust.

In outlining how the programme came about, the Organization Development Manager revealed a proactive role taken by the Organization Development Department in initiating the programme. The Organization Development Manager saw a lack of support from senior managers for management development, particularly in the early days following the gaining of trust status. He suggested that development programmes have suffered from a lack of integration with other organizational initiatives and criticized the organization for a one dimensional approach to training in the past. He claimed this programme was to be different in these respects. Some had previously obtained an Institute of Health Services Management qualification. The Organization Development Manager dismissed this as not relevant because it was very theoretical.

The Organization Development Manager commented that many of the desires expressed, particularly by senior managers, represented fairly simplistic views of how people and organizations develop. They felt that a couple of days of training would change people and produce the organizational outcomes desired.

Before the programme started, the Organization Development Manager suggested that the middle managers were saying the right things but were not ideologically committed to the change of role. He felt much of their behaviour was symbolic. Management development would encourage professionals to jump the fence, the fence being whether they are clinically or managerially orientated.

The Organization Development Manager saw the main aim of the programme as getting people on board and understanding our (managerial) reality. He saw it as an opportunity to promote reflection, development and personal change. He also invoked notions of identity and direction. The Organization Development Manager wanted them to think organizationally and identified what should be put across in the induction by facilitators. It was to be stressed that participants had responsibility as managers. They were to be 'champions' and take a proactive role in the management of culture in their areas. They were to have a corporate focus rather than a directorate focus. They would balance quality, resources and activity and initiate change where necessary. Cost improvements and people management were to be emphasized and the importance of information in taking decisions highlighted.

The competence approach was chosen by the Human Resources Department on the basis that it added value to the management development because one of the additional outcomes was a qualification for participants. The Organization Development Manager agreed with the model. He commented that it was what the typical academic model of management education had failed to crack. As a programme it was to be a mix of competences as defined by the MCI framework and bespoke Florence Hospital competences. The core competences were to be modelled on those existing nurse managers who exhibited 'champion' behaviours. The competence model adopted dealt with the behavioural element of the Service Manager's job.

A learning contract was to complement the programme. This was to be managerially orientated. However, at least in the planning stages there was sensitivity to the health care context. The Organization Development Manager requested that the School of Health and the School of Management of the providing organization work together in delivering the programme. He emphasized that the programme should bring together the professional and managerial approach.

The programme was seen by the Organization Development Manager to be a case of confirming competence for many of the prospective participants. He felt there would not be many skills gaps for the managers involved. He commented that if he had the opportunity to design the world he would concentrate on softer skills rather than the harder technical competences he saw the competence-based approach to be promoting. He suggested that the learning organization was the way forward. He felt that middle managers should be given a 'learning role'; that is, of counsellor, developer, facilitator. He suggested that the competence approach must be used to promote a move towards a learning culture in an organization.

Facilitators of the programme

There were two main facilitators observed: the lead facilitator and a second facilitator who was responsible for much of the initial delivery of the workshop content. A third facilitator helped run the development centres prior to the delivery of the programme. Other facilitators were responsible for finance inputs and information management inputs. In terms of outlining the objectives of the programme from the facilitator's viewpoint the lead facilitator is the main informant.

The lead facilitator had met frequently, prior to the delivery of the programme, with the Organization Development Manager. Therefore he might be expected to tell a similar story as to the objectives of the programme. The need for a paradigm shift in ways of looking at the organizational world was reiterated in the development centres by the lead facilitator. This was promoted via a video entitled, 'Paradigm Shift'. The idea of borders or fences which limit ideas and approaches was introduced. The message from the video was one that stated that managers should question the way they do things. The lead facilitator asked, following the video, whether participants were prepared to question their values and beliefs.

There was also a self-assessment questionnaire in the development centre entitled, 'Tender or Tough?' This reinforced an earlier suggestion that an objective of the programme was to create tougher managers. The need to become a champion for the role of Service Manager was also emphasized. In a workshop which aimed to develop the skills of handling a disciplinary interview the lead facilitator stressed that participants in the role play were focusing too much on the individual who was subject to the discipline. They were encouraged to focus on what was best for the organization. He wanted the participants to act 'harder' as managers and threw a metaphorical punch to illustrate the appropriate managerial response.

The lead facilitator stressed the management development programme was about creating people who saw themselves as managers. He also adopted the agenda of the Management Charter Initiative (MCI) who validated the programme. He identified the outcomes for the organization as being enhanced profitability and competitiveness. The programme was to be based on the personal competence model so that participants could say to themselves: 'I've proved myself good at my job.' There was an assumption that the participants were career-oriented in terms of wanting to progress up the hierarchy. In opposition to this assumption many participants had been with the organization for 15 years or more without any such behaviour in evidence.

Much of the facilitators' rhetoric in the development centres and workshops was value-laden. It sought to construct management as a body of knowledge. In a development centre prior to programme delivery, the personal competence model was promoted as breeding confidence allowing managers to become professional. The lead facilitator presented management as being something which relied on a unique body of knowledge. While he agreed participants were technically proficient, he stated management was something totally different from the work they were used to; for example, much of the work they were used to in their previous clinical roles had a distinct boundary in terms of activity and was a small part of a much larger process of care. He claimed that managing integrated a number of activities and was not divided into discrete elements in such a way.

The attempt to portray management as a profession was reinforced by a ritual at the end of the programme. There was to be an awards evening for all those participants who 'qualify' for the Institute of Management.

Participants

The participants as a stakeholder group interpreted the objectives of the programme as similar to those of the Executive Directors and the Organization Development Department, but viewed these objectives in a less positive light. Many of the participants commented that they felt 'coerced' to participate in the programme by their General Managers. Many felt they had been through similar management development programmes before.

In a formal activity of a 'hopes and fears' exercise, participants outlined their objectives. The Outpatient Services Manager in the Medical Directorate wanted to gain new knowledge relevant to her current role. A Patient Administration Manager wished to become more effective in her role and bring back her development to the team. The Orthotics Service Manager wanted to maintain a strong role in clinical aspects and felt the managerial role impacted on this. The Palliative Care Service Manager wanted specific skills in budget management but feared much of the content of the programme would clash with his philosophy of care. A Therapy Services Manager recognized a marriage of the two professions of management and professionals, and wanted to meet this challenge.

Some participants expressed similar expectations to the objectives set out for the programme by Executive Directors, Human Resource Department and the facilitators. A Service Manager in Surgical Services reiterated a problem with Nurse Managers as being that they don't see the wider picture. She saw them as suffering from paralysis, thus echoing the Chief Executive's desire that they become proactive managers. A Service Manager who was temporarily placed in the Florence Hospital also reinforced the perception of Nurse Managers as being narrowly focused on the patient and that they needed to take a much broader view. She also saw management development as contributing towards an identification with the organization rather than the NHS in general. A Physiotherapy Manager wanted to gain an awareness of the agendas that senior managers have in the hospital. All this reflected a desire to move away from narrow perspectives associated with professional or directorate membership.

The Private Patients Service Manager and the Palliative Care Service Manager became spokespersons for the group. They felt the programme needed to be delivered taking the existing culture and the feelings of the Service Managers into account. This contrasted with the desire of other stakeholders in the process who felt cultural change was necessary. The aforementioned 'hopes and fears' activity in an introductory session was seen as a management development ritual by participants. They were critical of attempts to develop generic management competences. The Service Manager for the Medical Directorate commented that following training, participants were expected to become all-singing and all-dancing managers.

Conclusion and Implications

The Executive Directors had expectations of cultural change as a result of the programme. Most of the thinking concerning the objectives of the programme, and the responsibility for its design, lay with the Organization

Development Manager. The objectives, as represented by him were ones which fed into desired organizational change for proactive, more business-like managers who identified with the organization. Linked to this was the rhetoric of a need for culture change but a recognition that this would take time. Both of these sets of stakeholders emphasized that Service Managers should jettison their narrow professionally- or directorate-based views of the organization. To a limited extent, participants identified with this agenda.

The facilitators represent another group of key stakeholders in the management development programme. While they share many of the objectives of the Executive Directors and the Human Resource Department, their concern lies more with the creation of a professional manager who exhibits generic competences. This objective is an arena for conflict as far as many of the participants are concerned. Their expectation is that the programme is sensitive to the health service context. This is reflective of participants' resistance to the agenda of culture change.

The conflict of objectives led to the programme being a failure both in terms of participation by managers and in the development of 'qualified' managers. Taking a prescriptive stance poses the question 'should the programme have been developed in a different way?' and 'what implications would this have for its design and delivery?'

The message here is that rather than using management development to promote overnight cultural change, sensitivity to context is important. While recognizing that every organization is unique, the uniqueness of a hospital trust lies in the history and professional elaboration of groups in the health service. The weaknesses of the competence approach, and insensitivity to context by the facilitators in particular, reinforce a deeper ideological conflict with managerialism. The implementation of a competence-based approach in this circumstance leads to the Service Managers distancing themselves from the organization instead of associating themselves with it, as desired by Executive Directors and the Human Resource Department. The off-the-shelf programme delivered in this case would have been more profitably replaced by a programme which recognized where the managers were starting from, rather than where the other stakeholders wanted them to go.

References

Albert, M. and Silverman, M. (1984a), 'Making management philosophy a cultural reality: Part 1', *Personnel*, Vol. 61 No. 1, pp. 12–21.

Albert, M. and Silverman, M. (1984b), 'Making management philosophy a cultural reality: Part 2', *Personnel*, Vol. 61 No. 2, pp. 28–35.

Brown, A.D. (1994), 'Politics, symbolic action and myth-making in pursuit of legitimacy', *Organisation Studies*, Vol. 15 No. 6, pp. 861–78.

DHSS (1983), *NHS Management Inquiry* (Griffiths Report); HMSO, London.

DHSS (1986), *Neighbourhood Nursing: A Focus for Care* (Cumberlege Report), HMSO, London.

DHSS (1989a), *Caring for People: Community Care in the Next Decade and Beyond*, HMSO, London.

DHSS (1989b), *Working for Patients* (White Paper), HMSO, London.

DoH (1991a), *The Health of the Nation*, HMSO, London.

DoH (1991b), *The Patient's Charter*, HMSO, London.

Ferlie, E., Ashburner, L., Fitzgerald, L. and Pettigrew, A. (1996), *The New Public Management in Action*, Oxford University Press, Oxford.

Hoggett, P. (1996), 'New modes of control in public services', *Public Administration*, Vol. 74 No. 1, pp. 9–32.

Holmes, L. (1995), 'HRM and the irresistible rise of the discourse of competence', *Personnel Review*, Vol. 24 No. 4, pp. 34–9.

Newman, J. and Clarke, J. (1994), 'Going about our business? The managerialisation of public services', in Clarke, J., Cochrane, A. and McLaughlin, E. (eds.), *Managing Social Policy*, Sage, London.

NHSTD (1991), *Bureaucracy to Enterprise*, NHS Training Directorate, London.

Pollitt, C. (1990), *Managerialism and the Public Services*, Blackwell, Oxford.

Ranade, W. (1995), 'The theory and practice of managed competition in the NHS', *Public Administration*, Vol. 73, Summer, pp. 241–62.

Reed, M. and Anthony, P. (1991), 'Between an ideological rock and a hard place', *International Privatisation: Strategies and Practices Conference*, University of Stirling, September.

Trice, H.M. and Beyer, J.M. (1993), *The Cultures of Work Organisations*, Prentice-Hall, Englewood Cliffs, NJ.

Williams, A., Dobson, P. and Walters, M. (1993), *Changing Culture: New Organisational Approaches*, IPM, London.

Part 4

Practising Leadership

12

Effective Leaders and Effective Schools

Kathryn Riley and John MacBeath

Effective schools can be good schools, and good schools must be effective
schools – but the two are not necessarily the same.

(Carl Glickman, 1987, quoted in Silver, 1994, p. 102)

Introduction

When we first began our project on school leadership, we adopted the title
'Effective School Leadership in a Time of Change'. In choosing such terminology, we wanted to reflect the shifting grounds of school leadership and
the rapid economic and social changes, in what is increasingly a globalised
context. The juxtaposition of the two words 'effective' and 'leadership' signi-
fied the growing emphasis on school outcome measures and the growing
acceptance of leadership as a key constituent in the 'effective' school
(Sammons *et al.*, 1995).

Leadership had become an urgent policy issue, an integral component of
the drive for more effective schools, raised achievement and public accountability. From a policy-maker's perspective, 'effective leadership' could perhaps
be seen as holding the key to resolving many of the problems which
appeared to be facing schools, but what assumptions lay behind that notion?
Were there some generic and resilient features of effective leadership impervi-
ous to changes in time and place? Were there common competencies? Could
leadership be constructed from a set of component parts?

The starting point for our research was how school leaders themselves conceptualised 'leadership', the expectations which they brought to that role and

Source: MacBeath, J. (ed.) (1998) *Effective School Leadership: Responding to Change*. London:
Paul Chapman. Edited version.

how their expectations meshed with those of other stakeholders. Differences in context and culture came to the surface because of the international nature of our project, and sharpened our awareness of how school leadership is shaped by socio-economic and political factors. It returned us persistently to the point where cultural history meets contemporary politics, and where globalisation confronts national identity (MacBeath *et al.*, 1996).

Exploring leadership, effective schools and their inter-relationship raised, for us, three fundamental questions:

- What do we understand by the terms 'effective' and 'good'?
- What is the relationship between effective leaders and effective schools?
- Are there models (of effective schools and effective leadership) which can be legitimately transferred?

These are the questions which we raise and attempt to answer in this chapter.

The 'Effective' Headteacher Recipe

The growing internationalisation of education has meant that the language of school effectiveness has become common currency amongst researchers, and has shaped the thinking of policy-makers. The climate of global competitiveness which now characterises much national thinking about education is receptive to the 'quick-fix' in school effectiveness, as in other areas. 'Policy borrowing', reinforced by a belief that education models are transferable, regardless of context, is becoming standard practice.

If we have learned one thing from our study it is that there is no one package for school leadership, no one model to be learned and applied in unrefined forms, for all schools, in all contexts – no all-purpose recipe. Nonetheless, there are clearly some common ingredients and the collaborative sharing of thinking and practice in which our study was rooted provided the opportunity for participating heads to look at the critical mix. From working alongside thirty heads from three countries – England, Scotland and Denmark – (and then forty as the Australian heads joined the study), it became increasingly obvious that successful school leaders do not learn how to 'do' leadership and then stick to set patterns and ways of doing things along a prescribed set of known rules. They are willing to change in response to new sets of circumstances – and to the differing needs of children, young people and teachers – and they are often rule breakers.

Notions of leadership are profoundly value-laden. They relate to national purposes, local context, as well as the skills and attributes of individuals, and the demands and expectations of school communities. Demands and expectations change over time. By and large, the role of the school principal or headteacher of a decade or two ago was to maintain a smooth-running organisation and harmonious staff relationships. Schools functioned in the belief that teachers were competent and needed to be left alone to teach. As Leithwood and Montgomery (1982) have shown in Canadian elementary schools, principals of the 1980s did not see it as their role to attempt to improve their schools' 'instructional effectiveness'. That was not the job they had set themselves, nor was it the one they were expected to do.

Expectations of headteachers have changed, or are changing, in many national and state contexts and the very notion of leadership is closely bound in with their culture and history. Some school systems give greater weight to it than others but for the four countries of our study, education reforms have brought issues of school effectiveness sharply into the foreground and along with it the accountability of principals for school performance. Denmark has perhaps felt this wind of change most. Denmark has always been a school system which believed in a bottom-up approach, priding itself on its democracy and its strong focus on teacher autonomy. In recent years, however, school leaders have acquired greater responsibilities for developing the professional competence of staff, at the same time holding on to their primary task of allowing freedom for the individual classroom teacher to develop his or her relationship with pupils and with their parents. This focus on the individual teacher is not unique to Danish schools. France and Switzerland, for example, have historically shared that perspective.

School principals in Queensland, like their counterparts in other parts of Australia (most notably Victoria), are being drawn increasingly into an accountability framework which will require them to take stronger professional leadership within their schools. In both Scotland and England, the power of the headteacher has been reinforced by increasing pay differentials between them and other staff. Headteachers in both countries are expected to be leading professionals within the school but this responsibility has to be balanced against major financial responsibilities and management demands. England, which has gone furthest down the road of self-government of the four countries in the study, places the most stringent governance and accountability framework on its headteachers.

The context and emphasis of school leadership may vary but increasingly it is the individual – the headteacher or school principal – who is placed in the spotlight. In England, for example, few of the headteachers of the 340 schools which had been designated as 'requiring special measures' following an Ofsted inspection, have remained in post after a critical inspection report (Riley and Rowles, 1996). But with all this focus on the individual, do we know what an 'effective' headteacher looks like? And is an 'effective' headteacher also a 'good' headteacher? How do those questions relate to the debates about what constitutes a 'good' school, as opposed to what constitutes an 'effective' school?

The 'Good' School and the 'Effective' School

The notion of what constitutes a good school is bound up in history, culture and local context.

> Good schools have been ones which have trained girls to be good wives and mothers, or which trained boys to serve the commercial ethic or the Empire. 'Good' has been an infinitely adaptable epithet, used of schools, of many kinds, by interested parties of many kinds.
>
> (Silver, 1994, p. 6)

The terms of 'good' and 'effective' are not neutral but contested. The notion of a good school is a social construct, shaped by national expectations and local aspirations. Equally, the notion of an effective school is socially constructed. Both notions rest on a belief that schools can make a difference but what those differences are may be at issue.

The basic assertion of the research literature on school effectiveness is that individual schools can make a difference to student achievement. Most of the early research on school effectiveness challenged the findings of James Coleman's highly influential US report on schools (Coleman *et al.*, 1966) which had reached the conclusion that differences between one school and another only accounted for a small percentage of the variance in pupil performance. Subsequent studies (Brimer *et al.*, 1978; Rutter *et al.*, 1979) concluded that there were differences in the 'effectiveness' of schools greater than those identified in the Coleman study. These findings were endorsed by a further study (Mortimore *et al.*, 1988) which examined primary schools in London and identified a range of variables (including leadership style) which could have positive effects on student outcomes.

The studies provided a welcome challenge to the social pathology of failure. They began to paint details into the portrait of what an effective school or classroom should look like (Silver, 1994, p. 93). Critics have argued, however, that research findings have become used as blanket recipes – solutions to the problems facing all schools. Research findings on school effectiveness were treated as 'laws of science that applied to all schools and all teachers' (Glickman, 1987, quoted in Silver 1994, p. 102). Purkey and Smith (1983), in one of the first such critiques, concluded that school effectiveness research tended to ignore school culture and issues of organisational change, and concluded that the characteristics which school effectiveness emphasised were

> unlikely to work in all schools, may not work as expected in many schools, and may in fact be counterproductive in some schools.
>
> (Purkey and Smith, 1983, pp. 440 and 447, quoted in Silver, 1994, p. 98)

More recently, critics have charged the movement with ignoring the social and economic content (Stoll and Riley, 1997, Whitty, 1997). Others have criticised it for being platitudinous, re-inventing the obvious; missing the fine-grain reality of school life; appropriating language (e.g. 'effectiveness') misdirecting attention from wider structural issues; confusing correlations and causes; offering little to school management or teachers; ignoring the problematic of the curriculum; and limited in its focus on the school as an entity (White and Barber, 1997).

By the very nature of its construction, school effectiveness research is vulnerable to such attacks. Its findings often seem no more than common-sensical. Its concern for quantifiable, reliable measures does limit its compass. Its focus on the internal workings of the school does, by definition, exclude home, community and wider political contexts. Silver (1994) has argued that schools operate within three sets of realities:

■ the community location (the social needs and neighbourhood context);
■ the policy context (set at the national: and state level); and
■ the internal workings (how the school perceives and acts upon its responsibilities).

Evidence from an English study of schools which have 'failed' Ofsted inspections (Riley and Rowles, 1996) suggests that a combination of pressures pushes schools along the downward spiral. Some of those pressures relate to weak leadership and isolated and disaffected staff (that is, the internal working of the school) but the study also demonstrated that many such schools served areas of deprivation and high unemployment (that is, the community location) and most of the secondary schools were in competition with selective grammar schools, or grant-maintained schools (that is, the policy context).

School effectiveness does, deliberately and specifically, focus on schools and has been unapologetically directed at explaining what goes on within the black box. Its strength and unique contribution to our understanding of schools is also its most singular weakness, however. The need to control the variables such as home background requires that these things are factored out, so risking the loss of data on the most significant area for enhancement of learning, the dynamic relationship between what pupils bring to school and what they take away from school (MacBeath, 1998).

The focus on individual schools is also a limiting factor. As Benn and Chitty (1996) have pointed out, the efforts of any individual school are affected by the organisation of other schools in the neighbourhood. The contextual effect, the critical mass, or the critical mix, is not just an intra-school phenomenon but an inter-school one. Effective schools are not just a product of the social dynamics within their four walls but a result of the wider social dynamic of the neighbourhood and the larger political and economic processes at work.

Attainment measures, however much used as proxies and surrounded by health warnings, may, nonetheless, reinforce a deeply-entrenched view of effective schools as those most efficient at improving exam scores. Where this happens, researchers may be wittingly or unwittingly complicit in diverting attention from wider structural issues and political agendas or fail to challenge retrogressive views of what education is or what schools might be for. In a critique of Rutter's (1979) work, Holtz, for example, argued that

> As we acknowledge the important contribution of 'Fifteen Thousand Hours' and other . . . research of its kind, it may be worth our while to remember that we once hoped that schools would create new models of community, encourage new commitments towards meaningful vocations, end racial discrimination, and open up new avenues out of poverty and unhappiness. Right now, it seems we rejoice if children can be caught to read.
>
> (Holtz, 1981, quoted in Silver, 1994, p. 102)

A similar view has been expressed by Gammage who argued that school effectiveness research, and its policy emphasis, obscured thinking about the 'good' school. This he characterised as one which focused on relationships, the nature of the school community, its essential values, and its capacity to enrich the lives of those who are a part of it:

> Perhaps therefore the good school is that which most successfully matches its curricular organisation and ethos to an expectation of high commitment by children . . . a school is 'good' not so much because of the specific nature of what is taught (though that is important) but through the manner in which a positive, supportive, richly and frequently interactive atmosphere is created.
>
> (Gammage, 1985, quoted in Silver 1994, p. 101)

The effective school is only one version of a good school and only one contributor to our understanding of what good schools are and how they come into being. Without a constant reminder of this, the danger is that broader notions of schooling and good schools drop off the policy and improvement agenda. In a paper on school effectiveness for the British Psychological Society, Raven (1997) made the case for deriving criteria on effectiveness from perceptions of the goals of education held by pupils, parents, teachers and employers. He argued that these give us better measures for differentiating 'more' from 'less' effective performance in occupational and life roles.

In fact there has been a growing rapprochement of school effectiveness and school improvement. A study for the National Union of Teachers (MacBeath *et al.*, 1995) which did derive effectiveness criteria from the stakeholders mentioned by Raven, found a close match between what parents, pupils and teachers wanted from their schools and what the mainstream of effectiveness research had identified. The school 'insiders' did, however, bring to those criteria, a depth of insight and elaboration of what learning and good schools meant. Good schools were those whose culture provided opportunities for growth, not only for pupils but for teachers and school leaders. The importance of such a culture is expressed by Per Dalin, the Norwegian educator, in these terms:

> The only way schools will survive the future is to become creative learning organisations. The best way students can learn how to live in the future is to experience the life of the learning school.
>
> (Dalin with Rolff, 1995, p. 19)

The work of Dalin and other school improvers in fact owes much to the effectiveness movement. It is a broadening church. It is more welcoming of practitioners and more willing to test its findings in school and classroom practice. The growing percentage of teachers and headteachers who attend and present papers at the annual School Effectiveness/School Improvement conferences is a vital sign of a learning movement which welcomes challenge and seeks a closer inter-relationship between theory and practice.

These are important issues to be borne in mind when considering the relationship between effective leadership and effective schools. They are in part about terminology but in larger part about values and paradigms, ways of thinking and ways of seeing.

Effectiveness of Leadership

Our use of the term 'effective' in terms of leadership is not derived from any empirical correlation with student attainment nor indeed from any outcome measures of school performance. Effectiveness, we recognise, is a contested notion and one that has to remain open to question, to challenge and to refinement. Deriving definitions of 'effectiveness' in leadership from the views of stakeholders, proved to be a useful starting place and the following 'expert' view from a group of nine year-olds in our project lays a useful groundwork. They described a good headteacher in these terms:

- Has a good education and is able to solve problems
- Is very experienced as a teacher
- Is able to understand children – what they can do at different ages
- Is easy going but firm
- Knows how to look after the building and create a nice environment and a safe place for children

- Knows how to take responsibility for things happening in the school and does not blame others
- Is able to make children, adults and the community feel confident about the things they do in school
- Provides a good example in their behaviour (by not smoking, or drinking in school)
- Is not racist and makes others see that the colour of their skin does not matter
- Keeps in touch with the local community, letting them know what is happening in the school
- Treats children equally
- Gives everyone the same advantages.

(Quoted in Riley, 1998a, p. 122)

The view of leadership offered by this group of children proved to be a consistent theme within our study. Effective leadership meant sustaining those relationships within a community in which all its members are heard, and taken account of. A happy and fulfilling school experience may stay with children right into their adult life and make it more likely that they would return to formal education as adults at a later stage. Paying attention to the inner life of the school was described as a requisite of leadership over a hundred years ago:

> The organisation of the school must be kept mobile to its inner life. To one who is accustomed to wind up the machine and trust it to run for fixed periods, this constantly shifting shape of things will seem unsafe and troublesome. And troublesome it is; for no fixed plan can be followed; no two schools are alike; and the same school is shifting, requiring constant attention and nimble judgement on the part of the (school leader).
>
> (Arnold Tomkins, education pioneer New York State, 1895,
> quoted in Louis *et al.*, 1995)

The school leadership paradigm which emerges from our study emphasises the capability of the school leader to sustain relationships. It is a model which ties in closely with much of the thinking about school improvement (e.g. Stoll and Fink, 1992) and which puts the heart and emotions of teaching at the centre (Hargreaves, 1997). The paradigm is also one of mobility and fragility. It rests on the assumption (inherent in Arnold Tomkins's analysis) that schools are constantly changing. The challenge is to be able to respond to the school's inner life – troublesome though it may be – as well to the demanding and constantly changing external context. It recognises that schools have to serve internal and external constituencies which are often in uneasy relationship with one another. It acknowledges that school leaders have to manage contested notions about achievement and cope with multiple interests and demands. It rests on uncertainty, as well as certainty, and is rooted in a deep understanding of context – national, local and school-based. It is because of this complexity that no single recipe will work.

The school leadership paradigm is also one of shared leadership. School leadership is beyond the undertakings of one heroic individual. It is simply not possible, and may not even be desirable, for one individual to undertake every leadership task within a school. Good school leaders are those who are able to maximise the diverse leadership qualities of others, enabling them to take on leadership within their areas of expertise. They lead by managing, motivating and inspiring people. This may come through individual one-to-one work with teachers, pupils, parents or governors, or through creating the impetus within an organisation that encourages and enables people to play an active part in school life. They are clear about 'the vision business' and recognise that whilst national targets and performance criteria have to be satisfied, those external goals can only be achieved by creating a professional community within the school. As one headteacher in our study concluded:

> My job is to try and develop the collegiate nature of the school and to create
> the opportunities for staff to develop professional relationships with colleagues
> in other schools.
>
> (Quoted in Riley, 1998b).

Good leaders who operate in this way recognise that teachers are more likely to become engaged in making changes within their own schools when more collaborative leadership models are the norm. As Gammage (1985) implied in his account of the good school, good leaders recognise the importance of relationships, enrichment and an interactive community. The style is also an inclusive one, for the reasons suggested by the findings from this North American study:

> Teachers' willingness to participate in school decision-making is influenced
> primarily by their relationships with their principals . . . Teachers appear more
> willing to participate in all areas of decision-making if they perceive their
> relationships with their principals as more open, collaborative, facilitative and
> supportive. They are less willing to participate in any decision-making if they
> characterize their relationships with the principals as closed, exclusionary, and
> controlling.
>
> (Smylie, 1992, p. 63, quoted in Murphy, 1994, p. 30)

The other key element in our paradigm is that school leadership is about making choices, deciding on priorities, and being willing to learn and change. The model cannot be transported from one situation, or context, to another because it is not a static model. It relies on the ability of the leaders to revise his or her approach and to learn and reflect. The capacity to be a continual learner is key.

School leaders have to make choices not only about what they do but about how they do it. The people with whom headteachers spend their time give telling insights into values, priorities, contexts and the underlying rationale for those choices. Danish headteachers in our study spent much more of their working day with teachers than Scottish or English heads. Scottish headteachers spent considerably more time with pupils than their Danish and English counterparts, while English heads were more likely to spend their time with outside agencies or individuals, managing external politics.

The people headteachers spend their time with does not, of course, indicate **how** they spend it. A headteacher who spends time with staff may be doing qualitatively different things, for example, nurturing, supporting, developing, or being task-orientated about specific elements of the school day (for example, the time-table). Time spent with pupils could imply disciplinary matters (poor performance); or personal issues (such as home pressures); or appreciation of educational achievements. Our analysis suggests that good headteachers are able to recognise how they spend their time, with whom and for what purposes, and then link their behaviour to their priorities. There are choices to be made and these choices may change, depending on the circumstances of the school, as well as the local and national environments. Effective leadership is about making those choices and about managing the 'fit' between the external world and the internal world of the school.

Analysis of the comparative data within and between the countries in our study suggests that there are a number of key dimensions which distinguish different approaches to leadership on the part of the headteacher. We have identified three that recur quite consistently. These are not all of the dimensions, nor are they necessarily definitive, but they do illustrate the complexities of leadership and its active and interactive nature. These three dimensions can be represented as three intersecting axes on which any given headteacher could be placed, or might place him/herself (Figure 12.1).

The internal–external dimension distinguishes between headteachers who look primarily inwards to the school community and those who look outwards to the local, or wider community. Philosophically, this might be distinguished by overt beliefs such as 'I believe I must protect and market the school', as against 'my job is to be with children and teachers'. Or it might spring less from conviction than circumstance and context.

The individual–collective dimension distinguishes between philosophy and behaviour which is orientated towards individual pupils and members of staff as against the broader collective. Some headteachers used staff meetings and collective occasions, such as school assemblies, to foster a corporate identity.

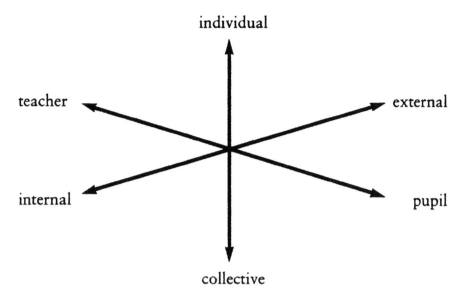

Figure 12.1

Some used self-evaluation, staff development and forward planning as collective mechanisms to demonstrate that decision-making was a corporate enterprise. At the other end of the spectrum, a headteacher might prefer a more individualistic style of influence, working through key individuals, using sanctions and rewards to promote (or marginalise) key players. Some school leaders spent time with individual pupils and with individual members of staff, encouraging, motivating, counselling, sanctioning and disciplining, and in some cases grooming individuals for promotion. As with the first dimension, these are tendencies, rather than diametrically-opposite patterns of behaviour, and the dimension could oversimplify what may be a complex and even inconsistent mix. Again, behaviour on this dimension is a matter of both national and local culture, as well as deriving from school-based factors.

The pupil-centred/teacher-centred dimension is even more difficult to see as ends of one continuous axis. However, we have tried to distinguish what has emerged clearly from the data – time priority given to being with pupils, or being with teachers. Some headteachers spent a great deal of the day with pupils, in either a teaching or counselling/disciplinary situation. Others saw little of pupils and spent more time with teachers, individually or collectively. This could reflect a difference in philosophy between those who saw pupils as the focus for development and those who saw teachers as the vehicle for change. Other school leaders put greater emphasis on time with staff and on staff needs. Their implicit or overt philosophy was that pupils would be the ultimate beneficiaries of an attempt to meet the needs of staff.

These three dimensions are complex, shifting, dynamically inter-related and real. They differ by country (which can be related to cultural and historic factors) and by school sector. Primary heads are more likely to spend time with pupils in a teaching–learning situation and with teachers on curriculum development than secondary heads. They report less lobbying and fewer tensions among group interests than their secondary colleagues (who have to contend with vertical department divisions, and layers of hierarchical responsibility).

We concluded that school leaders need to be aware of 'who' they are spending their time with, as well as the 'why' and the 'how'. The allocation of time reflects implicit priorities. Effective headteachers can match the two in ways that relate to their context, their own skills and attributes, as well as changing circumstances.

Concluding Thoughts

The exploration of school leadership presented in this chapter suggests that there are a number of tensions in thinking about models of leadership. Leadership is bound in context but whilst it does not lend itself to recipe swapping, discussions about common ingredients can be helpful. The conceptualisation of school leadership presented here acknowledges instability, the quixotic natures of schools and their political and social location, unlike some of the school effectiveness literature which has tended to deal in categoricals, and to focus on quantifiable outcomes and measurements of performance. 'Effective' school leaders are also 'good' leaders. They are distinguished by their vision and passion and by their capacity to bring a critical spirit into the complex and demanding job of headship, whilst at the same time focusing on staff and pupil performance, and on classroom pedagogy.

References

Benn, C. and Chitty, C. (1996) *Thirty Years On: Is Comprehensive Education Alive and Well or Struggling to Survive?*, David Fulton, London.

Brimer, A. *et al.* (1978) *Sources of Difference in School Achievement*, National Foundation for Educational Research, Slough.

Coleman, J.S. *et al.* (1966) *Equality of Educational Opportunity*, Department of Health, Education and Welfare, Washington DC.

Dalin, P. with Rolff, H.G. (1995) *Changing the School Culture*, Cassell, London.

Gammage, P. (1985) *What is a Good School?*, National Association for Primary Education, University of Nottingham.

Glickman, C.D. (1987) Good and/or effective schools: what do we want?, *Phi Delta Kappan*, Vol. 68, no. 8, pp. 622–624.

Hargreaves, A. (1997) Feeling like a teacher: The emotions of teaching and educational change. Paper submitted to *Phi Delta Kappan*.

Holtz, B.W. (1981) Can schools make a difference? (review of Rutterd *et al.*, *Fifteen Thousand Hours*), *Teachers College Record*, Vol. 83, no. 2, pp. 300–7.

Leithwood, K. and Montgomery, D (1982) The role of the elementary principal in program improvement, *Review of Educational Research*. Vol. 52 no. 3, pp. 309–339.

Louis, K.S., Kruse, S. and Associates (1995) *Professionalism and Community: Perspectives on Reforming Urban Schools*, Corwin Press, Thousand Oaks, California.

MacBeath. J., Boyd, B., Rand, J. and Bell, S. (1995) *Schools Speak for Themselves*, National Union of Teachers, London.

MacBeath, J., Moos, L. and Riley, K.A. (1996) Leadership in a changing world, in K. Leithwood, K. Chapman, C. Corson, P. Hallinger, and A. Hart (eds.) *International Handbook for Educational Leadership and Administration*, Kluwer, Dordrecht.

Mortimore, P. Sammons, P. Stoll, L., Lewis, D. and Ecob, R. (1988) *School Matters: The Junior School Years*, Open Books, London.

Murphy, J. (1994) Transformational change and the evolving role of the principal, in J. Murphy and K. Seashore Louis (eds.) *Reshaping the Principalship: Insights from Transformational Reform Efforts*, Corwin Press, Thousand Oaks, California.

Purkey, S.C. and Smith, M.D. (1983) Effective schools: a review, *The Elementary School Journal*, Vol. 83, no. 1, p. 429.

Raven, J. (1997) Education, educational research, ethics and the BPS, *British Psychological Society Education Section Review*, no. 21, pp. 3–10.

Riley, K.A. (1998a) *Whose School is it Anyway?* Falmer Press, London.

Riley, K.A. (1998b) Creating the leadership climate, *International Journal of Leadership in Education*, Vol. 1, no. 2.

Riley, K.A. and Rowles, D. (1996) *Learning from Failure*, London Borough of Haringey.

Rutter, M., Maughan. B., Mortimore, P., Ouston, J. with Smith, A. (1979) *Fifteen Thousand Hours: Secondary Schools and their Effects on Children*, Open Books, London.

Sammons, P., Hillman, J. and Mortimore, P. (1995) *Key Characteristics of Effective Schools: A Review of School Effectiveness*, Research for the Office of Standards in Education, London.

Silver, H. (1994) *Good Schools, Effective Schools*, Cassell, London.

Smylie, M.A. (1992) Teacher participation in school decision making: assessing willingness to participate, *Educational Evaluation and Policy Analysis*, Vol. 14, no. 1, pp. 53–67.

Stoll, L. and Fink, D. (1992) Effecting school change: the Halton approach, *School Effectiveness and School Improvement*. Vol. 3. no. 1, pp. 19–41.

Stoll, L. and Riley, K.A. (1998) School effectiveness and school improvement, *Country Report to the International Conference on School Effectiveness and Improvements*, Manchester, January.

White, J. and Barber, M. (eds.) (1997) *Perspectives on School Effectiveness and School Improvement*, Institute of Education, London.

Whitty, G. (1997) Social theory and education. Social policy: the Karl Mannheim Memorial Lecture, London Institute of Education.

13

Fostering Teacher Leadership

Kenneth Leithwood, Doris Jantzi and Rosanne Steinbach

Shared decision making and teacher professionalization are key elements of many school restructuring plans. Both elements require teachers routinely to exercise more leadership outside the classroom than traditionally has been expected of them. So facilitating the development of teacher leadership has become an important part of the role of those in formal school leadership positions. Summed up by Conley (1993: 246), the motivations for advocating such leadership include: the possibilities for reflecting democratic principles of participation in the workplace; enhancing teachers' satisfaction with their work; increasing teachers' sense of professionalism; stimulating organizational change; providing a route to increased organizational efficiency; and revitalizing teachers through increased interaction with their colleagues.

Like many others, we believe that developing teacher leadership is an important part of what those in formal school leadership roles should be doing. But specific practices helpful in facilitating such development will need to be crafted on the basis of a better understanding of two key matters: the relationship between formal and informal (or teacher) school leadership, and the nature of teacher leadership and factors influencing the perception of such leadership on the part of teacher leaders' colleagues. Based on a study fully described in Leithwood *et al.* (1997), this chapter addresses these two issues. Implications of the study for the development of teacher leaders are discussed in the final section of the chapter.

Teacher leadership

Leadership, suggest Sirotnik and Kimball (1996), does not take on new meaning when qualified by the term 'teacher'. It entails the exercise of influence

---

Source: Leithwood, K., Jantzi, D. and Steinbach, R. (eds.) (1999) *Changing Leadership for Changing Times*. Milton Keynes: Open University Press. Edited version.

over the beliefs, actions and values of others (Hart 1995a), as is the case with leadership from any source. What may be different is how that influence is exercised and to what end. In a traditional school, for example, those in formal administrative roles have greater access than teachers to positional power in their attempts to influence classroom practice, whereas teachers may have greater access to the power that flows from technical expertise.

Teacher leadership may be either formal or informal in nature. Lead teacher, department head, mentor – these are among the many designations associated with formal teacher leadership roles. Teachers assuming these roles are expected to carry out a wide range of functions. These functions include, for example: representing the school in district-level decision making (Fullan 1993); stimulating the professional growth of colleagues (Wasley 1991); being an advocate for teachers' work (Bascia 1997); and improving the school's decision-making processes (Malen *et al.*, 1990). Those appointed to formal teacher leadership roles are also sometimes expected to induct new teachers into the school, and to influence positively the willingness and capacity of other teachers to implement change in the school (Fullan and Hargreaves 1991; Whitaker 1995).

Teachers exercise informal leadership in their schools by sharing their expertise, volunteering for new projects and bringing new ideas to the school. They also offer leadership by helping their colleagues to carry out their classroom duties, and by assisting in the improvement of classroom practice. Teachers attribute leadership qualities, as well, to colleagues who accept responsibility for their own professional growth, promote the school's mission, and work for the improvement of the school or the school system (Smylie and Denny, 1990; Wasley 1991; Harrison and Lembeck 1996).

Empirical evidence concerning the actual effects of either formal or informal leadership is limited in quantity and mixed results are reported. Hannay and Denby (1994) found that department heads were not very effective as facilitators of change, largely due to their lack of knowledge and skill in effective change strategies. On the other hand, Duke *et al.* (1980) found that increased participation of teachers in school decision making resulted in a more democratic school. Increased professional learning for the teacher leader has also been reported as an effect of assuming such a role (Lieberman *et al.*, 1988; Wasley 1991).

The exercise of teacher leadership is inhibited by a number of conditions. Time taken for work outside the classroom probably interferes with time needed for students (Smylie and Denny 1990). When extra time is provided for leadership functions, it is usually not enough (Wasley 1991). Furthermore, the lack of time, training and funding for leadership roles (Cooper 1988; White 1992) interferes with teachers' personal lives, as well as their classroom work. Cultures of isolationism, common in schools, inhibit the work of teacher leaders with their teaching colleagues, as do the associated norms of egalitarianism, privacy, politeness and contrived collegiality (Sirotnik 1994; Griffin 1995). The effectiveness of teacher leaders is constrained by lack of role definition (Smylie and Denny 1990) and by requiring them to take on responsibilities outside their areas of expertise (Little 1995).

Transformational leadership

Uncertainties about the specific purposes and practices associated with many restructuring initiatives and the importance attached to fundamental organizational change call for commitment-building forms of school leadership with a systemic focus. What is most salient for the chapter is the claim that it leads to higher levels of personal commitment to organizational goals and greater capacities for accomplishing those goals. This, in turn, is assumed to result in extra effort and greater productivity.

The model of transformational leadership developed from our own research in schools conceptualizes transformational leadership along eight dimensions: building school vision; establishing school goals; providing intellectual stimulation; offering individualized support, modelling best practices and important organizational values; demonstrating high performance expectations; creating a productive school culture; and developing structures to foster participation in school decisions.

Most models of transformational leadership are flawed by their under-representation of transactional practices, which we interpret to be 'managerial' in nature, because such practices are fundamental to organizational stability. For this reason, we have added four management dimensions to our own model, based on a review of relevant literature (Duke and Leithwood 1994). These dimensions include staffing, instructional support, monitoring school activities and community focus.

We were curious about the extent to which teacher leadership reflected key managerial and transformational leadership practices typically associated with formal administrative leaders.

Leadership perceptions

A central premise for the design of this study is derived quite directly from the definition of leadership as an influence process. As Lord and Maher (1993) argue, such influence depends on a person's behaviour being recognized as, and at least tacitly acknowledged to be, 'leadership' by others who thereby cast themselves into the role of followers.

Lord and Maher (1993) offer a cognitive explanation for the judgements people make about whether or not someone is a leader. According to their account, salient information about people is processed in two possible ways. One way is to match that information to categories, or leadership prototypes (knowledge structures) already stored in long-term memory. This 'recognition' process on the part of the follower is triggered by observed or otherwise encountered information about the traits and behaviours of another person, who has the potential to be perceived as a leader. These observed traits and behaviours are compared with the traits and behaviours included in the relevant knowledge structure stored in the follower's long-term memory; his or her implicit or explicit leadership theory. Relatively high levels of correspondence between observed and stored traits and behaviours leads to the follower's perception of the other person as a leader.

Followers' assessments of correspondence may occur in a highly automatic fashion. This is likely in cognitively demanding, face-to-face encounters between followers and leaders. Followers may also develop perceptions of leaders through 'inferential' processes. Such processes depend on the opportunity for followers to observe events in which the potential leader is involved, to assess the outcomes of those events and to draw conclusions about the contribution of the potential leader to those outcomes. Perceptions of persons as leaders result from followers' judgements that those events were somehow salient, that they had desirable results and that the potential leader was instrumental in bringing about those results. Inferential processes may occur relatively, automatically or through more controlled processes.

Two studies using an adaptation of the Lord and Maher model (Jantzi and Leithwood 1996; Leithwood and Jantzi 1997) provide evidence concerning the factors that account for teachers' perceptions of transformational leadership among principals. These studies suggest that school conditions were the most powerful variables explaining teachers' leader perceptions.

These results led us to enquire about the extent to which perception of teacher leadership were influenced by factors similar to those that influence perceptions of transformational principal leadership.

School conditions or characteristics mediating leader effects on students

Most of the effects of school leadership on students are mediated by other characteristics of the school (Hallinger and Heck 1996). A significant challenge for both leadership practice and research is to identify those characteristics known to have direct effects on students and to inquire about the nature and strength of the relationship between them and leadership.

The seven school-level (non-classroom) characteristics selected as mediating variables were identified through a review of literature concerning school and district effects (Leithwood and Aitken 1995). These features or sets of conditions emerged from the review as having important consequences for school effectiveness. They included: the school's mission and vision; school improvement planning processes; culture; structures for decision making; information collection and decision-making processes; policies and procedures; and school–community relations.

The relationship between formal and informal school leadership

There are likely to be significant differences between formal leaders and teacher leaders both on the issues each are in the best position to address and the strategies available to each for addressing these issues. In this section we describe the relationship between the leadership provided by teacher leaders and those in formal leadership roles. We also describe characteristics of the school organization most likely to be influenced by those in formal leadership roles and by teacher leaders. We ask which aspects of the school are influenced most by the leadership of teachers, and what is the relative influence on the school of principal leadership compared with teacher leadership.

To address both of these questions, data were provided through a survey conducted with all elementary and secondary teachers in one large school district (4,456 teachers) in Ontario. Procedures used to analyse the data are described in detail in the original study (see Leithwood *et al.*, 1997).

Analysis of the survey responses indicated that teachers had a significant and at least moderately strong influence on all aspects of the school organization. Schools in which teachers were seen to provide more influential leadership were also schools perceived by teachers to be more effective and innovative. Teacher influence was most strongly related to school planning and school structure and organization.

The characteristics for which teacher influence accounted for the most variance were *school planning* and *structure and organization*. Not only were the variances most affected by the influence of teacher leaders, they were also two of the three characteristics for which the influence of principals had less effect than did that of teacher leaders. The explanatory patterns for school mission and school culture were almost identical: principal influence explained just over 20 per cent of the variation, and teacher influence explained about an additional 10 per cent.

Principals' influence was more strongly associated than teachers' influence with teachers' perceptions of the extent to which the leadership they experienced from all sources in the school was transformational in nature. Perceptions of transformational leadership practices explained 42 per cent of the variation in principals' leadership influence, compared with 33 per cent of the influence of teacher leaders. Similarly, principals' leadership influence was more strongly associated with perceptions of effective school management than was teacher leadership influence. These results suggest that school staffs tend to hold modestly different expectations for principal, as compared with teacher, leadership.

To summarize, the principal's leadership was more influential than the leadership exercised by teachers overall. But the leadership of teachers had a significant, independent influence on the school.

The Nature of Teacher Leadership

This section describes the forms of teacher leadership valued by teachers. Also described in this section are the factors that account for teachers' perceptions of the leadership of their colleagues.

Traits

Our research data identified six categories of traits: mood, values, orientation to people, physical characteristics, responsibility and personality. Table 13.1 indicates the frequency with which each of these categories was mentioned.

The most frequently mentioned category, values, encompassed ten specific items mentioned from 5 to 73 times. Three of these ten qualities were the most frequently mentioned across all categories of traits. Being committed to one's school and profession was mentioned most frequently, followed closely by the holding of strong beliefs and being committed to the welfare of students. Other values included in this category were: commitment to the community; fairness; concern for the morality of decisions made in the school; commitment to family; being a 'good' person; being humane; and ignoring personal biases.

The frequency with which personality characteristics were mentioned was second only to the frequency with which values were mentioned. Most mentioned in this category were openness, honesty and genuineness. Other personality traits identified were outspokenness, a pleasant but commanding presence and energy. Among the less frequently mentioned traits were creativity, humility, enthusiasm and confidence.

Orientation to people was the third most frequently mentioned category of traits that teachers associated with leadership. This category included being non-confrontational, being caring, having sensitivity to others and having good interpersonal and communication skills. This category also included being supportive, approachable, a good listener and easy to work with, having understanding of others and being appreciative and discreet. Four people mentioned not being defensive as an important orientation to people in those considered to be leaders.

The fourth most frequently mentioned category of traits was mood. Included in this category were quietness, positiveness, having a sense of humour, and being even tempered. Less frequently mentioned were gentleness, not taking oneself too seriously and being serious.

Some aspect of being responsible was mentioned next in frequency. Among the six facets of responsibility mentioned by teachers, being a hard worker dominated in frequency of mention. Also mentioned were being steady and conscientious, having a sense of responsibility and being dependable. Being indispensable was mentioned twice.

Table 13.1 Leadership categories: dimensions ranked in order of frequency*

Traits		Practices		Capacities		Outcomes	
Values	240	Performs administrative tasks	239	Procedural knowledge	110	Gains respect of staff and students	121
Personality	225	Models valued practices	187	Declarative knowledge	101	Things are implemented well	75
Orientation to people	202	Formal leadership responsibilities	150	Relationships with staff	57	Staff look to him/her for leadership	65
Mood	135	Supports the work of other staff	147	Problem solver	56	Enhances staff comfort level	52
Responsibility	98	Teaching responsibilities	114	Communication skills	53	Contributes to the culture of the school	45
Physical characteristics	10	Visible in the school	83	Relationships with students	47	Makes us want to emulate him/her	37
		Confronts issues directly/make hard decisions	64	Visionary	27	Has good effect on students	36
		Shares leadership with others	46	Organized	26	Staff will listen	33
		Personal relationships	28	Self-knowledge	16	Meets high expectations	14
		Takes initiative	27	Global thinker	13		
		Leader	22	Competent	12		
				Focused	10		
				Sets limits on self	8		
				Efficient	7		
Total	**910**	**Total**	**1107**	**Total**	**543**	**Total**	**478**

*Numbers indicate the number of times each leadership dimension was mentioned by all 57 interviewees.

People's physical features, the final set of traits, were mentioned a total of ten times as relevant to their perceptions of leadership; in particular being tall, and dressing like a leader.

Practices

What teachers perceive leaders actually to be doing is our meaning of the term 'practices'. The most frequently mentioned of these was the performance of administrative tasks, such as working administrative periods in the office, being on committees and organizing specific events.

Modelling valued practices was the next most frequently mentioned sub-category of practice. This included leading by example, interacting with students, being a motivator for staff and students and never missing a day of work. One teacher said, 'He sets the example that there are many teachers who have taught for a long time and who are excellent teachers'. Another said, 'He reminds us of our objectives'.

Formal leadership responsibilities were mentioned next in frequency. This set of practices reflects the number of times teachers were nominated as leaders because of their position; being a department head or being head of a particular committee. Supporting the work of other staff was mentioned almost as often as formal leadership; this referred to the help the teacher provided to his or her colleagues (for example, helps young teachers, helps with course outlines, helps with a difficult class) or the support given to staff (for example, 'kind of stroking people and saying you can do it', 'speaks out on our behalf whether we agree or disagree', 'allows people to vent').

The sub-category 'teaching responsibilities' was the fourth most frequently associated with leadership practices. Specific teaching practices (such as having lessons well prepared and being a good teacher) were mentioned often. Teachers felt that being visible in the school was an important dimension of leadership. Examples of this practice include presenting information at staff meetings, and being a leader in the school and not just in the department. Confronting issues directly, sharing leadership with others, personal relationships, taking initiative and simply 'leadership' were the last five sets of practices mentioned by the interviewees.

Capacities

The most frequently mentioned capacities or skills were associated with 'procedural' and 'declarative' knowledge. Procedural knowledge refers to knowledge teachers have about how to carry out leadership tasks, for example, making tough decisions, knowing how to run a meeting and dealing with administration. As several teachers said, '[She] can put out fires without too much trouble'; '[He] knows how to handle a situation without implicating anyone else; or '[She] knows how to evaluate our students, modify programmes, develop report cards'.

Declarative knowledge refers to knowledge about specific aspects of the profession; for example, knowledge about government education policy, knowledge about education in general; knowledge about the school, students and the community; knowledge about specific subjects; and knowledge about union issues.

Teachers' ability to work well with their colleagues, a valued category of leadership capacities, included statements about how a particular teacher can motivate staff, work effectively with others and be willing to moderate disagreements.

Being a good problem solver was also seen as an important leadership capacity. For example, one teacher said, '[She] can listen to a discussion and, in the end, filter it all down to what the real problems are'. Getting to the heart of the matter or being able to synthesize information was part of this sub-category. Dealing with difficulties well and being able to think things through are other examples of statements coded as problem-solving skills.

Having good communication skills was mentioned almost as frequently as problem solving. This dimension included being articulate and persuasive and having the capacity to relate well with students, in particular being able to motivate them and being able to understand them.

Other capacities identified by interviewees less frequently included being organized, being visionary, having self-knowledge, being a global thinker, being focused, being able to set limits on self and being efficient.

Perceived outcomes of teacher leadership

The outcomes perceived to be associated with leadership provide important clues about the basis for leader attributions under circumstances in which leadership is experienced long enough to draw inferences from leader effects on the organization. Outcomes of leadership identified by 'followers' tell us something about the needs people have that they hope leadership can meet.

Most frequently mentioned among different types of outcomes was gaining the respect of staff and students. Next most frequently identified as a leadership outcome was that activities involving the leader were invariably, implemented well ('it went off very well', or 'things always work out in the end', or 'he and [T] have taken the track team to extreme heights'). The fact that staff look to a person for leadership was also a frequently mentioned outcome of leadership. Said one teacher, 'I think he's someone they would turn to if they were looking for avenues to proceed'. Also mentioned frequently as leadership outcomes were enhancing staff comfort level, and contributing to the culture of the school.

An additional set of outcomes was mentioned less often in the interviews. That people 'listen' to the leader was mentioned: 'when she speaks up, people listen.' A desire to emulate the leader was also mentioned: 'You're just saying, "hey, if I could be like that".' Having a good effect on students and meeting high expectations are other types of outcomes mentioned.

Summary

Two purposes were served by this chapter. One purpose was to clarify the relationship between the formal leadership offered by those in school administrative positions and the leadership exercised by teachers. Evidence from a large-scale survey indicated that both principals and teachers had a significant influence on most aspects of the school organization but some aspects were typically influenced more by those in one role rather than another. The independent influence of teacher leaders was strongest (and stronger than the principals' influence) with respect to school improvement planning, and school structure and organization. Principal leadership exercised its strongest independent influence on school improvement planning and school structure and organization, as well as on school mission and school culture. Furthermore, teachers were more likely to associate their principals than their teacher-leader colleagues with effective management and transformational leadership.

The second purpose for the chapter was to clarify the nature of leadership exercised by those teachers perceived to be leaders by their teaching colleagues. Composite teacher leaders are strongly committed to their schools, the profession and the welfare of students. They have a positive orientation to their work, a sense of humour, and are warm, dependable and self-effacing. Teacher leaders are open and honest with their colleagues and students, and have well honed interpersonal and communication skills. In addition, they possess the technical and organizational skills required for programme improvement and use them in concert with a broad knowledge base about education policy, subject matter, the local community and the school's students. Armed with a realistic sense of what is possible, these people actively participate in the administrative and leadership work of the school. They are viewed as supportive of others' work and model those practices valued by the school.

Although less evidently than among principals, teacher leaders' practices were perceived to reflect many aspects of transformational school leadership. Most often mentioned were practices encompassed by the dimension of transformational leadership labelled 'individualized support', a set of practices also included in many other leadership models (for example, situational leadership; see Fernandez and Vecchio 1997). In addition, teacher leaders provided their colleagues with 'intellectual stimulation', 'modelled best practices', and helped 'develop structures to foster participation in school decisions'. Some teachers noted that their leader colleagues were visionary, a dimension of most models of transformational leadership. They also fostered extra effort on their part, a key goal of transformational leadership.

Perceptions of teacher leadership seem to be influenced primarily by the same variables that we found to be the most powerful influences on teachers' perceptions of principals' transformational leadership. What was of most influence was the opportunity to work with the leader on projects of significance to the school and to see evidence of the value of this work to the school. Evidence from the study, described in this chapter also suggests that colleagues' traits are important in forming teachers' perceptions of their leadership.

Implications for developing teacher leadership

In this concluding section of the chapter, we consider what those in administrative leader roles might do to further develop teacher leadership in their schools. Our primary focus is on informal teacher leadership, although much of what we suggest is also appropriate for the development of those assuming such formal teacher-leader roles as department head and lead teacher.

Just enough clarification of roles (and no more)

One of the conditions inhibiting the development and exercise of teacher leadership was lack of role definition (Smylie and Denny 1990). While this condition applies most obviously to formal teacher-leader roles, informal or temporary leadership roles (chairing a taskforce or leading a curriculum development committee, for example) may also be inhibited by this condition. So the implication for formal school leaders, in relation to both types of roles, is to work towards a level of clarity about duties and responsibilities that is suitable for the person assuming the role. Significant variation among teacher leaders in how much role definition is enough ought to be expected, however. Among other things, this variation is a product of teachers' earlier school leadership experiences, tolerances for ambiguity, professional goals and perceptions of colleagues' expectations. So clarifying the role is something that should be done in collaboration with the person assuming the role, in most cases.

In no case, however, should the role definition be so specific as to constrain the exercise of discretion in the role. Although teachers with little experience, for example, may benefit from relatively high degrees of clarity about their leadership duties and responsibilities at the outset, part of their development will entail the assumption of increased autonomy and discretion, and the provision of less external role specification. In a quite fundamental way, a 'well-defined leadership role' is an oxymoron.

Gaining a realistic perspective on time

Also identified as a condition inhibiting the development and exercise of teacher leadership, in our summary of the teacher leadership literature, were inadequate overall amounts of time allocated to teacher leadership functions (Wasley 1991), and the use, for teacher leadership, of time that teachers felt they should be devoting to their students (Smylie and Denny 1990). The implications of this obstacle to developing teacher leaders are complex. Clearly it is important that formal school leaders be realistic about the time required for the job and attempt to allocate sufficient amounts. But it is probably just as important to help those new to leadership roles to appreciate the demands of these roles, and the inevitable infringement on what they may consider to be personal time.

It is probably also important to help teacher leaders learn how to manage their time outside the classroom, including limiting the number of leadership initiatives in which they become involved. Realistically, one significant leadership initiative at a time, in addition to a substantial teaching load, will place sufficient demands on a teacher's time to preclude comfortably assuming other initiatives. Formal school leaders should act as consultants to teachers as they work out a realistic leadership load for themselves, stressing the importance of having time to reflect on and learn from each of their leadership initiatives.

Creating training opportunities out of leadership tasks

Reflection about on-the-job leadership experiences is one of the most powerful strategies for overcoming lack of training for teacher leaders. Those in formal school-leaders' roles can assist in the training of teacher leaders most directly by providing such leadership opportunities. Guided reflection may develop into more intensive coaching and mentoring relationships with teacher leaders, relationships that are themselves powerful tools for leadership development (Hart 1993).

Providing support for challenging leadership assignments

Each of these leadership development strategies begins to address another training-related obstacle identified in the literature concerning teacher leadership: assigning teacher leaders responsibilities outside their area of expertise (Little 1995). Without significant support, such assignments can have a debilitating effect on teacher leaders, undermining their sense of efficacy, reducing the likelihood of gaining satisfaction from their leadership experiences and eroding their motivation to further develop their leadership capacities. But it is precisely the effort required to meet the challenges of new leadership assignments that produces the greatest growth in leadership capacities. The implication is that the responsibilities of teacher leaders should not be restricted to challenges they have already mastered; they should be provided with novel leadership challenges, with support. Those in formal school-leader roles are often in the best position to provide such support.

Building a culture of collaboration

A frequently identified obstacle to the development of teacher leadership is the isolated professional culture common in schools, along with associated norms of egalitarianism, privacy, politeness and contrived collegiality (Sirotnik 1994; Griffin 1995). This means fewer opportunities for teachers to provide leadership to their colleagues, and little motivation for teachers to further develop their own leadership capacities. Such cultures present a significant challenge to formal school leaders in making the case with their staffs that teacher leadership would be a valuable addition to the school and ought to be further developed.

Truly collaborative cultures, in contrast, encourage the exchange of ideas and endorse mutual problem solving, thereby providing rich opportunities for the exercise of teacher leadership, and suitable motivation for potential teacher leaders to develop their capacities. Formal school leaders appear to be well positioned to exercise influence on the school's culture, at least from the perspective of teachers.

Research-based guidance about how to do this (for example Firestone and Wilson 1985; Rosenholtz 1989; Deal and Peterson 1990; Leithwood and Jantzi 1990) identifies at least five useful strategies:

1 Strengthen the typically 'weak' culture of the school. This is a culture in which there is little agreement with, or adherence to, common professional norms, values, beliefs and assumptions. Formal school leaders are in the best position to facilitate a sense of shared mission or purpose.

2 Use 'bureaucratic mechanisms'. For example, embed norms of sharing and mutual problem solving in the criteria used for teacher selection and evaluation procedures, and allocate teacher planning time to provide opportunities for mutual problem solving.

3 Create staff development opportunities that acknowledge what can be learned from one's immediate colleagues by engaging members of the school staff in the design and conduct of some of that staff development.

4 Use the many direct formal and informal communication opportunities available to formal school leaders to reinforce key cultural norms, values and expectations. This means that formal school leaders should talk a great deal to staff about the virtues of collaborative work and model such work in their approach to school administration.

5 Use symbols and rituals to support collaborative cultural values; for example by recognizing at staff meetings the collaborative work of groups of teachers and the positive outcomes of that work, and by providing positive feedback to individual teachers, thereby increasing their sense of professional self-efficacy, and along with it, their inclination to share their work with other teachers.

Selecting teachers who already have leadership qualities that are hard to develop

Some of the qualities emerging from the research data are much easier to develop than others. As a general rule, it is safe to assume a higher probability of developing the practices and capacities identified by our interviewees, than the traits. And while all three categories of leadership attributes are important, our study suggests that teachers' perceptions of the leadership provided by their teacher colleagues is very strongly influenced by these traits.

This has important implications for expanding the teacher leadership available within a school. When formal school leaders are able to participate in determining the choice of people for teacher-leader roles, our study recommends a preference for teachers who already display the traits associated with teacher leaders from among those who display comparable levels of development with respect to practices and capacities.

References

Bascia, N. (1997) Invisible leadership: teachers' union activity in schools, *Alberta Journal of Educational Research*, XLIII(2/3): 69–85.

Conley, D.T. (1993) *Roadmap to Restructuring: Policies, Practices and the Emerging Visions of Schooling*, University of Oregon, Eugene: ERIC Clearinghouse of Educational Management.

Cooper, M. (1988) Whose culture is it anyway?, in A Lieberman (ed.) *Building a Professional Culture in Schools*. New York: Basic Book.

Deal, T. and Peterson, K. (1990) *The Principal's Role in Shaping School Culture*. Washington, DC: US Department of Education, Office of Educational Research and Improvement.

Duke, D. and Leithwood, K. (1994) *Functions of School Leadership: A Review*, technical report prepared for the Connecticut State Board of Education, Leadership Standards Project.

Duke, D., Showers, B. and Imber, M. (1980) Teachers and shared decision making: the costs and benefits of involvement, *Educational Administration Quarterly*, 16: 93–106.

Fernandez, C.F. and Vecchio, R.P. (1997) Situational leadership theory revisited: a test of an across-jobs perspective, *The Leadership Quarterly,* 8(1): 67–84.

Firestone, W. and Wilson, B.L. (1985) Using bureaucratic and cultural linkages to improve instruction: the principal's contribution, *Educational Administration Quarterly*, 21(2): 7–30.

Fullan, M. (1993) *Change Forces: Probing the Depths of Educational Reform*. London: Falmer Press.

Fullan, M. and Hargreaves, A. (1991) *What's Worth Fighting For? Working Together for Your School*. Toronto: Ontario Public School Teachers Federation.

Griffin, G. (1995) Influences of shared decision making on school and classroom activity: conversations with five teachers, *The Elementary School Journal*, 96(1): 29–45.

Hallinger, P. and Heck, R. (1996) Reassessing the principal's role in school effectiveness: a review of empirical research 1980–1995, *Educational Administration Quarterly*, 32(1): 5–44.

Hannay, L.M. and Denby, M. (1994) Secondary school change: the role of department heads. Paper presented to the Annual Meeting of the American Educational Research Association, New Orleans, LA, 4–8 April.

Hart, A.W. (1993) Reflection: an instructional strategy in educational administration, *Educational Administration Quarterly*, 29(3): 339–63.

Jantzi, D. and Leithwood, K. (1996) Toward an explanation of teachers' perceptions of transformational school leadership, *Educational Administration Quarterly*, 32(4): 312–538.

Kouze, J. and Posner, B. (1996) Seven lessons for leading the voyage to the future, in E. Hesselbein, M., Goldsmith and R. Beckhard (eds.) *The Leader of the Future*. San Francisco, CA: Jossey-Bass.

Leithwood, K. and Aitken, R. (1995) *Making Schools Smarter: a System for Monitoring School and District Progress*. Thousand Oaks, CA: Corwin Press.

Leithwood, K. and Jantzi, D. (1990) Transformational leadership: how principals can help reform school cultures, *School Effectiveness and School Improvement*, 1(4): 249–80.

Leithwood, K. and Jantzi, D. (1997) Explaining variation in teachers' perceptions of principals' leadership: a replication, *Journal of Educational Administration,* 35(4): 312–31.

Leithwood, K., Begley, P. and Cousins, B. (1992) *Developing Expert Leadership for Future Schools*. London: Falmer Press.

Leithwood, K., Jantzi, D., Steinbach, R. and Ryan, S. (1997) Distributed leadership in secondary schools. Paper presented to the Annual Meeting of the American Educational Research Association, Chicago, March.

Lieberman, A., Saxl, E.R. and Miles, M.B. (1988) Teacher leadership: ideology and practice, in A. Lieberman (ed.) *Building a Professional Culture in Schools*. New York: Basic Books.

Little, J.W. (1995) Contested ground: the basis of teacher leadership in two restructuring high schools, *The Elementary School Journal*, 96(1): 47–63.

Lord, R.G. and Maher, K.J. (1993) *Leadership and Information Processing*. London: Routledge.

Reavis, C. and Griffith, H. (1993) *Restructuring Schools: Theory and Practice*. Lancaster, PA: Technomic Publishing Co.

Rosenholtz, S. (1989) *Teachers' Workplace*. New York: Longman.

Sirotnik, K. (1994) Curriculum: overview and framework, in M.J. O'Hair and S. Odell (eds.) *Educating Teachers for Leadership and Change*. Thousand Oaks, CA: Corwin Press.

Sirotnik, K. and Kimball, K. (1996) Preparing educators for leadership: in praise of experience, *Journal of School Leadership*, 6(2): 180–201.

Taylor, D.L. and Bogotch, I.E. (1994) School level effects of teachers' participation in decision making, *Educational Evaluation and Policy Analysis,* 16(3): 302–19.

Whitaker, T. (1995) Informal teacher leadership: the key to successful change in the middle school, *NASSP Bulletin*, January: 76–81.

White, P. (1992) Teacher empowerment under 'ideal' school-site autonomy. *Evaluation and Policy Analysis*, 14(1): 69–84.

14

Critical Studies on Men, Masculinities and Management

David L. Collinson and Jeff Hearn

In the study of work, organizations and management the critical analysis of men and masculinities is fundamentally important. Yet an examination of the literature reveals the recurring paradox that men are often an 'absent-presence' in organizational studies. The categories of men and masculinity are frequently central to analyses, yet they remain taken for granted, hidden and unexamined. Men are talked about but rarely the focus of interrogation rendered simultaneously explicit and implicit. Many scholars have seemed extraordinarily unaware of the men in organizations about whom they write. The study of management is a case in point. Most managers in most organizations in most countries are men (Collinson and Hearn, 1996). Yet the conditions, processes and consequences of men's historical and contemporary domination of management have received little scrutiny. There has been a strange silence, reflecting a taken for granted association, even conflation, of men with organizational power, authority and prestige. This association persists in both 'theory' and practice, with consequences for organizations, employees and managers. Although not all managers are men, the male domination, particularly of senior levels within management, tends to persist across different societies. The development of transnational organizations, communication and world financial systems could well reinforce the globalized nature of these male-dominated networks and processes.

The association of men and managements can be seen in the biographies and autobiographies of famous twentieth-century entrepreneurial male managers/owners, such as Ford (Ford, 1923; Sward, 1948), Iacocca (Iacocca, 1984), Geneen (Geneen, 1985), Hughes (Drosnin, 1987) and Maxwell (Davies, 1992). These accounts reveal evangelical, personal and lifelong pre-

---

Source: Davidson, M.J. and Burke, R.J. (eds.) (2000) *Women in Management: Current Research Issues*. London: Sage. Edited Version.

occupations with military-like efficiency, ruthless business practices based on bullying and coercion and autocratic control based on the humiliation of subordinates. Equally, they implicitly disclose the masculine assumptions and practices that frequently predominate in management. In the 1980s particularly aggressive forms of masculinity increasingly seemed to characterize managerial discursive practices. Highly autocratic managerial styles were widely celebrated as the primary means of generating corporate success. Journalistic profiles of male executives consistently emphasized their 'heroic' qualities of struggle and battle, a willingness to be ruthless and brutal, and an aggressive, rugged individualism (Neale, 1995). Managers and senior executives were often depicted and portrayed themselves as 'hard men', virile, swashbuckling and flamboyant entrepreneurs who had reasserted their managerial prerogative (Denham, 1991). Management came to be defined in terms of the ability to control.

In the 1990s gendered assumptions could still be discerned in managerial initiatives such as total quality management and business process re-engineering. The language of management was frequently gendered, for example, both in terms of its highly (hetero)sexualized talk about 'penetrating markets' and in the extensive use of sporting metaphors in rationalizing managerial decisions and practices (Cockburn, 1991). Equally, managerial presentational styles which emphasize 'professional', 'competent' and 'rational' self-images infused with an air of total confidence, detachment and control frequently reveal masculine assumptions, particularly when presenters use sexist jokes as 'ice-breakers' (Cockburn, 1991). Participations in male-dominated sports can still significantly shape managerial, social and business interactions and career progress within and between organizations, networks, labour markets and professional alliances (Collinson *et al.*, 1990; Kanter, 1997/1993).

Feminist writers have demonstrated how management often excludes women, especially those who are black and/or from ethnic minorities (Bell and Nkomo, 1992; Ibarra, 1995). This chapter attends to the other side, that is taken for granted in malestream discourses and is theorized implicitly and sometimes explicitly in feminist discourses: the problem of men, masculinities and managements. Its purpose is to examine critically the conditions, processes and consequences of men's persistent dominance of management. Why, when we 'think manager' do we still tend to 'think male'? (Schein, 1976). The first section below briefly illustrates how much of the literature on management has neglected issues of gender, men and masculinity. The main argument of the chapter is then developed through a review of studies that have begun to explore and analyse the complex gendered processes of power that characterize contemporary management. This review demonstrates how a more integrated analysis of gender, men and managements can facilitate a rereading of traditional issues in management. It suggests that a re-examination of themes such as power, structure and decision-making can produce challenging new insights, understandings and perspectives.

 ## A Gendered Management

The emergency of management as the central organizational activity of twentieth-century corporations is reflected in the burgeoning literature that explores the function's assumptions, responsibilities and practices (for example Drucker, 1979; Stewart, 1986; Reed, 1989; Grint, 1995). Despite – possibly even because of – the frequently pervasive association between men, power and authority in organizations, the literature on management has consistently failed to question its gendered nature. Whether adopting prescriptive, descriptive or critical perspectives, studies typically subscribe to images of middle and senior management that are imbued with particular notions of masculinity. This tendency can be seen in the development of management theory, from scientific management to human relations, systems and contingency theories, as well as population ecology and institutional perspectives. In conventional organizational psychology, where the major contribution to the prescriptive study of leadership has emerged, leadership is frequently assumed to be synonymous with men (Hearn and Parkin, 1988). For example, Bennis' (1989) prescriptions on how to 'become a leader' exclude women and fail to problematize men and masculinity in relation to leadership.

The influential work of Mintzberg (1973, 1975, 1983, 1989) challenges the prevailing highly rational and 'scientific' view of management. Mintzberg examines the political alliances and strategies played out by managers in their search for power, influence and organizational security. In many ways, such descriptions of managerial work are similar to those of Dalton's (1959) classic study that graphically examined the hidden agendas of intra-managerial collusion and conflict. While both authors may be writing primarily (or even exclusively) about men, they fail to analyse men and masculinities as socially produced, reproduced and indeed changeable. Minzberg uses 'manager' and 'he' interchangeably and even when he critiques the 'Great Man' theory for revealing 'almost nothing about managerial work' (1973: 12), he remains silent about its inherently gendered imagery and assumptions. He does not seem to recognize that within, between and across managerial and organizational hierarchies, masculine discourses and practices are often crucial basis for alliances, divisions and conflicts between men in senior positions.

More cortical studies of management examine the function's overriding concern with the control of labour and extraction of production and profit (Braverman, 1974; Edwards, 1979). They seek to make explicit and then to question management's extensive power and control (Alvesson and Willmott,

1996). Increasingly, critical writers have also contextualized managerial power and discretion within broader social, economic and political conditions (Willmott, 1987; Linstead *et al.*, 1996) and have examined the diversity, differences and contradictions that can characterize managerial hierarchies (Hyman, 1987; Jermier *et al.*, 1994). They show how managers may also be highly sensitized to career advancement in ways that can produce tension and conflict as managers seek to differentiate and elevate themselves and their departments (Watson, 1994). Outlining the patronage, intrigues and conspiracies characterizing relations within management, Jackail (1988) describes how managers seek to survive by 'currying favour' with senior managers and 'managing reputation' with colleagues. Yet even these more critical analyses of management rarely attend to the continued predominance of men in managerial positions, the relatively limited presence of women and the processes, networks and assumptions through which the latter are intentionally and unintentionally excluded and/or subordinated.

To summarize, whether we refer to the 'ideal' prescriptive models of management of early academic writers, descriptive accounts of managerial work or even more critical analyses, the masculine imagery of management and managers seems to be taken for granted, neglected, and thereby reproduced and reinforced. Having highlighted this tendency to ignore gender completely in the literature on management we wish to emphasize that our approach is not intended to be an extension of the 'women in management' literature (for example Helgesen, 1990; Rosener, 1990; Fagenson, 1993). Such analyses have also tended to neglect a critical examination of the hierarchical and gendered power of either men as managers or managers as men. Their recurrent emphasis upon women's different ways of managing and leading and the need to develop women's skills to fit into contemporary managerial hierarchies reflects a focus primarily upon women that is in danger of blaming the victim and or essentialism. Research has found few consistent differences between female and male managers in terms of managerial behaviours, commitment, decision style, stress or subordinates' responses (Donnell and Hall, 1980; Boulgarides, 1984). We subscribe to a much more critical approach to gender relations, as the following section outlines.

Gender, Feminism and Critical Studies on Men

Feminist studies constitute the major influence in developing the explicit analysis of gender in organizations. Some feminist writers (Cockburn, 1983; Walby, 1986) focus upon patriarchy as a separate system of men's control over women. They reveal how organized groups of male workers have historically opposed the entry of cheaper female labour by demanding the 'breadwinner wage' and by controlling both the provision of training and gendered definitions of skill (Phillips and Taylor, 1980). Other feminist analyses combine a focus on structure with that of agency, contradiction and difference (for example Hollway, 1984; Ferguson, 1984; Pringle, 1989). Examining the contradictions of male power and control, as well as highlighting female agency and resistance, such studies criticize theories of patriarchy for treating 'men' and 'women' as unified groups and undifferentiated categories. For Connell (1987), such 'categorical' theories about patriarchy neglect differences and relations that can shift over time and place. Post-structuralist feminism has increasingly recognized men's and women's diverse, fragmented and contradictory lives in and around organizations. Attention has focused on gendered subjectivities and their ambiguous, fragmented, discontinuous and multiple character within asymmetrical relations (Henriques *et al.*, 1984; Kondo, 1990).

Informed by the growing interest in gendered power, subjectivity and agency, critical studies on men highlight not only male power, but also the material and symbolic differences through which that power is reproduced (Brittan, 1989). While both men and masculinities are dominantly categories of power and social value, they are by no means homogeneous, unified or fixed categories but diverse, differentiated and shifting (Hearn, 1987, 1992b; Hearn and Morgan, 1990; Connell, 1995). Hence the use of the term 'masculinities', rather than just 'masculinity' (Carrigan *et al.*, 1985). Such studies also examine relations between men themselves as well as between women and men (Collinson, 1992; Morgan, 1992). Likely to vary in specific situations, in different historical times, particular masculinities may also be internally contradictory, in tension and differentiated by, for example, age; class; ethnicity; religion; sexuality; nationality; paternal/marital kinship status; occupation and size (Hearn and Collinson, 1994). Such debates have in turn led to critiques concerning the increasing diversity of what is meant by 'masculinity', the imprecise nature of some usages, and the need to focus on 'men's practices', material and discursive (McMahon, 1993; Hearn, 1996).

While many of the foregoing gender analyses have explored women's and indeed men's experience of subordination, and of being managed, comparatively less attention has been paid to the gendered conditions, processes and consequences of those who exercise considerable hierarchical power in organizations. Some feminist writers have examined the gendered character of the managerial function from the perspective and experience of women managers (e.g. Davidson and Cooper, 1983; Sheppard, 1989; Martin, 1990; Calás and Smircich, 1993; Marshall, 1995; Sinclair, 1995; Wajcman, 1998). Yet little attention has been paid to men in management. This is particularly surprising in the case of critical studies on men given the central focus in these studies on the way that 'hegemonic masculinities' (for example white, heterosexual, middle class) may dominate other masculinities (for example black, gay, working class). From the perspective of gender, hierarchy and class, men in management, especially those in accounting, engineering and strategic functions, often most closely represent 'hegemonic masculinity/ties' in the workplace. Accordingly, men's organizational dominance both 'as managers' and 'as men' requires further analysis.

Men, Masculinities and Management

Most of the work examined in the two previous sections has not explicitly considered the interrelations of gender, men and managements. This section discusses a growing number of studies attempting to 'break the silence' on men and management. It recognizes the seminal importance of Kanter's (1977/1993) groundbreaking work – one of the first studies explicitly to focus on the interconnections between men as managers and managers as men. The following discussion considers how other accounts of the connections between management, men and masculinities can shed new light on traditional themes in management writing and managerial practice. In what follows, we consider three 'classic' and closely interrelated issues in management: power, structure and discussion-making.

Power

In examining how the gendered nature of management is reproduced, Kanter describes the way that men managers can appoint in their own image and thereby exclude women. She then uses the term 'homosocial reproduction' (1977: 48) to characterize the processes by which certain men managers are selected according to their ability to display appropriate social credentials. In the former case, Kanter suggest that men are selected for managerial positions because they are perceived to be more reliable, committed and predictable, free from conflicting loyalties between home and work. In the latter case, she argues that the extensive pressures on managers to conform to corporate expectations and demands can exclude not only women, but also many men. The typical profile of managers, she argues, is 'invariably white and male, with a certain shiny, clean-cut look' (1977; 42). While Kanter's study usefully describes how elitist practices can characterize management, it is less valuable in analysing the gendered nature of these persistent interrelations and networks (see also Pringle, 1989; Witz and Savage, 1992). Kanter contends that what appear to be differences between men and women in organizations are related not to gender, but to work position and the structure of opportunity. In seeking to deny difference, she fails to recognize how organizational power relations are frequently heavily gendered. Her concern to separate 'sex' from 'power' (1977: 202), inevitably neglects the way that particular masculinities may help to reproduce and legitimize managerial power and authority (see also Collinson and Hearn, 1995).

Managerial power is both hierarchical and gendered. Typically, it is in the managerial function that organizational power formally (and often informally) resides. In most organizations, managerial prerogative over key decisions remains the taken-for-granted norm. Managerial prerogative can be seen as part of a highly masculine discourse. Indeed managerial masculinities are also hegemonic within organizations in the sense that those in senior positions enjoy comparatively high salaries and ancillary remuneration packages and other material and symbolic benefits (Pahl, 1995).

There are also innumerable ways in which the authority and status of managers can signify 'men' and indeed vice versa, just as there are many signs that can simultaneously signify the power of both 'manager' and 'men'. These cultural processes of signification include the company car, offices, the use or control of computers and the choice of clothing. Men's continued domination of senior positions results in many interconnections between particular masculinities and managerial practices. Specific managerial masculinities, such as paternalism or autocratic control methods, may not only reinforce the power of those men concerned, but also confirm the 'rights' of management and men to manage (Collinson and Hearn, 1994, 1996b; Hearn and Collinson, 1998).

In organizations where the manager is also the owner, power relations can be especially asymmetrical and gendered (Reed, 1996). Studies of entrepreneurialism also reveal the interdependence of organizational power, gender and the family. Mulholland (1996) found that, while men consistently claimed all of the credit for their business success, in practice their capital accumulation was highly dependent on the hidden household (and workplace) services provided by wives/women. Other studies report similar dynamics where men's managerial careers and identities are constructed through the invisible support of women as secretaries and wives (e.g. Finch, 1983; Grey, 1994).

In elaborating the connection between gendered power and subjectivity in management, Roper (1991,1994) describes how British men managers in the postwar era frequently identified strongly with machinery and products. Undervaluing the role of labour in the manufacture of products, male managers engaged in a kind of fetishizing of the masculine self through the idolization of products. These managers were persistently concerned to display a masculine air of confidence and control that concealed anxiety and self-doubt. Kerfoot and Knights (1996) examined the contemporary and privileged form of masculine identity associated with dominant management practice – abstract, rational, highly instrumental, controlling of its object, future-orientated, strategic and, above all, masculine and wholly disembodied. These masculine managerial subjectivities are typically expressed in aggressive and competitive practices concerned to master and dominate. Highlighting the self-defeating nature of the search for masculine and managerial identity in these discourses of control, Kerfoot and Knights also show how the desire for a secure and stable sense of self tends to reproduce rather than eliminate anxiety and insecurity.

Indeed man's asymmetrical control and authority as managers is more contradictory, precarious and heterogeneous than often it at first appears. For example, in the 1990s the security of gendered power relations and masculine identities was threatened by considerable social change. Equal opportunity initiatives, the need to compete with women for particular jobs, career bottlenecks and redundancies may all have constituted significant challenges to men managers' conventional gender identities. Widespread organizational downsizing, short-term contracts and work intensification seem to have reinforced the anxiety and insecurity of middle-range men managers in particular, who had to recognize that their working lives were constantly being evaluated and assessed. One central criterion of these evaluation practices is the masculinist concern with personal power and the ability to control others and self. Managers are increasingly assessed according to their ability to control their lives. Consequently men managers have frequently 'distanced' themselves from children and family responsibilities. Within organizations, such 'distancing' strategies are often interpreted in a positive light as evidence both of commitment to the company and of individual ability to control 'private life' (Collinson and Hearn, 1994). Accordingly, it is important to recognize that in the changing organizations of the 1990s, managers were self-evidently objects as well as subjects of the organization. These patterns that restructured gendered power relations require sophisticated analyses that incorporate the contradictory and ambiguous practices through which are reproduced the authority and status of men managers.

Organizational structure

Throughout the twentieth century organizational structures and managerial practices had been heavily influenced by the principles of scientific management and bureaucracy. Kanter (1977) argued that the emphasis in scientific management on rationality and efficiency is infused with an irreducible 'masculine ethic'. This assumes that only men hold the requisite qualities of the 'new rational manager': a tough-minded approach to problems, analytical abilities to abstract and plan, a capacity to subordinate personal concerns in order to accomplish the task and a cognitive superiority in problem-solving. Later contributions developed Kanter's interest in organizational structure by adding an analysis that is more sensitive to the connections between men, masculinities and managements. Rereading her own earlier work (Hollway,

1991) through the lens of competing masculinities, Hollway (1996) analyses the transition from the disciplining of bodies (scientific management) to self-regulation (human relations) in terms of diverse masculinities. Hollway pursues her approach through the application of psychoanalytic theory located within a social analysis of gendered power relations, both between women and men, and between men. Highlighting the reproduction of 'defensive masculinities', Hollway (1996: 40) outlines a variety of forms of splitting, desire for control and mastery over the other. Hearn (1992b) has also addressed the gendered conditions and consequences of management's establishment in the late nineteenth and early twentieth centuries.

Morgan(1996) critically reflects on the modern history of bureaucracy. Rereading classic sociological contributions, he identifies some of the concealed themes around gender that lie within these apparently genderless texts that subsequently influenced management theory and practice. Morgan shows how men have been and are more likely to carry out managerial functions within bureaucracies, while bureaucracies were, and are, major sites for the development and elaboration of modern masculinities. In marked contrast with Weberian bureaucratic models of impersonal relations, Roper (1996) suggests that organizations and managements are locales of emotion managed by men. He explores relations between men, not simply in terms of power, authority or competition, but specifically in terms of homosocial desire. Examining management as a complex series of processes that involve and invoke seduction and succession between men, his analysis suggests that these power relations may entail flows of power from the less formally powerful to the more formal, as well as vice versa. Roper argues that the relations between men in management can consist of circuits of desire.

The gendered nature of control and scientific management, and rationality and bureaucracy has also been examined by Burris (1996). Concentrating on the interrelation of technocracy, patriarchy and management and its specific implications for men and masculinities, she reviews the specific types of and shifts in patriarchy and their association with different forms of organizational control. In particular, she examines technocratic patriarchy – a new type of managerial practice that is highly gendered. Its key features include polarization of both occupational status and gender segregation; valuing of expertise as authority; 'adhocracy', informality; and technocratic patriarchal ideology. These developments, she contends, shape the gender identity of managers and the gendering of others. Increasingly, organizational structures have to be understood as part of global economic processes (Lehman, 1996). Connell (1998) has spelt out the form of transnational business masculinity. Woodward (1996) has examined 'rationality', in the context of the European Union administration, designed on the 'rational' principles of bureaucratic practice in order to be above national and party loyalties. Using a framework which emphasizes the interconnections of gender, organizations, systems, culture and power, Woodward has examined international organizations as gendered bureaucracies in which the 'male' norm is dominant and masculine practices of resistance to female leadership persist.

In the light of changing forms and practices of management worldwide, interrelations of men, masculinities and management in contemporary organizations are likely to be all the more important. On the one hand, these tendencies across private and public sectors for managerial work to be intensified, measured, evaluated and even delayered problematizes the view that management constitutes the most clear-cut form of hegemonic masculinity. On the other hand, working long hours in post-delayering cultures can become a test of manhood, with some men managers enjoying 'the buzz' of staying late at the office. Consequently management may be re-colonized as an inherently masculine function (Collinson and Collinson, 1997). Relatedly, it is possible that junior-level managerial positions, confined to national-level concerns, will continue to be feminized, downgraded and deskilled, while men appropriate the more powerful, prestigious and strategic globalized functions of transnational corporations (Calás and Smircich, 1993). The result will be the reinforcement of men's managerial hegemony at senior levels.

Decision-making

Yancey-Martin (1996) has demonstrated how managers' evaluations of employees can be shaped by particular masculinities. She identifies three evaluational frames which link masculinism and patriarchal masculinities: 'differing potential' (of men and women); 'normative legitimacy' (in rights to hierarchical power); and 'performance' (valuing men's and women's contributions and failures). She describes typical styles of gendered interactions: 'promotion of men', 'requests for paternalistic aid', 'open criticism of women, not men', and 'ganging up on a woman'. By studying managerial decision-making, she reveals the cultural and structural embeddedness of gender in organizations, the importance of power as a constitutive aspect of gender relations in organizations, and the proactive gendering of individuals through the discursive, relational and material dynamics and arrangements of organizations. Similarly, in our own work we have explored the ways that (men) managers can routinely discriminate against women in recruitment and promotion practices whilst privileging male candidates (Collinson et al., 1990; Hearn and Collinson, 1998). We have also examined how men managers can mismanage cases of sexuality and sexual harassment as a result of flawed decision-making shaped by deep-seated misconceptions about gender (Collinson and Collinson, 1989, 1992, 1996).

The potentially negative and indeed disastrous impact of hegemonic masculinities on key managerial decisions has been graphically documented in relation to the *Challenger* space shuttle explosion (Messerschmidet, 1996;

Maier and Messerschmidet, 1998). This research reveals that the flawed decision-making leading up to the disaster took a specifically gendered form via an all-male management team because risk-taking was embedded in their managerial masculinity.

Thus conventional managerial decision-making can be shaped by multiple masculine subjectivities that, in turn, can result in intensified competition, hostility between employees, increased anxiety and, fundamentally, flawed decision-making. However these perspectives on the socially constructed and gendered nature of men managers and men's management also raise the possibility of anti-oppressive and even pro-feminist management by men (Hearn, 1989, 1992a, 1994).

Conclusion

This chapter has attempted to demonstrate the growing importance to organizational analysis of critical perspectives on men, masculinities and managements. It has shown how the literature in this area enables us to re-examine traditional issues relevant to the study of management, such as power, structure and decision-making. In turn studies make general questions for management. For example, could the continued dominance of management by men and masculinities and the exclusion of alternative views actually constitute crucial barriers to 'effective', 'efficient' and 'rational' decision making and organizational practices? Will women managers challenge or reproduce the masculine hegemony of management? Conversely, how is men's power in management maintained by the gendered structuring of largely unpaid domestic work and childcare? Less obviously, what are the implications for both women and men of the tendency for increasing organizational power in management to be associated with growing encroachments of business into personal and domestic time? These studies also raise important issues about the impact of gender on the historical emergence of particular managerial functions (marketing, production, sales, etc.) and in relation to the different (gendered) meanings and values associated with managements in and across cultures and societies. There is also a need to explore the possible connections between workplace bullying, sexual harassment and violence and managerial masculinities. In sum, studies of men, masculinities and managements have the potential to develop new forms of analysis of power in management organizations.

All of these issues suggest major changes in the theorizing of management. Management theory itself until recently has remained very much a domain of men. These arguments raise important questions: what perceptions and priorities are emphasized and neglected by men management educators?

Why do men as management and organization theorists find so many 'good reasons' for avoiding these issues? Self-reflexive questions such as these speak to the very heart of management theory and practice as it has been constructed historically. Not least, they critically examine what counts as 'theory', and how 'theory' is developed, defined, written, refereed, rejected or acclaimed, published and circulated. The practice of critical self-reflexivity is an important precondition for the development of management theorizing. There is a need for explicit, critical, feminist/pro-feminist and self-reflexivity studies on the enduring dominance and interrelations of men, masculinities and managements. How is it that the 'great' and 'classic' theories of management consistently managed to avoid these obvious questions?

References

Alvesson, M. and Willmott, H. (1996) *Making Sense of Management*, Sage, London.

Bell, E.L. and Nkomo, S.M. (1992) 'Re-visioning women managers' lives', in A. Mills and P. Tancred-Sheriff (eds.), *Gendering Organizational Theory*, Sage, Newbury Park, CA, pp. 235–47.

Bennis, W. (1989) *On Becoming a Leader*, Warren Bennis, Wilmington, MA.

Boulgarides, J.D. (1984) 'A comparison of male and female business managers', *Leadership and Organisation Development Journal*, 5(5): 27–31.

Braverman, H. (1974) *Labour and Monopoly Capital*, Monthly Review Press, New York.

Brittan, A. (1989) *Masculinity and Power*, Basil Blackwell, Oxford.

Burris, B. (196) 'Technocracy, patriarchy and management', in D.L. Collinson and J. Hearn (eds.), *Men as Managers, Managers as Men*, Sage, London, pp. 61–77.

Calás, M. and Smircich, L. (1993) 'Dangerous liaisons: the "feminine-in-management" meets "globalization"', *Business Horizons*, March–April: 73–83.

Carrigan, T., Connell, R.W. and Lee, J. (1985) 'Toward a new sociology of masculinity', *Theory and Society*, 14(5): 551–604.

Cockburn, C. (1983) *Brothers*, Pluto Press, London.

Cockburn, C. (1991) *In the Way of Women. Men's Resistance to Sex Equality in Organizations*, Macmillan, London.

Collinson, D.L. (1992) *Managing the Shopfloor: Subjectivity, Masculinity and Workplace Culture*, Walter de Gruyter, Berlin.

Collinson, D.L. and Collinson, M. (1989) 'Sexuality in the workplace: the domination of men's sexuality', in J. Hearn, D. Sheppard, P. Tancred-Sheriff and G. Burrell (eds.), *The Sexuality of Organization*, Sage, London and Newbury Park, CA, pp. 91–109.

Collinson, D.L. and Collinson, M. (1992) 'Mismanaging sexual harassment: blaming the victim and protecting the perpetrator', *Women in Management Review*, 7(7): 11–17.

Collinson, M. and Collinson, D.L. (1996) 'It's only Dick: the sexual harassment of women managers in insurance', *Work, Employment and Society*, 10(1): 29–56.

Collinson, D.L. and Collinson, M. (1997) 'Delayering managers: time-space surveillance and its gendered effects', *Organization*, 4(3): 275–408.

Collinson, D.L. and Hearn, J. (1994) 'Naming men as men: implications for work, organization and management', *Gender, Work and Organization*, 1(1): 2–22.

Collinson, D.L. and Hearn, J. (1995) 'Men managing leadership? *Men and Women of the Corporation* revisited', *International review of Women and Leadership*, 1(2): 1–24.

Collinson, D.L. and Hearn, J. (eds.) (1996a) *Men as Managers, Managers as Men*, Sage, London.

Collinson, D.L. and Hearn, J. (1996b) "Men" at "Work": multiple masculinities in multiple workplaces', in M. Mac an Ghail (ed.), *Understanding Masculinities: Social Relations and Cultural Areas*. Open University Press, London.

Collinson, D.L., Knights, D. and Collinson, M. (1990) *Managing to Discriminate*, Routledge, London.

Connell, R.W. (1987) *Gender and Power*, Polity Press, Cambridge.

Connell, R.W. (1995) *Masculinities*, Polity Press, Cambridge.

Connell, R.W. (1998) 'Globalization and masculinities', *Men and Masculinities*. 1(1): 3–23.

Dalton, M. (1959) *Men Who Manage*, John Wiley & Sons, New York.

Davidson, M. and Cooper, C. (1983) *Stress and the Woman Manager*, Martin Robertson, Oxford.

Davis, N. (1992) *The Unknown Maxwell*, Pan Macmillan, London.

Denham, D. (1991) 'The "Macho" management debate and the dismissal of employees during industrial disputes', *Sociological review*, 39(2): 349–364.

Donnell, S.M. and Hall, J. (1980) 'Men and women as managers: a significant case of no significant difference', *Organizational Dynamics*, 8: 60–77.

Drosnin, M. (1987) *Citizen Hughes*. Henry Holt, New York.

Drucker, P. (1979) *The Practice of Management*, Heinemann, London.

Edwards, R. (1979) *Contested Tarrair: The Transformation of the Workplace in the Twentieth Century*, Heinemann, London.

Fagenson, E. (1993) 'Diversity in management: introduction and the importance of women in management'. in E.A. Fagenson (ed.). *Women in Management: Trends, Issues and Challenges in Managerial Diversity*, Sage, Newbury Park, AC, pp. 3–19.

Ferguson, K.E. (1984) *The Feminist Case against Bureaucracy*, Temple University Press, Philadelphia, PA.

Finch, J. (1983) *Married to the Job: Wives' Incorporation in Men's Work*, Allen & Unwin, London.

Ford, H.(1923) *My Life and Work*, Heinemann, London.

Geneen, H.S. (1985) *Managing*, Collins, London.

Grey, C. (1994) 'Career as a project of the self and labour process discipline', *Sociology*, 28(2): 479–98.

Grint, K. (1995) *Management: a Sociological Introduction*, Polity Press, Cambridge.

Hearn, J. (1987) *The Gender of Oppression: Men, Masculinity and the Critique of Marxism*, Wheatsheaf, Brighton. St Martin's, New York.

Hearn, J. (ed.) (1989) 'Men, masculinities and leadership: changing patterns and new initiatives', special issue, *Equal Opportunities International*, 8(1).

Hearn, J. (1992a) 'Changing men and changing managements: a review of issues and actions', *Women in Management Review and Abstracts*, 7(1): 3–8.

Hearn, J. (1992b) *Men in the Public Eye. The Construction and Deconstruction of Public Men and Public Patriarchies*, Routledge, London and New York.

Hearn, J. (1994) 'Changing men and changing managements: social change, social research and social action', in M.J. Davidson and R. Burke (eds.), *Women in Management – Current Research Issues*, Paul Chapman, London, pp. 192–209.

Hearn, J. (1996) 'Is masculinity dead? A critique of the concept of masculinity/masculinities', in M. Mac and Ghaill (ed.), *Understanding Masculinities. Social Relations and Cultural Arenas*, Open University Press, London.

Hearn, J. and Collinson, D.L. (1994) 'Theorizing unities and differences between men and between masculinities', in H. Brod and M. Kaufman (eds.), *Theroizing Masculinities*, Sage, Newbury Park, CA and London, pp. 148–62.

Hearn, J. and Collinson, D.L. (1998) 'Men, masculinities, managements and organisational culture', *Zeitschrift für Personalforschung*, 12(2): 210–222.

Hearn, J. and Morgan, D.H.J. (eds.) (1990) *Men, Masculinities and Social Theory*, Unwin Hyman, London and Boston.

Hearn, J. and Parkin, W. (1988) 'Women, men and leadership: a critical review of assumptions, practices and change in the industrialized nations', in N.J. Adler and D. Izraeli (eds.), *Women in Management Worldwide*, M.E. Sharpe, New York, pp. 17–40.

Hearn, J. and Parkin, W. (1995) *'Sex' at 'Work': The Power and Paradox of Organisation Sexuality*, Prentice Hall/Harvester Wheatsheaf, London. St Martin's, New York.

Helgesen, S. (1990) *The Female Advantage: Women's Ways of Leadership*, Doubleday, New York.

Henriques, J., Hollway, W., Urwin, C., Venn, C. and Walkerdine. V. (1984) *Changing the Subject*, Methuen, London.

Hollway, W. (1984) 'Gender difference and the production of subjectivity', in J. Henriques, W. Hollway, C. Urwin, C. Venn, and V. Walkerdine. (1984) *Changing the Subject*, Methuen, London, pp. 227–63.

Hollway, W. (1991) *Work Psychology and Organizational Behaviour*, Sage, London.

Hollway, W. (1996) 'Masters and men', in D.L. Collinson and J. Hearn (eds.), *Men as Managers, Managers as Men*, London, Sage, pp. 25–42.

Hyman, R. (1987) 'Strategy or structure? Capital, labour and control'. *Work, Employment and Society*, 1(1): 25–55.

Iacocca, L. (1904) *Iacocca: An Autobiography*, Bantam, New York.

Ibarra, H. (1995) 'Race, opportunity, and diversity of social circles in managerial networks', *Academy of Management Journal*, 38(3): 673–703.

Jackall, R. (1988) *Moral Mazes: The World of Corporate Managers*, Oxford University Press, New York.

Jermier, J., Knights, D. and Nord, W. (eds.) (1994) *Resistance and Power in Organizations*, Routledge, London.

Kanter, R.M. (1977) *Men and Women of the Corporation*, Basic Books, New York (republished in 1993).

Kerfoot, D. and Knights, D. (1993) 'Management masculinity and manipulation: from paternalism to corporate strategy in financial services in Britain', *Journal of Management Studies*, 30(4): 659–79.

Kerfoot, D. and Knights, D. (1996) 'The best is yet to come? The quest for embodiment in managerial work', in C.L. Collinson and J. Hearn (eds.), *Men as Managers, Managers as Men*, Sage, London, pp. 78–98.

Kondo, D. (1990) *Crafting Selves: Power, Gender and Discourses of Identity in a Japanese Workplace*, Chicago University Press, Chicago.

Lehman, C. (1996) 'Quiet whispers: men accounting for women, west to east', in D.L. Collinson and J. Hearn (eds.), *Men as Managers, Managers as Men*, Sage, London, pp. 150–66.

Linstead, S., Grafton Small, R. and Jeffcutt, P. (eds.) (1996) *Understanding Management*, Sage, London.

Maier, M. and Messerschmidt, J. (1998) 'Commonalities, conflicts and contradictions in organizational masculinities: exploring the gendered genesis of the *Challenger* disaster', *Canadian Review of Sociology and Anthropology*, 35(3): 325–44.

Marshall, J. (1995) *Women Managers Moving On*, Routledge, London.

Martin, J. (1990) 'Deconstructing organizational taboos: the suppression of gender conflict in organizations', *Organizational Science*, 1(4): 339–359.

McMahon, A. (1993) 'Male readings of feminist theory: the psychologization of sexual politics in the masculinity literature', *Theory and Society*, 22: 675–95.

Messerschmidt, J. (1996) 'Managing to kill: masculinities and the space shuttle *Challenger* explosion', in C. Cheng (ed.), *Masculinities in Organizations*, Sage, London, pp. 29–53.

Mintzberg, H. (1973) *The Nature of Managerial Work*, Prentice Hall, Englewood Cliffs, NJ.

Mintzberg, H. (1975) 'The manager's job: folklore and fact', *Harvard Business Review,* July/August: 49–61.

Mintzberg, H. (1983) *Power in and around Organizations*, Prentice Hall, Englewood Cliffs, NJ.

Mintzberg, H. (1989) *Mintzberg on Management*, Macmillan, New York.

Morgan, D.H.J. (1992) *Discovering Men*, Unwin Hyman/Routeledge, London and New York.

Morgan, D.H.J. (1996) 'The gender of bureaucracy', in D.L. Collinson and J. Hearn (eds.), *Men as Managers, Managers as Men*, Sage, London, pp. 29–53.

Mulholland, K. (1996) 'Entrepreneurialism, masculinities and the self-made man', in D.L. Collinson and J. Hearn (eds.), *Men as Managers, Managers as Men*, Sage, London, pp. 123–49.

Neale, A. (1995) 'The manager as hero'. Paper presented at Labour Process Conference, Blackpool, April.

Pahl, R. (1995) *After Success: Fin-de-Siècle Anxiety and Identity*, Polity Press, Cambridge.

Phillips, A. and Taylor, B. (1980) 'Sex and skill: notes towards a feminist economics', *Feminist Review*, 6(7): 79–83.

Pringle, R. (1989) *Secretaries Talk*, Verso, London.

Reed, M. (1989) *The Sociology of Management*, Harvester Wheatsheaf, London.

Reed, R. (1996) 'Entrepreneurialism and paternalism in Australian management: a gender critique of the self-made man', in D.L. Collinson and J. Hearn (eds.), *Men as Managers, Managers as Men*, Sage, London, pp. 99–122.

Roper, M.R. (1991) 'Yesterday's model: product fetishism and the British company men 1945–85', in M.R. Roper and J. Tosh (eds.), *Manful Assertions, Masculinities in Britain since 1800*, Routledge, London and New York, pp. 190–211.

Roper, M.R. (1994) *Masculinity and the British Organization Man since 1945*, Oxford University Press, Oxford.

Roper, M.R. (1996) 'Seduction and succession; circuits of homosocial desire in management', in D.L. Collinson and J. Hearn (eds.), *Men as Managers, Managers as Men*, Sage, London, pp. 210–26.

Rosener, J. (1990) 'Ways women lead', *Harvard Business Review*, 68(6): 119–25.

Schein, V.E. (976) 'Think manager – think male', *Atlanta Economic Review*, March–April: 21–24.

Sheppard, D. (1989) 'Organizations, power and sexuality: the image and self-image of women managers', in J. Hearn *et al.*, *The Sexuality of Organization*, Sage, London. pp. 139–58.

Sinclair, A. (1995) 'Sex and the MBA', *Organization*, 2(2): 295–319.

Stewart, R. (1986) *The Reality of Management*, Heinemann, London.

Sward, K. (1948) *The Legend of Henry Ford*, Russell & Russell, New York.

Wajcman, J. (1998) *Managing Like a Man*, Polity Press, Cambridge.

Walby, S. (1986) *Patriarchy at Work*, Polity Press, Cambridge.

Watson, T. (1994) *In Search of Management*, Routledge, London.

Willmott, H. (1987) 'Studying managerial work: a critique and a proposal', *Journal of Management Studies*, 24(3): 249–70.

Witz, A. and Savage, M. (1992) 'The gender of organizations', in M. Savage and A. Witz (eds.), *Gender and Bureaucracy*, Blackwell, Oxford, pp. 3–62.

Woodward, A.E. (1996) 'Multinational masculinites and European bureaucracies', in D.L. Collinson and J. Hearn (eds.), *Men as Managers, Managers as Men*, Sage, London, pp.167–85.

Yancey-Martin, P. (1996) 'Gendering and evaluating dynamics: men, masculinities and managements', in D.L. Collinson and J. Hearn (eds.), *Men as Managers, Managers as Men*, Sage, London, pp. 186–209.

15

Cross-Cultural Perspectives on School Leadership: Themes from Native American Interviews

Miles T. Bryant

Introduction

Hallinger (1995) has noted that in studies of educational leadership culture has been a missing variable. This is not entirely true. Hofstede, for example, has pursued an extensive research agenda exploring how culture influences such variables as (1) the manner in which individuals in a group handle variation in equality; (2) the degree to which individuals are dependent upon a group (collectivism vs. individualism); (3) the manner in which individuals cope with uncertainty; and (4) the manner in which cultures assign gender roles (Hofstede, 1980, 1991). As part of these studies. Hofstede examined the preference for managerial or leadership style.

However, there remains much to learn about cultural understandings of leadership. Administrative textbooks rarely touch upon the expectations that culture creates for leaders. Thus, Hallinger's criticism is well aimed. Lacking a knowledge of the cultural base from which the leadership theories of educational administration spring, the teaching of leadership in the field tends to reify the topic and to place it beyond the group of concepts that we regularly scrutinize for cultural bias.

Scholars who have researched leadership behavior from a western perspective have continued to focus on the leader as a key in organizational performance. Transformational leadership (Burns, 1978) outlined the ability of the leader to change subordinates by maximizing the talents of each individual; this was to be done through a leadership posture sensitive to the needs of others. Deming held that it was critical for leaders to develop their human

---

Source: Educational Management & Administration, Vol. 26, no. 1, 1998, pp. 7–20. Edited version.

resources (Deming, 1992). Others have suggested that leadership occupies a central role in organizational performance: that organizations need leaders who exhibit profound ethical knowledge and principled behavior (Covey, 1991; Sergiovanni, 1992); that true leaders have the capacity to serve others (Greenleaf, 1977); that leaders must possess the ability to design systems (Senge, 1990); and that, paradoxically, leaders must have an ability to bring about decentralized, organic and intuitive organizations (De pree, 1992; Wheatley, 1994). In all of these scholarly explorations, culture is at work both inspiring and constraining conceptions of leadership. Yet, our scholarly literature has not interpreted our conceptions of leaders as culturally derivative.

Clearly one issue of great importance to those who seek to help other countries develop their administrative and organizational systems is the match between western conceptions of leadership and local culture. How is leadership understood by other cultures? Are there places where western cultural values naturally conflict with the requirements of local culture? How can local cultural expectations of leadership be accommodated by imported theories? What aspects of leadership transcend cultural boundaries? These important questions can only be answered by cross-cultural comparisons.

This chapter reports on an exploration of how leadership is understood from the varied perspectives of members of six different Native American tribes. While Native Americans abide within the embrace of the larger American culture, many tribes retain a tribal culture that is quite separate from the majority one. Thus, Native American understandings of leadership provide one useful contrast to usual American conceptions of leadership.

▎ The Study

This study was undertaken as a class research project by eight graduate students and their instructor. The simple question guiding the members of this class was: how do selected Native American individuals understand leadership?

Individual Native Americans who were knowledgeable about their tribal culture were chosen to be interviewed. Participants came from the tribes indicated in Table 15.1. Twelve interviews were conducted. Each interview lasted approximately an hour. Six men were interviewed and six women.

Several basic questions were asked of all participants but no set schedule of questions was used. It was felt that each individual came to the interview from very different circumstances and that it was best to try to understand the context from which the individual described his or her understandings of leadership. At some point during the interview all participants were asked to describe how they understood Native American leadership and to give examples of behaviors that illustrated that concept of leadership.

Table 15.1 *Tribal affiliations of participants*

Tribe	No. of participants interviewed
Northern Ponca	2
Taos Pueblo	1
Winebago	1
Omaha	3
Lakota	4
Dakota	1
Total	12

In the case of most participants, considerable care was taken to create an interview environment that would signal to the participant that the researcher(s) were interested in their opinions and did not want them to try to speak for any other individual or group. Several of the interviews were conducted on an Indian reservation. Notes were not taken in all interviews. In several instances, the practice of taking out paper and pencil and recording the dialogue about leadership would have been inappropriate. Because, in most instances, a number of us participated in the interview, a number of memories were able to reconstruct what had been said. A disadvantage was that we were often unable to record the actual words of our subjects.

Data were also gathered about Lakota concepts of leadership by spending three days helping one traditional tribal leader prepare for a Sun Dance, one of the important religious ceremonies of the Lakota. As we worked side by side, informal discussions about traditional ways were possible. By participating in one of the Lakota religious ceremonies, we were able to appreciate at an emotional level the cultural differences between our American culture and this more traditional one.

The resulting data provided much diverse information. While more interviews need to be conducted in order to determine if there are certain themes about leadership that are general to Native American culture or even to particular tribes, the following ideas appeared in sufficient numbers of interviews to warrant a preliminary analysis. The data were coded and themes were developed after several iterations and reductions of categories. The themes we identified have been reviewed by our subjects for veracity and have been authenticated through this process.

Analysis of Interview Data

A caveat

In Native American cultures on the Great Plains, a guiding value that we experienced frequently was that of modesty. One does not presume to speak for others. Thus, as we interviewed different members of different tribes, we typically heard a person state that they would not speak about leadership for others. One in particular frequently began his observations with the phrase, 'I know my traditions. I cannot speak for others'. We would have our words tempered by this same value that hesitates to speak for others.

Yet to honor this value as we write about Native American conceptions of leadership poses a methodological problem. How does a scholar construct meaning from qualitative interview data if that same scholar must refrain from speaking for others? 'Speaking for others' by constructing meaning is at the very heart of qualitative research. To read the transcripts of interviews and isolate themes in those interviews is, in fact, to speak for another.

Native leaders with whom we interacted provided a route around this tortuous dilemma. One goes ahead and speaks, but first one asks forgiveness for the mistakes and misinterpretations that one will inevitably make. We begin our discussion of Native American leadership with such a request for forgiveness. The themes that we have identified are not intended to be representative of how all Native Americans understand leadership nor how particular tribal communities understand leadership. Rather, these themes surfaced as we analyzed and discussed what the participants in our study said. Our findings may be instructive but they should not be regarded as conclusive.

Leadership themes

From the data gathered six thematic areas emerged. These are as follows: decentralized leadership, immanent value of all things, non-interference, self-deflecting image projection, Indian time, and collectivist decision-making. Each of these is discussed below. Because this study is exploratory in nature, no attempt is made to quantify these data and arrange these themes in any particular priority. Nor are these themes necessarily of equal strength. We saw elements of all of these leadership themes in the interviews with almost all the Native Americans with whom we spoke.

Decentralized leadership

Clark and Clark note that they have learned that 'leaders must emerge and play a role at every level of the organization if that organization is to use the full energy of all followers in achieving objectives' (1990: 71). This conception of leadership is found everywhere in American culture. From Frederick

Taylor to Robert Young and his leadership secrets of Attila the Hun, the idea that every organization or human group must have a person in charge predominates. This idea is the simple one that in every organization or human group there must be a place where the 'buck stops', a common American phrase used to capture the necessity of hierarchical authority.

Native Americans spoke of a different kind of leadership. It was a leadership that is decentralized. Every person has a role to play. Each person's role is important to the whole. No other person can make the exact same contribution. The total contribution is an organic whole that can only be understood over life cycles. One Lakota Sioux member suggested to us that one of his jobs was to put on a Sun Dance, but not to interfere with the work of sweatlodge leaders whose work, while integral to the successful Sun Dance, was separate and special. No single entity supervises all other individual entities in some hierarchical fashion.

This understanding of one's relationship to the whole as decentralized seemed significantly different from those common in western culture. When asked about leadership in his tribal culture, one participant said

> people don't crave to be leaders. You don't get leaders because one person beats another person out. You inherit it; it comes to you. You internalize the culture and when you can show how well the culture has taught you, maybe you will become a leader.

In the language of this tribe the closest word for leader meant only 'one who goes first'. This resembles the transient position of the leader in some contemporary images of decentralized systems.

Resnick (1994), for example, provided a powerful image of decentralized leadership. He likened it to a flock of swallows. Such a flock swoops and veers across the sky, all moving together yet never having the same leaders. One may be in front for a while but never for long. Belasco and Stayer (1993) captured this same concept of decentralized leadership with their metaphor of the flock of geese. In such a flock, leadership changes repeatedly. De pree used the Native American watercarrier as a metaphor for decentralized leadership. The watercarrier is the person who does what needs to be done when it needs to be done, regardless of role authority. De pree cited an inscription next to a sculpture of a watercarrier at his company: 'The tribal watercarrier in this corporation is a symbol of the essential nature of all jobs, our interdependence, the identity of ownership' (De pree, 1992: 65). Wheatley (1994) has written a book about the necessity for a paradigm shift from centralized to decentralized leadership.

In the minds of our Native American participants, decentralized leadership was natural to their communities. Another participant said that leadership is very fluid. Different leaders will surface at different times. We don't have a word for chief. We have people who have responsibilities for specific things. Like if the council met about a hunting trip, one person might be appointed as responsible for the hunt.

Among these Native Americans, there was no necessity for a final arbiter or authority. Authority was tied to the particular situation and ended when the need for it ended.

Immanent value

In a Lakota sweatlodge, the phrase 'mitakuye oyas'in' has much meaning. An English translation is rendered as 'for all my relatives'. In the spiritual cosmology of the Lakota, all things are relations. People, animals, trees, rocks – every creature and thing is a part of the universe and has a spirit. Therefore it has value quite apart from any utilitarian purpose it might serve and therefore it requires understanding in its own right. Brooke Medicine Eagle noted that this phrase, 'mitakuye oyas'in', is used to represent the full circle of sacred life and this circle includes

> not only two legged relatives of all colors and persuasions but also all the peoples with four legs, those with wings and fins, the green standing [tree and plant] people, the mineral and stone people, those that live within and crawl upon the earth, everything both known and unknown, for we are one. (Eagle, 1991)

Rob Patterson (1995) referred to this as the idea of immanent value. All that is in the universe has a purpose and a place and a worth. The Native Americans with whom we spoke often described rocks or animals or other races as relatives and as animate objects. In one instance where we helped a tribal group slaughter a buffalo, a very respectful prayer was offered not only to the animal we were about to butcher but to the entire 'buffalo nation'. In the sweatlodge, the hot rocks that heat the lodge were portrayed as challenging relatives and sometimes called the ancient ones.

A Native American from the Taos Pueblo helped us see how this concept of immanent value influences Native American leadership. He pointed out that a Native American does not appoint himself or herself as leader. One grows into such a position and is gradually accepted into such a position. 'How well we translated the mother culture was what determined our leaders.' The foundation of respect for a Native American leader rests on that person's knowledge of how things work. That knowledge in turn is based on a person forever being a student of the trees and the rocks and the river. There are lessons everywhere. 'Nature becomes your teacher; water becomes your teacher; the trees become your teacher.' The wise and respected person will be he or she who can help the rest of us understand those lessons. Knowledge and an ability to interpret the events of the world, to understand the immanent value of all things, were important aspects of leadership in the minds of most of those with whom we spoke.

For our participants there was an understanding that the contributions of the whole, of all the relations, creates an organization of decentralized leadership that does not rank people or things in a hierarchy. Everything has a unique and, when understood, powerful worth.

Responsibility for others

In a typical American public school district of any size, staff development will be a major task of the administrative staff. Usually a great variety of developmental resources are brought to the teachers and staff of a district. Teachers and staff are then expected to educate themselves by participating in seminars and classes and workshops. This model of staff development presents individuals with information that they are expected to learn. Some person has decided what knowledge is needed and has brought this knowledge to the learner (Byrne and Bryant, 1995; Miller *et al.*, 1994).

Such administrative behavior reveals an acceptance of responsibility for the learning and development of others. Leaders are responsible for others. There is great variety in how this basic responsibility for others is understood by leaders. For some it is a paternalistic obligation; for others it is a caring, and nurturing expression; and for others still it is a belief that others are deficient and must be improved. But no matter how the feeling of responsibility for others is expressed, western leadership accepts this as one of its charges, i.e. to be responsible for followers or fellow workers or subordinates.

From our interviews with Native Americans, we conclude that the Native American leader may have a responsibility for the welfare of the collective (the family, the tribe, the people) just as the superintendent in a large school district has. One participant suggested that leaders are 'caretakers of the future of the collective'. But that responsibility appears to be exercised differently. From one Lakota woman came the notion of non-interference, the term she used to discuss this issue of responsibility for others. It is a value-laden term but one that we use to bring out differences in American and Native American conceptions of leadership. She noted that the Native American leader might believe that another person needs something, that an intervention is necessary, that, for example, teachers would benefit from a particular kind of staff development. But that native leader would be unlikely to take any action without permission from the individual needing help. Consequently, the native leader would not assume a responsibility for others. Rather, the native leader might hope that a person will come to desired levels of understanding.

Wax *et al.*, wrote that 'conservative Indians do not subscribe to a Protestant ethic's conception of the human character as a phenomenon that may (and ought to) be modeled and changed' (1989: 20). The value of non-intervention has many implications for leadership behaviors. For example, how would a value of non-intervention shape attitudes toward personnel evaluation or program evaluation? How would a value of non-intervention impact strategic planning?

What does a value of non-intervention say about trust? As could be deduced from the earlier discussion of western research in leadership, trust is one of the factors that has concerned leaders. How does one secure the trust of others? Francis Fukuyama in a book called *Trust* (1995) claims the warp and woof of western society is being shredded by a lack of trust among people. Amitai Etzioni's communitarian movement (1993) seeks to develop community structures that produce trust among members.

Perhaps one of the precursors to trust is a willingness not to interfere in how others construct their understandings. Interference implies a lack of trust: someone must do something for someone else because otherwise some important act will not be done. Interference suggests that one party is super-ordinate to another in terms of establishing an agenda for action. Non-interference, on the other hand, may suggest trust. Certainly, when one person is granted or assumes the authority to design changes in another person, there is a hierarchical relationship between those two parties.

One Lakota member told us, this value of non-interference does not mean ignoring the needs of others. Displeasure with behaviors or positions can be communicated in many ways. Nor does it mean that help or assistance is not provided. The Lakota value holds with the old folk adage that 'you can lead a horse to water but you cannot make him drink'. This is similar to what Hofstede suggested (1980) about collectivist cultures where members control others not through internal pressure but through external societal pressures or norms. Thus, there is a felt sense of responsibility for others, but that sense of responsibility is expressed in a different way in Lakota society. Pressure to conform and to change in acceptable ways comes not from an individual but from the culture around the individual. This has strong implications for organizational cultures.

Image projection

Western leaders have a tendency to see themselves as strategic players seeking to advance their own purposes. One of the baldest examinations of this aspect of leadership was Machiavelli's *The Prince*. Here the leader was exhorted to be a wise prince who understood the need to be merciless at times. The prince must be aware of the forces that swirl about him and be able to manipulate those forces to personal gain. One of the long honored thoughts of politics is that if one would exert influence one must be around long enough to do so. From an American perspective, leaders are helped to remain in their roles by manipulation of their image. Leaders are expected to look like leaders in American culture. They are expected to make more money, have more well-appointed offices, wear more expensive clothes, and be more visible in public meetings. Leaders are expected to look for opportunities to display their talents and to do so when these opportunities are located. They are expected to seek advanced education and to volunteer their skills in community organizations. American culture accepts these kinds of self-aggrandizing behaviors as appropriate leader behavior whereas in another culture such behavior might appear to be too self-centered.

In some Native American cultures there is what amounts to an imperative requiring the leader not to stand out, not to seek advancement, and not to manipulate image in self-aggrandizing ways. When one is singled out as a leader, one can accept and feel honored at that recognition. But if one actively promotes one's self, that action is likely to result in disrespect. One participant noted:

> the leader was not the person who could amass and sit upon the biggest pile of toys. It was the leader who gave away everything that he had and his family had. If you look at a traditional or pre-European contact leader, it might be the guy who is riding the scruffiest horse and living in the scruffiest tent because he had given away everything to those who needed it.

Perhaps for this reason, leaders in Native American cultural events are not always obvious. An example of this would be the behavior of singers and drummers at powwows. Men will sit in a circle about a large drum. No single individual will appear as a leader. One must look and listen very carefully if one hopes to identify a leader. Songs are begun by different individuals; breaks are signaled by different individuals; no one person will stand out in the group. However, there will be a leader or two that are respected as such by the others.

Another example of this value in action is seen in the story that one Lakota spiritual leader told us. Several years ago he was speaking with a woman who praised him for the wonderful things that had happened to her husband as a result of his participation in a Sun Dance. The Lakota spiritual leader replied: 'I told her, I had done nothing; it was all done by that tree out there. I pointed to the tree that is at the center of our Sun Dance ceremonial grounds. Go talk to that tree. It is what changed your husband.'

The practice of deflecting praise to something or someone else appeared in several interviews. As in decentralized systems, the Native American approach to image seemed to be one that downplays the importance of an individual. Put slightly differently, the image that is created is one of humility and self-deprecation. The sense of a need to display the symbols of personal agency or power and authority so characteristic of mainstream conceptions of leadership (Gronn and Ribbins, 1996) is absent from these traditional Native American contexts.

In the Native American context, the leader is an exemplar as well. One participant suggested that 'you were the leader only as long as you could influence people through role modeling, through good deeds. You couldn't really be a coercive leader because you couldn't coerce everybody.' Others told us that the leader was a student. It was the wisdom of the leader, accumulated through some period of learning, that impressed others. Through that student's own learning, others learned. That learning was voluntary. It was a never-ending process.

Time

Western culture requires that leadership be oriented toward the future (Bruno, 1995). We have many, many examples of this. Strategic plans, mission statements, information systems, forecasting are all common to top organizational leadership. All are oriented toward the future, either toward a future goal or to analyzing possible trends. Reducing future uncertainty through an ability to predict events is very much the job of top leadership in modem organizations. In fact, the way in which the members of a culture live with or seek to avoid future uncertainty is a major dimension one can use to distinguish leadership behavior (Hofstede, 1980). In some cultures, the leader is expected to help others reduce future uncertainty. In other cultures, this concern with the future is muted.

The Native Americans with whom we spoke described a different leadership in terms of time orientation. For the Native American leader there was a deep connection to the present. Often this connection was linked with an ability to see and comprehend the meaning of natural events. The traditional Native American leader has a strong spiritual component that seeks to understand the lessons provided by daily experience. More frequently, the individuals with whom we interacted tended to treat the present as a time to be appreciated and enjoyed. Few people were in a hurry to get to something else. One morning we were waiting to help a group go gather rocks for the sweatlodges. After two hours of standing around pick-up trucks listening to different individuals tell stories, we began to wonder if the work would ever commence. It finally did, but there was no hurry about it.

For us, coming from a white culture, patience was a necessary virtue. In our interviews with Native Americans during the formal part of the class, a cognizance of time was not mentioned as an important aspect of leadership. Based on our field experiences, we would have to conclude that an allegiance to a predetermined time scheme is not a significant factor. Following a predetermined schedule was unimportant and not done. There were things that had to occur at particular parts of a day, but these were dictated by the nature of the events, not by the leadership. For example, when the group slaughtered a buffalo, the animal had to be butchered immediately or the meat would spoil. Some sweatlodge services had to happen at particular times based on ritual obligations. Generally, however, leaders organized work in a relaxed fashion and one set off to do something when everyone was ready and able to do it. Thus, we found no evidence that an awareness of time or a consciousness of time's importance played a role in Native American leadership.

Decision-making

Organizations, in western management theory, are tools to get work done (Weber, 1974; Scott, 1981). We understand organizations as instruments. American organizational decision-making is frequently portrayed as a rational process in which an attempt is made to maximize goal attainment while minimizing the expenditure of resources. Goal clarity is seen as an essential part of this rational process. In such a process, goals are identified and then decisions are made in keeping with those goals.

Karl Weick suggested a far more complicated world. Goals become important as a means to justify past behaviors (Weick, 1969), not just as a way to justify future behavior. James March suggested that 'a description that assumes that goals come first and action comes later is frequently radically wrong' (March and Olsen, 1976: 72). They were proposing a different explanatory perspective to that perspective that views the goal as central to organizational and leader behavior. In the organizational world that March, Olsen and Wieck described, decisions were as dependent upon who was involved in making the decisions and the circumstances surrounding them as they were oriented toward an organizational goal. This diffuse decision-making process, the garbage can model, resembles group decision-making in the Native American context. Said one participant, decision-making 'depends on the person, depends on the situation. Consensus is the best way. That's why you have a council of seven and not a king of one.' Another participant said that it was the

> elders who would make the final decision, but only after a lot of talk. Decisions were consensual and everybody gets their point of view out there. Everybody ends up knowing how it is going to work before the decision is made.

We were told that when a group or a tribe needed to make an important decision, the method of arriving at that decision was through talk. All participated. All listened. Decisions were arrived at when the talk had exhausted the issue and a direction for action was established. It appeared to be very much a consensual model.

One Native American said that leadership is a 'touchy subject'.

> When they say I'm a leader of my clan, that's really hard to define because – I'll give you an example – I know this much about my culture. That leader of that clan could … and there's this much to learn, that leader of that clan could know

this much even though he may be 88 years old, he does not know everything there is to know about his culture. He may know some stuff and somebody who is forty-five may know some other stuff. So collectively everyone becomes the leaders, so that the collective unconscious becomes the leader so that in the community individuals don't shine out as leaders because they know everything; they've studied everything, done everything there is to know and can say I am the leader. It is a society that becomes successful by all of them participating to be the questioners and answerers at once. That's how a society becomes successful. Because that leader can't do everything by himself. He needs the society members.

Decision-making as understood by this participant was a collective behavior in which all participated, with no one standing out as a leader.

Conclusion

There are many cultural aspects of Native American leadership that remain to be uncovered. Different tribal perspectives need to be explored. A rich literature by Native American authors exists and frequently contains information that suggests how Native Americans view leadership differently. For example, Paula Gunn Allen argued that in traditional times in some tribes, women's leadership was the major component in tribal governance, a form of governance she labeled gynocracy (Allen, 1992: 30–42). In such a woman-centered context, one imagines leadership will be understood and practiced differently.

Finally, Native American culture can be unsettling. Simple values that we take for granted are sometimes turned upside down. Nepotism is a good example. In western culture, and particularly in rational organizational culture, the notion of doing things that benefit family and relatives is seen as unethical. In some places there are laws forbidding nepotism. Yet, in Native American cultures, taking care of family and relatives is one of the first obligations of a leader. Nepotism becomes a positive value. Giving money with the expectation that some future benefit will eventually be bestowed on the giver is another example of a behavior acceptable in one culture's political context and unacceptable in the others.

Many contrasts become evident as one studies leadership from differing cultural perspectives. These differences become important conceptual tools that allow us to examine more carefully the characteristics of leadership in our institutions.

Note

This chapter was written with the assistance of Rochelle Ashley, Elaine Gardner, Nancy Johnson, Toni Gammage, Ellen Patterson, Rob Patterson and Darlene Williams at the University of Nebraska-Lincoln.

References

Allen, Paula Gunn (1992) *The Sacred Hoop*. Boston, MA: Beacon Press.

Bruno, James (1995). 'Organizational Leadership in an Era of Time Scarcity', Faculty Symposium Lecture, Ben Gurion University of the Negev, BeerSheva, Israel, November.

Burns, J.M. (1978) *Leadership*. New York: Harper and Row.

Byrne, Marilyn and Bryant, Miles (1995) 'The Professional Development Seminar: An Addition to School District Staff Development Activities'. *Leadership Nebraska* 4(2): 34–7.

Clark, Kenneth and Clark, Miriam (1990) *Measures of Leadership*. West Orange, NJ: Center for Creative Leadership.

Covey, Stephen (1991) *Principle-Centered Leadership*. New York: Summit Book.

Deming, W. E. (1992) *Quality Productivity Competitive Position*. Rochester, NY: Industrial Management Council.

De pree, Max (1992) *Leadership Jazz*. New York: Dell Publishing.

Eagle, Brooke Medicine (1991) *Buffalo Woman Comes Singing*. New York: Ballantine Books.

Etzioni, Amitai (1993) *The Spirit of Community*. New York: Crown Publishing.

Fukuyama, Francis (1995) *Trust: The Social Virtues and the Creation of Prosperity*. New York: The Free Press.

Gronn, P. and Ribbins, P. (1996) 'Leaders in Context: Postpositivist Approaches to Understanding Educational Leadership', *Educational Administration Quarterly* 32(3): 452–73.

Greenleaf, Robert (1977) *Servant Leadership: Journey into the Nature of Legitimate Power and Greatness*.

Hallinger, Phillip (1995) 'Culture and Leadership: Developing an International Perspective on Educational Administration', *UCEA Review*, 36(2).

Hofstede, Geert (1980) *Culture's Consequences: International Differences in Work Related Values*. Newbury Park, CA: Sage.

Hofstede, Geert (1991) *Culture and Organizations: Software of the Mind*. New York: McGraw-Hill.

March, James and Olsen, Johan (1976) *Ambiguity and Choice in Organizations*. Bergen: Universitetsforlaget.

Miller, B., Lord, B., and Dorney, J. (1994) *Staff Development for Teachers*. Newton, MA: Education Development Center.

Patterson, Rob (1995) 'Medicine Rocks: Challenges to the Rhetorical Tradition', *Communication Studies Paper*. Lincoln, NE: University of Nebraska-Lincoln.

Senge, Peter (1990) 'A Leader's New Work', *Sloan Management Review*.

Sergiovanni, Thomas (1992) *Moral Leadership*. San Francisco, CA: Jossey-Bass.

Wax, Murray, Wax, Rosalie and Dumont Jr., Robert (1989) *Formal Education in an American Indian Community*. Prospect Heights, IL: Waveland Press.

Weick, Karl (1969) *The Soical Psychology of Organizing*. Reading, MA: Addison-Wesley.

Wheatley, Margaret (1994) *Leadership and the New Science: Learning about Organizations from an Orderly Universe*. San Francisco, CA: Berrett-Koehler Publishers, Inc.

16

Managing Ambiguity in Further Education

Denis Gleeson and Farzana Shain

Introduction

This chapter critically examines the complex and contradictory role played
by academic 'middle' managers, as *mediators of change*, in the reconstruction
of professional and managerial cultures in the Further Education (FE) sector.
With few notable exceptions (Ainley and Bailey, 1997), FE research has subsumed the experiences of lecturers and managers within a managerialist
imperative (Elliott, 1966a and b., Elliott and Crossley, 1994; Randle and
Brady, 1994; 1997), without sufficient attention paid to their narratives and
experiences of the FE workplace.

   In this chapter we explore the role played by middle managers as an ideological 'buffer' between senior managers and lecturers through which market
reform is *filtered* in the FE workplace. The chapter examines volatile working
conditions in FE, which give rise to ambiguity and connect lecturers and
senior managers in a complex duality of control and support (Hetherington
and Munro, 1997; Watson, 1997). In so doing, we consider the way such duality finds expression in the 'double' identities of middle managers, as they
broker materiality and meaning in their work. We also connect this to the regulation and reconstruction of lecturers' work (Dale, 1989; Avis *et al.*, 1996;
Seddon, 1997), in the context of economic, political and cultural change in
the FE workplace (Casey, 1995; Labier, 1986). The term 'middle manager' is
employed to denote a diverse group commonly referred to within FE as
'middle management'. Specifically, within their various institutions, they are
known by one of the following broad titles: programme manager, programme
developer, co-ordinator, head of school, sector head or programme leader. Our

Source: The Sociological Review 1999, pp. 461–90. Edited version.

use of the term 'middle' manager here, therefore, describes members of the FE workforce who assume managerial responsibility for the co-ordination of courses, people management, budgets and income generation, often having originally entered FE as classroom teachers.

Background: The Changing Policy Context

The 1992 Further and Higher Education (FHE) Act granted FE institutions independent corporate status, governed by non-elected boards drawn mainly from business and industry. The Further Education Funding Council (FEFC) was initiated by Government with the task of ensuring the 'adequacy' and 'sufficiency' of provision in the sector.

Despite an increase in autonomy, FE colleges were controlled by central government principally through funding mechanisms (Randle and Brady, 1997). The new funding formula meant that funds could be 'clawed back', if colleges failed to meet targets, retain students or if students did not successfully complete courses.

These changes, however, cannot be attributed solely to the 1992 FHE Act; neither can they be seen as suddenly imposed. FE has historically operated in a voluntaristic fashion in the marketplace and centralisation has been a gradual process (Elliott, 1996b).

Following Labour's election defeat in 1979 the momentum was taken up by Thatcherism and the new right, with its emphasis on traditional values, market discipline and the doctrine of tight fiscal controls over public expenditure. It was also during this period that a new discourse of education workers had been constructed, sparked by the Ruskin speech of 1976. In this speech, the then Labour Prime Minister, James Callaghan, identified the teaching profession as complacent and failing to pay sufficient attention to skills and attitudes required to regain Britain's declining prosperity (Esland, 1996). Thus, by the time Margaret Thatcher's new right government had been elected, images of teachers as self serving and monopolistic were already being reworked in common sense, to justify greater state control and regulation of education (Ozga, 1995).

During the 1980s and 1990s, a period of recession and mass unemployment (Friend and Metcalf, 1982), this reassertion of control has been achieved through direct state intervention in education, while paradoxically leaving education to market forces. By privileging the market, reforms both realigned relations between teachers and the State and subjected teacher professionalism to externally imposed surveillance and funding control, thereby disconnecting teachers from any semblance of post-war consensus (Ranson, 1994).

The FHE Act 1992, according to Gleeson (1996) created a framework of market competition in FE by:

- removing local authority control by transferring funding to the Further Education Funding Council.
- granting FE and 6th Form Colleges independent status.
- introducing a competitive user-provider system linking colleges and student recruitment with Training and Enterprise Councils, industry, business and commerce.
- initiating management systems which equated growth, units of resource and convergence, with lowering average levels of funding (ALFs); and by
- redistributing the subsidy from the supplier (colleges) to the customer (the student). (Evans, 1992)

Arising from this framework, education and training reforms, enacted by successive governments since 1979, have had two different but related objectives. Esland (1996) sees the first as economic in attempting to meet the demands from employers for a more vocationally relevant curriculum and assessment system, as part of the task of preparing young people for a flexible workforce; the second, politically connected with the ambitions of the new Right, is concerned with the necessity to attack and replace the critical and liberal democratic basis of education, and to destroy its potential for undermining the free-market economy. Successive education reform in both schools and FHE has according to Esland (1996:48)

> ... substantially redrawn the lines of responsibility and accountability which have led to greatly increased regulation of professional workers and intensification of work loads. At the same time the introduction of a marketisation system of course provision and output related funding has heightened competitive relations between different institutions. (Esland, 1996)

Central to the processes of regulation and intensification is the discourse of *managerialism* (Clarke and Newman, 1997). This discourse has pervaded the new management of FE in an attempt to elicit the compliance of professionals in new modes of control over their work. It is to this aspect that we now turn.

Managerialism and cultural change in the further education sector

Ostensibly, managerialism has been introduced into education and the public sector as a rational process, linked with new principles of funding, efficiency and professionalism. A number of features of managerialism have been outlined in the research (Pollitt, 1993; Fergusson, 1994; Clarke and Newman,

1997), which associate its economic rationalism with ulterior motives. These include, on the one hand, its control over professionals, by reasserting 'managements right to manage'. On the other, it conveys the notion that good management resides only in the private sector and by implication, that the public sector is characterised by liberalism and dogged sloth. This 'economising of education' brings with it the discipline of the market into the workplace, and the legitimising language that goes with it (Kenway, 1994). Through its discourse of Human Resources Management (HRM) and Total Quality Management (TQM), such 'economising' represents a powerful mechanism for both the internalisation of control, and surveillance of professionals in education and elsewhere in the public sector. Another controlling feature is the way in which managerialism turns senior professionals, who might be resistant to loss of professional autonomy, into managers.

The process by which professionals can be reconstructed as managers of reform is of strategic importance to the implementation of market and managerial initiatives in education. Not only do academic managers play a crucial role in the manufacture of consent, between professional and managerial interests, but also their reading of situations closely mirrors changes in their own identities, which are as important as the reform process itself (Fergusson, 1994). Thus, contrary to an emphasis in some FE research, which views professionalism and managerialism as opposed (Elliott, 1996; Randle and Brady, 1997), this chapter examines connections between the two as they are mediated by changing identities in the work place. In this way we focus on the role academic managers play in constructing the meaning of FE, through their cultural activities at college level. As Senior Management Teams decrease in size as part of cost-cutting, and increasingly concern themselves with strategic planning, middle managers appointed from the lecturing ranks, are taking on broader managerial roles. They not only manage budgets and people in the pursuit of greater efficiency, but also mediate tensions and dilemmas associated with rapid and unpredictable change (Clarke and Newman, 1997). Among lecturers, reduced autonomy, insecurity, new contracts and longer hours, have further complicated the middle managers' remit. For senior managers budgetary deficits, pressure to attract more students and to compete with other providers, sharply focus decision making in colleges. Moreover, preoccupation with corporate identity, mission statements and strategic planning have, according to Randle and Brady (1994; 1997), estranged many senior managers from their staff.

Such factors have signalled to many professionals working in FE its transformation from a public to a private sector of education (General Educator, 1997). In addition the language of FE has changed to reflect the new 'business' ethos, with students referred to as 'customers' or 'clients', teaching as 'the management of learning', and desks as 'work stations'. Perhaps the most significant aspect arising from such change has been the struggle over meaning and identity of professionals in the reconstruction of the FE workforce. To comprehend this involves recognition that FE is occupied by competing visions and cultures intimately connected with wider social and economic change. In short, there is a crisis of professional identity in FE.

The study focused on the impact of government policy on FE (FHE Act, 1992), with particular reference to changing professional, teaching and managerial perceptions. Fieldwork was conducted from January 1997 to March 1998, across five colleges in three countries in the Midlands region. Semi-structured interviewed were conducted with a cross section of individuals, including principals, governors, senior and middle managers, lecturers, support staff and union representatives. In addition, documentary data was analysed and observations were recorded of key meetings.

We have sought to illuminate different narratives which express recurring themes among participants across the colleges. In theoretical terms we have endeavoured to analyse such data in terms of the wider policy context outlined at the beginning of this chapter, which connects managerialism with the identities and experiences of professionals 'on the ground'. Thus, any claims made for the authenticity of this study reside less in conventional notions of representativeness, and more in the qualitative complexities of analysing changing professional and managerial cultures. The section which follows takes further the notion of *mediation* among middle managers, to which we now turn.

Mediating Change

Caught in the middle

Many of the middle managers interviewed spoke of being 'caught in between' senior management and lecturers. They also spoke of being at the sharp end of service delivery where both job and identity were being squeezed.

In addition to the sense of being 'squeezed from the top and from underneath', there is also a perceived lack of support from senior management which presents its own problems. Consequently many middle managers feel they are being asked to perform an impossible task, without the necessary tools for the job. This at times has left them open to criticism from both senior managers and lecturers:

> Chris: we have become the people who are linked very much with the staff, and get the blame from the staff and also unfortunately suffer the blame from the Senior Management Team for things we are not able to manage.

The sense of being squeezed in the middle relates not only to the experience of being 'caught between' senior managers and lecturers, but also in relation to the problem of balancing, finance with curriculum issues, particularly where devolved budgets are in operation:

> William: we are in the middle because we have strict instructions to make sure that whatever we do, we do profitably, against providing what is a reasonable curriculum basket of provision for those people we come across.

Managing ambiguity

Another key concern relates to the ambiguitous territory which middle managers occupy between lecturers and senior managers, and whose recognised identity as a 'manager' is not fully understood by lecturers or senior management, or even among middle managers themselves:

> Jenny: The staff don't really know where we fit in and I don't think the senior management really know where either ...

Promoted from the ranks, many 'middle' managers retain often heavy teaching commitments and, at the same time, are expected to 'hold the line' between lecturers and senior managers in brokering change. If their strategic influence is in mediating messages between senior managers and lecturers, they are in many ways more 'managed' than those who they allegedly manage (see Watson, 1997).

Ambiguity, in the form of being neither senior lecturer nor lecturer, allows middle managers some room for manoeuvre. However it can often be at a cost, particularly when financial pressures come to the fore. In this context middle managers are not victims or simply 'middlemen' but deal with complex moral and ethical decisions on a daily basis, often bounded by severe financial constraints. Though potentially flatter neo-Fordist work practices threaten their future, they effectively remain key intermediaries in potentially conflictual relations between professional and managerial interests. Evidence for this is to be found in the 'double identities' which middle managers account for in their work, and in their perceptions of themselves. This equivocal stance, referred to by Watson (1997) as a *double control problem*, shifts between a fascination for, and an ambivalence to, managerially driven reform. The nature of this duality of control which we call 'double identities' connects both with the communicative contingencies of the job and its meaning in middle managers' lives.

The management of consent – the translation of policy into practice

In the narratives of middle managers it is strikingly noticeable how highly they regard achieving effective working relations with teachers and senior managers. On the one hand, this demands working closely with senior management in implementing often controversial policies and, on the other, it involves communicating and enlisting the co-operation of lecturers in carrying these out. They filter change in both directions between senior management and lecturers, buffering potential conflict and resistance from lecturing staff.

A key function of the middle manager is then tied to the management of consent in work practices that operate within an environment of increasing public scrutiny and accountability, based on a principle of 'more for less'.

The task of policing potential conflict is not made easy by a tendency for teachers and senior managers to display polarised identities, in the defence of either pedagogy or in the promotion of management interests (Elliott, 1996a). In brokering such interests the language of *becoming* a 'good' academic manager displays all the tensions which link colleges with wider education policy, an issue to which we now turn.

Facing the constant threat of redundancy and living with vulnerability

The culture of reorganisation, delayering or restructuring poses a threat to the life span of the FE middle manager. It also serves as a reminder to all staff in the FE organisation that they can be removed, or demoted in the interests of greater efficiency and economy. Although some middle managers were more willing to talk openly about this vulnerability than others, lecturers were in no doubt as to the increasing uncertainty and unpredictability that impacts on both lecturers and managers in the FE workplace.

The narratives underline a deepening industrial relations crisis in FE since Incorporation. With year on year savings in college budgets many FE lecturers experienced reductions in their pay, security, academic freedom and job satisfaction, accompanied by increases in their work load (Beckett, 1998). This coupled with some colleges' insolvency, sporadic strike action and financial mismanagement, has in a short period, turned FE into an industrial relations battlefield. For those in posts prior to Incorporation the combination of efficiency gains and restructuring has had a marked effect on morale and career prospects.

Even those middle managers who had recently received promotion felt vulnerable. Bill, one of the most ambitious and well paid managers interviewed also expressed such vulnerability despite his apparent success on the career ladder.

> Bill: Personally speaking, I feel extremely vulnerable. I am quite highly paid as
> a college manager. My job could be done by somebody younger who
> would have a lower salary than me.

A number of further questions arise from such accounts, as to how middle managers resolve such ambiguity and vulnerability in the workplace. It is, for example, too simplistic to view middle managers as either 'puppets' or 'free agents' in their dealings with the sharp end of user–provider reforms in education or elsewhere. At the same time middle managers are neither victims or 'honest brokers', but have to deal with complex moral, administrative and pragmatic decisions on a daily basis, often bound by severe financial constraints. Though restructuring and delayering practices threaten their future, they remain effectively key intermediaries in potentially conflictual relations between professional and managerial interests. Despite their ambivalence about being 'caught in the middle' of budgetary, staffing and management constraints, many middle managers view their new responsibilities positively. Those whose established middle tier posts (for example, as heads of department or subject leaders) became subsumed in wider management reforms, or who had promotion thrust upon them often tend to view the job more instrumentally and individualistically. However, middle managers do not constitute a neat homogenous group. Their responses to, and perceptions of, their work varies in relation to institutional effects, age, gender, qualifications and work experience, none of which alone tells the full story. In the section which follows, we seek to make further sense of our data by developing a heuristic model for analysing narratives around recurring responses of compliance: willing, unwilling and strategic. These are not intended to be exhaustive or fixed and draw on recurring themes identified by participants in the study.

■ Manager Responses to Change

Willing compliance

Willing compliance is characterised by the expression of a deep commitment to the FE institution and its corporate image. Managers frequently used the terms 'we', 'us' or 'our' to communicate their individual identification with the college. Willing compliers are typically ambitious and have either been recently promoted, or are seeking promotion within the organisation. Often they are pursuing further management qualifications to aid their promotion prospects. Although a minority retain direct contact with students, either through teaching or tutorial work, the majority have moved into management roles precluding their direct contact with students. A defining feature of this response is a conscious alliance with the corporate aims of the institution in line with a managerialist work ethic. This involves immersion in a discourse of 'business speak', with middle managers making frequent references to efficiency and effectiveness, and referring to students as customers or clients.

The dominant managerialist discourse is consciously internalised and guides the daily working practices of those involved. Incorporation is thus spoken of in both positive and realistic terms as offering the only possibility of strategic direction and change in the changing business climate of FE. Changes in the corporate appearance of the college are also cited approvingly as indicative of a new professional era. In such accounts 'professional' is used synonymously as a noun or adjective that is uncoupled semantically from *profession* to denote the business of FE in terms of efficiency, reliability, compliance and a no-nonsense anti-intellectualism (Ainley and Bailey, 1997). In this discourse of professionalism, skill is given priority over knowledge and compliance over judgement.

> Monica: In the main there is a growing feeling of professionalism. We attempt
>   to be as professional to our public as we can.

Middle managers such as Monica view flexibility and working long hours positively in exchange for possible recognition and promotion. The constant and rapid change referred to so far, though a source of fear and frustration to many managers, is viewed as positive, challenging and exciting by willingly compliant managers.

> Karen: I like challenges and so I find this restructuring is very exciting.

Such compulsive optimism about organisational change, and one's role within it, is congruent with Casey's *colluded self* (Casey, 1995), where the strategy is used as a psychic buffer to filter competing messages and impulses. Following the corporate line provides some managers with a modern focus on which to build their professional identity. Key phrases from mission statements are often internalised and reproduced in the interview situation. This adoption of the corporate line also involves close identification with senior managers' assessment of the new found freedoms that go with incorporation. In line with the corporation's official views, competition between colleges is viewed as healthy. As Karen put it, 'These people are our competitors'. Resultant changes in the conditions of teachers' work are viewed as inevitable and necessary for the overall of the system.

Another associated characteristic of willing compliance finds expression in the corporate style of dress adopted by some managers. Suits in neutral and safe colours (navy and grey) are often worn by both men and women middle managers in preference to smart casual gear.

Significantly, a majority of those middle managers interviewed in this category are women. The emerging less male-orientated culture of FE is seen by them to offer new opportunities in exchange for long hours of service and total dedication to the organisation. This contrasts with, or perhaps complements, research emphasising the 'macho' culture of management in FE (Kerfoot and Whitehead, 1998). Female middle managers find the prospect of promotion a challenge that bonds them to the organisation but which, at the same time, *trades* on their womanly skills and ambitions (Casey, 1995).

In the process of seeking promotion, female middle managers find themselves at the sharp end of service delivery, managing and resolving tensions in the workplace resulting from budget cuts and contraction in resources and services. They work long hours to cover staff shortages and resultant conflicts which surface amid a climate of cut-throat competition.

Willing compliers express commitment to the college, frequently referring to meetings and conversations with Principals or senior managers, who are referred to by first name. Karen identifies strongly with her new Principal whom she regards as 'dynamic'.

Elsewhere, Patricia's compulsive optimism – linked with a positive sense of family – represents a strong antidote to the perceived pressures involved in her work.

> Patricia: ... I feel a deep commitment to the college on many levels. As a
> parent, as a member of the community and as a member of staff as well.

Despite expressing such high levels of commitment to the organisation, few middle managers felt able to escape totally from the vulnerability that is an essential part of their new corporate life. Not all our respondents were willing to speak openly about this vulnerability.

Monica detects gender discrimination in the way the organisation operates, which makes her feel uncertain about her position in the institution, and hence extremely vulnerable:

> The college has just appointed a new Director and he is in the Senior
> Management Team, but is also called Director. I am a director and so is Beth but
> we are not in the Senior Management Team, so I think that has got to be cleared
> up ... I don't know what level I'm on.

Unwilling compliance

If a characteristic of willing compliers is their level of interest and optimism in the organisation, the 'unwilling complier' is altogether more sceptical and disenchanted with the new FE ethos. Paradoxically, those values and challenges which most excite the willing compliers are those which unwilling compliers find most difficulty in relating to. Anger and frustration with one's lot is discernible, across the age, gender, qualifications and range of experience. It is a response which shares much in common with Casey's 'defensive self' (Casey, 1995), among those who have moved sideways, become stuck or who have been passed over for promotion – though not exclusively so. For younger managers like Andrew, recently recruited from industry, the college is not perceived to be 'business like' enough. Though he accepts the new corporate image of FE, he believes the college is not responsive enough to new 'business' principal. Following a number of suggestions rejected by senior management about how to improve things, he has become bitter and resentful of the work culture in his college. He has become frustrated by the lack of support received from senior management, which affects his ability to respond to what he terms elsewhere as the 'cut throat' nature of his work.

> Andrew: ... I have worked in business and the college wants to be a business but the college is miles off being a business ... If something is going bad the buck stops with you, down at the bottom. The load is so high you just can't cope with it anymore ... It is not a very good environment to work in.

For more experienced academic managers like Martin, unwilling compliance can result from the experience of demotion of some sort within the organisation. Delayering and restructuring often means that middle managers face the prospect of redundancy or applying for their own or redesignated posts. This can be accompanied by a reduction in status and pay as in Martin's case. often with an enlarged responsibility:

> Martin: I feel quite resentful.

Since being 'reappointed' Martin has found it difficult to reconcile the loss of professional autonomy and status that had originally attracted him to FE. His despair is evident as he talks of the way in which senior management and the control mechanisms operate, in order to elicit compliance with new working arrangements.

> Martin: I think we are much more at the mercy of senior managers now than we used to be ... Also ... we have had thrown at us the threat of redundancy which is a sort of macho management strategy.

He also spoke of what he saw as the callous way in which professionals were being treated in FE institutions. Despite feeling used and abused by the organisation, Martin complained that he had little option but to remain within his college. However, like Andrew he did not relish the thought of arriving at work each morning:

Martin: There are very few promotion prospects. I think people need to have a sense that if they work hard enough they will get some sort of recognition either through promotional prospects or through increased salary ... or being treated properly by their managers.

In Hayley's case, who experienced a loss of professional and financial status (due to job reallocation), bitterness and resentment is aimed at the system rather than the college. She has found it difficult to overcome the financial loss which she has experienced in and out of work, in both her professional and personal life:

Hayley: ... How was I going to live, after my salary was cut by nearly half from £20,000 a year ... I felt very very angry towards the system.

If Hayley's case is not typical of those interviewed, the perceived threat of redundancy or job reallocation was uppermost in many lecturers' and managers' accounts. While there is no evidence in the study that willing compliers are any more or less advantaged than unwilling compliers in the job market, both groups are vulnerable in not possessing *strategies* for reconciling work and non work tensions. In different ways both display individualised and marginalised accounts of their relationship with work and non work situations. By contrast the strategic often displays a strategic 'reading' and interpretation of chance to their own and the organisation's advantage.

Strategic compliance

The vast majority of middle managers interviewed in the project complied strategically. This response is perhaps best explained as a form of artful pragmatism which reconciles professional and managerial interests. In their study of a Technical and Further Education (TAFE) college in Australia, Seddon and Brown (1997) describe such strategic compliers as possessing innovative strategies for dealing with the pressures of income generation, flexibilisation and work intensification while, at the same time, continuing their commitments to educational or other professional values of student care, support and collegiality. In this study, strategic compliers also retain their professional values and bend with change in order to protect their staff. Although they accept some aspects of the new FE work culture as non-negotiable (for example, new contract conditions) they attempt to work around these conditions within their own sectors, in different ways. They also maintain a strong sense of student and staff perspective, although variations exist in the approaches adopted by strategic managers. Some are beginning to get caught up in the competitive environment following the logic of economic rationalism so far described. For example, Ken believes that it is logical to close down certain sections of the college because they are inefficient. However. he speaks of his determination to protect staff from administration in order that they may get on with the job of teaching:

> Ken: I think my job is to protect lecturers and the Heads of Section from the administration, and they concentrate on teaching.

Unlike willing compliers, middle managers such as Ken do not identify strongly with the corporate image of their respective institutions. They recognise that a major part of their role involves 'selling' the party line to lecturers as crisis and stress are pushed further down the line (Watkins. 1993). At the same time they also maintain a personal and professional distance from senior management, in order to retain their credibility with *their* staff. In doing so they manage and maintain context specific identities in their routine practices at work.

> Chris: We have been told that we are managers. As a result we do protect the college as much as maybe the senior managers might do. I hope I'm not seen by my staff as too closely linked to senior management because that would not do my credibility any good, and yet I regularly have to put their line across to the staff.

Strategic compilers do not readily accept the 'party line' on definitions of quality as measured by output, or of professionalism as predetermined by service delivery. Although they comply strategically by switching identities in different contexts, they are also conscious of being consumed by managerial preoccupations and paperwork:

> Isabel: I fear I could be removed totally from the person that I originally was . . . I think the culture is now that everybody is trying to prove that they deserve their job . . . and one of the physical manifestations of the job is proving to have a pile of paper coming through.

For Isabel real quality is defined in terms of a 'no frills' model, that is distinct from what she calls 'paper' quality:

> Isabel: . . . I believe in] . . . the 'Kwik save model' of education, so that there are no frills; no frills so that you don't sink up to your belly button in carpet as soon as you come into the place or there is a razzmatazz lounge for the students to lounge around in . . . because I think ultimately the resources should go into materials and teaching . . . What I would term as quality is the time for focus groups, where lecturers can get together and talk about non administration issues, but there is very little time.

In this case such group meetings are sometimes held without the knowledge of senior managers. For middle managers such meetings are seen as essential for retaining some measure of professional autonomy based around educational values. In Chris's college, middle managers attempted to meet as a separate group in order to develop innovative strategies to deal with pressures of work intensification and income generation. Paradoxically, such action posed a threat to the dominant managerial culture of the college and was swiftly halted by the Principal.

> Chris: I brought together the Sector heads' rogue meetings. The Principal said we couldn't meet. He misunderstood the reason why we met; we met to share ideas and most of the time to develop the college.

While this group drew on residual elements of professional and collegial culture in embracing the business culture of FE they were, at the same time, reminded of where power lies in the new corporate structure. Paradoxically their innovative 'reading' of how best to broker market and professional concerns in the interests of the college reveals conflict with senior management over how this is best achieved. Thus, if at one level middle managers are becoming more skilfully handling tasks which senior managers throw at them such actions – as those of the Principal – reinforce the ambiguity of their occupational role. However, without access to the necessary financial and other data middle managers have become adept at 'reading' signs and signals which connect the top to the bottom of the organisation, a factor often more important than the financial detail itself. Having an ear close to both senior managers and lecturers allows middle managers to interpret the 'middle ground' while, at the same time, maintaining distance between both groups allowing room for manoeuvre. Walter, for example, prefers to identify himself as a third layer of management, not part of the lecturing staff or senior management but near to both; though significantly with roots in teaching.

> Walter: . . . I am not basically a through and through manager . . . I enjoy being able to generate new projects but still nevertheless be near to the staff. I mean not part of the staff but near to them, able to share in what goes on and see things from their point of view . . . and to promote teaching and learning . . . We are managers, we accept that now, but I think our roots are in teaching.

Unlike willing or unwilling compliers, such middle managers demonstrate a broader interpretation of their work, which is less defensive, optimistic and obsessive. In the context of the study, the different responses referred to signify the complexities of similar groups culturally interpreting the (FE) workplace in different ways. As Seddon and Brown (1997) note, decentralisation and marketisation drive diverse responses, shifting the patterns of education provision and practice in ways which are often double edged:

> Neither advocates nor critics of reform, capture this complexity sufficiently.
> Exciting developments in the application of technology in pedagogy and
> innovative assessment practices exist alongside and *because of* huge
> intensification, casualisation and the erosion of teachers' working conditions.
> (Seddon and Brown, 1997, emphasis in original)

Thus, to draw attention simply to the processes of deprofessionalisation without reference to its relationship to the processes of professional reconstruction
is to misrecognise ways in which narrative and context and give 'voice' to
new reworkings of identity and professionalisation in the education workplace. However, focusing primarily on the effects of deprofessionalisation is
reactive and implies that education is driven by external forces and that education workers are just victims of history (Seddon, 1997). While it is certainly
the case that ongoing battles involving public sector workers (teachers, nurses,
health, social workers and others) are being accommodated through managerialist principles, the process is by no means complete, uncontested or static.
To see middle managers, therefore, as either fully fledged members of the corporation, as victims or malcontents, is to ignore how different cultures and
identities are formed within and by changing work practices and, importantly,
how they also influence those practices.

   This brings us full circle to the central theme of the chapter. If at one level,
market and managerial reform in FE is seen to have undermined professionalism and collegiality, at another, it has paradoxically exposed anomalies and
myths surrounding the very existence of such values. That being the case
what new constructions of professionalism are emerging from a system
acknowledged by many to be in crisis? If there was no 'golden age' of FE how
are we to make sense of what subsequently happened? In addressing these
questions we seek to provide a synthesis of some of the theoretical and substantive issues raised in the chapter, as they bear on changing professional
and managerial cultures in the wider context of education reform.

Conclusion

This chapter has examined the role that middle managers play in the process
of filtering market reform in the post-incorporated education sector. In a climate of rapid and unpredictable change, in which struggles over the
meaning, identity and ethos of FE have been to the fore, we have argued that
middle managers play a crucial role in mediating change in the education
workplace. In doing so, they are actively involved in the reconstruction of
professional and managerial cultures in this volatile sector. Not only do they
mediate different tensions between, for example, funding and curriculum,
but they also filter competing messages from 'above and below', in the trans-

lation of policy into practice, effectively 'buffering' potential conflict between senior managers and lecturers. The dilemmas that middle managers face possess a materiality and meaning which cannot be disassociated from the interventionist role of the state. The accounts to which we have referred articulate the contradictions experienced by professionals in mediating tensions over funding, contracts and working conditions, which find their expression in a managerial state (Clarke and Newman, 1997), and in the identities of those who work for it. In the attempt to steer the economy to international competitiveness, education policy has shifted its corporate responsibilities onto individuals and institutions. Thus, in transferring the burden of bureaucracy and financial accountability onto schools and colleges, such institutions have become 'liable' for their own autonomy. However, in order to accomplish this steering role the contracting state has shrunk the public sector, making institutions self managerial in the process. Though obscured, the economic rationalism which underpins this process of control reveals itself in democratic forms associated with devolution and de-regulation. At the same time this process transfers responsibility for policy effectiveness and, in particular policy failure, from government to institutions themselves.

What we have sought to demonstrate are the ways in which such transference of power and control finds expression among professionals in the education workplace. However, the ambiguous territory occupied by middle managers in their various institutions is compounded by a vulnerability that gives rise to different professional responses within and across the loose categories of 'middleness' and 'duality'. Though there is some evidence of managers being incorporated into the dominant managerialist discourse of professionalism (that emphasises loyalty to organisations above collegiality; competence over knowledge, compliance over judgement and outcome over process), this is by no means complete. A majority of middle managers in this study, for example, adopted an approach of strategic compliance in dealing with pressures from above and below while, at the same time, maintaining a commitment to educational and other professional values in support of student care and collegiality. In maintaining a personal and professional distance from 'the corporation' they thereby managed and adopted context specific identities in their routine practices at work. By drawing on residual elements of public sector professionalism and reworking these values within the context of an incorporated and marketised model of FE, strategic compliers present a challenge to managerialism suggesting that professionalism is not a fixed or static concept but is rather subject to social, political and cultural definition. One interpretation of such mediation is to view it as an artful form of self preservation, in response to potentially conflictual relations between lecturer and senior manager interests. Another possibility is to see it as a basis for rethinking professionalism in the FE sector and for raising new questions about the way in which professionalism can be reworked and pursued (Grace, 1995; Seddon. 1997).

If a combination of market and managerialist policies currently restrict the possibilities of professionals seeking common purpose, they also draw attention to ways in which this can happen. Paradoxically, the limitations of devolved managerialism both negate and draw attention to the conditions which give rise to a variety of professional responses in the education workplace. As we have sought to demonstrate, the majority of middle managers in this study operated strategically to ensure that their staff were protected and that educational values were promoted as far as possible within the new management culture of FE. We would conclude by arguing that the accounts of middle managers discussed here say much about two things: first, they point to the ways in which new professional identities arise from ambiguities and contradictions in the education workplace; and, second, they show how a variety of identities and responses, though shaped and influenced by managerialism are not determined by it. This suggests that managerialism is not as complete or uncontested as is often assumed, and that we should look for innovative signs of professional life in new ways and places.

Acknowledgements

The authors wish to acknowledge the support of the Economic and Social Research Council in funding the research on which this chapter is based (ESRC award number R000236713). We are grateful to the staff in our case study colleges who took part in the research.

References

Ainley and Bailey, (1997), *The Business of Learning*, London: Cassell.

Avis, J., (1996), 'The Enemy Within: Quality and Managerialism in Education', Avis *et al.*, *Knowledge and Nationhood*, London: Cassell.

Beckett, F., (1998), 'A Chance to Build Peace', *Guardian Education*, 20.1.98.

Casey, C., (1995), *Work, Self and Society: After Industrialism*, London: Routledge.

Clarke, J. and Newman, J., (1997), *The Managerial State*, London: Sage

Dale, R., (1989), *The State and Education Policy*, Milton Keynes: Open University.

Elliot, G., (1996a), 'Educational Management and the Crisis of Reform in Further Education', *Journal of Education and Training*, 48(1): 5–23.

Elliot, G., (1996b), *Crisis and Change in Vocational Education and Training*, London: Jessica Kingsley.

Elliot, G. and Crossley, M., (1994), 'Qualitative Research, Education Management and the Incorporation of the Further Education Sector', *Educational Management and Administration*, 22(3): 188–97.

Esland, G. (1996), 'Education, Training and Nation-State Capitalism: Britain's Failing Strategy', in Auis *et al.*, *Knowledge and Nationhood*, London: Cassell.

Evans, B., (1992), *The Politics of the Training Market: From Manpower Services Commission to Training and Enterprise Councils*, London: Routledge.

Fergusson, R., (1994), 'Managing Education', in J. Clarke, A. Cochrane and E. McLaughlin (eds.), *Managing Social Policy*, London: Sage.

Friend, A. and Metcalf, A., (1992), *Slump City: the Politics of Mass Unemployment*, London: Pluto.

General Educator, (1997), *Journal of the NATFHE General Education Section*, Sheffield: NATFHE.

Grace, G., (1995), *School Leadership: Beyond Educational Management*, London: Falmer Press.

Hetherington, K. and Munro, R., (1997), *Ideas of Difference: Stability, Social Spaces and the Labour of Division*, Oxford: Blackwell Publishers.

Kenway, J., (1994), (ed.), *Economising Education: The Post-Fordist Directions*. Deakin University: Deakin University Press.

Labier, D., (1986), *Modern Madness: The Hidden Link between Work and Emotional Conflict*, New York: Simon and Schuster.

Ozga, J., (1995), 'Deskilling a Profession: Professionalism, Deprofessionalism and the New Managerialism', in H. Busher and R. Saran, *Managing Teachers as Professionals in Schools*, London: Kogan Page.

Pollitt, C., (1990), *Managerialism and the Public Services*, Oxford: Blackwell.

Randle, K. and Brady, N., (1994), 'Further Education and New Managerialism', *Journal of Further and Higher Education*, 22(2): 229–39.

Randle, K. and Brady, N., (1997), 'Managerialism and Professionalism in the Cinderella Service', *Journal of Vocational Education and Training*, 49(1): 121–39.

Ranson, S., (1994), *Toward the Learning Society*, London: Cassell.

Ranson, S. and Nixon, J., (1997), 'Theorising Agreement: The Moral Bases of the Emergent Professionalism within the New Management of Education', *Discourse*, 18(2): 197–214.

Seddon, T., (1997), 'Education: Deprofessionalised? Or Reregulated, Reorganised and Re-authorised?', forthcoming in *Australian Journal of Education*.

Seddon, T. and Brown, L., (1996), 'Teachers' Work and Professionalisation. Towards 2007', unpublished paper, University of Melbourne, Australia.

Watkins, R., (1993), 'Pushing Crisis and Stress Down the Line: The Self-Managing School', in J. Smyth (ed.), *A Socially Critical View of the Self-Managing School*, London: The Falmer Press.

Watson, T., (1997), 'The Labour of Division: Manager as "self" and "other",' in K. Hetherington and R. Munro, *Ideas of Difference*, Oxford: Blackwell.

17

Between Hierarchical Control and Collegiality: The Academic Middle Manager in Higher Education

David Hellawell and Nick Hancock

We interviewed 14 academic middle managers in three of the nine faculties of one of the 'newer' UK universities about the nature of university middle management, as they perceived it. These managers were at the level of Dean, Associate Dean and Head of Department (HOD) or its equivalent. Interestingly, none of our interviewees objected to our use of the term 'academic middle manager' to define their roles when we gave them the opportunity to do so, and they all appeared to accept that it was an accurate depiction of their positions in the university. One interviewee did, however, add the afterthought that he would prefer to be seen as an academic and a manager rather than an academic manager. On balance, they tended to feel they were being pushed by external and internal pressures to become more 'managerial', but the majority clearly wished to maintain some academic profile, generally regretting that it could not be a greater one. Only one of these interviewees was female which reflects the fact that there are relatively few female academic managers in Higher Education (HE). We promised anonymity to all our interviewees; so to protect the anonymity of this lone female, all our respondents are referred to in the singular by the male gender. This does have the benefit of underlining the overwhelmingly male composition of our opportunity sample.

One of the clusters of questions we posed to the interviewees in the course of the semi-structured interviews centred on the extent to which collegiality was still a significant factor in the university's internal decision-making processes. The cluster was prefaced by a reference to collegiality as 'decision-making by discussion among equals rather than by hierarchical level' and was followed by the questions:

Source: *Research Papers in Education*, Vol. 16, no. 2, 2001, pp. 183–97. Edited version.

To what extent does collegiality still exist in the management here? Do you have a view on the pros and cons of collegiality?

No other cluster of questions raised responses that went more to the heart of the interviewees' perceptions of their roles, although the chapter does also draw upon the responses to a wide range of other questions.

Our reading, as well as our experience of working in schools and HE as middle managers, shaped our own view of collegiality. A definition of the term in the UK school context is the following by Bush (1995; p. 52), which states that collegiality:

> assume(s) that organisations determine policy and make decisions through a process of discussion leading to consensus. Power is shared among some or all members of the organisation who are thought to have a mutual understanding about the objectives of the institution.

It might, however, be useful for the purposes of this chapter also to quote some key phrases from a statement first issued in 1987 by the California State University, Sacramento about their revised policy on collegiality at that time. They add some helpful 'acts of faith' about the subject which are intended to inform the working practice of an HE organization.

> Collegiality consists of a shared decision-making process and a set of values which regard the members of the various university constituencies as essential for the success of the academic enterprise . . . Collegial governance allows the academic community to work together to find the best answers to issues facing the university . . . Collegiality rests on a network of interlinked procedures jointly devised, whose aim is to assure the opportunity for timely advice pertinent to decisions about curricular and academic personnel matters . . . faculty recommendations are normally accepted, except in rare instances and for compelling reasons . . . Central to collegiality and shared decision-making is respect for differing opinions and points of view, which welcomes diversity and actively sponsors its opinions. (California, 1996; p. 1)

The fact that this policy statement was revised and available on the Internet, suggests that the university in question has not abandoned its traditional views on collegiality. There may, nevertheless, be a gap between the public rhetoric and the past and present educational practice. One obvious point to make in this respect is that collegiality was, in the present writers' experience, in reality never meant to apply to administrative staff in the UK context. We also have some limited personal experience of the possibly even wider gap in North America between 'faculty' (i.e. academic staff) and university administrative staff who certainly did not see themselves as part of the 'academic community' as far as collegiality was concerned. For this reason, this chapter refers only to the management of academic staff, although it is interesting to note that some of the managers we interviewed did indeed make sharp distinctions between the management of the two categories of staff. One of them caricatured the general distinction as having to manage, on the one hand, academic staff who did not want to be managed at all, and, on the other hand, too many administrative staff who wanted to be directed to an excessive degree!

A possible erosion of traditional university collegiality could be implied in the way we phrased the issue to our interviewees, but we would defend ourselves against the argument that the questions were unduly leading. It has been widely accepted that the 'new' UK universities, established in general from the former polytechnics, have managerial systems that are much more hierarchical in nature than the traditional collegial model. This trend away from traditional collegiality has, in any case, been seen by some as endemic across the whole university system in the UK and elsewhere (see e.g. Smyth, 1995; Wilmott, 1995; Sizer, 1998). In the particular new university where we interviewed, for example, the annual appraisal system introduced in the late 1980s was from its outset of a top-down nature where it was usual for the individual to be appraised by his or her line manager. The middle managers are all now appointments in the case study university and not, as in some cases in the older universities, post-holders elected from and by their colleagues. (Although it is important to note that the academic middle manager posts have varied backwards and forwards between 'permanent' and 'fixed-term' appointment in the case study university over the last decade and more.) Not to have acknowledged these sorts of realities in the way that the question was put would, we argue, have laid us open to an accusation of naiveté from our interviewees.

In any case, the UK university system is not alone in having its academic critics who allege that there has been what they tend to see as a general and, in their view, unfortunate shift away from collegial towards more hierarchical models of decision-making in their countries. (See for example such writers about Australian university management as Penington, 1991; Williams, 1992; Stockley, 1993.) We do not argue that the operation of collegiality in the university in this case study is necessarily representative of all universities. We do, however, argue that something can be learned from it which can add to our understanding of the concept of collegiality and give us insights into the extent to which it is still applicable to HE organizations in general. Furthermore, the responses of our interviewees on the subject appear to us to highlight some wider conceptual issues concerning the role of the middle manager in HE, which was the major preoccupation of our research. What we are not going to dwell upon in this chapter are the well-known *generic* problems of middle managers stemming from differing expectations of them by their superiors and their subordinates. Indeed, our interviewees themselves seemed to take it for granted that we would understand that their being between a rock and a hard place was endemic in this respect, and they only touched upon this *general* issue in passing. What they did dwell upon at length were the *particular* (and very special) issues in HE as regards the nature of managerial control at levels above and below them in the hierarchy. These issues *will* recur throughout this chapter and in the concluding sections we will attempt to generate some hypotheses about the conceptual nature of these issues.

Difficulties with Collegiality

It is possible to summarize one aspect of the responses we received from our interviewees relatively easily. At the lower levels of the organization the majority of the respondents certainly felt that collegiality was still viewed as the norm in interpersonal relations even where there were obstacles to it. As they viewed the various levels up the hierarchy, however, the interviewees felt that collegiality decreased. One of the problems of promoting cross-faculty and even intra-departmental collegiality even at grassroots levels, advanced by a number of the interviewees, was the practical logistical difficulty of communication in a large university with many buildings and many sites. One Dean pointed to the fact that the faculty academic staff who had to work together in designing and delivering courses had until recently been widely scattered across a large building, although he was now trying to remedy this by reallocating tutorial accommodation. Such reallocation was, however, not a possibility open to another Dean who had staff in separate faculty departments, which were in different buildings altogether. Similarly, a third Dean simply took it as axiomatic that his HODs were compelled to operate their departments separately for most of the time because they were even more widely geographically scattered and could in no way be described as even being on the same campus. He did acknowledge, however, that his perception was that some of these departments operated in more hierarchical ways than others, so physical location may not be the determinant of the degrees of collegiality *within* departments. Nevertheless, the members of the traditional 'collegium' in the universities of yesteryear were indeed usually housed together, and it is obviously difficult to have a faculty, for example, working collegially if some of its academic tutors have no physical proximity with each other. Size also seemed to be a key variable according to those we interviewed, because they felt that the most collegial relationships were at the course team level, where the smaller the course team the more likely it was that the staff would operate in close collaboration.

It may not be possible for all staff of a faculty to work collegially together because of the physical separation referred to above. Our impression was that there were those among the middle managers who actually welcomed the opportunity for individual sections to 'go it alone'. It would, however, still be possible for a faculty board, for example, to meet in a regular fashion and to operate collegially to a greater or lesser extent. Many of the responses were, therefore, directed at the degree to which those who did meet on a regular face to face basis in the university were operating collegially or not, and the extent to which collegial decision-making was either desirable or practicable.

Imperfections of collegiality

There were certainly those who saw many imperfections in collegial decision-making. One which was noted by a number of the academic managers we interviewed was that it was possible for vocal and articulate individuals to sway the decision-making process so that apparently collegial decisions were driven by some of the staff who had their own 'agendas'. These agendas were viewed as negative in some instances. So one manager talked of those who wanted to throw 'spanners in the works'. Writers on collegiality in other contexts have commented on such behaviour. Brundrett (1998, p. 311), for example, writes:

> In effect individuals and groups seek to realise their values and goals at the expense of others but seek to legitimate their power through assuming the cloak of the moral legitimacy lent to them by the apparent use of democratic procedures.

This tendency was also linked by our interviewees to some staff who had been members of the university for a long time. As one of them put it, 'they tend to have a lot of influence because of their experience'. In one particular faculty there was a clear consensus among the managers that there were long-serving members of staff who had grievances which went back a long way and who would act in negative ways if they could. One manager in particular linked this to the way the old 'Silver Book' contract terms had been done away over a decade previously for new entrants to the university. He considered that even some of those longer-serving members of staff, who had also been persuaded (by financial as well as other incentives) to sign up for the new contracts, still used the issue as a focal point for dissent. In one department in this faculty, which had been managed by another of our interviewees, over half the staff were, in any case, still on the old 'Silver Book' contract. He and other managers elsewhere in the university pointed to some of the difficulties this caused for themselves and others when, for example, they were unable to rely upon such staff to be available once the students had departed on vacations, because of the former's generous 'holiday' allowances.

This kind of resistance to change has been noted much more frequently in the research literature on the FE colleges in England since their 'incorporation' in 1993. A good example of this can be found in Elliott (1996, p. 4) when he writes:

> . . . it appeared to the writer, working with lecturers in the FE sector that they could draw upon a repertoire of strategies to thwart attempts to impose systemic and specific changes perceived to be at variance with their core values.

Our experience might suggest that the prevalence of a 'compliance culture' whereby academics have supinely complied with the progressive 'fragmentation, stratification and alienation' of academic work (Smyth, 1995) has been overestimated by some commentators on trends in HE. The examples given by our interviewees seem to point to resistance to such trends not only at the formal level of refusal to sign new contracts, but also in the form of a potent 'underground' influence exerted by some of those who have indeed signed these contracts. It should be pointed out, however, that while our middle managers were understandably preoccupied with those members of staff who were unduly resistant to change (implicitly the minority), they acknowledged that there were others who enthusiastically responded to new challenges. With these latter staff, it was implied, collegial forms of management worked well.

In general though, there was an acceptance by almost all the managers we interviewed that achieving decisions through collegiality could be a slow and difficult process with some staff, which at times could be very demanding for the managers concerned. One of our interviewees likened it to 'walking through treacle'. There was a widespread acceptance that it called for abilities to listen, persuade, cajole and, in general, act with considerable patience in the face of what were sometimes seen as quite unreasonable objections by some members of staff. To a middle manager who had a vision, which he wished the unit to both share and pursue with some urgency, this could be extremely frustrating. Staff were seen as having the means to 'bog down' the decision-making process so that the implementation of policies was delayed or, in some cases, actually prevented. Managers talked of having to 'play a long game' and seeing persuasion often as a long, slow process. Even when a consensus had been achieved on a particular plan of action, it was noted that some members of staff did not always feel personally obliged to go along with it at the implementation stage. This was, however, seen as a distinct over-stepping of the collegial mark, and one where tutors should be made aware in no uncertain terms of the error of their ways. There was some feeling among our middle management interviewees that some of these academic staff identified themselves with fellow 'professionals' such as lawyers and doctors when it came to resisting the kind of directive line man-

agement thought to be more commonly experienced in industry or commerce. They were, however, also perceived as often unwilling to accept some
of the stringent responsibilities which members of those other professions
were generally supposed to carry.

Bypassing or Subverting the Collegial Process

It is hardly surprising, therefore, that some of our interviewees felt that the
collegial processes were often bypassed, subverted or simply ignored. There
was a general view that this happened more frequently further up the hierarchy. An instance commonly cited by our interviewees was one where the
Vice Chancellor (VC) was perceived to have taken an unwise managerial
decision (most unusually it was implied) many years earlier on behalf of the
university. Our interviewees considered this to have been largely a personal
decision despite the fact that the Senate and the Governing Body had formally approved it. There was explicit and implicit criticism of the ability or
desire of these latter bodies to resist strong pressures of this kind from the
VC. One of our managers in particular saw the Senate as much less collegial
in practice, as far as the academic staff were concerned, than had been the
Academic Board under previous polytechnic directors. This was an issue
which appeared to have some strong emotive elements for the manager concerned because he used terms such as 'sycophants' to describe the kind of
people he now felt were attracted to serve on Senate. He was, however,
echoed in his views by one of the few other managers in our group also able,
by virtue of length of service, to make comparisons between such bodies in
the university and the former polytechnic. The latter manager talked of
Senate as now being a 'rubber-stamping' instrument for 'Directorate decisions' and he also felt that the constitution of the former polytechnic
Governing Body had been much more representative as far as the staff of the
university were concerned. The more general criticism being made here was
that at the upper levels of the university there was insufficient 'timely advice'
being taken onboard before decisions were made. It has to be stated as a
counter to this, however, that one of the managers who had only had recent
experience of Senate and the Deans Directorate meetings found them to be
'more open and supportive and more helpful/developmental than I'd antici-
pated'. This was an unusual response because the much more common
reaction of our interviewees was that these meetings had far too many people
present to be effective, which consequently left the steering of decision-
making firmly in the hands of the Directorate. (The majority of our middle
managers had to be relying mainly, if not entirely, on hearsay evidence as
regards the effectiveness of Deans-Directorate meetings, because only the
Deans of those we interviewed were regular attendees.)

It has to be constantly borne in mind that we interviewed nobody below the head of department level and so it is perhaps not surprising that the criticisms of this kind tended to be of 'abuses' of the collegial processes above that level. If we had interviewed 'grassroots' members of staff we would no doubt have received criticisms of a similar kind levelled against heads of department. There may well be a widespread human tendency to act 'managerially' to one's subordinates but to resist the managerial tendencies of one's superiors! Nevertheless, there may be some general validity in the claim by one HOD that his role meant that he had to be 'closer' to his staff and carry them with him. He implied that this might not have been the case if he had occupied a more elevated position in the hierarchy where he could have been more remote from the 'chalk face'. To some extent, the HOD at least still has to have 'subject credibility' in the eyes of the members of that department if he is to offer academic leadership as well as exert managerial control. It should also not be forgotten that in their teaching capacity (however small this might have now become in some cases), these middle managers are also the colleagues of those they manage, and may even play subordinate roles within particular course teams.

To be seen to be acting in a non-collegial fashion may, therefore, cause more difficulties for the HOD in this respect than it might for those higher up the hierarchy. Even so, the person at the next level up in this hierarchy, the Dean, has to step very carefully in this respect, at least as regards his managerial subordinates. One Dean in particular had apparently established an 'executive' group in the management structure of the faculty which in effect excluded the HODs and made the latter feel, we were told, that managerial decisions were taken above their heads with any subsequent consultation with them being of a token nature. It was argued that the Dean concerned had taken the criticism which they had expressed on board, but only to the extent of renaming the 'executive' as the 'advisory' group. We were informed that the HODs involved saw this as more cosmetic than real in its response to their concerns.

In this instance we were aware of general feelings among our interviewees that this Dean had reservations about the collegial approach to decision-making, and he did express some of these in his own interview. According to our other interviewees, he tended to circumvent it with devices such as that cited, so that the consultation process was sometimes perceived as more of a mechanism for persuasion than for genuine listening to views before positions were taken up. There was nevertheless some sympathy for this approach both on the grounds of the problems of collegiality already referred to, and also on the grounds that the Deans themselves were perceived as pressured by the Directorate in some non-collegial ways. One of our interviewees alleged that it was quite a frequent message received from the Directorate that 'managers should manage' which he interpreted as an injunction to achieve results with staff more speedily. To use our own analogies, middle managers in the university might have to behave more like facilitating trainers in their handling of their subordinates but they themselves often felt as if they were treated as 'non-commissioned officers' by their own superiors. They felt that they would soon be in trouble, however, if they acted like sergeant majors with their own staff.

In another faculty a former Dean was seen by some of his erstwhile subordinates whom we interviewed as having acted in what were described as authoritarian ways to achieve his objectives. There was considerable resentment expressed by two of his former subordinates at the 'dictatorial' behaviour of this Dean. They argued that it had often led to ill-considered decisions, which had not been sufficiently thought through in advance and had led to some very unfortunate consequences. In fact, the most charitable epithet applied to this former Dean's managerial style by *any* of his erstwhile subordinates was 'autocratic', and this was attributed by a number of them to his various alleged personal characteristics such as insecurity. Individual psychology may, therefore, play a part in the nature of the managerial control that is exercised. It is interesting, however, that not one interviewee considered that this style of management could even be contemplated as functional at HOD level, and nobody thought it had ultimately been productive when employed by this particular Dean. Nor did any of our interviewees advance psychological reasons for the 'strong' management alleged to be exercised at times by the Directorate. This did seem to be perceived as a sociological/organizational rather than a psychological issue.

Positive Views about Collegiality

In this next section, we must, however, record the positive views about collegiality, which were expressed by the majority of these middle managers, including even those who could also see the downsides. To a perhaps surprising extent in the light of some of the comments referred to above, collegiality was still seen by nearly all our interviewees as the most effective form of decision-making for higher education. As one HOD expressed it, collegiality could generate spontaneous creativity arising from shared ideas in a non-managerial environment. He did not feel it was possible to direct staff to be creative or to be good teachers. Those qualities could only emerge from within a professional environment of the traditional collegial kind.

Partly however, this allegiance to collegiality may only have been an acceptance on the part of some managers of the perception that academics would resist and effectively undermine all other forms of managerial control. The nature of the teaching and learning processes was seen as such that only staff who were engaged and committed would ensure successful outcomes.

The majority of our middle managers saw this kind of commitment as achievable only if the 'hearts and minds' of staff were won over in favour of the policies proposed. As one middle manager put it, it was no use *telling* staff that the VC had decided that things had to be done in a particular way, 'because it won't work'. To this extent at least the middle managers we interviewed still saw the university, at least *below* their managerial level, as what Charles Handy (1977) called an 'organization of consent':

> For the distinction between the organization of consent and the traditional hierarchical organization is that the authority in the former is granted by those below whereas in the hierarchical state authority is conferred by these above. Your official role in the organization of consent gives you little effective power – that is only won by the consent of those you seek to manage. Nor does this consent, once given, hold good for all time or for all circumstances. It needs constant ratification. (Ibid.; p. 251)

Williams (1989, p. 80) has outlined the moral dimension of this concept:

> The moral character of an exercise of authority is based on the presence of consent on the part of those subject to its jurisdiction . . . Where consent is not made a condition of authority, then we are not speaking of moral authority, but of the exercise of power, or purely formal or legal authority.

It is, however, interesting nevertheless to note that there was a perception that middle managers might be 'told' what they had to achieve by *their* managers in the Directorate. (Indeed the pressures 'from the top' placed on middle managers to 'deliver' were described by one of them as 'beyond what is reasonable', and others echoed that sentiment without using those precise words.) They just did not think it was possible to do their own jobs effectively by simply passing the Directorate message down the line without an attempt to persuade their staff of its virtues. In effect, they could be argued to be implicitly making the point that the 'organization of consent' still began from the bottom up but now stopped at their level.

One of our middle managers argued that he could use collegiality as a means of putting pressure on individual members of staff and to this extent it could be an agency of control as well as of resistance. Their own colleagues would not let them have, for example, unduly favourable timetables if the process of timetable allocation was transparent to the extent that the staff team itself had to decide collectively how the total allocation of timetabled hours for a course should be divided up. Others accepted that the official authority of their roles gave them some opportunity to 'drive policy' but only if they had been seen to listen to the views of their colleagues first. To this extent they saw themselves as occupying positions where they were first among equals, facilitating cooperative working. Nevertheless, those heads of department who had previously been course team leaders felt they had at least more authority in the former than in the latter roles where the *only* weapons at their disposal had been persuasion and exhortation. One Dean argued that at the end of the day he had to take some decisions where no consensus had been possible. His position gave him the authority to do that, but for those decisions to be effective that could only be done after a lengthy process of consultation and discussion had taken place.

The Vulnerability of the Academic Middle Manager

We will now go on to argue that in the context of the newer universities in the UK in particular all this puts the academic middle manager in a relatively vulnerable position when it is compared to that occupied by their subordinates. There are, in our view, many dilemmas facing academic middle managers in HE now that they are increasingly expected in some universities to be at least as much resource managers and fund-raising entrepreneurs as they are academic leaders. This is particularly true in some of the newer universities where a new breed of VC emerged over the period when these former polytechnics were taking on university status and severing their links with their former LEA controllers. In certain respects these new VCs were more inclined to run their institutions as quasi-businesses. Much more overtly than was the case in the traditional universities, these VCs operated as though the universities were what Roger Harrison (1972) and Charles Handy (1976) originally designated as 'power cultures'. As Handy describes it:

> This culture depends on a central power source, with rays of power and
> influence spreading out from that central figure. They are connected by
> functional or specialist strings but the power rings are the centres of activity and
> influence. (Handy, 1976; p. 178)

At that time Handy did not, as we have already noted, see universities as having that kind of culture at all. Indeed, the university culture of consent that he described was much more akin to his notions of 'existentialist' or 'people' cultures. These are cultures where the individual is more important than the organization and the organization attempts to control these individuals closely at its peril. He saw the power culture, on the other hand, as much more closely associated, for example, with the kinds of 'robber baron' commercial and industrial companies of the USA of the nineteenth century. He noted, however, that these were 'strong' organizations which had certain advantages:

They have the ability to move quickly and can react well to threat or danger. Whether they do move in the right direction will, however, depend on the person or persons in the centre. (Ibid.; pp. 178–9)

One could argue that the universities in the 1980s and 1990s were very much more under threat than had previously been the case as the levels of govern- ment funding were steadily reduced. The dangers of this were very promptly seen by many of the new breed of HE leaders who were equally quick to pursue policies of very rapid expansion of student numbers when this was financially advantageous to the institutions concerned.

The individuals who had to deliver this expansion were, however, the middle managers. Only they were close enough to the staff and the students to know which existing courses could be rapidly expanded, or which new courses could be almost as rapidly designed, validated and promoted to fit the new niches in the markets which they had the expertise to identify. So a new breed of middle manager was also called for in these new power cul- tures. The spider at the centre of the web of a power culture (to use another image from Handy) is often keen *not* to 'micro-manage' so that the subordi- nates are allowed to have considerable degrees of autonomy. But the spider retains central control of the key threads (usually financial) which link the outer and inner circles of the web. The managers whom we interviewed did indeed feel that the key area of decision-making in the university where they felt most in the dark was that of financial control and allocation from the centre. As Handy (Ibid.; p. 179) again writes of these cultures:

Individuals employed in them will prosper and be satisfied to the extent that they are power-orientated, politically minded, risk-taking, and rate security as a minor element in their psychological contract.

This is not a description of the traditional academic middle manager that would have sprung readily to the minds of many of the commentators on the *modus vivendi* of the university professor of yesteryear. Certainly as depicted in the literature of much of the nineteenth and twentieth centuries, professors were often seen as somewhat unworldly eccentrics so concerned with the pursuit of 'truth' that the worlds of business and commerce were very distant from the planets on which they resided. To some extent this was always a caricature and writers who had inside experience of even the most venerable of the HE institutions tended to be much more aware of the sharp- ness and the cruelty of academic politics.

Nevertheless, their particular brands of skulduggery and chicanery were conducted, at least on the surface, through the traditionally slow-moving collegial decision-making channels of working parties and committees which were supposed to come to conclusions largely based on consultation if not consensus. These are not the ways in which power cultures operate, and the consequences for middle managers can be very serious. To take a final quotation from Handy:

> These cultures put a lot of faith in the individual, little in committees. They judge by results and are tolerant of means. Often seen as tough or abrasive, though successful they may well suffer from low morale and high turnover in the middle layers as individuals fall or opt out of the competitive atmosphere. (Ibid.; p. 179)

Discussion

It is our contention that this may well be what has happened in the ranks of the middle managers in the newer universities. In some ways these middle managers are more vulnerable than the staff they manage, a point explicitly made by more than one of those we interviewed. The majority of members of the full-time staff on 'permanent' contracts are usually on standard career grades with a fixed incremental salary scale, so financial sanctions of a negative or positive kind are very difficult to apply to them. (This also makes the point that when the management of academic staff has been referred to in this chapter, we have not been discussing issues related to staff on short-term temporary contracts or 'visiting lecturers' etc. The interviews tended to confirm that such lecturers were not generally central to the preoccupations of the managers we interviewed: most of the latter claimed to have delegated this aspect of their management to others.) Similarly, these full-time academic staff have traditionally had little to lose in the way of formal status so that any threat to remove their non-teaching responsibilities from them on the grounds of poor performance might be perceived by some of them as more of a potential reward than a punishment.

The middle managers we interviewed felt that they had very few sanctions of any kind available to them when dealing with the full-time academic staff nominally under their control. Time and again they referred to the limits of their managerial control with academic staff they considered to be underperforming. Despite the ending of the traditional security of tenure for the majority of academic staff in the UK, it is still notoriously difficult to sack them for other than serious breaches of the disciplinary code. These problems of dealing with non-productive academic staff appear to be common to many developed countries (Jackson and Muir, 1994). This protection against dismissal from the university may also hold good for middle managers as far as their academic positions are concerned, but to them their managerial status *is* very important partly because this is linked to their salaries. If a restructuring process is undertaken in the course of which a HOD, for example, loses that position, his or her prestige within the institution will be severely affected and the HOD element of that salary may be, at the very least, frozen at that point. Others may have held their HOD positions on fixed-term contracts, and so lose completely that (often-significant) element of their salary previously linked to their managerial roles. So the demoted HOD, for example, could be bypassed in one way or another whenever future financial rewards of a specifically HOD nature are handed out.

All this can effectively turn the ex-HOD into somebody akin to what the Japanese describe as a 'window man'. This term may also apply, albeit to a lesser extent, to the demoted HOD still employed by the university but holding no significant managerial role any more. In the Japanese business community, the larger national and international organizations have also traditionally given effective security of tenure through their 'lifetime job guarantee'. In such circumstances, a manager may be reshuffled out of managerial responsibility but still continue working for the organization. The term 'window man' then signifies that the individual in question has been reallocated a desk placed near a window out of which he has little to do but gaze all day because nothing of any managerial significance is channelled through him any more. In a society where 'loss of face' is particularly shameful, this can be a very brutal sanction to employ.

In UK universities it may be less unbearable to become a window man because it is possible to return to a more significant academic role. Nevertheless, the extent of the psychological, and, to a lesser extent, financial punishment for a certain kind of striving and ambitious middle manager should not be underestimated. To that extent the middle manager is more vulnerable to the sanction of demotion than those at subordinate levels. One might well suspect that some of the revisions of organizational structures in universities have been undertaken with the primary purpose of removing some middle managers who have been perceived to be underperforming in one way or another. In the case study university some of these 'demotions' have simply been the non-renewal of fixed-term appointments, but in other cases some 'permanent' middle managers have had to reappraise their understanding of the meaning of permanence. (It is interesting to note, in passing, that some of the middle managers we interviewed felt that some of these demotions had followed resentment about the middle management expressed by the 'rank and file' to the middle managers' superiors. In other words, the middle managers' positions were, they felt, vulnerable to attack from below as well as above.) Some demotions of this kind at middle manager levels in the case study university were referred to by more than one of our interviewees as 'humiliations' of a very public kind. The sentiments of other interviewees clearly echoed that view even where in some cases they themselves had gained promotion as a consequence. Where circumstances have allowed, early retirements, or transfers to other organization altogether, have sometimes followed these demotions. (It is worth noting that all those who were inter-viewed were current middle management post-holders, none of whom, as far as we are aware, had themselves suffered these kinds of demotions at the time of the interviews. They must, nevertheless, have been aware of their own future vulnerability if past experience were to be repeated.)

It may be, however, increasingly difficult for the middle manager not to 'under-perform' in some aspect or other of a job which is becoming more and more complex and multifaceted. The traditional view of the middle management job as simply listening to, understanding and interpreting the strategic plans of senior management and then seeing that these plans are communicated to, and implemented by, the rank and file, is becoming obso-lescent if not obsolete (Floyd and Wooldridge, 1996). As the universities have been compelled by government funding decisions to become more entrepre-neurial and service-orientated, so that they are increasingly customer-driven rather than producer-driven, the management of relationships with the external world has become more and more vital. The budgetary issues alone, which stem from an increasing reliance on overseas students, fully funded and franchised courses etc., have multiplied in number and complexity in recent years. They are now, as a number of our interviewees pointed out, such as to require skills and expertise in financial matters that middle man-agers in the past were not required to display to anything like the same degree. Even with the assistance of administrative finance officers, much responsibility has to lie with the middle manager negotiating the contractual terms of new initiatives. The middle manager with his or her subject and resource expertise now plays a crucial role in following business precepts by ensuring that the organization stays 'close to the customer' so that 'repeat business' can be ensured (Peters and Waterman, 1982). It is interesting to note that in the case study university there has been none of the de-layering which had 'flattened' so many of the organizational structures of industrial and commercial enterprises in the 1980s and 90s. The arguments for the re-evaluation and reinstatement of the vital role of middle managers made in both learned journals and the practitioner literature (e.g. Jackson and Humble, 1994; Dauphinais and English, 1996; Mintzberg, 1996) appeared to have been heeded throughout this period in this university at least. Individual post-holders may have come and gone, but, by and large, the middle-management posts themselves have remained or even increased.

The needs and wants of the university's customers, whether or not this term is used to include the students themselves, are generally considered to be changing at rates unheard of in by-gone decades. This is particularly true of the knowledge-based sector in which the university is firmly based (Drucker, 1995). Keeping up with the trends in the customer's world is ever more demanding for the middle manager. For these reasons, the role is a cru-cial boundary-spanning one as well as an internal managerial function. This latter role has, however, also been made much more complex by the growing rates of change. There is more likely to be a lack of consensus among staff about the directions in which they and the organization should be moving as the choices proliferate. In universities which, as our middle managers argued, still operate to some extent collegially at least at the grassroots levels, gaining general consent for the ways forward is likely to be much more difficult. Yet it still appears to our interviewees a vital part of the middle manager's job in HE to gain the cooperation of the staff, despite the fact that the rate of innovation may be making interpersonal relationships more fraught.

Conclusion

We have avoided the use of lengthy quotations from the interviews in this chapter, up to now, but it might be appropriate to end on one as it sums up so well the general views of our interviewees on the rapidly changing role of the academic middle manager in HE. This came at the very end of the interview when the interviewee (generally regarded in our perception as an exceptionally competent and successful middle manager with a potentially lengthy career still ahead of him) was asked if he'd anything else to add:

> . . . I think the only thing I'd say about it, and I guess you'll probably find the same if you go and talk to the Heads of Department and other middle managers . . . is how the job has changed since I started, and that's only five or six years ago. It bears no relationship whatsoever hardly to where I was in 1992 and if it continues at that speed you've got to have pretty good reflexes to stay with it. And I think that the pace and range of things that I now have to deal with are just way beyond what they were in the past. And I think the main characteristic of the job at the moment is continual change and a continual attempt really to come to terms with that. And I don't think that's going to alter in the next few years. In fact, it's bound to get more and more complex.

References

Brundrett, M. (1998). 'What lies behind collegiality, legitimation or control?', *Educational Management and Administration*, 26, 3, 305–16.

Bush, T. (1995). *Exploring Collegiality: Theory, Practice and Structure. E 326 Managing Schools; Challenge and Response.* Milton Keynes: Open University Press.

California (1996). 'Policy statement on collegiality', *Manual of California State University, Sacramento.* Available online: http://www.csus.edu/admbus/umanual/UMC02250.htm (accessed 21 November 1999).

Dauphinais, B. and English, M. (1996). 'The renaissance of the middle manager', *Australian Accountant*, July, pp. 30–2.

Drucker, P.F. (1995). *Managing in a Time of Great Change*. Oxford: Butterworth-Heinemann.

Elliot, G. (1996). *Crisis and Change in Vocational Education and Training*. London: Jessica Kingsley.

Floyd, S.W. and Wooldridge, B. (1996). *The Strategic Middle Manager*. San Francisco: Jossey-Bass.

Handy, C.B. (1976). *Understanding Organizations*. Harmondsworth: Penguin.

Handy, C.B. (1977). 'The organizations of consent'. In Piper, D.W. and Glatter, R. (eds.) *The Changing University*. Slough: NFER, pp. 249–56.

Harrison, R. (1972). 'Understanding your organisation's character', *Harvard Business Review*, May/June 1972, reprinted in the *1975 Annual Handbook for Group Facilitators University Associates Publishers, Inc.*

Jackson, D. and Humble, J. (1994) 'Middle managers: new purpose, new directions', *Journal of Management Development*, 13, 3, pp. 15–21.

Jackson, J. and Muir, W. (1994). 'Managing non-productive university faculty members', *Educational Management and Administration*, 22, 3, 184–87.

Mintzberg, H. (1996). 'Musings on management', *Havard Business Review*, 74, 4, 61–8.

Pennington, D. (1991). 'Australia's universities: through the looking glass', *Journal of Tertiary Educational Administration*, 13, 2, 80–92.

Peters, T. and Waterman, R. (1982). *In Search of Excellence*. London: Harper and Row.

Sizer, J. (1998). 'The management of institutional adaptation and change under conditions of financial stingency'. In Eggins, H. (ed.) *Restructuring Higher Education*. Buckingham: Open University Press, pp. 80–92.

Smyth, J. (ed.) (1995). *Academic Work: The Changing Labour Process in Higher Education*. Buckingham: SRHE/Open University Press.

Stockley, D. (1993). 'Being productive, being clever: the enchanted forest of intellectual property', *Australian Journal of Education*, 37, 1, 96–111.

Williams, B. (1992). *What Now is a University?: Higher Education Policy Changes in Australia and Britain*. Working Papers in Australia Studies No. 73.

Williams, K. (1989). 'The case for democratic management in schools', *Irish Educational Studies*, 8, 2, 73–86.

Willmott, H. (1995). 'Managing the academics: commodification and control in the development of university education in the UK', *Human Relations*, 48, 993–1025.

Part 5

Dilemmas in Leadership and Management

18

The Emotional Side of Leadership

Rick Ginsberg and Timothy Gray Davies

As anyone who has lived in the southeast United States knows, hurricanes are circular structures around an eerily calm eye. As a hurricane passes through, we experience the storm, then the calm, and then the storm again. I write this account from the eye of the hurricane (a community college president).

Introduction

Studies of leadership have examined a variety of issues related to leadership styles, including traits and behaviors, situations and contingencies, gender issues and cultural issues (see, e.g. Hoy and Miskel, 1996). Research has examined the symbolic side of leadership (Bolman and Deal, 1991), ethical and moral issues (London, 1999), the ambiguity in leader decision-making (Cohen and March, 1974) and proposed roles such as servant leader (Greenleaf *et al.*, 1996) and instructional leader in schools (Greenfield, 1987). Based on the work of Dan Golemen (1995), the importance of emotional intelligence (or EQ) has surfaced as important for good decision-making and successful and satisfying lives. Emotions have come to be seen as significant for organizational success most prominently reflected in the work of Peters and Austin (1985), who see workplace emotions and feelings as necessary ingredients for managerial success. Peters (1989), in *Leadership and Emotion*, urged leaders to be enthusiastic about the products of the company, suggesting that they even laugh, cry and smile in order to be effective.

Other scholars focus on leadership issues related to emotions. Argyris (1977) emphasized the importance of intuition in organizational manage-

Source: Commissioned.

ment, while Barnard (1938) discussed the non-scientific non-logical processes as important for managerial success. Indeed, in Barnard's seminal work on leadership, he recognized that leaders' emotions can impact their behavior. He suggested that when an executive's moral code faces conflict, the result may be emotional feelings potentially leading to paralysis.

Organizational and leader behavior studies often have relied on psycho-dynamic theories to explain corporate culture behavior. Morgan (1998, p. 192) argued that organizations are not shaped solely by their environments, but also by 'the unconscious concerns of their members and the unconscious forces shaping the societies in which they exist'. Fineman (1993, p. 25), in discussing research on leaders and managers, asks 'To what extent do repressed, "unresolved" early-life emotional struggles re-emerge in the organizational forms they create?' He goes on to show how the work of leaders like Frederick Taylor and Henry Ford were shaped by their background and temperament.

Research on emotions in organizational life has been prominent for decades. Hochschild's (1983) examination of flight attendants, perhaps the most influential work in this area, introduced the terms 'emotional work' and 'emotional labour'. Emotional work is the effort individuals put into keeping their private feelings suppressed or presented in socially acceptable ways. Emotional labor relates to the wearing of the organization's accepted 'mask', what Putnam and Mumby (1993, p. 37) describe as 'the way roles and tasks exert overt and covert control over emotional displays'. Emotional labor, they explain, is experienced most strongly when individuals must express emotions that clash with their inner feelings. But even recognizing the importance emotions play in organizational behavior, the research has generally ignored the emotion's specific impact on individuals. Fineman (1993, pp. 9–10) explains:

> 'the student of organizations would find little in existing organizational theory to reveal the detail of such phenomena [emotions], despite an enormous shift from a strictly rationalistic view of organizations . . . We find little or no mention of how feeling individuals worry, envy, brood, become bored, play, despair, plot, hate, and so forth.'

Similarly, Mangham (1998, p. 51) argues:

> The general neglect of emotions by contemporary writers on behaviour in organizations seems largely due to an acceptance of the common managerial perception that 'feelings' (a term often used pejoratively) have no place in institutions that are committed to considering judgment and rational action. They get in the way and cloud the issues.

Cooper and Sawaf (1996) developed the executive EQ as a means for examining the emotional intelligence in organizational leaders. They argued (ibid., p. xv) that emotional intelligence is important for leadership as emotions are 'the primary source of motivation, information (feedback), personal power, innovation and influence.' They contend (ibid, p. xiii) emotional intelligence's importance is based on a definition of EQ as the 'ability to sense, understand, and effectively apply the power and acumen of emotions as a source of human energy, connection and influence'. In educational settings, the significance of social and emotional learning for leaders has emerged as significant for leader effectiveness (Chemiss, 1998). Research on transformational leadership (Burns, 1978), caring leadership (Sernak, 1998) and leadership for K-12 schools (Sergiovanni, 1996) has implored educational leaders to apply their emotions and morals in positive ways. Others have emphasized the importance of understanding the worker maturity in organizations (Hersey and Blanchard, 1982) and even the significance of developing 'followership' (Evans, 1996) and caring (Sernak, 1998) to enhance effectiveness.

Studies of influence and power (French and Raven, 1960; Mechanic, 1962) generally considered leaders' decisions in a top-down manner without considering the impact such decisions may have on the leaders themselves. In other words, whether it is ethical, moral, transformational, symbolic, servant, instructional or even emotionally intelligent leadership that is being applied, leaders must make decisions and live with the consequences. An organization's members react to decisions in a variety of ways, and leaders invariably react to these reactions. Studies of how leaders should behave also need to understand ways that leaders react to their subordinates in any organizational setting.

The bulk of related research, therefore, has either ignored the impact of emotions on organizational behavior or suggested behaving in specified emotional ways as an ingredient affecting leadership success. More recently, research has examined the importance of emotional intelligence on behaviour. However, little research has specifically examined the impact that emotional experiences have on those in leadership roles. The purpose of our research was to understand better the emotional side of leadership decision-making as it affects those in positions of authority. Two main questions guided the research:

1. What kinds of decisions evoke the strongest emotional response from leaders in schools, community colleges and universities?
2. In what ways do leaders in schools, community colleges and universities react to decisions that arouse an emotional response on their part?

Methodology

A qualitative research design utilizing retrospective stories (Wallace, 1996) was employed with leaders from K-12 schools, community colleges and universities. The targeted sample included high-school principals and superintendents from school districts from one mid-western state, community college presidents or vice-presidents from across the USA, and deans of schools/colleges of education in universities throughout the country. While not designed necessarily to capture a representative sample of leaders, stories were sought from those in a variety of leadership roles in educational organizations. Therefore, 30 high-school principals, superintendents, community college administrators and deans of schools/colleges of education were identified. Twenty-three leaders submitted stories (approximately 20 per cent of those contacted). Of those submitting stories, 53 per cent were male, 47 per cent female. The breakdown of roles was as follows:

- Community college president – 40 per cent.
- Other community college administrator – 13 per cent
- Dean/director of education – 27 per cent
- Principal (high school) – 7 per cent
- Superintendent – 13 per cent.

Data were analyzed in two ways. First, responses were compiled that specifically answered the first research question. Secondly all stories were read independently by the two researchers to identify first-order data categories or codes; then key themes and patterns characterizing the stories were identified. Cross-case displays were developed, which included individual story analyses and common themes that transcended the stories (Miles and Huberman, 1994). Validity in the analysis and quality control (Goetz and LeCompte, 1984) was heightened by each story having two independent analyses which were compared, discussed, then reconciled for any differences.

Findings

The first research question asked participants which decisions evoked an emotional response. Here, a clear pattern emerged. Fully two thirds selected a story involving a personnel matter, usually related to the dismissal (or in a few cases the reassignment) of an employee. In each instance, the specifics that instigated the need for the dismissal differed. However, the two most common causes for personnel dismissal or reassignment were due to incompatibility between employee and responsibilities or budget cutbacks and financial exigencies. Other issues included disobeying rules, sexual harassment and unacceptable job performance. In about 25 per cent of these cases, the person being terminated or reassigned was a close personal friend of the leader. These were especially emotional experiences for the leaders. But in all the stories, the leaders emphasized the concern for people in their organization that the experience engendered. Thus, there was always anxiety about having to deal with a colleague even if his or her performance was unacceptable given the possible financial and career impact that a dismissal or reassignment can cause. Concern for student well-being was expressed in many cases but most especially where sexual harassment was involved. Student well-being was not separated in the leaders' minds from the care and concern they had exhibited toward faculty and staff.

The other issues causing a leader's emotional response were divided evenly among a variety of circumstances, including dealing with a tragedy (shooting) at a school, being elected to a major office as the first non-white female in the organization's history, implementing a new governance approach and working with colleagues in less than honest ways. These issues shared a common ingredient with the personnel-related stories of involving a series of human interactions that created the emotional response. The shooting potentially could have an unsettling impact on students and faculty across campus, not to mention the tragedy brought upon the families of the victims. The election story involved unsavory interactions with those unaccustomed to having a minority female in a position of authority. The new governance approach required new thinking about how the organization operated, challenging old ideas and feelings. Thus a key theme which emerged from this analysis was the human toll that emotionally laden experiences had on all the leaders.

The second research question asked how leaders reacted to situations causing an emotional response. Five major themes emerged that characterized the stories. These include what we call 'The agony of decision making', 'Finding order out of chaos', 'Communication is the key', 'Follow your heart' and 'Showing the right face.' 'The agony of decision-making' referred to the high levels of stress and anxiety the various situations evoked. 'Finding order out of chaos' reflects the fact that, despite all the emotion and pain, something good came from these situations, not the least of which was personal growth and learning. 'Communication is the key' was a message that emerged from nearly every story – that being open in communication was important for organizational and individual health and success. 'Follow your heart' captured the sense that the leaders often felt pretty good about the decisions they had rendered. Though the experiences they described were never easy, there was a clear belief that they had acted in ways to benefit their institutions. Finally, 'Showing the right face' was a theme that characterized a smaller number of stories, where the leaders expressed the need to wear a certain leadership face or mask in order to serve the needs of the organization. Each theme will be discussed separately.

The agony of decision-making

In each story the leader expressed considerable anxiety relative to the circumstances surrounding the decision and the decision itself. Some leaders were new to their positions and were concerned about the impact the decisions might have. For other leaders there was the concern of making organizational changes that might not be well received. Most prominently, there was anxiety concerning the affect their decision would have on the others' lives. But no matter the intervening variables, the leaders discussed their deeply felt emotions, sleepless nights and high levels of anxiety. They cared about their work; they cared about their employees; and they cared about the impact on everyone in the organization. Note these remarks from our leaders:

> I was faced with a real dilemma. My old friend had made some decisions due to his family situation. I didn't necessarily agree with his approach, but I was empathetic toward him. Several nights each week I lay awake agonizing about what was the right thing to do. I felt bad for his daughter and family, but really felt as if he had held me and the entire faculty in the school hostage to his own poor decision making. I am required to provide renewal/non-renewal letters for untenured faculty by May 1 of each year, and I chose not to renew his contract. That would give him one more year as a faculty member, after which he would be gone . . . This was a very tough decision for me, but the school had needs which weren't being met, the faculty were looking at me to resolve the situation, and I felt that Dr P would let this drag on as long as he could to 'get the university back' . . . The whole affair had an emotional toll on me.

> I am in the middle of this excruciating process, dismantling pieces of the college, perhaps risking the position to which I aspired for so long. For several weeks I have tossed and turned at night, rising to make notes to myself about points I should make, people to whom I needed to talk . . . I cannot escape the heaviness of heart that I feel. I exercise each morning to try to take care of myself, but I talk less about my work with my husband, as I am just emotionally spent.

> But for me, I was in a state of higher anxiety. I knew I had started a process that was now beyond my power to stop. I bore the responsibility but none of the control. I took long walks at night to try and unwind and sleep. I couldn't confide in anyone on campus and was too new to the state to have established a support network among the other community college administrators. I

remember being gripped by my own fears: for faculty who might have to be released, for their families, for the college's image in our community, and in all honesty, for my own professional position. Could I, would I be made the scapegoat for this problem?

After this brief discussion with the board chairman I realized that there was absolutely no reason for me to stay in the district. I went back to my office and prepared a resignation. I had no job in mind but I knew I could no longer work in this district and with this board of education. They had violated every principle I knew in protecting children. I was emotionally spent mostly because of what happened to these kids. Now, I had no relationship with the board and I had no job. This was a very difficult emotional time worrying about finding a job on such short notice and what was going to happen to these poor children that had been betrayed . . . As I write this story, emotions flood back into my head and the nauseating truth of what happened in that district will always remain with me. I am a Vietnam veteran who saw my share of misery and suffering, but I don't think any of the experiences, no matter how awful they were, compared to the disgusting feelings I still have about this incident.

The emotional depth and intensity the leaders experienced was quite dramatic. Characterizing the emotions and pain felt in a school-related incident to the misery witnessed in the Vietnam war is telling. Being a leader and making difficult decisions can cause a great deal of pressure and agony.

Finding order out of chaos

Research on complex adaptive systems (Prigogine and Stengers, 1984; Waldrop, 1992; Holland, 1995) teaches us that open systems can spontaneously self-organize, are adaptive in turning circumstances to their advantage and are dynamic in their complexity, spontaneity and disorder or flux while bringing the disorder into a special kind of balance (sometimes referred to as the 'edge of chaos'). These complex systems' characteristics take on human-like qualities in their non-linear and non-predictable reaction to inputs. Much as the science of complexity has described how such systems actually work, these leaders were adaptive in finding something positive out of the very difficult and often nerve-racking circumstances they confronted. Their ability to respond and find balance was remarkable. They found order out of chaos.

The most common reaction that falls under this theme of 'Order out of chaos' was the learning that took place. Many leaders discussed what they learned and how they evolved due to this emotional experience. Similarly, but less often, the leaders discussed how the experience forced them to reassess their values – also a learning experience for them. This learning is depicted in the comments of several of the leaders:

Things I learned included that no location can be isolated from this type of incident. Procedures must be in place, even on rural campuses. Everyone must be prepared. Also, take into account the human factor. There are many ways that people respond to things, including family dynamics. Finally, never underestimate the length of time and the intensity of the reverberations. The past comes alive, situations come to the fore, and things are triggered. There is connectiveness of the human race: people respond to what happens to someone else and the personal agony relating to it. And put aside expectations for the way people relate. It can be very surprising, but however it manifests itself, it must be taken seriously.

At each level, I learned and I grew and I benefited. One of the things that I say to people all the time – as a leader, don't be afraid to learn. Because you constantly will be faced with obstacles or situations that you have not faced before. You've got to deal with those. You are going to be facing people who don't believe in you, don't trust you, or for whatever reason are trying to tear you down. As long as you know what you're doing is the right thing and you're doing the best you can, you just keep doing it. Bring people together. Work with people because you are there because they put you there.

Probably the greatest lesson I learned was that you can be straightforward, as helpful as providing lots of assistance to the person, but unless the person knows and comes to expect the fact that they need to change, they won't . . . you have to learn those things the hard way.

Although I learned many lessons from that experience, five have affected the way I live my life to this day. First, I cannot replenish myself by myself. For me there has to be a higher power. Second, I learned that in leadership you sometimes have to suffer in the short run to bring people along with you for the whole journey. Third, I learned that being polite, courteous, compassionate and caring no matter what is said to me or about me in return costs nothing. My own self-respect remains intact and that is worth everything. Fourth, I learned that underneath people's ugliness, hostility, and nasty behavior there is fear. Fear of losing a job, fear of being rejected. Fear can take on so many disguises that I have learned to always look for that first in a really contentious situation. Fifth, I have finally learned that when we talk about ethics we are talking not about 'right' and 'wrong,' but 'right' and 'right.'

I lost someone who I thought was a friend, but learned the lesson that you can't put individual friendship above treating the larger whole with the respect they deserve.

So, what have I learned? That it's very important as an administrator to understand what situations might potentially 'push our buttons'. These buttons are very ingrained in us because of past experiences, our personalities, and our value systems. I've realized that I actually like to fight – indeed, I am a fighter and a survivor. But when I don't keep that trait in check when carrying out administrative tasks and responsibilities, I do not serve myself well.

Clearly, the leaders in our study were a resilient group who grew from the emotional experiences they described. They were very self-referent in examining what had transpired and taking lessons from the scenario to improve their leadership. Ultimately, the growth that took place for the leaders in this study was the basis for their being able to move beyond what for many was a terribly devastating experience. They adapted and learned in finding some order from the events and emotional chaos.

Communication is the key

The majority of experiences the leaders described were personnel-related matters. A common thread running through each story was the open communication used with the organizational membership. Where some privacy was necessary due to the nature of the events (e.g. dismissal of an employee), the leaders shared information to the extent possible. There was a common belief that shared information benefited the entire organization. Many saw this as very self-protective; their own position could be compromised by the event itself and the resulting action, so sharing information was crucial to everyone's understanding what the decisions were and why they were being made. Comments from the leaders clarify this issue:

Knowing how quickly bad news spreads, I inserted this issue into the agenda for my scheduled faculty meeting at the end of the week. This gave me time to update the president's cabinet on Wednesday and the Faculty Senate on Thursday before the Friday faculty meeting. I knew ahead of time that the gallows humor would be rampant about an early Christmas present and Scrooge and the rest that goes with an end of fall term negative announcement. But I also realized that what I had to say about the overstaffing issue, the information I had gathered, and faculty involvement would be more positive than the gloom and doom the grapevine would spew forth.

How to handle the media becomes critical in traumatic situations – because you can be sure that the media will be there. You must be fast, and you must be the initiator or it puts you in a vulnerable situation . . . it is also essential for any community relations people to do a good job . . . informing students about college resources is critical. There are services available in any kind of crisis situation, any kind of jeopardy, for any kind of problem.

I believe in inclusion, in the importance of all to the whole, in the importance of the process of creation. In November, I sent out communications focusing on the importance of recruiting and cautioning against unnecessary spending . . . I met with groups and individuals, sent out memos and e-mails, and solicited input, ideas and feedback. The open communication elicited great suggestions.

The leaders regarded open communication as essential for dealing with these issues. Open communication helped the leaders survive a difficult time and protected them as they worked with their colleagues. It often made the decisions feel as if they were 'ours' and not just the leaders'. According to the leaders, the open communication provided damage control to the organization and to the leader.

Follow your heart

There is no doubt these leaders made difficult decisions, but the common thread throughout was that they believed they took the correct action. For about half the leaders in this study, there was a sense that their action was consistent with the organization's collective good. In 'following their hearts', these leaders expressed confidence that they were performing in appropriate ways. The words of the leaders characterize this feeling:

The whole affair was very hurtful, as I felt I was overly supportive of someone who didn't treat me with equal respect. I left the situation quite dismayed, but with a strong sense that I had done what was right for the School of Education. The faculty were very supportive of me and angry at the way Dr P had dealt with them . . . In the end, I gathered a good deal of strength in the knowledge that I was doing what was right, and although it was okay to lend a colleague some help, the ultimate decision had to be related to the collective good.

I do not know the long-term impact this will have. I have worked hard to be open, fair, forthcoming. I have acted in good faith. I have tried to be inclusive, to take advantage of the talent and knowledge across the institution. Yet, I accept responsibility for all the decisions that have been made . . . my hopes for the future and my dreams for the college – for my college – are increasingly clear. I still have the passion . . .

As I was wont to do in those days I took a long weekend alone and went to the ocean. I wanted to reconnect with my soul. It didn't take long to realize how incredibly saddened I was by what we were doing and by what was going to have to take place. I felt angry and resentful that previous leaders had dropped the ball and had let the faculty down. That they didn't have the courage it took to make tough decisions along the way. On and on this righteous indignation went until I remembered those walks to campus last summer when I, too, was praying for a miracle. Anything, Lord, that would save me from having to make tough decisions. Suddenly, I was filled with a compassion I had not felt before. I realized that those projects were their man-made miracles!

These leaders' decisions were difficult to make. Yet, in the end, they felt they had done what was correct, and felt some solace realizing that they had acted in their institutions' best interests. These leaders were true to their heart, and carried out decisions that felt right.

Showing the right face

Finally, the literature on emotion speaks to the work that many employees contain their emotions to meet their organization's expectations (Hochschild, 1983). Some have referred to this as wearing the company's 'mask' Putnam and Mumby, 1993). Some leaders felt they had to present themselves in a particular way in order to maintain and convey their stature as the leader in the organization. Note these remarks by several of the leaders:

> There is no question that I felt great grief during this situation, but a president must find private time for these emotions . . . in this situation, one must steel oneself, because you must act on behalf of others, making sure of their well being and safety. You cannot do this if you abdicate your leadership by indulging your emotions. If and when you decide to fall apart you must do it someplace else, later on. People need to know that whoever is in the leadership position is operating from a point or position of strength. When they lose that confidence, where can they turn? So I think the person in a leadership role must be steadfast – must be strong.

> The faculty returned in the fall and I laid out for them what we had accomplished in the summer. I promised that we would go to each division and present our findings so that every faculty member would know exactly where his or her division and department stood and to show how the criteria were applied to everyone in a full time faculty line. No one was exempt from the process . . . I was walking the line between the feelings and compassion for the individuals and the lawyers telling me what I could and could not say, could and could not do. The final outcome was worse than even I expected.

The leaders expended a great deal of energy in presenting themselves and information in ways that they felt were in the organization's best interest. Hochschild (1983) labeled these actions as emotional labor, and it can cause great distress when the emotional face one must present conflicts with one's innermost feelings. While we didn't sense emotional labor in most of the situations presented to us, we did find that the leaders spent energy and effort presenting themselves within what they believed to be their proper role.

Conclusions

This study began with two research questions aimed at better understanding how leaders react to emotional experiences in the workplace. From stories presented by 23 leaders from community colleges, school districts and school/colleges of education, we learned that the most emotionally laden experiences derive from matters related to personnel decisions. And even when the emotional experience did not directly involve a personnel decision (such as a termination or a job reassignment), the experience did involve interactions with people in the organization and the impact on those individuals was generally the cause for some consternation among the leaders. We label this as the 'human toll' from which emotional experiences derive.

The second research question dealt with the leaders' reactions to the emotional experiences and decisions. Five themes characterized these reactions: 'The agony of decision-making', 'Finding order out of chaos', 'Communication is the key', 'Follow your heart', and 'Showing the right face'. We draw several conclusions from the findings to the research questions.

First, as noted in the literature on emotions, leaders discussed the energy expended and the emotional pain endured when making significant emotionally laden decisions. This was most obvious in the theme 'The agony of decision-making', but all themes demonstrated the effort required to make the required decision. Hochschild (1983) and others identified this emotional work and emotional labor of an organization's employees. Clearly, leaders experience this emotional effort as well – whether it be from the decision-making process itself, the background work needed to chart a new direction, the effort required in opening communication among participants or the energy attached to putting forward the right face to the world. Emotional decision-making is hard work.

Secondly, the leaders were sensitive and caring individuals clearly dedicated to their positions. They were concerned for their employees and their organization and the impact the decision would have on each. For several this was their first high-level leadership opportunity. So they were also pragmatic and were concerned the decision could impact their own career negatively. Still, the leaders' stories could not belie their feelings and their care for other people. The experiences they described were people oriented. These leaders worried about hurting other people.

Thirdly, it appeared that leaders rarely were prepared for the emotionally heavy experiences they described. Many leaders' stories described the solitude they experienced when making these decisions and experiencing their emotional impact. Several even talked about isolating themselves from potential support providers (e.g. a spouse). But while it often is 'lonely at the top' for leaders, it seems unhealthy and counter-productive to be isolated when making these very difficult decisions. This is an area that future research should examine in more detail. Whether some case-based training, further emphasis in MBA or educational leadership programs or creating avenues for leaders to share their concerns with peers could be beneficial, it is clear that these and other approaches should be studied and tested.

Finally, the results of this study suggest a need to research emotions and leader decision-making. These leaders' stories were not derived from a randomly selected group of leaders. There were no analyses comparing reactions based on gender, race or level or type of organization. Though the stories from men and women or leaders from different educational organizations did not appear to differ greatly here, a larger sample would allow for careful comparisons. At the same time, leaders from non-educational organizations could also be examined to see if the findings here compare to private sector experiences. With the growing interest in understanding emotions in organizational behavior, and widening appeal of issues like emotional intelligence, the impact of significant emotionally laden decisions by leaders of organizations is important to understand. This research is a beginning in that process.

Notes

An earlier version of this chapter was presented as a paper at the American Educational Research Association Annual Meeting, Seattle, Washington, April 10, 2001.

References

Argyris, C. (1977) Double loop learning in organizations. *Harvard Business Review.*

Barnard, C.I. (1938) *The Functions of the Executive.* Cambridge, MA: Harvard University Press.

Bolman, L. and Deal, T. (1991) *Images of Leadership.* Washington, DC: US Department of Education, Office of Educational Research and Improvement, Educational Resources Information Center.

Burns, J.M. (1978) *Leadership.* New York: HarperCollins.

Cherniss, C. (1998) Social and emotional learning for leaders. *Educational Leadership* 55: 26–28.

Cohen, M. and March, J. (1974) *Leadership and Ambiguity.* Boston, MA: Harvard Business School Press.

Cooper, R. and Sawaf, A. (1996) *Executive EQ: Emotional Intelligence in Leadership and Organizations.* New York: Grosset/Putnam.

Evans, R. (1996) *The Human Side of School Change.* San Francisco, CA: Jossey-Bass.

Fineman, S. (1993) *Emotion in Organization.* Newbury Park, CA: Sage.

French, J. Jr and Raven, B. (1960) The bases of social power. In D. Cartwright and A. Zanders (eds.) *Group Dynamics.* Evanson, IL: Northwestern University Press.

Goetz, J.P. and LeCompete, M.D. (1984) *Ethnography and Qualitative Design in Educational Research.* New York: Academic Press.

Goleman, D. (1995) *Emotional Intelligence.* New York: Bantam Books.

Greenfield, W. (1987) *Instructional Leadership*. Boston, MA: Allyn & Bacon.

Greenleaf, R.K., Frick, D. and Spears, L. (1996) *On Becoming a Servant Leader*. San Francisco, CA: Jossey-Bass.

Hersey, P. and Blanchard, K. (1982) *Management of Organizational Behavior: Utilizing Human Resources*. Englewood Cliffs, NJ: Prentice-Hall.

Hochschild, A. (1983) *The Managed Heart*. Berkeley, CA: University of California Press.

Holland, J.H. (1995) *Hidden Order: How Adaptation Builds Complexity*. Reading, MA: Addison-Wesley.

Hoy, W. and Miskel, C. (1996) Leadership. In W. Hoy and C. Miskel (eds.) *Educational Administration: Theory, Research and Practice*. New York: Random House.

London, M. (1999) Principled leadership and business diplomacy. A practical value-based direction for management development. *Journal of Management Development* 18: 170–92.

Mangham, I.L. (1998) Emotional discourse in organizations. In D. Grant *et al.* (eds.) *Discourse and Organization*. Thousand Oaks, CA: Sage.

Mechanic, D. (1962) Sources of power of lower participants in complex organizations. *Administrative Science Quarterly* 7: 349–64.

Miles, M. and Huberman, A.M. (1994) *Qualitative Data Analysis*. Thousand Oaks, CA: Sage.

Morgan, G. (1998) *Images of Organizations*. Thousand Oaks, CA: Sage.

Peters, T.J. (1989) *Leadership and Emotion*. California: TPG Communications.

Peters, T.J. and Austin, N. (1985) *A Passion for excellence*. New York: Bantam Books.

Putnam, L.L. and Mumby, D.K. (1993) *Organizations, emotion and the myth of rationality*. In S. Fineman (ed.) *Emotion in Organizations*. Newbury Park, CA: Sage.

Sergiovanni, T.J. (1996) *Leadership for the Schoolhouse*. San Francisco, CA: Jossey-Boss.

Sernak, K. (1998) *School Leadership: Balancing Power with Care*. New York: Teachers College Press,

Waldrop, M.M. (1992) *Complexity: The Emerging Science at the Edge of Order and Chaos*. New York: Simon & Schuster.

Wallace, D. (ed.) (1996) *Journey to School Reform: Moving from reflection to Action through Story Telling*.

19

Leadership Challenges and Ethical Dilemmas in Front-Line Organisations

Patrick Duignan and Victoria Collins

Introduction

Leaders in contemporary service organisations are confronted by external and internal challenges and expectations that make demands on their time, expertise, energies and emotional well-being. They are, increasingly, being held accountable for their performance and are expected to comply with ethical and moral standards in their relationships and practices (Taylor, 1991; Starratt, 1993; Terry, 1993; Duignan and Bhindi, 1987). Many leaders, as well as other professionals in service organisations, face increasingly demanding clientele who may have unrealistic expectations of the quality of service to be provided.

While leaders may experience confusion, even frustration, in their attempts to respond productively to these pressures, the current emphasis in many service organisations on corporate management values, strategies and practices has contributed to a persistent feeling among many organisational members of being used, devalued, cheated, even demeaned. This perception of 'excessive managerialism' has led to a call for the transformation of managers and administrators into leaders who focus more on issues related to culture and people in organisations (Little, 1997).

At the heart of these 'people' issues are values and ethics (Karpin, 1995; Ryan, 1997). There is an emerging concern with 'the paralysis of moral patterns' of life (Pirsig, 1992, p. 357) and a yearning to reclaim the moral, ethical and spiritual domains of leadership (Hodgkinson, 1991; Covey, 1992; Sergiovanni, 1992; Conger and associates, 1994; Duignan, 1997; Handy, 1997). It was within such a framework of concern that the Service

Source: Commissioned.

Organisation Leadership Research (SOLR) project was conceived, developed and implemented.

The SOLR project is a three-year Australian Research Council funded study involving leaders in four service organisations, namely, the New South Wales (NSW) Police Service; the NSW Department of Education and Training (DET, which includes the Technical and Further Education System); the Catholic Education System of the Diocese of Parramatta; and the Australian Conference of Leaders of Religious Institutes (ACLRI). Leaders at executive, middle and front-line levels from the different organisations were invited to participate in the study.

The main research questions included:

1. What are the contemporary challenges for leaders in front-line human service organisations?
2. How are leaders responding to these challenges?
3. What are the ethical dilemmas and underlying values involved in making these responses?

Such a complex study required a methodology and methods that would be comprehensive in scope yet sufficiently focused and integrated to generate a coherent view of contemporary leadership challenges, dilemmas and practices. To achieve these, the study incorporated four complementary data collection stages, namely, questionnaire, interviews, critical leadership incident and electronic dialogue on an interactive website (Duignan and Collins, 2001).

Key Findings Related to Challenges and Dilemmas

A selection of key findings are presented in this chapter in the form of *tensions* that leaders face, especially when making difficult choices that involve competing values and ethical dilemmas. These findings are derived, primarily, from the critical incidents written by leaders, describing the dilemmas they face daily. While these tensions are identified using different and distinctive labels, they are not necessarily discrete, having many characteristics in common. Given the complex nature of the tensions, particular examples from the data may fit into one or more of them. The key lessons that emerge from the data can be regarded as guidelines which may be applied to the resolution of multiple tensions.

The findings indicate that the most difficult challenges facing leaders in contemporary front-line service organisations present themselves as dilemmas, paradoxes or *tensions*. These tensions are usually people centred and involve contestation of values.

The leaders in this study reported that they frequently have to make choices about people in situations where there are no obvious 'right' and 'wrong' answers. Mostly there are degrees of 'right' on both sides. It is not a matter of choosing one side or value over another (either/or approach) but, more likely, the most effective outcomes will reflect concerns for all people and values involved (both/and approach).

Kidder (1995) makes this point well when discussing the problems for leaders and others making choices in situations where values and ethical considerations are paramount. He states (ibid., p. 16): 'Tough choices, typically, are those that pit one right value against another. That's true in every walk of life – corporate professional, personal, civic, international, educational, religious, and the rest.' He points out that right-versus-right values are at the heart of most difficult choices. While there are numerous right-versus-wrong situations, they are, for the most part, more easily discernible, and therefore more easily dealt with by honest, well intentioned people than are right-versus-right situations. As Kidder (ibid., p. 17) suggests: 'Only those living in a moral vacuum will be able to say, "On the one hand is the good, the right, the true and noble. On the other hand are the awful, the wicked, the false, and the base. And here I stand, equally attracted to each".' On the contrary, he argues (ibid., p. 18) that: 'The *really* tough choices, then, don't centre upon right versus wrong. They involve right versus right. They are genuine dilemmas precisely because each side is firmly rooted in … core values.'

Such dilemmas usually present tensions between competing sets of values where each can be interpreted as 'right' and justified in a given situation. Many of the tensions faced by leaders in the SOLR project fall into this category of right-versus-right.

Tensions

While a number of tensions were identified from the data in the SOLR project, three will be discussed in this chapter, namely:

1. The rights of the individual versus those of the group or community.
2. The provision of a quality service versus the efficient use of scarce resources.
3. The exercise of compassion versus rigidly following the rules.

Tension 1: individual versus group interests

This was one of the most frequently discussed tensions. There are tensions involved when deciding whether to support decisions which promote the good of the group or community as against the rights of the individual and vice versa. Generally, the 'community' was perceived by respondents in educational organisations to be the wider student body while individuals were usually teachers.

The two main causes of tensions in the choices between the good of the community and the rights of the individual included:

1. staff ineffectiveness; and
2. student misbehaviour.

While no definite trends were evident in the outcomes of whether principals decide to retain or expel students, or retain or dismiss ineffective staff, all situations caused tension and anxiety for them.

In every case involving student discipline, principals noted the need to provide for student welfare, safety and educational outcomes. In these examples, the principal's decision to suspend or expel was influenced by the detrimental effects of student misbehaviour on the school community. One principal stated: 'I learnt as well a benchmark for when the price for individual "good" is too high in relation to the "good" of the whole group.' It should be noted, however, that students were not expelled without consultation and/or without conscientious attempts to address the problems they were having.

In every case of a tension in this area, principals expressed concern for the welfare of the individual, whether student or teacher. In cases where principals refused to expel students, the choice not to expel was governed by concern for that individual's welfare and the basic right of every child to receive an education.

In the case of ineffective staff, long and loyal service was acknowledged but was generally outweighed by the concern for the needs of the student body whose education was being impacted upon by their ineffectiveness in teaching. One principal concluded that the task of removing a long-serving and loyal teacher was too difficult and decided to 'wait it out'. This decision was, in hindsight, regretted and the principal acknowledged that the decision to move the teacher on should have been made earlier. He stated:

> I should have put her on an improvement programme. Her students deserved better. If she didn't make a change, it would affect her superannuation, retirement and staff morale. Some staff considered my lack of action weak as she was also undermining my decisions . . . I made this choice because the process is difficult, time consuming and stressful. I thought about the years of good and loyal service she had given. I should have acted earlier before it got to the stage that there was only one or two years to go before retirement. I have learnt that the process of looking at duty and obligations in ethical dilemmas is really important and I let down the people who are my first responsibility, the children. Being a principal carries with it some truly difficult decisions requiring head power not heart power.

Another principal decided that it was too difficult to fight an ineffective staff member who was applying for voluntary redundancy for the second time. Whilst the principal did not believe that this payout should be approved, she concluded:

> I would have preferred to terminate his services. In the end, I approved his voluntary redundancy. I weighed up the time and effort involved in trying to bring an unwilling and uncommitted staff member up to speed against the other priorities I had, together with the emerging initiatives and projects which were in the planning stage. I also thought very carefully about where my time would be better spent in terms of staff development, change management, redirecting the organisational culture and re-positioning the site for the future. I also know what it is like to prove incompetence in the area I work in. I believe I made the 'right' choice. I have worked in the public sector for many years and I have seen and experienced time, money and emotions spent on people and projects with absolutely no progress or outcomes. I have seen and experienced policies applied to the letter and in very inflexible ways all to no great effect other than to disillusion the people involved and create unbridgeable gaps among staff. I have used the time I have 'saved' in this case, to foster innovations and work with people who are committed and wish to be involved and do a good job.

Principals were asked about the lessons they had learned when attempting to resolve such tensions. The following quotations are examples of the main points made.

> Sometimes there needs to be a clinical approach to situations. Compassionate leadership should be the norm but sometimes a less soft approach is the best.

> When the going gets difficult and you know you're right, you need to stick with your decision. I believe that surviving this 'ordeal' has made me more aware of individual/school and community needs and expectations.

> Leadership must demonstrate a human side as well as a task-oriented side.

> Always be guided when making ethical decisions by what you believe is 'right' and 'good'.

> I also learnt that at the end of the day you need to own the decision and be able to give sound reasons for it. At times I found it hard to distinguish between my personal reasons (her intimidation of me) and the communal reasons (the effect she was having on others).

Tension 2: service versus efficiency

This tension focused on those instances where respondents believed that the imperatives of economic rationalism (such as having to do more with less; increased accountability; restructuring; and merging of organisational structures) had a negative impact on their core business – i.e. providing a high-quality education which is a fundamental right of all students.

In each of the critical incidents in leadership related to this tension, the emphasis was on 'meeting the bottom line' or responding to increased accountabilities. It appears that the service end of the tension is often implied and is not discussed directly when dealing with the tension. It is implied in the fact that the increased emphasis on efficiency has negative implications for the level of service that can be provided. Examples of the tensions reported by principals include:

■ Parents pleading questionable financial difficulties and wanting reduced fees, yet able to afford a new car.
■ An organisation *driven* by performance and accountability without consideration of the emotional impact on staff.
■ Funds allocated to those areas targeted as being high priority by the system, despite requests from staff for other priorities.
■ Funding needed for special needs students but resources allocated to improve academic outcomes.
■ Rational economic corporate management style not compatible with individual leadership style of principal.

One principal captured the essence of the tensions related to a corporate management approach to leadership in a collegial, collaborative educational context:

> I think it's because of the complete change in culture and the way in which the organisation now operates. It's quite different from what we previously experienced. For example, it used to be a much more open and collaborative style and it has become quite different to that now, so that there is much less openness, much less collaboration, much less information. But it's of a different nature, it's very limited and not exploratory type information, just facts and figures type information. It's quite different. It resembles a shift from say collaborative professionalism to a rational economic corporate management style. I think that's happening in a lot of organisations as people are consumed and absorbed by this sort of budget-driven approach to management.

Another principal explained the tension and its possible solution:

I had the job of handing out to two-thirds of the staff a big white envelope that said 'Would you like a voluntary redundancy? 'If you want to put your name forward this is what you'll get. . .' The impact on your support staff, your gardeners is great . . . Very difficult! Trying to keep the ship going and, at the same time, not always believing in these values. I'm the messenger, I've got to stand up in front of the staff and say that this is what we are doing and this is why we are doing it and, at the same time, not believing that it was the best thing in every aspect. So that's very hard to do and it is very hard not to overlay your own perspective and undermine it . . . so this is difficult for me to get up and say that this is what our hierarchy has decided and then not say, 'Well I think it stinks'. Conveying to staff the message from on high is not very palatable for me. My beliefs are in the individual. I think an educational organisation is based on teaching individuals and every person within it should be treasured and valued and cultivated and you just shouldn't be saying to people that we really don't need your sort any more. We should be saying, perhaps, 'your profile is not what we actually need but we can look around for another position for you, we can retrain you', but we've moved away from that to being a more typical private sector.

Principals were asked what lessons they had learned when attempting to resolve such dilemmas. Most claimed that 'you have to be true to yourself and live your values'. You have to live with yourself at the end of the day. They also advised that honesty and openness when deciding on such tensions are always the best policy. Deceptiveness and playing politics are not recommended.

Despite budget restrictions and economic imperatives, it is always possible to exercise care and concern for those with whom you work. A recommendation was to be fair in relationships and provide others with the reasons for why you decided the way you did. Honesty, it appears, is the best policy according to the respondents in the SOLR study.

Tension 3: compassion versus rules

Principals continually face decisions in which choices can be influenced by considerations for either 'compassion' or 'strictly following the rules'. Compassion encompasses looking at the individual circumstance and making a decision that puts care and concern for the individual above all rules and policies, if these should be contrary. Rules or policies provide guidelines for leaders on how to make decisions. Some respondents in this study, however, argue that by complying with rules, they are also fulfilling their duty of care to students and, therefore, do not recognise any tension.

The main causes of these tensions in the SOLR study involved instances of:

1. student discipline;
2. teacher incompetency; and
3. parental complaints.

The resolution of these tensions tended to be either positive or negative depending on the personal circumstances of the individuals involved. The cases were positive for students where their personal safety and interests were protected; or special provision in the form of support programmes and structures were provided.

The cases often tended to have negative outcomes for teachers (the majority of instances in this study). For example:

■ A teacher disciplined a student for breach of rules on a school camp. In order to placate the parents the teacher was disciplined despite the fact that staff and indeed the principal agreed that the teacher had a solid reputation and acted appropriately.
■ A teacher was falsely accused of sexually assaulting an infant student. The teacher was a valued member of staff and the accusation was found to be baseless. The teacher, however, suffered loss of reputation and trust from the principal and system.

In some of the cases the rules were emphasised while in others compassion was given priority. When rules were used to determine the outcome of the tension, attention was usually given to the feelings of both parties. When rules were ridgidly adhered to, principals appeared to have no alternative but to commit to system or departmantal rules and guidlines or to legislation.

When leaders enforced the rules, they appeared to be, especially, mindful of the litigious nature of contemporary society:

■ A student with aggressive behaviour was suspended with allegations of drugs at home. The principal noted that a detailed record of all interactions and decisions was kept in case of complaint or legal challenge.
■ In the two cases of sexual assault discussed in the study, both principals followed procedural guidelines strictly because of the stringent laws in this area.
■ In two cases involving violent parents, principals adhered strictly to departmental guidelines.

In these cases, principals consulted widely with appropriate authorities such as departmental personnel, welfare agencies, police and other members of staff. They needed to 'cover these tracks' as well as their backs.

Where students were suspended or expelled, the rules were followed in order to protect the body of students but it was considered also in the best interests of the individual student, who would learn from the strict adherence to rules and discipline.

In outcomes where compassion was emphasised, rules were suspended when principals considered that a care outcome was the optimal solution to the tension. A disadvantaged student was disciplined and, because of the nature of the offence, the policy proclaimed that he should miss out on a major sporting event. The senior executive disregarded the policy and the student was allowed to compete. This was said to be a once in a lifetime experience for the student who needed the affirmation from sport because of an unsupportive family life. The principal described the incident:

> Our school has a policy where, if a student has received more than one 'blue slip', that student is not allowed to participate in special activities such as excursions, visits or play sports until his/her behaviour has improved. If it is their first 'blue slip', the ban is for one week only. One student, who is a talented athlete, had reached eligibility to participate at regional level. The student had received no support from home (we are a low SES school) and has been known to run in bare feet! One week prior to the regional carnival he earned, fairly, his first 'blue slip'. Technically the full week was up the day after the carnival. The dilemma of allowing this child a chance at the carnival was taken to the Executive who decided he should go.

Another case, described in detail by a principal, demonstrates the complexity of leadership challenges, the tensions involved and the difficulty of making the 'right' choice. While this is a rather lengthy case, it is worth describing in full because it presents a picture of the complex and challenging nature of dilemmas faced by leaders, such as principals. These complex leadership challenges and dilemmas are, usually, not amenable to simple solutions.

In this case, the principal, in fact, disregarded regulations in order deliberately to influence the 'abduction' of a child by her grandfather. The principal felt that this was in the best interests of the child and, according to him, the end result proved his judgement to be correct. On reflection, however, the principal concluded that this would probably not be a course of action that he would repeat in similar circumstances. The risks were too high and, with maturity and experience, he would handle the matter differently. The principal told the story:

> The incident took place in a small village of around 150 people. This is the school of which I am principal. There was a child who attends the school; her mother who is a drug addict; and her grandfather who is a prominent magistrate. The child's mother was not neglecting the child involved. However, her lifestyle was not, initially, providing the child with the best opportunity for long-term success at school. As the grandfather lived in another part of the state, my contact with him was limited to twice a year face-to-face meetings, and fortnightly phone calls.

There were a series of incidents involving the child that started to concern me. She was coming to school having no food, she was not being picked up in the afternoons and her personal hygiene was being neglected. I contacted the Department of Community Services, as I am required to do, but nothing was done. I called the grandfather and told him about my concerns as well.

A week later, there was a fire at the child's house, due to the drugs that the child's mother had been taking. It could have been fatal. Later that week, the grandfather called to the school and asked to speak to the child. This is not in line with departmental policy, but I allowed the child to come to the phone. That afternoon she was taken from the local park by her grandfather to an aunt in another part of the state. Two days later, the child's mother came to the school looking for her daughter.

This incident presented two ethical choices. The first was to allow the child to speak to her grandfather. This choice had to be made on the spot. I knew it was not within normal operating guidelines, but I felt it would be in the best interest of the child. I personally trusted the grandfather. This made the choice more difficult.

The second choice was after the child had been taken and her mother had come to ask if I knew where she was. I was prepared for this choice. I knew that it would come. I could tell her what had happened, tell her where her child was, or claim that I had no knowledge of the incident.

The choices that I made were made with the best interests of the child in mind. In the first instance with the phone call, I decided to allow the child to speak with her grandfather. Knowing full well that I would be doing so outside the guidelines that were set down. When I was questioned by the child's mother as to her daughter's whereabouts, I decided to deny all knowledge of the incident while knowing that I should have reported it.

The first choice was made for a number of reasons. I was becoming increasingly concerned for the child. I was actually relieved when I got the phone call and he asked to speak to his grandchild. I was hoping that it would result in an improved home situation for the young girl.

The second choice, regarding what I would say if I were ever questioned regarding the child's removal, was an easier one, because I had time to think the situation through. I knew that other people in the village had seen the grandfather take the child and that it would only be a matter of time before she found out. I decided that no information that may lead to the child being returned to her mother would be coming from me. This decision was also formed partly due to my breach of guidelines in the first instance with the phone call.

With the benefit of hindsight, I'm not sure that I did make the right choices. The end result could not have been better. The child is now in a warm, safe environment and her mother's visits are short and supervised. No action was taken against anyone, and all parties are happy with the new situation. But I don't think that I can judge my actions purely on the basis of the final outcome. As a leader, I should have been able to work within the guidelines to bring about a favourable result. I think I showed inexperience. I was fortunate that the repercussions of my actions, and inactions, were positive. If I were faced with the same situation in the future, I would hope that I would handle the situation with a much greater sense of professionalism. In fact, I am confident that I would handle the situation differently.

This case reflects the complexity of many tension situations where the determination of which choice to make is not always clear. Despite rules and regulations to the contrary, there may be a number of choices that could be perceived by different people as being 'right'. When a situation appeals to the heart, choice may be based more on care and compassion than on strict adherence to rules.

Conclusions: Formation of Leaders to Meet Contemporary Challenges

The challenges facing leaders in contemporary service organisations, including principals, are complex and multidimensional. Many challenges present themselves as tensions where choices are often between 'right-and-right', rather than 'right-or-wrong' alternatives.

Often, finding optimal resolutions to such tension situations demands mindsets and approaches based on both/and rather than either/or thinking and actions. Leaders who have to make choices in such paradoxical situations require more than management skills and competencies. They require creative, intuitive frameworks based on in-depth understanding of human nature and of the ethical, moral, even spiritual dimensions inherent in human interaction and choice. Above all, they need sound judgement and a wisdom derived from critical reflection on the meaning of life and work. They have to be people with heart who are emotionally mature enough to 'encounter others well' (Jones, 1998) and develop mutually productive relationships.

They need to be 'depthed' people with a spirituality shaped by the warp and weft of life's experiences. They tend to have spiritual scars from having battled with the perplexing dilemmas and tensions of life and work. They are morally courageous, unafraid to question unfair and unjust processes and practices when conformity would be the easier path.

While they need to be competent and skilled in a number of management and leadership dimensions, the tensions inherent in the leadership challenges identified in this chapter call for qualities, mindsets and dispositions that help them form creative frameworks for choice and action that transcend competencies and management skills.

Such a view begs the question of how leaders, such as principals, can be better prepared, or can prepare themselves, to make informed choices in complex, tension situations. Perhaps, instead of thinking in terms of education and training for leaders, it would be more useful, first, to focus on their formation as 'depthed' human beings. Duignan (2002) argues for a 'formation' approach to the leadership preparation and development of principals. Such formation approaches and programmes should adopt an interdisciplinary approach in order to expand their horizons and to get them to appreciate better that intelligence is 'holistic', connecting them to the universe of knowledge and to their wholeness as human beings. Leaders, today, should not only be good managers and corporate citizens but also good human beings. As Kelly (2000, p. 19) so eloquently states: 'In this respect it is not merely a matter of knowing something, but becoming someone, not just a matter of knowing relevant things, but of becoming a relevant person. . .'

Formation processes should assist principals develop their own ethical and moral frameworks for the study and analysis of the complex problems and tensions they face each day. The challenge for such programmes is to combine the intellectual and the moral into frameworks that help transcend knowledge generation and skills development to one of reflective critique of contemporary dilemmas, and personal and professional growth and development through an exploration of what it means to be human. Hesburgh (1994, p. 8) argues for such a combination of the intellectual and moral when discussing the special focus of the programmes of Notre Dame University in the USA:

> . . . we are united in believing that intellectual virtues and moral values are important to life and to this institution. I take it that our total community commitment is to wisdom, which is something more than knowledge and much akin to goodness and beauty when it radiates throughout a human person.

The following are some suggested dimensions for a formation programme for principals based on a combination of the intellectual and moral virtues. They are meant to be a beginning framework only and require considerable discussion and development. However, they reflect the main themes presented in this chapter.

A formation programme should develop leaders who are:

1. critically reflective – reflect on life, work and learning;
2. intellectually challenging – disciplined mind, knowledgeable, rigorous in method;

3. competent – have knowledge, understanding, skills of leadership and management;
4. emotionally mature – able to engage others in mutually beneficial relationships; use heart as well as head;
5. ethically literate – capable of applying ethical frameworks and standards to complex and perplexing value situations;
6. spiritually courageous – depthed human beings who have struggled with 'the meaning of life' and who have the spiritual scars to show for it;
7. intuitively connected – able to tap into the wisdom distilled from the warp and weft of life's experiences;
8. culturally sensitive – to discern differences and respond with consideration and empathy to individuals/groups, especially within the culture of their organisations.

Such programmes are more likely to form leaders who can meet the complex challenges and tensions of leadership in contemporary service organisations.

Note

This chapter reports on the findings of an Australian Research Council funded, three-year research project involving the Australian Catholic University, the NSW Police Service, the NSW Department of Education and Training, the Catholic Education Office, Parramatta, and the Australian Conference of Leaders of Religious Institutes (ACLRI).

Patrick Duignan is the Chief Investigator of the project and members of the research team include: Anne Benjamin, Charles Burford, Elizabeth Cameron-Traub, Victoria Collins, Lyn Coulon, Mary Cresp, Tony d'Arbon, Michael Fagan, Jack Flanagan, Michael Gorman, Ron Ikin, Aengus Kavanagh, Lynne Stallard.

References

Conger, J.A. and associates (1994) *Spirit at Work: Discovering the Spirituality in Leadership*. San Francisco, CA: Jossey-Bass.

Covey, S. (1992) *Principle Centred Leadership*. New York: Simon & Schuster.

Duignan, P.A. (1997) *The Dance of Leadership: At the Still Point of the Turning World*. ACEA Monograph Series 21. Melbourne: ACEA.

Duignan, P.A. (2001) The managed heart: the price of professional service in contemporary organisations. *Improving Schools* 4(3): 33–9.

Duignan, P.A. (2002) Formation of authentic educational leaders for Catholic schools. In D. Duncan and D. Riley (eds.) Melbourne: HarperCollins.

Duignan, P.A. and Bhindi, N. (1997) Authenticity in leadership: an emerging perspective. *Journal of Educational Administration* 35(3–4): 195–209.

Duignan, P.A. and Collins, V. (2001) Leadership challenges and ethical dilemmas in frontline service organisations. Paper presented at the British Educational Research Association Conference, Leeds, September.

Handy, C. (1997) *The Hungry Spirit: Beyond Capitalism*. London: Hutchison.

Hesburgh, T.M. (ed.) (1994) *The Challenge and Promise of a Catholic University*. Notre Dame, IN: University of Notre Dame Press.

Hodgkinson, C. (1991) *Educational Leadership: The Moral Art*. Albany, NY: University of New York Press.

Jones, C. (1998) *An Authentic Life: Finding Meaning and Spirituality in Everyday Life*. Sydney: ABC Books.

Karpin, D. (1995) *Enterprising Nation: Renewing Australia's Managers to Meet the Challenges of the ASIA Pacific Century. Report of the Industry Task Force on Leadership and Management Skills*. Canberra: Australian Government Publishing Service.

Kelly, T. (2000) *Researching Catholicity at an Australian Catholic University*. Draft paper, ACU Sub-faculty of Theology.

Kidder, R.M. (1995) *How Good People Make Tough Choices: Resolving the Dilemmas of Ethical Living*. New York: William Morrow.

Little, A.D. (1997) *Managing Change – the Australian Experience: Survey Results*. Sydney: Arthur D. Little International.

Pirsig, M. (1992) *Lila: An Inquiry into Morals*. London: Corgi Books.

Ryan, P. (1997) Address to Australian Institute of Training and Development. Sydney, March.

Sergiovanni, T. (1992) *Moral Leadership: Getting to the Heart of School Improvement*. New York: Jossey-Bass.

Starratt, R.J. (1993) *Building an Ethical School: A Practical Response to the Moral Crisis in Schools*. London: Falmer Press.

Taylor, C. (1991) *The Ethics of Authenticity*. Cambridge, MA: Harvard University Press.

Terry, R.W. (1993) *Authentic Leadership: Courage in Action*. San Francisco, CA: Jossey-Bass.

Index

academic managers *see* middle managers

accession, career model of leadership, 128

accountability, 4–5, 175

action level, management activity, 66, 67

active consent, 52

Adey, K., 134

Adler, P.S. and Borys, B., 149

administrative knowledge, 54, 58t

administrators
  dealing with conflict, 147, 151–2
  effective, 153–4, 156
  formalization, 150–51

affective conflict, 148

aggressive masculinities, management, 202

agonism, 100

aikido, 101–2

Alderfer, C.R., 31

alienative compliance, 55

Allen, P.G., 227

ambiguous territory, middle managers, 234, 244

anxiety, decision-making, 272–3

apathy, 22

Argyris, C., 267

assumptive world, 50

attainment measures, 178

attributes, leadership, 27, 33, 34–5

Australia
  principal training programmes, 118–24
  school principals, 175

Australian Principals Centre (APC), 120

awareness, subject leader training, 136–9

Barnard, C.I., 268

Baron, A., 30

behaviours
  leadership, 27–8, 34–5, 40
  managerial, 64–5

subject leader training, 136–9

Bell, D., 76

Benn, C. and Chitty, C., 177

big-five model, personality, 33

Blake, R.R. *et al.*, 28

Bolman, L. and Deal, T., 50, 62, 67, 68, 69, 70, 145

boundary management, leadership, 40

Brown, T., 40

Brundrett, M., 251

bureaucracy, 209

Burns, J., 144, 146

Burrell, G., 52

Bush, T., 248

Caldwell, B., 119

Callaghan, J., 230

capacities, teacher leadership, 193–4

capillary power, 100

career model, of leadership, 127–8

Catholic schools, funding, Scotland, 21–2

centralization, in education, 112

cerebral aspects, management, 66

challenging assignments, support for, 197

change
  affecting headteachers, 111
  managing knowledge networks during, 82–3
  middle managers as mediators of, 233–6
  organizational culture, 29–30, 56–7
  technological, 75

change agents, 152–3, 160

chief executives, corporate culture, 53

choices, in leadership, 181–2, 283

Clark, K. and Clark, M., 219

Clausewitz, C. Von, 100

Clegg, 52

codification, tacit knowledge, 77

coercive formalization, 148; 149

cognition, knowledge networks, 81–2

cognitive conflict, 147, 148
cognitive frames, 75
Cohen, A.P., 96
collaborative cultures, 198–9
collaborative leadership, 181
collectivist cultures, 223
collegiality
    bypassing or subverting
        process, 253–5
    difficulties with, 250–1
    imperfections of, 251–3
    internal decision-making, 247–50
colluded self, 237
colonization
    of lifeworld, 18–19
    in Rio Vista, 19–21
    further examples, 21–3
command and control models,
        leadership, 38
commitment
    middle managers, 238, 256
    teacher leadership, 191
communication
    effective administrators, 155
    persuasive, 102–5
    shared information, 275–6
    teacher leadership, 194
community, 23
community of followers, 93
community narrative/myth, 97
community of practice, 35
compassion, versus rules, 287–91
competency frameworks
    for headteachers, 121–4
    use of, 9
competency movement, 65
compliance
    middle managers, 236–43, 252
    power resources, 54–5
compulsive optimism, middle
        managers, 237, 238
concern for output, 28
concern for people, 28
conductors, musical, 6–7
conflict
    as constructive force, 145
    as destructive force, 144–5
    formalization, 148–9
    occurrence, 143
    responses to, 143–4

in schools, 150–1
strategy and tactics, 145–6
types of, 146–7
Conley, D.T., 186
Connell, R.W., 205, 209
consent, management of, 235
constitutive approach, to
        leadership, 89, 90–1
constructive conflict strategy, 147
constructivism, 35, 94–6
contingency approach, to
        leadership, 89, 90
contingency theories,
        leadership, 28–9
control, management theory, 65
Cooper, R. and Sawaf, A., 269
Cormack, M., 20, 21
corporate culture, chief executives, 53
Corwin, R.G., 150
Cowen, E., 123
creative leaders, 15
Creemers, B.P.M., 44
Crevola, C., 120
critical reflection, 139
cultural change
    in further education, 231–3
    management development
        programme, 159–68
cultural players, 53
cultural reproduction, 17
culture, 23
    of consent, universities, 257
    management, leadership, 30
    power as dynamic linking structures
        and, 53–59
    see also collaborative cultures;
        collectivist cultures;
        organizational culture; power
        cultures; reculturing; school
        culture; subcultures
Cuthbert, R.E. and Latcham, J., 65

Dalin, P. and Rollf, H.G., 179
Daresh, J. and Male, T., 111–12
Davis, B., 112, 120
Deal, T.E., 53
decentralization, in education, 113
decentralized leadership, 219–21
decision-making, 155
    agony of, 272–3

Native American perspective, 226–7
in organizations, 210–11
teacher participation, 187
declarative knowledge, 194
defensive self, 239
Dell, M., 102
Deming, W.E., 216
demotion, middle managers, 239, 260
Denmark, school system, 175
dependence, fostering, 6–7
Dew, J., 40
Deweyian perspective, conflict, 145
DiPaola, M.E., 150
disciplinary power, 52
discretion, 50
divestiture, career model of leadership, 128
Donnelly, R.G. and Kezsbom, D.S., 40
double control problem, 234
Drath, W.H. and Palus, C.J., 35, 39
dress style, willing compliance, 237
dynamic equilibrium, 48

Earley, P. and Fletcher-Campbell, 132
Early Literacy Research Project (ELRP), 120
economic rationalism, 232, 240–1
economic resource
power, 54, 55, 57, 58t
education
centralisation and
decentralisation, 113
see also further education;
higher education
education systems, uniformity in, 8
educational leadership
fostering dependence, 6–7
fostering of homogeneity, 8–10
procedural illusions of effectiveness, 3–5
values and action in, 14–24
educational reform, 231
effective headteachers, 174–5
effective schools, 176–9
effectiveness
of leadership, 179–84
procedural illusions of, 3–5
subject leader training courses, 136–9
efficiency, versus service, 286–7
Eisner, E., 10

emotional intelligence, 267, 269
emotional labour, 268
emotional work, 268
emotionality study, leadership, 267–79
conclusions, 278–9
findings, 270–8
methodology, 270
enabling formalization, 148, 149
England, principal training
programmes, 113–18
entrepreneurialism, power relations, 207
equity theories, 31
Esland, G., 231
expectancy theory, 31
explicit knowledge, 77, 79
external agency, training, 140
external assessment, 5
external factors, structural responses to, 49–50

failure, leadership, 34
families, 17
Fayol, H., 46, 64
FE see further education
Feinstein, L., 8
female middle managers, 238
feminist studies, gender in
organizations, 204–5
Fiedler, F.E., 28
filtering, information, 104
financial status, loss of, middle
managers, 240
Fineman, S., 268
firms, knowledge in, 75–6
Fleming, Admiral Klas, 12
Flesch, C., 6
flexibility, leadership, 28
Florence Hospital, management
development programme, 159–68
followers
community of, 93
compensating for leaders' errors, 92
contingency theory, 29
ensuring compliance from, 101
imagination of, 98
line between leaders and, 38
motivation of, 103
recognition of leadership, 188–9
forging of identities, 94, 96

formal leaders, 37
formal leadership, 187, 190, 193
formation, leadership, 127–9, 291–3
Foucault, M., 52, 53, 100, 104
framing, 67–71
Frohman, M., 40
Fullan, M., 116
funding, schools, 21–2
funding formula, FE, 230
further education
    changing policy context, 230–3
    middle managers
        mediating change, 233–6
        responses to change, 236–43
Further and Higher Education Act
    (1992), 230, 231

Galway, J., 7
Gammage, P., 178, 181
Gardner, J.W., 32, 144
gender discrimination, middle
        managers, 238
gendered assumptions, managerial
        initiatives, 202
gendered management, 203–4
    feminist studies, 204–5
gendered power, in
        management, 207–8
goal setting theory, 31
goals, 226
Gonzalez, E., 20
government reforms, management
        development, 159–60
Graen, G., 29
Granovetter, M.S., 83
Gray, J. *et al.*, 45
Greenfield, T. B., 15
Griffiths Report, 159–60
Grint, K., 63
Gronn, P., 63
group interests, versus individual
        interests, 283–5
group purpose, leadership, 32
group-think, 145–6
Gunter, H., 115
gynocracy, 227

Habermas, J., 16–17, 23
Hackman, J.R., 37
Hales, C., 54

Hallinger, P., 216
Handy, C., 256, 257, 258, 259
Hanna, D., 45
Hannay, L.M. and Denby, M., 187
Hansen, M.T., 79
Hansson, Capt. Sofring, 11
Hay McBer programmes
    Australia, 121
    competency approach, 65
    England, 9, 116–17
Hayek, F.A. von, 77, 81, 82
headteachers
    competency frameworks, 9
    effective, 174–5
    interest in role of, 111–13
    training programmes
        Australia, 118–24
        England, 113–18
        Hong Kong, 124–5
        international initiatives, 127
        Sweden, 125–6
    see also leaders; leadership
Heck, R.H. and Marcoulides, G.A., 51
hegemony, 52
Heifetz, R.A., 92
Heiney, R., 5
Heraclitus, 74
Hermosa, F., 20
Herzberg, F., 30–1
higher education, 247–62
    collegiality
        bypassing process, 253–5
        difficulties with, 250–1
        positive views about, 255–7
    institutions, subject leader training,
        134–5
    middle managers, vulnerability
        of, 257–9
Hill, P., 120
Hochschild, A., 268, 277, 278
Hofstede, G., 223
Hollway, W., 207–8
Holtz, B.W., 178
homogeneity, fostering of, 8–10
homosocial reproduction, 206
Hong Kong, principal training
        programmes, 124–5
Hoy, W.K. and Miskel, C.G., 155
human resource frame, 68
hygiene factors, 30–1

identity, constructing, 92–6, 105
image projection, 223–5
imaginary communities, 92–3
imagination
    of followers, 98
    leadership, 97
immanent value, 221–2
improvisation, 83–4
in-group, 29
incorporation, willing compliance, 237
incumbency, 128
individual interests, versus group
        interests, 283–5
individual-collective dimension,
        leadership, 182–3
ineffective staff, 284–5
influence process, leadership, 188
informal leadership, 187, 190
information, filtering, 104
information level, management
        activity, 66, 67
innovation programmes,
        implementation, 4
insightful aspect, 66
Institute of Educational Administration
        (Victoria), 119–21
institutional leaders, 15
institutional norms, organizational
        culture, 56
integrative cultures, 51
interference, 223
internal/external dimension,
        leadership, 182
international initiatives, headteacher
        training, 127
interpersonal relations, power, 49–50
inventive management, 70–1, 72

Jackall, R., 204
James, S., 93
James and Whiting, 112
Joyce, B. and Showers, B., 136, 140

Kanter, R.M., 206, 208
Kelly, T., 292
Kerfoot, D. and Knights, D., 207
Kidder, R.M., 283
Knight, F., 74
knowledge
    constructivism, 35

in firms, 75–6
subject leader training, 136–9
see also declarative knowledge;
        procedural knowledge; tacit
        knowledge
knowledge networks, 78–81
    cognition, 81–2
    managing during uncertainty, 82–4
    recommendations for designing, 85
    stability in uncertainty, 75
knowledge resource power, 54, 55, 58t
knowledge society, 75, 78
Kolb, J.A., 40
Koslowski, S.W.J. et al., 40
Kreiner, K., 76
Kushner, S., 5

Labour, B., 100
language
    construction of truth, 95
    of management, 202
Lappas, G.E., 33
leaders
    creative, 15
    formation of, 127–9
        to meet contemporary challenges,
        291–3
    successful, 33–4, 69, 92
    see also headteachers; school leaders;
        subject leaders
leadership
    challenges and dilemmas, 281–93
    constitutive approach, 89, 90
    contingency approach, 89, 90
    contingency theory, 28–9
    development, 154
    effectiveness of, 179–84
    emotionality study, 267–79
    identity, 92–6
    management, 62–72
    Native American Study, 216–27
    organizational tactics, 99–102
    persuasive communication, 102–5
    perceptions of, 188–9
    as performance, 104
    situational approach, 89, 90
    Socratic thinking about, 89–90
    strategic vision, 97–9
    tensions in, 283–91
    theories, review of, 27–41
    trait approach, 89, 90

leadership (*continued*)
   see also educational leadership;
      teacher leadership
Leadership and Emotion, 267
Leadership Programme for Serving
      Heads, 65, 116–17
learning, leadership, 273–5
Least Preferred Co-worker scale, 28
Lebrecht, N., 6
legitimacy, power resources, 55–7
Leithwood, K. *et al.*, 186
Leithwood, K. and Jantzi, D., 198
Leithwood, K. and
      Montgomery, D., 175
Levačić *et al.*, 46, 69
Levicki, C., 63–4, 69, 70
lifeworld, 16–17
   center position, 17–18
   colonization of, 18–19
   culture, community and person, 23–4
Little, Chris, 5
local education authority, subject
      leader training courses, 134–5
loosely coupled system, 45
Lord, R.G. and Maher, K.J., 188–9
Loudon, W. and Wildy, H., 121–2, 123
Louis, M.R., 14

McClelland, D., 117
Machiavelli, N., 93
management
   leadership, 62–72
   men, masculinities and, 201–12
   tacit knowledge, 77
   theory, 64–7
management development programme
      case study, 159–68
   conclusions, 167–8
   context, 160–1
   executive directors, 163
   human resource department, 164–5
   participants, 166–7
   programme facilitators, 165–6
   programme objectives, 162–3
   programme outcomes, 161–2
   research design, 161
managerial masculine
      subjectivities, 207–8
managerial power, 206–8
managerialism, in FE, 231–3
managers
   inventive, 70–1, 72
   motivators of an organization, 69
   see also middle managers
Mangham, I.L., 268
manifest needs theory, 31
Manz, C.C. and Sims, H.P., 32, 35, 39
March, J., 226
market competition, in FE, 231
Marx, K., 100
masculinities, and
      management, 201–12
Maslow, A.H., 31
Matsson, Joran, 11–12
meaningfulness, school lives, 16
mechanistic views,
      organizations, 46, 48
Melbourne Diocesan Synod report, 6
members, organizations, 47
men, and management, 201–12
methods, emphasis on, 16
Meyer, J. and Rowan, B., 3
Meyerson, D. and Martin, J., 51, 68–9
middle management, paucity of
      research into, 132–3
middle managers
   further education, 229–45
      changing policy context, 230–3
      mediating change, 233–6
      response to change, 236–43
   higher education, 247–62
      bypassing collegial process, 253–5
      difficulties with collegiality, 250–1
      imperfections of collegiality, 251–3
      positive views about
         collegiality, 255–7
      vulnerability, 244, 257–9, 260–1
Middle Years Research and
      Development Project (MYRAD),
      120
Millett, A., 115
Millikin, J.P., 39
Mintzberg, H., 65–6, 70–1, 203
mitakuye oyas' in, 221
modelling valued practices, 193
mood, teacher leadership, 191
Moorman, C. and Miner, A.S., 83
Morgan, D.H.J., 209
motivation
   employees, team leadership, 33
   of followers, 103

leadership, 30–2
Mullholland, K., 207
mutuality, 16

National College for School
    Leadership, 118
National Health Service (NHS), cultural
    change process, 159–68
national identities, 93, 94
National Professional Qualification for
    Headship (NPQH), 65, 113–16
National Standards, 65
  for Headteachers, 114
  for Subject Leaders, 131–2
Native American leadership
    study, 216–27
natural systems, 45
need theories, 31
nepotism, 227
neutralization, opposition's resources,
    101
New Zealand, funding of schools, 22
Newman, V. and
    Chaharbaghi, K., 63, 70
Nias, J, 21
non-interference, 223
non-intervention, 222–3
normative resource power, 54, 55, 58t
norms
  organizational culture, 51, 53
  power as source of, 52
NPQH see National Professional
    Qualification for Headship

Olson, L., 113
open communication, 275–6
open systems, 45–6, 48, 273
organization, of knowledge, 77
organization of consent, 256
organizational culture
  change and stasis, 56–7
  defined, 50–1
  distinctive, 51
  externally generated norms, 51
  four-frames model, 67–71
  institutional norms, 56
  leadership, 29–30
  power, 52–3
organizational structures, 208–10
organizational tactics,

leadership, 99–102, 105
organizational theory, school
    effectiveness, 44
organizations
  constructivism, 35
  knowledge in, 75–6
  knowledge networks
    managing, 82–4
    recommendations for designing, 85
  members, 47
  organic views of, 46, 48
  power resources, 58t
  purpose, 47
  resources, 47–8
  as self-regulatory systems, 65
  structures
    as dynamic entities, 48–50
    and tasks, 48
  as systems, 45–6
  team leadership, 36–40
organized complexity, 82
orientation to people, 191
Orton, J.D. and Weick, K.E., 45
Ouston, J., 116
out-group, 29
outcomes, teacher leadership, 194

partnerships, leadership programmes,
    127, 135, 140
path-goal theory, 29
patriarchy, in organizations, 204–5, 209
Patterson, R., 221
people cultures, 257
people level, management
    activity, 66, 67
performance management, subject
    leaders, 132
performance management system,
    leadership programmes, 122
Performance Standards for School
    Headteachers, 122–3
performative approach, to
    communication, 103
person
  leadership as a, 37
  lifeworld dimension, 23
personal capacity, successful
    leadership, 69
personal framing, 70
Personalising Evaluation, 5

personality
  big-five model, 33
  teacher leadership, 191
persuasive communication, 102–5
physical resource power, 54, 55, 57, 58t
physical structures, 48
planning, training, 153
play, 83
Poet, The, 104–5
Polanyi, M., 77
political frame, 68
political theorists, conflict, 145
popular individuals, 94
post–industrial society, 75–6
Powell, W.W., 78
power
  dynamic linking structure and
      culture, 53–59
  in management, 206–8
  organizational culture, 52–3
  sources of norms, 52
power cultures, 257
power relations
  as agonism, 100
  in organizations, 207
  structures, 49–50
power resources, 54
  compliance, 54–5
  conflict and exchange, 57–9
  legitimacy, 55–7
practices, teacher leadership, 193
preparation programs, 153–5
presentation *see* self-presentation
Prince, The, 223
principals *see* headteachers
problem solving skills, 194
procedural knowledge, 193
process, leadership as, 35, 37, 39
product development teams,
      knowledge sharing, 79–80
productive conflict, 147
productivity, and leadership, 33–4, 39
professional status, loss of, middle
      managers, 240
professionals, managers of
      reform, 232
promotion seeking, female middle
      managers, 238
psychodynamic theories,
      organizational and leadership
      behaviour, 268

pupil-centred dimension,
      leadership, 183
purpose, organizations, 47
Putnam, L.L. and Mumby, D.K., 268

rational management models, 65
rational open systems model, 45
rational systems, 45, 144
rational technicist view, 46
rationality, leadership, 66
Raven, J., 178
real communities, 93
reculturing, 153
reductionist approaches, in education,
      8–9
redundancy, threat of, middle
      managers, 235–6
relationships, 152
religious schools, Scotland, 22–3
research
  emotional side of leadership, 267–79
  Native American study,
      leadership, 216–27
  subject leader training, 131–41
Resnick, 220
resource inversion, leadership, 102
resources
  organizations, 47–8
  see also power resources
responsibility for others, 222–3
rhetoric, persuasive, 104
Ribbins, P., 128
Rio Vista, 19–21
Roper, M.R., 207, 209
rules, versus compassion, 287–91
Ruskin speech, 230

Sawatzki, Max, 119
Schein, E.A., 53
school culture, 14–16
school effectiveness
  internationalisation of
      education, 174
  rational open systems model, 45
  research, 44, 176–9
school improvement
  open systems, 45–6
  research, 44
School Leader Education Project
      (SLEP), 126

school leaders, 143–56
  conflict, 150–1
  effective administrators, 152–3
  training and practice, 153–5
  types of formalization, 147–50
schools
  conflict in, 150–1
  funding, 21–2
  lifeworld in center position, 17–18
  mediating leader effects on students,
      189
Schools of the Future, 119
Schultz, M., 78
scientific management, 64, 208–9
Scotland, Catholic and religious
      schools, 22–3
Scott, W.R., 45
search for knowledge, 79
Seddon, T. and Brown, L., 240
self-awareness, 38
self-directed teams, 36–7
self-interest, followers, 98
self-leadership, 35, 39
self-presentation
  leadership, 277
  managerial, 202
Selznick, P., 15–16
Senge, P. et al., 38
senior management teams, 232
service, versus efficiency, 286–7
Service Organisation Leadership
      Research (SOLR), 281–2
shared knowledge, 77, 79, 81–2
shared leadership, 181
sibling rivalry metaphor, 63
Sirotnik, K. and Kimball, K., 186–7
situational approach, to
      leadership, 89, 90
situational favourability, 28–29
skills, democratic leadership, 40
Smith, A., 77
Smylie, M.A., 181
Smyth, J., 140
social discourses, identity, 95
social identities, 93
societal significance, leadership, 63
sporting arena, organizational
      characteristics, 101
Spring, G., 122
Stacey, R., 116

staff, ineffective, 284–5
standards
  competency frameworks, 121–4
  see also National Standards
Steadman, S. et al.1, 139–40
Steinberg, L. et al., 23
Stinson, R., 20
strategic action, 18
strategic compliance, 240–3
strategic skills, 40
strategic vision, 97–9, 103, 105
strong ties
  improvisation in organisations, 83
  knowledge sharing, 79, 80, 81
structural aspects, leadership, 40
structural frame, 68
structural responses, external
      factors, 49–50
structures
  as dynamic entities, 48–50
  in education, 4
  organizational tasks in, 48
  power as dynamic linking culture
      and, 53–9
students
  eroding lifeworld forces, 23–4
  school leadership, 189
subcultures
  organizational, 51
  students, 23–4
subject leaders, effective training study,
      131–41
  conclusions, 139–40
  effective training approaches, 136–9
  findings, 134–5
  research design, 133–4
successful leadership, 33–4, 69, 92
SuperLeadership, 32, 39
Sweden, principal training
      programmes, 125–6
symbiotic relationships, 16
symbolic construction, of community, 96
symbolic frame, 68
systems, organizations as, 45–6
systemsworld, 16, 17

tacit knowledge, 77, 78–9
tactical skills, 40
task structures, 49
tasks, organizations, 48

Taylor, F.W., 46, 64, 91
teacher leadership, 186–99
  effects on students, 189
  formal and informal, 190
  implications for developing, 196–9
  role definition in, 196
  nature of, 191–4
  perceptions of, 188–9
  role definition in, 196
  transformational, 188
teacher-centred dimension, leadership,
    183
teacher/administrator conflict, 151
teachers' work groups, 7
teaching responsibilities, 193
Teaching Standards Framework
    (DfES), 132
team leadership, 36–40
technical knowledge, 54, 58t
technical-instrumental domain, 15
technocratic patriarchy, 209
technological learning networks, 78
technology, as knowledge, 75
teleological action, 18
tensions, of leadership, 283–91
Thatcherism, 230
theatrical performance, mobilizing
    followers, 103
theoretical knowledge, 76
time
  allocation, teacher leadership, 196–7
  headteachers' use of, 182
  Native American perspective, 225–6
Tjosvold, D., 145
Tomkins, A., 180
training
  providing leadership
    opportunities, 197
  school leaders, 153–5
  subject leaders, 131–41
traits, leadership, 89–90, 191–3
transactional leadership, 32
transfer of knowledge, 79
transformational leadership,
    32, 188, 216
trial by ordeal, 4–5
Trust, 223
truth, construction of, 92–6
two–factor model, of leadership, 28

uncertainty, managing knowledge
    networks during, 82–4

understanding, subject leader training,
    136–9
uniformity, education systems, 8
universities
  culture of consent, 257
  expansion of, 258
  leadership programmes, 127
unpredictability, dealing with change,
    84
unwilling compliance, middle
    managers, 238–40
utopian thought, leadership, 97

values
  central zones, schools, 16
  postmodern society, 112
  teacher leadership, 191
values domain, 15
Vasa, 10–12
vertical dyad linkage theory, 29
Vice Chancellors, 257
Victoria, principal training
    programme, 119–21
Vroom-Yetton theory, 29
vulnerability, middle managers, 235–6,
    244, 260–1

war, identity construction, 94
Wax, M. *et al.*, 222
weak ties
  knowledge sharing, 79, 80, 81
  play in organizations, 83
Whitworth, L., 20, 21
*Who's Who Among American High
    Schools*, 23
Wieck, K., 226
Williams, K., 256
willing compliance, middle managers,
    236–8
Wilson, J.M. and Wellins, R.S., 40
window man, 260
wise leadership, 70
work structures, 48–9
work teams, leadership, 36
workplace, linkage between workshop
    and, 140
Wright, G., 78

Yancey-Martin, P., 210
Young, 50